Critical Government Documents on the Environment

CRITICAL DOCUMENTS SERIES

Critical Government Documents on the Environment

DON PHILPOTT

CRITICAL DOCUMENTS SERIES

Lanham • Boulder • New York • London

Published by Bernan Press
An imprint of The Rowman & Littlefield Publishing Group, Inc.
4501 Forbes Boulevard, Suite 200, Lanham, Maryland 20706
www.rowman.com
800-865-3457; info@bernan.com

Unit A, Whitacre Mews, 26-34 Stannary Street, London SE11 4AB

Library of Congress Control Number: 2015936608

ISBN: 978-1-59888-747-1
E-ISBN: 978-1-59888-748-8

∞™ The paper used in this publication meets the minimum requirements of American National Standard for Information Sciences—Permanence of Paper for Printed Library Materials, ANSI/NISO Z39.48-1992.

Printed in the United States of America

Summary Contents

Contents

Acknowledgement

This book is one of a series that looks at critical issues of our times. The subject of this book is the environment and a review of many of the major environmental issues facing us today. The book does not offer any new science or attempt to take sides. This book has relied heavily on the vast wealth of information that is in the public domain. Almost all the material comes from federal, state and local public domain websites as well as environmental groups, energy companies and trade associations and politicians. These include the Department of the Interior, Environmental Protection Agency, Department of Health and Human Services, the White House, Natural Resources Defense Council, Audubon Society, Heartland Institute, Heritage Foundation, U.S. National Academies of Science, NASA, National Oceanic & Atmospheric Administration, American Association of Petroleum Geologists, Intergovernmental Panel on Climate Change, United Nations Environment Programme and many more. The sources for the material contained herein are presented at the end of each chapter under the heading "Source Material." Sources that are summarized or used for research, but not quoted directly, are listed under "Further Reading."

Introduction

The environment is everything around us. We are all part of the environment and have an impact on it whether we realize it or not. All the components of the environment—land, water, air, plants and animals—have their own individual and collective impacts on it and on us.

Although the earth has been around for millions of years, man has only been seriously interested in protecting and preserving the environment for less than 200 years and the terms conservationism and environmentalism are little more than 100 years old.

For most of history mankind was too busy surviving to worry about anything other than putting food on the table, staying warm in the winter, protecting the family and keeping enemies at bay. The industrial revolution changed all that. In the late-eighteenth century new power-driven manufacturing processes created millions of jobs. The mechanization of cotton spinning powered by steam or water increased the output of one worker about a thousand fold. Cotton replaced wool as the main textile material and demand led to huge plantations around the world and especially in the southern United States.

There was an exodus from low paying rural jobs to higher paid jobs in factories and mills. Productivity reached spectacular highs. Urban populations rocketed and while there was still poverty, most people saw their living standards gradually rise. More spending power meant greater demand for goods and services which helped sustain the economic prosperity. An abundance of cheap coal led to larger and more efficient steam engines and machine tools in the factories. Stream powered trains and ships were able to bring raw materials to the factories and transport the finished products to consumers worldwide. Other byproducts of the industrial revolution were steel and cement, mass produced chemicals and fertilizers and, of course, pollution.

Factories were poorly regulated, child labor was used and accidents and death at work were regular occurrences. Most industrial waste as well as sewage was pumped into rivers and lakes—leading to epidemics of diseases like cholera and typhoid—while factory chimneys belched out thick black smoke. This smoke combined with fog to become a killer smog. In one week in 1873 over 700 died in London because of the air pollution (The first Clean Air Act wasn't passed in the UK until 1956).

Many industrialized nations around the world took steps to reduce air and water pollution from the factories and continue to try to protect the environment from other threats as well. However, other developing countries who are still trying to catch up with their industrialized competitors don't place such a high priority on curbing pollution, especially if the cost of doing so is perceived as too high.

THE BIG QUESTION

Of course the first issue is to determine whether this pollution and all the other environmental threats are as serious as some scientists suggest. There are some scientists who argue that global warming is a myth. They say that since the beginning of time the earth has gone through cycles of warming and cooling and that we are just going through another of those cycles. On the other hand, many scientists can show evidence of melting ice caps, record high temperatures, freak weather patterns, and rising ocean levels. Who is right?

There are scientists who argue that the ozone layer is being depleted because of greenhouses gases which poses a threat to our very survival while others say there is evidence that the ozone layer is actually healing itself and the gap is now smaller.

The aim of this book is to offer the arguments for and against many of the leading environmental issues currently under discussion. All the material in this book is from published sources—from scientific journals and government reports to political manifestos and lobby group publications. This book does not offer any new science but attempts to present both sides of the argument so that you can make informed choices.

A LITTLE BACKGROUND

During the Industrial Revolution forests were chopped down and coal mines were developed to provide the fuel needed to power the new machines. Some of the deforested land was used for agriculture but without the trees to hold the soil, it often became barren. Collieries and open cast mining also led to huge tracts of despoiled land. At the time, it was considered a small price to pay when weighed against the greater good of the economic boom.

It wasn't until the early twentieth century that people started to seriously discuss the damage that was being caused to the environment. Basically there are four camps in the environmental debate.

There are those who just don't care. There are those who believe that if they own the land they should be able to do whatever they wish on it. There are those who recognize that the land and its resourced need to be conserved and finally, there are the environmentalists who generally believe that the land has to be protected at all costs.

The don't-care brigade are the ostriches with their heads in the sand—the "it will never happen to me" types. The next group are the property owners who believe they have the right to do as they please on their land. In the early twentieth century this principle was known as *laissez-faire* which literally means "let them do." It argues that land owners should be free to chop trees, mine and whatever else they want without government restrictions and interference.

On the other side are the conservationists and environmentalists. Although not the first, the most famous early conservationist was President Theodore Roosevelt. He understood that natural resources had to be conserved is they were to be used as an asset. This was best done, he argued, by acquiring land so that it came under federal protection and by developing long terms sustainability plans for its natural resources.

While President Roosevelt was not opposed to using natural resources, the fourth camp—the environmentalists—definitely were. John Muir, regarded as the father of American environmentalism, argued that nature was there to be enjoyed not to be pillaged. The environment was too important and needed to be protected and preserved at all costs. That is why this camp is also referred to as the 'preservationists'. Within the latter three camps there are, of course, many different positions from moderate to ultra-extreme.

One reason we should all be concerned with what is happening to and in the environment is that until we can colonize some distant planet, our earth is all we have got. In the last 2,000 years the world's population has exploded from around 300 million to over 7 billion. That is a lot of people trying to make do with diminishing resources and depending which camp you are in that has created many environmental problems—or not. You decide.

World Population Growth	
6000 BC	5 million (estimate)
1 AD	300 million (estimate)
1650	500 million
1820	1 billion
1930	2 billion
1960	3 billion
1974	4 billion
1987	5 billion
1999	6 billion
2011	7 billion
2025	8 billion (estimate)
2043	9 billion (estimate)
2083	10 billion (estimate)

KEY MOMENTS ALONG THE ENVIRONMENTAL HIGHWAY

When America was first settled there was enough land and natural resources for all. Livestock grazed on common land and water was pumped from rivers and lakes for human consumption and agriculture. Most disputes were settled by local councils.

As the rural population grew so did demand for land. Forests were cleared and sawmills often dammed rivers depriving towns and farmers downstream of water while fish could no longer travel to upland communities that relied on fisheries. Large landowners prevented other ranchers from grazing on their land leading to range wars and bitter disputes over water rights.

Apart from the obvious physical changes to the environment, scientists started to observe other changes as well. For instance, deforestation often lead to soil erosion and fewer nesting birds so insect populations increased damaging crops. In 1864 George Perkins Marsh published Man and Nature, considered by many to be the first scientific attempt to analyze and mitigate environmental impacts.

From the 1870s to early twentieth century it was the sportsmen and hunters who led the conservation movement. They were largely interested in the scientific management of wildlife and they argued for the creation of national parks as one means of achieving this. They took their case to Washington and this signaled the start of the shift from local to state and federal control.

Theodore Roosevelt was a passionate hunter and knew first hand that uncontrolled hunting was threatening large numbers of species. He advocated for long-term plans for both land and species management. He and George Bird Grinnell formed the Boone and Crockett Club in 1887 pulling together conservationists, scientists, intellectuals and politicians. By the time he became President, Roosevelt was already a committed conservationist. He put more than 230 million acres of land under federal protection and set aside more Federal land for national parks and nature preserves than all of his predecessors combined. He also established the United States Forest Service, signed into law the creation of five National Parks, and signed the 1906 Antiquities Act, under which he proclaimed 18 new U.S. National Monuments. He also established the first 51 Bird Reserves, four Game Preserves, and 150 National Forests, including Shoshone National Forest, the nation's first.

Roosevelt and John Muir butted heads on many occasions and their disagreements while visiting Yosemite illustrate the differences between the conservationists and the environmentalists. Muir wanted nature preserved for its natural beauty with minimal commercial use of water resources and forests. Roosevelt wanted "to make the forest produce the largest amount of whatever crop or service will be most useful, and keep on producing it for generation after generation of men and trees."

Franklin Delano Roosevelt, cousin of Theodore, was also a passionate conservationist and introduced many programs in the 1930s to end wasteful land-use, mitigate the effects of the Dust Bowl, and efficiently develop natural resources in the West. Conservationists are not against the use of natural resources they are opposed to inefficient, wasteful and damaging practices. Roosevelt also established the Civilian Conservation Corps which put two million poor young men to work in rural and wilderness areas, mostly on conservation projects.

As American industrialization increased after World War II, conservationists became more active to prevent encroachment in wilderness land and they were responsible for preventing a number of projects including the Bridge Canyon Dam that would have backed up the waters of the Colorado River into the Grand Canyon National Park.

One of the most influential gatherings occurred in 1948. The Inter-American Conference on the Conservation of Renewable Natural Resources bought together almost 200 scientists from all over country. The post conference declaration was "No generation can exclusively own the renewable

resources by which it lives. We hold the commonwealth in trust for prosperity, and to lessen or destroy it is to commit treason against the future."

A number of events occurred during the 1950s, 1960s and 1970s that
raised public awareness about possible man-made harm to the environment.
In 1954, the 23 man crew of the Japanese fishing vessel Lucky Dragon was
exposed to radioactive fallout from a hydrogen bomb test at Bikini Atoll,
and in 1969 there was an ecologically catastrophic oil spill from an offshore
well in California's Santa Barbara Channel. Perhaps the most significant of
all, however, was the publication of Rachel Carson's *Silent Spring* in 1962.
Suddenly issues about air and water pollution, solid waste disposal, declining
energy resources, radiation and pesticide poisoning were in the news and
being discussed as matters of concern.

People started to protest—about the proliferation of nuclear weapons and
nuclear power stations and the threats they posed; about ground water contamination and air pollution; about pesticides in food and toxins in the environment.

Politicians took note and in 1970 the Clean Air Act was passed followed
by the Water Pollution Control Act of 1972. For the first time this new legislation took the onus for clean air and water away from individual states and
made it the responsibility of the federal government. Other significant legislation was the 1970 National Environmental Policy Act (NEPA) which established the Environmental Protection Agency; the 1972 Marine Protection,
Research, and Sanctuaries Act; the 1973 Endangered Species Act, the 1974
Safe Drinking Water Act, the 1976 Resource Conservation and Recovery Act
and the 1977 Water Pollution Control Act Amendments which became
known as the Clean Water Act.

Because the new laws were controlled by the federal governmental many
conservation and environmental groups switched from being active locally
and regionally to becoming national government lobbyists. New groups such
as the Natural Resources Defense Council and Environmental Defense were
founded to target Congress and the relevant federal agencies.

The 1980s were challenging for environmental protection. President Ron-
ald Reagan appointed James G. Watt as Secretary of the Interior. According
to Greg Wetstone, the chief environment counsel at the House Energy and
Commerce Committee during the Reagan administration, who subsequently
served as director of advocacy at the Natural Resources Defense Council,
Watt "was one of the two most intensely controversial and blatantly anti-
environmental political appointees" in American history. The other, he said,
was Anne Gorsuch, director of the EPA at the time.

One effect of the two appointments, however, was that environmental organizations saw a dramatic increase in membership and funding. Environmentalism which had until that point largely been the domain of sportsmen, hunters, conservationists and scientists was now mainstream with growing support from urban areas.

Today environmental groups command widespread public support, especially in areas such as air and water pollution. Politicians are beginning to realize this and the major parties environmental manifestos are likely to play an important role in the 2016 elections.

THE CURRENT POLITICAL SITUATION

Today's Republican Party by and large still believes in a laissez-faire attitude to the environment and land management while the Democrats and the current administration are conservationists at heart.

THE ADMINISTRATION

According to the White House, "The Obama Administration is committed to protecting the air we breathe, water we drink, and the land that supports and sustains us. From restoring ecosystems in the Chesapeake Bay and the Everglades, to reducing mercury pollution from power plants, we are bringing together Federal agencies to tackle America's greatest environmental challenges."

"The President established the America's Great Outdoors Initiative to foster a twenty-first century approach to conservation that responds to priorities of the American people. When he signed the Omnibus Public Land Management Act of 2009, President Obama marked the most extensive expansion of land and water conservation in more than a generation, designating more than two million acres of federal wilderness, thousands of miles of trails, and protecting more than 1,000 miles of rivers. In addition, the President has used his authority under the Antiquities Act 11 times to permanently preserve some of America's most treasured landscapes, most recently designating the Organ Mountains—Desert Peaks National Monument in New Mexico.

"Wilderness, parks, forests, monuments, and other public lands help support local economies through tourism. Recent estimates also show that over

$50 billion were added to the economy from visits to public lands in 2012 alone. In fact, a recent study says that this national monument could double the number of visitors to the region and help grow the local economy by more than 70 percent. Protected public lands also attract businesses interested in relocating to areas with beautiful scenery, outdoor opportunities, and a high quality of life. These businesses can bring high-paying jobs, which helps explain why, on average, western non-metro counties' per capita income increases when there is more protected public land in the area. The outdoor recreation industry supports 6.1 million jobs nationwide," added the White House spokesperson.

THE ADMINISTRATION'S ENVIRONMENTAL POLICY

Supporting Land Conservation

Protecting our Oceans

The health of our oceans is under threat on multiple fronts, from overfishing to carbon pollution. President Obama has established the first comprehensive National Policy for the Stewardship of the Ocean, our Coasts, and the Great Lakes. The National Ocean Policy helps us prioritize our efforts and resources to address the most critical issues facing our oceans and establishes a comprehensive, collaborative, regionally based planning process to ensure healthy ocean and coastal resources for the many communities and economies that rely on and enjoy them.

America's oceans and coastal regions support tens of millions of jobs and contribute trillions of dollars a year to the national economy. In June of 2014, the President announced new steps to protect world-class marine areas as well as a comprehensive program to combat illegal fishing and support fishermen.

Prioritizing Clean Water

The Administration is taking comprehensive action to ensure the integrity of the waters Americans rely on every day for drinking, swimming, and fishing, and that support farming, recreation, tourism and economic growth. We have issued draft Federal guidance to clarify which waters are protected by the Clean Water Act nationwide; launched innovative partnerships and

programs to improve water quality and water efficiency; and created initiatives to revitalize communities and economies by restoring rivers and critical
watersheds. The Administration has also proposed to modernize the guidelines that govern Federal water resource planning, calling for water resources
projects based on sound science, improved transparency, and consideration
of the variety of community benefits of projects.

Restoring Treasured Great Ecosystems

- Gulf of Mexico
- California's Bay Delta
- Chesapeake Bay Protection and Restoration
- Great Lakes Restoration
- Everglades Restoration

Working towards Environmental Justice

Because we all deserve the chance to live, learn, and work in healthy
communities, the Obama administration is committed to ensuring that
communities overburdened by pollution—particularly minority, low-income
and indigenous communities—have the opportunity to enjoy the health and
economic benefits of a clean environment. After more than a decade of inac-
tion, the Administration reconvened the Environmental Justice Interagency
Working Group and engaged more than 100 environmental justice leaders at
a White House forum. Federal agencies signed a Memorandum of Understanding formally committing to environmental justice, and have since taken
steps to integrate environmental justice into federal decision-making and
programs in areas such as transportation, labor, health services, housing and
others.

In September, 2014 President Obama announced a series of executive
actions to reduce carbon pollution, prepare the U.S. for the impacts of climate change, and lead international efforts to address global climate change.

The following is the press release released by the White House on September 23, 2014:

THE U.S. CONTINUES TO LEAD INTERNATIONAL EFFORTS TO COMBAT GLOBAL CLIMATE CHANGE AND PREPARE FOR ITS IMPACTS

Today, at the United Nations Climate Summit in New York, President Obama announced a
new set of tools to harness the unique scientific and technological capabilities of the United

States to help vulnerable populations around the world strengthen their climate resilience. The United States also announced its leadership and participation in more than a dozen new climate change partnerships launched at the Climate Summit.

The tools for global resilience announced by the President include improved and extended extreme weather risk outlooks to help avoid loss of life and property; data, tools and services to enable countries to better prepare for the impacts of climate change, including a new release of global elevation data; and an announcement of a new public-private partnership to ensure that the climate data, tools, and products made available by U.S. technical agencies are useful to developing countries. The President also announced a new Executive Order requiring Federal agencies to factor climate resilience into the design of their international development programs and investments.

New international climate change partnerships in which the United States has played a key role in launching include the Global Alliance for Climate-Smart Agriculture, the Oil and Gas Methane Partnership, the Pilot Auction Facility for Methane and Climate Change Mitigation, and the Cities Climate Finance Leadership Alliance.

These actions build on the President's Climate Action Plan, which includes unprecedented efforts by the United States to reduce carbon pollution, promote clean sources of energy that create jobs, and protect American communities from the impacts of climate change.

The Climate Action Plan is working. In 2012, U.S. greenhouse gas emissions fell to the lowest level in nearly two decades. Since the President took office, wind energy production has tripled, and solar energy has increased by a factor of ten. The Environmental Protection Agency has proposed the first carbon pollution standards for existing power plants, which account for a third of U.S. carbon pollution. And the President is empowering state and local leaders to reduce carbon pollution and prepare for the impacts of climate change in their communities through initiatives including a $1 billion National Disaster Resilience Competition and the State, Local, and Tribal Leaders Task Force on Climate Preparedness and Resilience.

Internationally, the United States continues to press for an ambitious, inclusive, and pragmatic global climate agreement in 2015, and intends to put forward a robust post-2020 climate commitment in the context of other major economies doing the same. Through our leadership of the Major Economies Forum and the Clean Energy Ministerial as well as our bilateral relationships, we continue to press the scientific and economic case for strong climate action. U.S. leadership has helped spur international action to address the health and climate impacts of short-lived climate pollutants, to launch free trade talks on environmental goods, and to cut donor country financial support for new coal-fired power plants. Going forward, the United States will continue to help develop, launch, and implement practical, action-oriented international initiatives such as those announced at today's U.N. Climate Summit.

NEW U.S. ACTIONS TO STRENGTHEN GLOBAL RESILIENCE TO CLIMATE CHANGE

Executive Order on Climate-Resilient International Development

President Obama announced an Executive Order on Climate-Resilient International Development, requiring agencies to factor climate-resilience considerations systematically into the U.S. government's international development work and to promote a similar approach with multilateral entities. U.S. financial support for adaptation activities in developing countries has increased eightfold since 2009; such dedicated funding is critical. At the same time, the magnitude of the challenge requires not just dedicated adaptation finance flows but also a broader, integrated approach. Development investments in areas as diverse as eradicating malaria, building hydropower facilities, improving agricultural yields, and developing transportation systems will not be effective in the long term if they do not account for impacts such as shifting ranges of disease-carrying mosquitoes, changing water availability, or rising sea levels, thereby reducing the effectiveness of taxpayer money. This new Executive Order will:

- Improve the resilience of the Federal Government's international development programs, projects, investments, overseas facilities, and other funding decisions through consideration of current and future climate-change impacts, as appropriate;
- Share knowledge, data, tools, information, frameworks, and lessons learned in incorporating climate-resilience considerations; and
- Complement efforts by the Federal Government to reduce greenhouse gas emissions at home and globally.

Releasing Powerful New Data to Enable Planning for Resilience

To empower local authorities to better plan for the impacts of severe environmental changes such as drought, glacial retreat, flooding, landslides, coastal storm surges, agricultural stresses, and challenges concerning public health, today the National Aeronautics and Space Administration (NASA), the National Geospatial-intelligence Agency (NGA), and the U.S. Geological Survey (USGS), as part of an ongoing commitment to open data and international data sharing through the inter-governmental Group on Earth Observations, will release a collection of higher-resolution elevation datasets for Africa. Datasets covering other global regions will be made available within one year, with the next release of data providing more accurate elevation information for Mexico, Central and South America, and the Caribbean. Until now, elevation data for Africa were freely and publicly available only at 90-meter resolution. The datasets being released today, and during the course of the next year–which are based on data collected by sensors designed by an international partnership and carried on the U.S. Space Shuttle–resolve to 30-meters and will be used worldwide to improve environmental monitoring, climate change research including sea-level rise impact assessments, and local decision support. These datasets are being made available via a user-friendly interface on USGS's Earth Explorer website. With a commitment from the Secure World Foundation, and in collaboration with the Committee on Earth Observation Satellites, USGS, NOAA, and NASA plan to offer online training and regional workshops to further enable users to take advantage of these data resources.

Developing New Outlooks for Extreme-Weather Risk

To reduce harm from extreme-weather events occurring throughout the world, the Obama Administration announced its intent to begin a coordinated U.S. effort, led by NOAA, to develop reliable extreme-weather risk outlooks on time horizons that are currently not available. This effort will initiate the planned development of new extreme-weather outlooks in the 15-30 day range, beyond the 14-day limit of current reliable weather forecasts and will explore producing information products for longer time-scales at which climate change influences risk. Currently available weather and climate information from NOAA empowers decision-makers, communities, farmers, and business owners to make smart decisions as they plan and prepare for the future. This new effort will seek to increase the information available to these decision makers in the 15-30 day timeframe with new kinds of actionable information to use as they plan and prepare for the future. To kick off the effort this year, NOAA will begin issuing weekly 3-4 week precipitation outlooks and will extend its current extreme-heat index product from the current 6-to-10-days-out to 8-to-14-days-out, giving communities several additional days to prepare for potential life threatening heat waves.

Equipping Meteorologists in Developing Nations with the Latest Tools and Knowledge

To help connect meteorologists in developing nations with the best-available tools, knowledge, and information resources, NOAA will seek to significantly expand the reach of its highly successful international "Training Desk" program, which brings developing-country meteorologists to the United States for state-of-the-art training and education at NOAA's National Weather Service Climate Prediction Center. Since 1992, more than 300 meteorologists from 35 nations have completed NOAA's training desk program, helping both to build capacity at meteorological institutions in their home countries for climate prediction, monitoring, and assessments, and to feed local observational climate data back to NOAA upon returning to their home countries. This effort will increase the number of meteorologists from developing countries in Africa, the Caribbean, South America, and Southeast Asia who will participate in the training desks and will expand the curriculum from weather and climate to include the important water challenges (predicting how much, how little and what quality) that are now confronting the global community.

Launching a Public-Private Partnership on Climate Data and Information for Resilient Development

President Obama announced that the United States will develop and launch a new public-private partnership focused on connecting actionable climate science, data, tools, and training to decision-makers in developing countries. This partnership will enhance capacity within developing countries to assess impacts and vulnerabilities associated with climate change, boost resilience, and achieve their own development goals in the context of a changing climate. Building on the skills and investments of USAID's climate change and development programming, including leveraging the newly announced Global Resilience Partnership; expertise from international and scientific agencies, including the agencies of the U.S. Global Change Research Program; and the innovation of U.S. universities, NGOs, and the private sector, this new partnership will:

- Make existing climate data, scientific information, outlooks, tools, and services more accessible to decision-makers around the world;
- Identify and address targeted climate information and capacity gaps, including by providing targeted training opportunities;
- Create a global community of practice that links climate data, climate change adaptation efforts, and international development; and

- Commit to the timely development of new products to support decision-making targeted at the needs of specific climate-vulnerable countries.

The Global Alliance for Climate-Smart Agriculture

The United States is joining the Global Alliance for Climate-Smart Agriculture as a founding member. The Alliance brings together governments, businesses, farmers' organizations, civil society groups, research bodies and intergovernmental entities to address food security in the face of climate change. The United States will bring its existing food security and climate programs to this multi-stakeholder effort, including:

Feed the Future

"Feed the Future"–the U.S. Presidential initiative for food security, invests in technologies to deliver drought tolerant seeds, fertilizer and water efficiency technologies, and other tools to help farmers become more climate-smart in achieving its objectives of inclusive agricultural sector growth and improved nutrition.

Climate and Clean Air Coalition

The United States co-chairs the Agriculture Initiative of the Climate and Clean Air Coalition (CCAC), which seeks to reduce methane and black carbon emissions while promoting agricultural livelihoods and advancing broader climate change objectives on adaptation and mitigation.

USDA Regional Climate Hubs

The Department of Agriculture's Regional Climate Hubs will deliver information to American farmers, ranchers and forest landowners to help them adapt to climate change and weather variability.

Launch of CCAC Oil and Gas Methane Partnership

The United States has played an integral role in launching the Oil and Gas Methane Partnership, an innovative public-private initiative bringing together governments, leading oil and gas companies, and other stakeholders in a partnership focused on cost-effective reduction of methane emissions. The Partnership, an initiative of the Climate and Clean Air Coalition (CCAC), provides involved companies with a systematic, cost-effective approach for reducing their methane emissions and for credibly demonstrating to stakeholders the impacts of their actions.

Global Green Freight Action Plan

The United States is helping to lead the development and implementation of a Global Green Freight Action Plan together with over 20 countries plus NGOs, international organizations, and companies. This effort will result in fuel and cost savings for businesses and consumers as well as emission reductions of climate and air pollutants such as black carbon, carbon dioxide, and particulate matter.

Indonesia Palm Oil Pledge

The United States applauded the signing of the landmark Indonesia Palm Oil Pledge by the CEOs of Cargill, Asian Agri, Golden Agri-Resources, Wilmar, and the Indonesian Chamber of Commerce and Industry. This Pledge includes industry-leading benchmarks such as proactive government engagement on policy reform and a principle of no planting on peat lands, and go beyond the companies' existing sustainability commitments. By applying these principles to third-party suppliers and covering the signatories' operations worldwide, these companies are creating best practices for their industry. The U.S. Government looks forward to working with the signatories, civil society and the Government of Indonesia to follow and promote implementation of the Pledge.

Pilot Auction Facility (PAF) for Methane and Climate Change Mitigation

The United States will announce the intention to provide a $15 million contribution to the Pilot Auction Facility for Methane and Climate Change Mitigation (PAF), an innovative, World Bank-managed climate finance instrument that will use auctions to maximize the efficiency of public resources for climate change mitigation. The PAF will pioneer an innovative, results-based climate finance model with potential to support low-carbon investment in ways that provide better value and lower risk for the taxpayer. The United States drove this concept forward from the time of our G8 presidency in 2012 to its launch by the World Bank this month.

Power Africa Cooperation Agreement with Sustainable Energy for All Initiative

The United States has signed a Cooperation Understanding Agreement with the Sustainable Energy for All (SE4All) Initiative to further strengthen collaboration between the President's Power Africa Initiative and the UN- and World Bank-led SE4All activities in Africa. Building on Power Africa's Beyond the Grid component, the cooperation will focus on expanded energy access, as well as development of renewable energy projects. At the August 2014 U.S.-Africa Leaders' Summit, President Obama announced new aggregate goals for Power Africa to add 60 million new electricity connections and 30,000 megawatts of clean energy generation in Africa. Working with the countries on investment strategies and reducing barriers to project development will be a high priority of the collaboration.

The Cities Climate Finance Leadership Alliance

The United States is a founding member of the Cities Climate Finance Leadership Alliance, a new initiative aimed at helping cities around the world access financial tools for low carbon, climate resilient infrastructure. The Alliance will bring together cities, national governments, financial institutions, NGOs, and other stakeholders. The United States will contribute experience, best practice and lessons learned from ongoing efforts such as the National Disaster Resilience Competition and Climate Resilient Transportation System.

National/Subnational Cooperation on Climate Change

Enhanced cooperation and coordination among national and subnational levels of government is essential to forge coherent, effective, and efficient responses to climate change. The United States has been at the leading edge of efforts to connect these national and subnational efforts through its State, Local and Tribal Leaders Task Force on Climate Preparedness and Resilience and other programs, and announced a range of initiatives at the Climate Summit including:

Climate Action Champions

The Climate Action Champions initiative will recognize local and tribal government entities that are leading emission reductions and climate resilience efforts domestically. The initiative will enhance opportunities for financial and technical assistance, as well as facilitated peer-to-peer networking and mentorship, to support and advance their climate mitigation and resilience objectives.

Public Transportation Resilience Projects

The U.S. Federal Transit Administration announced the awarding of nearly $3.6 billion for climate resilient transportation infrastructure projects in the states impacted by Hurricane Sandy that were competitively selected.

Federal-Tribal Climate Resilience Partnership

The Department of the Interior's Bureau of Indian Affairs launched a new $10 million program for delivering adaptation training.

First Green Guaranties Issued by the Overseas Private Investment Corporation (OPIC)

By providing "Green Guaranties," OPIC (the U.S. government's development finance institution) joins other public and private sector institutions in supporting climate-friendly investments. OPIC's first Green Guaranties were offered to eligible U.S. investors in the domestic debt capital markets on September 17, 2014. These U.S. government-guaranteed certificates of participation adhere to the Green Bond Principles of 2014, which have been collaboratively developed with the guidance of leading capital markets issuers, investors, underwriters and environmental groups. The placement enables OPIC to boost an asset class that is rapidly becoming an attractive investment for generating both social and financial returns. Proceeds raised under these Green Guaranties will total an initial $47 million to be deployed in the construction of the Luz del Norte solar project in Chile—which, when completed, will be the largest photovoltaic project in Latin America.

Phasing down Climate-Potent Hydrofluorocarbons

Hydrofluorocarbons (HFCs) are potent greenhouse gases used in refrigerators, air conditioners, and other industrial applications as replacements for ozone-depleting substances. At the Climate Summit, a large group of governments and civil society partners agreed to support phasing down consumption and production of HFCs through a Montreal Protocol amendment; promoting public procurement of climate-friendly alternatives to high-GWP HFCs; and welcoming new private sector led initiatives aimed at reducing HFC emissions, including a Global Cold Food Chain Council, and a Global Refrigerant Management Initiative. In the summer of 2014, EPA proposed two new rules under the Significant New Alternatives Policy (SNAP) program that would smooth transition to climate-friendly alternatives to HFCs in the United States by expanding the list of acceptable alternatives and limiting use of some of the most harmful HFCs where lower risk alternatives are available. The Obama Administration also announced new private sector commitments and executive actions that will reduce the equivalent of 700 million metric tons of carbon pollution globally through 2025. Companies committed to introducing new climate-friendly alternatives, transitioning production lines and cold food chain equipment–the equipment that brings food from farm to market–away from potent HFCs.

City Action to Reduce Methane and Black Carbon from Municipal Solid Waste

The United States, in cooperation with over 60 country, city, non-government, and private sector partners, is taking action to reduce harmful methane and black carbon from municipal solid waste through a global city network that seeks to catalyse action in 1,000 cities by 2020. The United States is providing direct technical assistance to cities to improve waste and emissions data, design waste policies and programs, and conduct project studies. American cities like San Diego and San Francisco are also doing their share by building partnerships with cities overseas to help them apply our world-class practices in their own cities.

U.S. Leadership on Forest Preservation

The United States joined other governments, the private sector, civil society, and indigenous people's organizations in signing the New York Declaration on Forests. Supporting the Declaration reaffirms the ongoing commitment of the United States to protecting the world's forests and restoring degraded lands, including our pledge to restore 15 million hectares (ha) of forest land domestically as our contribution to the Bonn Challenge global goal to restore 150 million ha of forests and degraded lands by 2020. The United States government has committed over $1.3 billion to support REDD+ (Reducing Emissions from Deforestation and forest Degradation) since 2010. The United States was a co-founder of the BioCarbon Fund Initiative for Sustainable Forest Landscapes (ISFL), which seeks to promote reduced greenhouse gas emissions from the land sector, from REDD+, and from sustainable agriculture, as well as smarter land-use planning, policies and practices. The ISFL co-founders announced at the Climate Summit that they have agreed to establish the first two large-scale, public-private programs in the Oromia Regional State of Ethiopia and the Luangwa Valley of Zambia.

New International Energy Partnerships

At the Climate Summit and SE4All events in New York, the United States announced its support for three group initiatives:

- The Africa Clean Energy Corridor is a regional project in East Africa aimed at accelerating renewable energy development and complements the Administration's Power Africa initiative;
- A coalition of foundations and private companies is launching "energy efficiency accelerators" to pursue policy reforms and commercialization of new technologies in buildings, appliances and lighting, and transport. The United States will support these accelerators through the Clean Energy Ministerial's (CEM) Clean Energy Solutions Center and other CEM initiatives; and
- The SIDS Lighthouse Initiative complements U.S. efforts in Hawaii and the Virgin Islands and the new Caribbean Energy Security Initiative.

On November 12, 2014 President Obama and Chinese President Xi Jinping signed an historic agreement to reduce greenhouse gas emissions driving climate change in the post 2020-period.

A White House statement read:

> This announcement is a unique development in the U.S.-China relationship. The world's two largest economies, energy consumers, and carbon emitters are reaching across traditional divides and working together to demonstrate leadership on an issue that affects the entire world.
>
> By making this announcement well in advance of the deadline set out in the UNFCCC negotiations, the two leaders demonstrated their commitment to reducing the harmful emissions warming our planet, and urged other world leaders to follow suit in offering strong national targets ahead of next year's final negotiations in Paris.
>
> President Obama believes we have a moral obligation to take action on climate change, and that we cannot leave our children a planet beyond their capacity to repair. Over the last year, a spate of scientific studies have laid

out the scope and scale of the challenge we face in the starkest of terms. "Climate change, once considered an issue for a distant future, has moved firmly into the present," says the U.S. National Climate Assessment. "Without additional mitigation efforts...warming by the end of the 21st century will lead to high to very high risk of severe, widespread, and irreversible impacts globally," the Intergovernmental Panel on Climate Change concludes.

In Copenhagen in 2009, President Obama pledged that the United States would reduce its greenhouse gas emissions in the range of 17 percent below 2005 levels by 2020. We're on track to meet that goal while growing the economy and creating jobs, thanks to the historic fuel economy standards enacted during the President's first term; the measures to reduce carbon pollution, deploy more clean energy, and boost energy efficiency through the President's Climate Action Plan; and the leadership demonstrated by a growing number of U.S. businesses, who have increased their investment in clean technologies and pledged to phase down the potent greenhouse gases known as HFCs.

After 2020, the United States will reduce its net greenhouse gas emissions to 26-28 percent below 2005 levels by 2025. This goal is both ambitious and achievable, grounded in an intensive analysis of what actions can be taken under existing law, and will double the pace of carbon pollution reduction in the United States from the pre-2020 period. It also means the United States is doing its part to contain warming to 2 degrees Celsius, though achieving that global outcome will require global ambition and commitments from all economies.

THE REPUBLICANS

The Republican Party Environmental manifesto over the years has argued that conservation is a conservative value—as long as it is properly balanced with economics.

They consider human health and safety to be the first and most important issue in environmental concerns, as humans are our country's most valuable resource, and argue that any policy that supports conservation must equally address economic growth and development, as well as private property rights, in order for it to be practical.

The party also supports public access to public lands for hunting, fishing, and recreational shooting. Republicans believe in environmental policies that are tailored to the needs of the localities that they regulate, and that focus on achieving results processes. To this end, they support developing the technology to meet the nation's environmental needs by providing market-based incentives to advance said technology.

Republicans believe that environmental causes have been advanced best on private lands, and therefore consider the security of private property to be essential to any environmental agenda. Most environmental degradation has happened under government control they say which is why they safeguard private property rights by supporting the enforcement of the Takings Clause of the Fifth Amendment, which guarantees a private property owner compensation for any pubic use of their land that is justified by eminent domain.

Republicans are generally opposed to the EPA arguing that its regulations have cost businesses and consumers tens of billions of dollars in the last few years. The Republican Party believes these regulations create regulatory uncertainty, preventing new projects from moving forward, discouraging investment, and preventing job creation.

Republicans on the Environment

Lisa Murkowski, the ranking Republican on the Senate Committee on Energy and Natural Resources, explains the Republican viewpoint on energy and the environment in a 2013 committee report, *Energy 20/20: A Vision for America's Energy Future*:

> America's energy and natural resources policies must be re-imagined as we move toward the year 2020. Dramatic changes have taken place in global and national economic conditions. There is a heightened awareness of our energy production and consumption which moves us towards greater environmental responsibility (1).
>
> I believe we can secure a future in which energy and natural resources are affordable and abundant from secure and diverse sources; the air and water are cleaner in our own country and around the world; and Americans enjoy a healthy economy and preserve their ability to live and to pursue happiness (2).
>
> Our nation contains the largest deposits of oil shale in the world. The Green River Formation's 11 million acres in Colorado, Utah, and Wyoming contain the equivalent of more than one trillion barrels in oil. Assessments fluctuate, but DOE estimates that combined U.S. oil shale deposits may hold as much as six trillion barrels of oil equivalent. While most of these

are non-recoverable, the fact that global proven crude reserves amount to a mere 1.5 trillion barrels should give us pause. Whether recoverable barrels from these deposits stand at 800 billion or 1.8 trillion, America truly is the Saudi Arabia of oil shale (28).

It is important to face questions about the risks of energy and resource development including questions about climate change. We need to discuss these questions openly and find common ground on prudent steps to take in the face of uncertainty. What is certain is that we can best address environmental challenges if we are prosperous and secure. Affordable, abundant, secure energy is not the problem; it is part of the answer (4).

She outlines five principles that Republicans believe must be part of any future energy or environmental policies, as reported by the Senate Republican Policy Committee:

- **Affordable, reliable, and efficient energy**. Washington Democrats favor renewable energy as a substitute for, not a supplement to, fossil fuels. This results in higher gasoline prices for cars and higher heating, cooling, and electricity prices for homes and businesses. A Republican-led Senate would implement a true all-of-the-above strategy that embraces coal, oil, gas, and nuclear as baseload power, encourages development of renewables as supplementary power, and promotes deployment of energy efficiency measures. This would reorient gasoline, electricity, cooling, and heating prices to more affordable levels, while strengthening energy reliability.
- **Produce American energy**. The federal government restricts access to federal onshore and offshore energy resources. A Republican-led Senate would reform federal leasing plans to empower producers to responsibly develop fossil and renewable energy resources throughout the nation's federal lands, including in Colorado and other energy-rich western states; off the Atlantic, Pacific, and Gulf coasts; and in Alaska.
- **Certainty in energy project permitting**. The federal government suffocates energy projects by slow-walking, politicizing, and rejecting routine permits like the Keystone XL pipeline. A Republican-led Senate would restore certainty in energy project permitting by streamlining applications, insulating reviews from politics and manipulation by ideologues, requiring regulators to render decisions by specified deadlines, and prohibiting preemptive and retroactive permit vetoes.
- **Energy innovation**. The federal government underwrites handpicked renewable projects like Solyndra with billions in taxpayer dol-

lars to enhance their appeal in the marketplace. A Republican-led Senate would refocus federal support away from commercial deployment and toward basic research and development. It would task public and private-sector research institutions with leading an energy innovation economy focused on scientific and technological breakthroughs that must be achieved before emerging energy technologies can be commercially viable.

- **Protecting energy infrastructure from emerging threats**. The federal government's current programs do not adequately protect our nation's electric grid, pipelines, and other energy infrastructure. A Republican-led Senate would coordinate public and private-sector resources to adequately secure America's energy infrastructure from physical and cyber threats.

Her energy and natural resources vision include the following federal government initiatives:

- Identify and remove barriers in federal law and policy that are hindering rapid and competitive deployment of clean energy. For example, provide for swift and certain leasing and perming structures for wind, solar, and geothermal leases. Create fair and competitive royalty systems for these energy sources on public lands (32).
- Hydropower is the largest source of clean, renewable electricity in the United States. It is an under-developed resource. Further development of this cost-effective, clean energy option will support economic development and local job creation (33).
- Accelerate the development of renewable wave, current, and dal energy across the nation (35).
- Technologies that bring down the cost of storing solar energy are needed. Cost-effective energy storage will likely unlock the full potential of solar power. Rather than force solar power into the electricity supply through mandates or quotas, we should endeavor to use solar power where it naturally fits: in remote applications, to complement baseload and intermediate supply, and to diversify our energy portfolio. Meanwhile, we should continue to fund R&D to discover and develop tomorrow's solar technologies (37).
- Wind power is abundant and renewable. To make wind power cost-competitive we should focus on R&D for energy storage technologies (39).

- Geothermal power is an emerging factor in in the diversification of US energy supply. More research is needed to bring geothermal costs in line with the costs of fossil fuels in the future (43).
- Biomass is organic material that can be processed into transportation fuel, used to generate electricity, or harnessed in other ways to provide energy. Innovative technologies are starting to allow biomass to emerge as a viable source of renewable chemicals as well, further extending its range of potential applications. Congress, we should continue to find cost–effective ways to utilize this resource, while also making several common sense reforms to existing policies (46).
- Nuclear power is one of the most reliable sources of baseload electricity, one of the lowest–cost producers of electricity, and one of the cleanest sources of energy, emitting no pollutants or greenhouse gases in electricity generation and with lifecycle emissions comparable to wind and hydropower. In addition, the nuclear industry is a source of good–paying jobs and large–scale job creation. Nuclear energy must remain a viable contributor to America's power supply (48).
- Establish as the policy of the United States the promotion of an adequate, reliable, domestic, and stable supply of critical minerals, produced in an environmentally responsible manner, to strengthen and sustain our nation's economic security (54).
- We should aim to use energy more wisely – by using less and less energy per capita and per unit of gross domestic product. Using energy efficiently is part of, not in conflict with, abundant and affordable energy. Energy experts have correctly called energy efficiency "the fifth fuel." Using energy more efficiently is akin to developing more fuel (62).
- While emerging technologies can prosper by relying on government–provided finance for set periods of me, perpetual reliance on subsidies can actually inhibit the growth and development of new technologies. By 2020, we need to eliminate most of the government's current subsidies and implement a new system of clean energy finance that is cost–effective, technology–neutral, and conducive to private investment (73).
- The combined use of horizontal drilling and hydraulic fracturing ("fracking") techniques has allowed the oil and gas industry to develop and produce resources that were unrecoverable less than 10 years ago. The federal government should consider the efficacy of self–regulation before mandating new blanket regulations that may not work in every state. The economic benefits associated with the "shale boom"

in the U.S. are clear: more jobs, higher wages, and increased revenues to federal, state and local governments (92).

- Economic uses of federal lands are now heavily restricted by regulation which has caused significant harm to many rural communities. It is imperative that DOI partner with states to achieve the best possible use of public lands. Current federal regulations pit DOI against the states in never-ending legal and political battles over land use. This arrangement is wasteful and contrary to DOI's mission (93).
- Initiate a regulatory moratorium across the board for a reasonable me to assess the impact of regulations on the economy generally and energy security specifically. During the moratorium, agencies should identify duplicative or burdensome regulations that should be removed (96).

Everything we do has environmental consequences. We never notice nor consider most of these. Everything we do also uses energy, and the environmental consequences of energy development tend to be more visible than the consequences of many of our other actions.

We should be proud of this, and strive to continue to have the best environmental standards. We absolutely should pay close attention to the environmental consequences of energy development. In doing so, however, we need to make our evaluations fairly in respect to actual impact per unit of energy produced, the practicality and cost of alternatives, and the effect of not having sufficient affordable energy (106).

The United States should be proud of its record on the environment, because it is a record of tremendous progress most often forged through bipartisan legislation and sensible regulation. Rivers no longer catch fire because of the waste dumped into them. Our skies are blue—less often clouded by particulate matter or haze. Emissions from power plants have declined considerably, and vehicle efficiency has been increasing since 2005. The air in America is dramatically cleaner than it was thirty years ago, while the air pollution in China, a country so often cited as a model, has become a major health hazard. Still, there is more work we can do, and the key to success will be striking the right balance between the need for energy production and the desire for environmental standards (107).

THE ENVIRONMENTAL MOVEMENT

The environmental movement in the United States is tens of millions strong. The majority are not activists or campaigners but opinion polls regularly show that they are concerned about water quality, pollution, renewable energy and sustainability. It is useful, therefore, to talk about two elements—the organized environmental movement and the vast silent majority.

The organized movement is largely represented by groups known as nongovernmental organizations (NGOs)—the Sierra Club, Green Peace, Audubon Society, Nature Conservancy and many more. These NGOs can operate at local, regional and national and even international levels.

In the late 19th and early 20th centuries the focus was on conservation—conserving fisheries, wildlife, water, soil and forests. Today environmentalism also covers air and water pollution, preservation and protection of wilderness areas, sustainable use of natural resources and biodiversity—the variety and number of different organisms within an ecosystem.

Thanks to the media—written, electronic and social—there is greater awareness of environmental concerns especially major issues such as global warming, ozone depletion, natural resource exploration and pollution.

THE ANTI-ENVIRONMENTALISTS

The Anti-environmentalists argue that there really is nothing to worry about, that the earth is not as fragile as the environmentalists would have us believe. They are much more concerned with wealth building and job creation by exploring for oil, mining raw materials, building pipelines, forestry, and construction and so on.

In 1988 a Wise Use Campaign was introduced by Republican senator, Mark Hatfield. It advocated unrestricted access to timber and other resources and effectively launched the anti-environmentalism movement.

The economic recession that began in 1990 enhanced anti-green and pro-industry views. A group called Alliance for America was created with 125 anti-environment and pro-industry groups. In 1994, the United States declined to pass a Biodiversity Treaty. Another group formed called Earth Day Alternatives labelled environmentalists as "anti-human and extremists." They promoted three things—privatization of resources for exploitation, the 'trading' of pollution between companies, and to discredit environmental science.

Today's anti-environmentalists include chemical manufacturers, oil producers, mining producers, timber companies, real estate developers, nuclear power industries, electric utilities and politicians. They view environmentalism as "an attack on middle-class American capitalism."

At a Heartland Institute anti-environmentalism conference held in 2011, President Barack Obama's campaign promise to make America more environmentally cautious was labelled as a plan toward National Socialism. Former Republican Senator Harrison Schmitt accused environmentalism of sacrificing humans for the sake of the weather. Larry Bell, an anti-environmental speaker claimed that the point of environmentalism is to destroy capitalism. Many anti-environmental activists portray environmentalism as a "the ambitions of communist central planners to control the entire society."

SOURCE MATERIAL

Murkowski, Lisa. *Energy 20/20: A Vision for America's Energy Future*. Report prepared for the US Senate Committee on Energy and Natural Resources. 113th Cong., 1st Sess., 2013. http://www.energy.senate.gov/public/index.cfm/files/serve?File_id=c691a024-1004-4d49-8de9-a976ceo d2bf3.

Podesta, John and John Holdren. "The U.S. and China Just Announced Important New Actions to Reduce Carbon Pollution." *The White House Blog*. November 12, 2014. https://www.whitehouse.gov/blog/2014/11/12/us-and-china-just-announced-important-new-actions-reduce-carbon-pollution.

Senate Republican Policy Committee. "Republican Solutions: Energy." May 21, 2014, http://www.rpc.senate.gov/policy-papers/republican-solutions-energy.

The White House. "FACT SHEET: President Obama Announces New Actions to Strengthen Global Resilience to Climate Change and Launches Partnerships to Cut Barbon Pollution." Office of the Press Secretary. September 23, 2014. https://www.whitehouse.gov/the-press-office/2014/09/23/fact-sheet-president-obama-announces-new-actions-strengthen-global-resil.

FURTHER READING

The White House. "Executive Order—Climate Resilient International Development." Office of the Press Secretary. September 23, 2014. https://www.whitehouse.gov/the-press-office/2014/09/23/executive-order-climate-resilient-international-development.

1

Global Warming

This chapter reproduces the argument that climate change is happening and is caused by human activities, as presented by the US Global Change Research Program and the US Environmental Protection Agency.

OUR CHANGING CLIMATE

Many independent lines of evidence demonstrate that the world is warming and that human activity is the primary cause. Other changes flow from this warming, including melting of snow and ice, rising sea level, and increases in some types of extreme weather, such as extreme heat and heavy downpours. How much climate change we will experience in the future depends largely on the global emissions pathway.

Observed Change

Climate is defined as long-term averages and variations in weather measured over a period of several decades. The Earth's climate system includes
the land surface, atmosphere, oceans, and ice. Many aspects of the global
climate are changing rapidly, and the primary drivers of that change are human in origin. Evidence for changes in the climate system abounds, from the
top of the atmosphere to the depths of the oceans. Scientists and engineers
from around the world have compiled this evidence using satellites, weather
balloons, thermometers at surface stations, and many other types of observing systems that monitor the Earth's weather and climate. The sum total of
this evidence tells an unambiguous story: the planet is warming.

Temperatures at the surface, in the troposphere (the active weather layer
extending up to about 5 to 10 miles above the ground), and in the oceans
have all increased over recent decades. Consistent with our scientific understanding, the largest increases in temperature are occurring closer to the
poles, especially in the Arctic. Snow and ice cover have decreased in most
areas. Atmospheric water vapor is increasing in the lower atmosphere, because a warmer atmosphere can hold more water. Sea levels are also increasing. Changes in other climate-relevant indicators such as growing season
length have been observed in many areas. Worldwide, the observed changes
in average conditions have been accompanied by increasing trends in extremes of heat and heavy precipitation events, and decreases in extreme
cold.

Natural drivers of climate cannot explain the recent observed warming.
Over the last five decades, natural factors (solar forcing and volcanoes) alone
would actually have led to a slight cooling.

The majority of the warming at the global scale over the past 50 years can
only be explained by the effects of human influences, especially the emissions from burning fossil fuels (coal, oil, and natural gas) and from deforestation. The emissions from human influences that are affecting climate include
heat-trapping gases such as carbon dioxide (CO_2), methane, and nitrous oxide, and particles such as black carbon (soot), which has a warming influence, and sulfates, which have an overall cooling influence. In addition to
human-induced global climate change, local climate can also be affected by
other human factors (such as crop irrigation) and natural variability.

The conclusion that human influences are the primary driver of recent
climate change is based on multiple lines of independent evidence. The first
line of evidence is our fundamental understanding of how certain gases trap
heat, how the climate system responds to increases in these gases, and how

other human and natural factors influence climate. The second line of evidence is from reconstructions of past climates using evidence such as tree rings, ice cores, and corals. These show that global surface temperatures over the last several decades are clearly unusual, with the last decade (2000-2009) warmer than any time in at least the last 1300 years and perhaps much longer.

The third line of evidence comes from using climate models to simulate the climate of the past century, separating the human and natural factors that influence climate. When the human factors are removed, these models show that solar and volcanic activity would have tended to slightly cool the earth, and other natural variations are too small to explain the amount of warming. Only when the human influences are included do the models reproduce the warming observed over the past 50 years.

Another line of evidence involves so-called "fingerprint" studies that are able to attribute observed climate changes to particular causes. For example, the fact that the stratosphere (the layer above the troposphere) is cooling while the Earth's surface and lower atmosphere is warming is a fingerprint that the warming is due to increases in heat-trapping gases. In contrast, if the observed warming had been due to increases in solar output, Earth's atmosphere would have warmed throughout its entire extent, including the stratosphere.

In addition to such temperature analyses, scientific attribution of observed changes to human influence extends to many other aspects of climate, such as changing patterns in precipitation,, increasing humidity,, changes in pressure, and increasing ocean heat content.

Natural variations in climate include the effects of cycles such as El Niño, La Niña and other ocean cycles; the 11-year sunspot cycle and other changes in energy from the sun; and the effects of volcanic eruptions. Globally, natural variations can be as large as human-induced climate change over timescales of up to a few decades. However, changes in climate at the global scale observed over the past 50 years are far larger than can be accounted for by natural variability. Changes in climate at the local to regional scale can be influenced by natural variability for multiple decades. This can affect the interpretation of climate trends observed regionally across the United States.

Globally averaged surface air temperature has slowed its rate of increase since the late 1990s. This is not in conflict with our basic understanding of global warming and its primary cause. The decade of 2000 to 2009 was still the warmest decade on record. In addition, global surface air temperature does not always increase steadily. This time period is too short to signify a change in the warming trend, as climate trends are measured over periods of decades, not years. Such decade-long slowdowns or even reversals in trend have occurred before in the global instrumental record (for example, 1900-1910 and 1940-1950), including three decade-long periods since 1970, each followed by a sharp temperature rise. Nonetheless, satellite and ocean observations indicate that the Earth-atmosphere climate system has continued to gain heat energy.

There are a number of possible contributions to the lower rate of increase over the last 15 years. First, the solar output during the latest 11-year solar cycle has been lower over the past 15 years than the past 60 years. Second, a series of mildly explosive volcanoes, which increased stratospheric particles, likely had more of a cooling effect than previously recognized. Third, the high incidence of La Niña events in the last 15 years has played a role in the observed trends., Recent analyses suggest that more of the increase in heat energy during this period has been transferred to the deep ocean than previously. While this might temporarily slow the rate of increase in surface air temperature, ultimately it will prolong the effects of global warming because the oceans hold heat for longer than the atmosphere does.

Climate models are not intended to match the real-world timing of natural climate variations—instead, models have their own internal timing for such variations. Most modeling studies do not yet account for the observed changes in solar and volcanic forcing mentioned in the previous paragraph. Therefore, it is not surprising that the timing of such a slowdown in the rate of increase in the models would be different than that observed, although it is important to note that such periods have been simulated by climate models, with the deep oceans absorbing the extra heat during those decades.

Future Climate Change

A certain amount of continued warming of the planet is projected to occur as a result of human-induced emissions to date; another 0.5°F increase would be expected over the next few decades even if all emissions from human activities suddenly stopped, although natural variability could still play an important role over this time period. However, choices made now and in the next few decades will determine the amount of additional future warming. Beyond mid-century, lower levels of heat-trapping gases in scenarios with reduced emissions will lead to noticeably less future warming. Higher emissions levels will result in more warming, and thus more severe impacts on human society and the natural world.

Confidence in projections of future climate change has increased. The wider range of potential changes in global average temperature in the latest generation of climate model simulations used in the Intergovernmental Panel on Climate Change's (IPCC) current assessment—versus those in the previous assessment—is simply a result of considering more options for future human behavior. For example, one of the scenarios included in the IPCC's latest assessment assumes aggressive emissions reductions designed to limit the global temperature increase to 3.6°F (2°C) above pre-industrial levels. This path would require rapid emissions reductions (more than 70 percent reduction in human-related emissions by 2050, and net negative emissions by 2100) sufficient to achieve heat-trapping gas concentrations well below those of any of the scenarios considered by the IPCC in its 2007 assessment. Such scenarios enable the investigation of climate impacts that would be avoided by deliberate, substantial reductions in heat-trapping gas emissions.

Projections of future changes in precipitation show small increases in the global average but substantial shifts in where and how precipitation falls. Generally, areas closest to the poles are projected to receive more precipitation, while the dry subtropics (the region just outside the tropics, between 23° and 35° on either side of the equator) expand toward the poles and receive less rain. Increases in tropical precipitation are projected during rainy seasons (such as monsoons), especially over the tropical Pacific. Certain regions, including the western United States (especially the Southwest) and the Mediterranean, are presently dry and are expected to become drier. The widespread trend of increasing heavy downpours is expected to continue, with precipitation becoming less frequent but more intense.,,, The patterns of the projected changes of precipitation do not contain the spatial details that characterize observed precipitation, especially in mountainous terrain, because the projections are averages from multiple models and because the effective resolution of global climate models is roughly 100-200 miles.

One important determinant of how much climate will change is the effect of so-called "feedbacks" in the climate system, which can either dampen or amplify the initial effect of human influences on temperature. One important climate feedback is the loss of summer Arctic sea ice, allowing absorption of substantially more of the sun's heat in the Arctic, increasing warming, and possibly causing changes in weather patterns over the United States.

The observed drastic reduction in sea ice can also lead to a "tipping point"—a point beyond which an abrupt or irreversible transition to a different climatic state occurs. In this case, the dramatic loss of sea ice could tip the Arctic Ocean into a permanent, nearly ice-free state in summer, with repercussions that may extend far beyond the Arctic. Such potential "tipping points" have been identified in various components of the Earth's climate system and could have important effects on future climate. The extent and magnitude of these potential effects are still unknown.

Recent US Temperature Trends

There have been substantial advances in our understanding of the US temperature record since the 2009 assessment. These advances confirm that the United States annually averaged temperature has increased by 1.3°F to 1.9°F since 1895. However, this increase was not constant over time. In particular, temperatures generally rose until about 1940, declined slightly until about 1970, then increased rapidly thereafter. The year 2012 was the warmest on record for the contiguous United States. Over shorter time scales (one to two decades), natural variability can reduce the rate of warming or even create a temporary cooling. The cooling in mid-century that was especially prevalent over the eastern half of the United States may have stemmed partly from such natural variations and partly from human influences, in particular the cooling effects of sulfate particles from coal-burning power plants, before these sulfur emissions were regulated to address health and acid rain concerns.

Since 1991, temperatures have averaged 1°F to 1.5°F higher than 1901-1960 over most of the United States, except for the Southeast, where the warming has been less than 1°F. On a seasonal basis, long-term warming has been greatest in winter and spring.

Warming is ultimately projected for all parts of the nation during this century. In the next few decades, this warming will be roughly 2°F to 4°F in most areas. By the end of the century, US warming is projected to correspond closely to the level of global emissions: roughly 3°F to 5°F under lower emissions scenarios involving substantial reductions in emissions, and 5°F to 10°F for higher emissions scenarios that assume continued increases in emissions; the largest temperature increases are projected for the upper Midwest and Alaska.

Future human-induced warming depends on both past and future emissions of heat-trapping gases and changes in the amount of particle pollution. The amount of climate change (aside from natural variability) expected for the next two to three decades is a combination of the warming already built into the climate system by the past history of human emissions of heat-trapping gases, and the expected ongoing increases in emissions of those gases. However, the magnitude of temperature increases over the second half of this century, both in the United States and globally, will be primarily determined by the emissions produced now and over the next few decades, and there are substantial differences between higher, fossil-fuel intensive scenarios compared to scenarios in which emissions are reduced. The most recent model projections of climate change due to human activities expand the range of future scenarios considered (particularly at the lower end), but are entirely consistent with the older model results. This consistency increases our confidence in the projections.

Lengthening Frost-free Season

The length of the frost-free season (and the corresponding growing season) is a major determinant of the types of plants and crops that do well in a particular region. The frost-free season length has been gradually increasing since the 1980s. The last occurrence of 32°F in the spring has been occurring earlier in the year, and the first occurrence of 32°F in the fall has been happening later. During 1991-2011, the average frost-free season was about 10 days longer than during 1901-1960. These observed climate changes have been mirrored by changes in the biosphere, including increases in forest productivity, and satellite-derived estimates of the length of the growing season. A longer growing season provides a longer period for plant growth and productivity and can slow the increase in atmospheric CO_2 concentrations through increased CO_2 uptake by living things and their environment. The longer growing season can increase the growth of beneficial plants (such as crops and forests) as well as undesirable ones (such as ragweed). In some cases where moisture is limited, the greater evaporation and loss of moisture through plant transpiration (release of water from plant leaves) associated with a longer growing season can mean less productivity because of increased drying and earlier and longer fire seasons.

The lengthening of the frost-free season has been somewhat greater in the western United States than the eastern United States, increasing by two to three weeks in the Northwest and Southwest, one to two weeks in the Midwest, Great Plains, and Northeast, and slightly less than one week in the Southeast. These differences mirror the overall trend of more warming in the north and west and less warming in the Southeast.

In a future in which heat-trapping gas emissions continue to grow, increases of a month or more in the lengths of the frost-free and growing seasons are projected across most of the United States by the end of the century, with slightly smaller increases in the northern Great Plains. The largest increases in the frost-free season (more than eight weeks) are projected for the western United States, particularly in high elevation and coastal areas. The increases will be considerably smaller if heat-trapping gas emissions are reduced, although still substantial. These increases projected to be much greater than the normal year-to-year variability experienced today. The projected changes also imply that the southern boundary of the seasonal freeze zone will move northward, with increasing frequencies of years without sub-freezing temperatures in the most southern parts of the United States.

US Precipitation Change

Since 1900, average annual precipitation over the United States has increased by roughly 5 percent. This increase reflects, in part, the major droughts of the 1930s and 1950s, which made the early half of the record drier. There are important regional differences. For instance, precipitation since 1991 (relative to 1901-1960) increased the most in the Northeast (8 percent), Midwest (9 percent), and southern Great Plains (8 percent), while much of the Southeast and Southwest had a mix of areas of increases and decreases.

While significant trends in average precipitation have been detected, the fraction of these trends attributable to human activity is difficult to quantify at regional scales because the range of natural variability in precipitation is large. Projected changes are generally small for central portions of the United States. However, if emissions of heat-trapping gases continue their upward trend, certain global patterns of precipitation change are projected to emerge that will affect northern and southwestern areas of the United States. The northern United States is projected to experience more precipitation in the winter and spring (except for the Northwest in the spring), while the Southwest is projected to experience less, particularly in the spring. The contrast between wet and dry areas will increase both in the United States and globally—in other words, the wet areas will get wetter and the dry areas will get drier. As discussed in the next section, there has been an increase in the amount of precipitation falling in heavy events, and this is projected to continue.

The projected changes in the northern United States are a consequence of both a warmer atmosphere (which can hold more moisture than a colder one) and associated changes in large-scale weather patterns (which affect where precipitation occurs). The projected reduction in Southwest precipitation is a result of changes in large-scale weather patterns, including the northward expansion of the belt of high pressure in the subtropics, which suppresses rainfall. Recent improvements in understanding these mechanisms of change increase confidence in these projections. The patterns of the projected changes of precipitation resulting from human alterations of the climate are geographically smoother in these projections than what will actually be observed because: 1) the precise locations of natural increases and decreases differ from model to model, and averaging across models smooths these differences; and 2) the resolution of current climate models is too coarse to capture fine topographic details, especially in mountainous terrain. Hence, there is considerably more confidence in the large-scale patterns of change than in local details.

In general, a comparison of the various sources of climate model data used in this assessment provides a consistent picture of the large-scale projected precipitation changes across the United States. Multi-model average changes in all three of these sources show a general pattern of wetter future conditions in the North and drier conditions in the South. The regional suite generally shows conditions that are somewhat wetter overall in the wet areas and not as dry in the dry areas. The general pattern agreement among these three sources, with the wide variations in their spatial resolution, provides confidence that this pattern is robust and not sensitive to the limited spatial resolution of the models.

Thus, despite subtle difference between various sets of projections, the overall picture remains the same: wetter conditions in the North and drier conditions in the Southwest in winter and spring. Drier conditions are projected for summer in most areas of the contiguous United States but, outside of the Northwest and south-central region, there is generally not high confidence that the changes will be large compared to natural variability. In all models and scenarios, a transition zone between drier (to the South) and wetter (to the North) shifts northward from the southern United States in winter to southern Canada in summer. Wetter conditions are projected for Alaska and northern Canada in all seasons.

Heavy Downpours Increasing

Across most of the United States, the heaviest rainfall events have become heavier and more frequent. The amount of rain falling on the heaviest rain days has also increased over the past few decades. Since 1991, the amount of rain falling in very heavy precipitation events has been significantly above average. This increase has been greatest in the Northeast, Midwest, and upper Great Plains—more than 30 percent above the 1901-1960 average. There has also been an increase in flooding events in the Midwest and Northeast where the largest increases in heavy rain amounts have occurred.

Warmer air can contain more water vapor than cooler air. Global analyses show that the amount of water vapor in the atmosphere has in fact increased over both land and oceans. Climate change also alters dynamical characteristics of the atmosphere that in turn affect weather patterns and storms. In the mid-latitudes, where most of the continental U.S. is located, there is an upward trend in extreme precipitation in the vicinity of fronts associated with mid-latitude storms. Locally, natural variations can also be important.

Projections of future climate over the U.S. suggest that the recent trend towards increased heavy precipitation events will continue. This is projected to occur even in regions where total precipitation is projected to decrease, such as the Southwest.

Extreme Weather

Heat waves are periods of abnormally hot weather lasting days to weeks. Heat waves have generally become more frequent across the United States in recent decades, with western regions (including Alaska) setting records for numbers of these events in the 2000s. Tree ring data suggests that the drought over the last decade in the western United States represents the driest conditions in 800 years. Most other regions in the country had their highest number of short-duration heat waves in the 1930s, when the multi-year severe drought of the Dust Bowl period, combined with deleterious land-use practices, contributed to the intense summer heat through depletion of soil moisture and reduction of the moderating effects of evaporation. However, the recent prolonged (multi-month) extreme heat has been unprecedented since the start of reliable instrumental records in 1895. The recent heat waves and droughts in Texas (2011) and the Midwest (2012) set records for highest monthly average temperatures, exceeding in some cases records set in the 1930s, including the highest monthly contiguous US temperature on record (July 2012, breaking the July 1936 record) and the hottest summers on record in several states (New Mexico, Texas, Oklahoma, and Louisiana in 2011 and Colorado and Wyoming in 2012). For the spring and summer months, 2012 had the second largest area of record-setting monthly average temperatures, including a 26-state area from Wyoming to the East Coast. The summer (June-August) temperatures of 2012 ranked in the hottest 10 percent of the 118-year period of record in 28 states covering the Rocky Mountain states, the Great Plains, the Upper Midwest, and the Northeast. The new records included both hot daytime maximum temperatures and warm nighttime minimum temperatures. Corresponding with this increase in extreme heat, the number of extreme cold waves has reached the lowest levels on record (since 1895).

Many more high temperature records are being broken as compared to low temperature records over the past three to four decades—another indicator of a warming climate. The number of record low monthly temperatures has declined to the lowest levels since 1911, while the number of record high monthly temperatures has increased to the highest level since the 1930s. During this same period, there has been an increasing trend in persistently high nighttime temperature. There are various reasons why low temperatures have increased more than high temperatures.

In some areas, prolonged periods of record high temperatures associated with droughts contribute to dry conditions that are driving wildfires. The meteorological situations that cause heat waves are a natural part of the climate system. Thus the timing and location of individual events may be largely a natural phenomenon, although even these may be affected by human-induced climate change. However, there is emerging evidence that most of the increases of heat wave severity over the United States are likely due to human activity, with a detectable human influence in recent heat waves in the southern Great Plains, as well as in Europe, and Russia. The summer 2011 heat wave and drought in Texas was primarily driven by precipitation deficits, but the human contribution to climate change approximately doubled the probability that the heat was record-breaking. So while an event such as this Texas heat wave and drought could be triggered by a naturally occurring event such as a deficit in precipitation, the chances for record-breaking temperature extremes has increased and will continue to increase as the global climate warms. Generally, the changes in climate are increasing the likelihood for these types of severe events.

The number of extremely hot days is projected to continue to increase over much of the United States, especially by late century. Summer temperatures are projected to continue rising, and a reduction of soil moisture, which exacerbates heat waves, is projected for much of the western and central United States in summer. Climate models project that the same summertime temperatures that ranked among the hottest 5 percent in 1950-1979 will occur at least 70 percent of the time by 2035-2064 in the United States if global emissions of heat-trapping gases continue to grow. By the end of this century, what have previously been once-in-20-year extreme heat days (one-day events) are projected to occur every two or three years over most of the nation., In other words, what now seems like an extremely hot day will become commonplace.

There are significant trends in the magnitude of river flooding in many parts of the United States. When averaged over the entire nation, however, the increases and decreases cancel each other out and show no national level trend. River flood magnitudes have decreased in the Southwest and increased in the eastern Great Plains, parts of the Midwest, and from the northern Appalachians into New England.

These regional river flood trends are qualitatively consistent with trends in climate conditions associated with flooding. For example, average annual precipitation has increased in the Midwest and Northeast and decreased in the Southwest. Recent soil moisture trends show general drying in the Southwest and moistening in the Northeast and northern Great Plains and Midwest. These trends are in general agreement with the flood trends. Although there is a strong national upward trend in extreme precipitation and not in river flooding, the regional variations are similar. Extreme precipitation has been increasing strongly in the Great Plains, Midwest, and Northeast, where river flooding increases have been observed, and there is little trend in the Southwest, where river flooding has decreased. An exact correspondence is not necessarily expected since the seasonal timing of precipitation events makes a difference in whether river flooding occurs. The increase in extreme precipitation events has been concentrated in the summer and fall when soil moisture is seasonally low and soils can absorb a greater fraction of rainfall. By contrast, many of the annual flood events occur in the spring when soil moisture is high. Thus, additional extreme rainfall events in summer and fall may not create sufficient runoff for the resulting streamflow to exceed spring flood magnitudes. However, these extreme precipitation events are often associated with local flash floods, a leading cause of death due to weather events.

Research into the effects of human-induced climate change on flood events is relatively new. There is evidence of a detectable human influence in recent flooding events in England and Wales and in other specific events around the globe during 2011. In general, heavier rains lead to a larger fraction of rainfall running off and, depending on the surface conditions, more potential for flooding.

Higher temperatures lead to increased rates of evaporation, including more loss of moisture through plant leaves. Even in areas where precipitation does not decrease, these increases in surface evaporation and loss of water from plants lead to more rapid drying of soils if the effects of higher temperatures are not offset by other changes (such as in wind speed or humidity). As soil dries out, a larger proportion of the incoming heat from the sun goes into heating the soil and adjacent air rather than evaporating its moisture, resulting in hotter summers under drier climatic conditions. Under higher emissions scenarios, widespread drought is projected to become more common over most of the central and southern United States.

Changes in Hurricanes

There has been a substantial increase in most measures of Atlantic hurricane activity since the early 1980s, the period during which high-quality satellite data are available. These include measures of intensity, frequency, and duration as well as the number of strongest (Category 4 and 5) storms. The ability to assess longer-term trends in hurricane activity is limited by the quality of available data. The historic record of Atlantic hurricanes dates back to the mid-1800s, and indicates other decades of high activity. However, there is considerable uncertainty in the record prior to the satellite era (early 1970s), and the further back in time one goes, the more uncertain the record becomes.

The recent increases in activity are linked, in part, to higher sea surface temperatures in the region that Atlantic hurricanes form in and move through. Numerous factors have been shown to influence these local sea surface temperatures, including natural variability, human-induced emissions of heat-trapping gases, and particulate pollution. Quantifying the relative contributions of natural and human-caused factors is an active focus of research. Some studies suggest that natural variability, which includes the Atlantic Multidecadal Oscillation, is the dominant cause of the warming trend in the Atlantic since the 1970s, while others argue that human-caused heat-trapping gases and particulate pollution are more important.

Hurricane development, however, is influenced by more than just sea surface temperature. How hurricanes develop also depends on how the local atmosphere responds to changes in local sea surface temperatures, and this atmospheric response depends critically on the cause of the change. For example, the atmosphere responds differently when local sea surface temperatures increase due to a local decrease of particulate pollution that allows more sunlight through to warm the ocean, versus when sea surface temperatures increase more uniformly around the world due to increased amounts of human-caused heat-trapping gases. So the link between hurricanes and ocean temperatures is complex. Improving our understanding of the relationships between warming tropical oceans and tropical cyclones is another active area of research.

Changes in the average length and positions of Atlantic storm tracks are also associated with regional climate variability. The locations and frequency of storms striking land have been argued to vary in opposing ways than basin-wide frequency. For example, fewer storms have been observed to strike land during warmer years even though overall activity is higher than average, which may help to explain the lack of any clear trend in landfall frequency along the US eastern and Gulf coasts. Climate models also project changes in hurricane tracks and where they strike land. The specific characteristics of the changes are being actively studied.

Other measures of Atlantic storm activity are projected to change as well. By late this century, models, on average, project a slight decrease in the annual number of tropical cyclones, but an increase in the number of the strongest (Category 4 and 5) hurricanes. These projected changes are based on an average of projections from a number of individual models, and they represent the most likely outcome. There is some uncertainty in this as the individual models do not always agree on the amount of projected change, and some models may project an increase where others project a decrease. The models are in better agreement when projecting changes in hurricane precipitation—almost all existing studies project greater rainfall rates in hurricanes in a warmer climate, with projected increases of about 20 percent averaged near the center of hurricanes.

Changes in Storms

Trends in the occurrences of storms, ranging from severe thunderstorms to winter storms to hurricanes, are subject to much greater uncertainties than trends in temperature and variables that are directly related to temperature (such as snow and ice cover, ocean heat content, and sea level). Recognizing that the impacts of changes in the frequency and intensity of these storms can easily exceed the impacts of changes in average temperature or precipitation, climate scientists are actively researching the connections between climate change and severe storms. There has been a sizeable upward trend in the number of storms causing large financial and other losses. However, there are societal contributions to this trend, such as increases in population and wealth.

Severe Convective Storms

Tornadoes and other severe thunderstorm phenomena frequently cause as much annual property damage in the U.S. as do hurricanes, and often cause more deaths. Recent research has yielded insights into the connections between global warming and the factors that cause tornadoes and severe thunderstorms (such as atmospheric instability and increases in wind speed with altitude). Although these relationships are still being explored, a recent study suggests a projected increase in the frequency of conditions favorable for severe thunderstorms.

Winter Storms

For the entire Northern Hemisphere, there is evidence of an increase in both storm frequency and intensity during the cold season since 1950, with storm tracks having shifted slightly towards the poles. Extremely heavy snowstorms increased in number during the last century in northern and eastern parts of the United States, but have been less frequent since 2000. Total seasonal snowfall has generally decreased in southern and some western areas, increased in the northern Great Plains and Great Lakes region, and not changed in other areas, such as the Sierra Nevada, although snow is melting earlier in the year and more precipitation is falling as rain versus snow. Very snowy winters have generally been decreasing in frequency in most regions over the last 10 to 20 years, although the Northeast has been seeing a normal number of such winters. Heavier-than-normal snowfalls recently observed in the Midwest and Northeast United States in some years, with little snow in other years, are consistent with indications of increased blocking (a large scale pressure pattern with little or no movement) of the wintertime circulation of the Northern Hemisphere. However, conclusions about trends in blocking have been found to depend on the method of analysis, so the assessment and attribution of trends in blocking remains an active research area. Overall snow cover has decreased in the Northern Hemisphere, due in part to higher temperatures that shorten the time snow spends on the ground.

Sea Level Rise

The oceans are absorbing over 90 percent of the increased atmospheric heat associated with emissions from human activity. Like mercury in a thermometer, water expands as it warms up (this is referred to as "thermal expansion") causing sea levels to rise. Melting of glaciers and ice sheets is also contributing to sea level rise at increasing rates.

Since the late 1800s, tide gauges throughout the world have shown that global sea level has risen by about eight inches. A new data set shows that this recent rise is much greater than at any time in at least the past 2000 years. Since 1992, the rate of global sea level rise measured by satellites has been roughly twice the rate observed over the last century, providing evidence of additional acceleration.

Projecting future rates of sea level rise is challenging. Even the most sophisticated climate models, which explicitly represent Earth's physical processes, cannot simulate rapid changes in ice sheet dynamics, and thus are likely to underestimate future sea level rise. In recent years, "semi-empirical" methods have been developed to project future rates of sea level rise based on a simple statistical relationship between past rates of globally averaged temperature change and sea level rise. These models suggest a range of additional sea level rise from about two feet to as much as six feet by 2100, depending on emissions scenario. It is not clear, however, whether these statistical relationships will hold in the future, or that they fully explain historical behavior. Regardless of the amount of change by 2100, however, sea level rise is expected to continue well beyond this century as a result of both past and future emissions from human activities.

Scientists are working to narrow the range of sea level rise projections for this century. Recent projections show that for even the lowest emissions scenarios, thermal expansion of ocean waters and the melting of small mountain glaciers will result in 11 inches of sea level rise by 2100, even without any contribution from the ice sheets in Greenland and Antarctica. This suggests that about one foot of global sea level rise by 2100 is probably a realistic low end. On the high end, recent work suggests that four feet is plausible. In the context of risk-based analysis, some decision makers may wish to use a wider range of scenarios, from eight inches to 6.6 feet by 2100. In particular, the high end of these scenarios may be useful for decision makers with a low tolerance for risk. Although scientists cannot yet assign likelihood to any particular scenario, in general, higher emissions scenarios that lead to more warming would be expected to lead to higher amounts of sea level rise.

Nearly five million people in the United States live within four feet of the local high-tide level (also known as mean higher high water). In the next several decades, storm surges and high tides could combine with sea level rise and land subsidence to further increase flooding in many of these regions. Sea level rise will not stop in 2100 because the oceans take a very long time to respond to warmer conditions at the Earth's surface. Ocean waters will therefore continue to warm and sea level will continue to rise for many centuries at rates equal to or higher than that of the current century. In fact, recent research has suggested that even present day carbon dioxide levels are sufficient to cause Greenland to melt completely over the next several thousand years.

Melting Ice

Rising temperatures across the United States have reduced lake ice, sea ice, glaciers, and seasonal snow cover over the last few decades. In the Great Lakes, for example, total winter ice coverage has decreased by 63 percent since the early 1970s. This includes the entire period since satellite data became available. When the record is extended back to 1963 using pre-satellite data, the overall trend is less negative because the Great Lakes region experienced several extremely cold winters in the 1970s.

Sea ice in the Arctic has also decreased dramatically since the late 1970s, particularly in summer and autumn. Since the satellite record began in 1978, minimum Arctic sea ice extent (which occurs in early to mid-September) has decreased by more than 40 percent. This decline is unprecedented in the historical record, and the reduction of ice volume and thickness is even greater. Ice thickness decreased by more than 50 percent from 1958-1976 to 2003-2008, and the percentage of the March ice cover made up of thicker ice (ice that has survived a summer melt season) decreased from 75 percent in the mid-1980s to 45 percents in 2011. Recent analyses indicate a decrease of 36 percent in autumn sea ice volume over the past decade. The 2012 sea ice minimum broke the preceding record (set in 2007) by more than 200,000 square miles. Ice loss increases Arctic warming by replacing white, reflective ice with dark water that absorbs more energy from the sun. More open water can also increase snowfall over northern land areas and increase the north-south meanders of the jet stream, consistent with the occurrence of unusually cold and snowy winters at mid-latitudes in several recent years., Significant uncertainties remain at this time in interpreting the effect of Arctic ice changes on mid-latitudes.

The loss of sea ice has been greater in summer than in winter. The Bering Sea, for example, has sea ice only in the winter-spring portion of the year, and shows no trend in surface area covered by ice over the past 30 years. However, seasonal ice in the Bering Sea and elsewhere in the Arctic is thin and susceptible to rapid melt during the following summer.

The seasonal pattern of observed loss of Arctic sea ice is generally consistent with simulations by global climate models, in which the extent of sea ice decreases more rapidly in summer than in winter. However, the models tend to underestimate the amount of decrease since 2007. Projections by these models indicate that the Arctic Ocean is expected to become essentially ice-free in summer before mid-century under scenarios that assume continued growth in global emissions, although sea ice would still form in winter. Models that best match historical trends project a nearly sea ice-free Arctic in summer by the 2030s, and extrapolation of the present observed trend suggests an even earlier ice-free Arctic in summer. However, even during a long-term decrease, occasional temporary increases in Arctic summer sea ice can be expected over timescales of a decade or so because of natural variability. The projected reduction of winter sea ice is only about 10 percent by 2030, indicating that the Arctic will shift to a more seasonal sea ice pattern. While this ice will be thinner, it will cover much of the same area now covered by sea ice in winter.

While the Arctic is an ocean surrounded by continents, Antarctica is a continent surrounded by ocean. Nearly all of the sea ice in the Antarctic melts each summer, and changes there are more complicated than in the Arctic. While Arctic sea ice has been strongly decreasing, there has been a slight increase in sea ice in Antarctica., Explanations for this include changes in winds that directly affect ice drift as well as the properties of the surrounding ocean, and that winds around Antarctica may have been affected by stratospheric ozone depletion.

Snow cover on land has decreased over the past several decades, especially in late spring. Each of five recent years (2008-2012) has set a new record for minimum snow extent in June in Eurasia, as did three of those five years in North America.

The surface of the Greenland Ice Sheet has been experiencing summer melting over increasingly large areas during the past several decades. In the decade of the 2000s, the daily melt area summed over the warm season was double the corresponding amounts of the 1970s, culminating in summer surface melt that was far greater (97 percent of the Greenland Ice Sheet area) in 2012 than in any year since the satellite record began in 1979. More importantly, the rate of mass loss from the Greenland Ice Sheet's marine-terminating outlet glaciers has accelerated in recent decades, leading to predictions that the proportion of global sea level rise coming from Greenland will continue to increase. Glaciers terminating on ice shelves and on land are also losing mass, but the rate of loss has not accelerated over the past decade. The dynamics of the Greenland Ice Sheet are generally not included in present global climate models and sea level rise projections.

Glaciers are retreating and/or thinning in Alaska and in the lower 48 states. In addition, permafrost temperatures are increasing over Alaska and much of the Arctic. Regions of discontinuous permafrost in interior Alaska (where annual average soil temperatures are already close to 32°F) are highly vulnerable to thaw. Thawing permafrost releases carbon dioxide and methane—heat-trapping gases that contribute to even more warming. Recent estimates suggest that the potential release of carbon from permafrost soils could add as much as 0.4°F to 0.6°F of warming by 2100. Methane emissions have been detected from Alaskan lakes underlain by permafrost, and measurements suggest potentially even greater releases from thawing methane hydrates in the Arctic continental shelf of the East Siberian Sea. However, the response times of Arctic methane hydrates to climate change are quite long relative to methane's lifetime in the atmosphere (about a decade). More generally, the importance of Arctic methane sources relative to other methane sources, such as wetlands in warmer climates, is largely unknown. The potential for a self-reinforcing feedback between permafrost thawing and additional warming contributes additional uncertainty to the high end of the range of future warming. The projections of future climate shown throughout this report do not include the additional increase in temperature associated with this thawing.

Ocean Acidification

As human-induced emissions of carbon dioxide (CO_2) build up in the atmosphere, excess CO_2 is dissolving into the oceans where it reacts with seawater to form carbonic acid, lowering ocean pH levels ("acidification") and threatening a number of marine ecosystems. Currently, the oceans absorbs about a quarter of the CO_2 humans produce every year. Over the last 250 years, the oceans have absorbed 560 billion tons of CO_2, increasing the acidity of surface waters by 30 percent. Although the average oceanic pH can vary on interglacial timescales, the current observed rate of change is roughly 50 times faster than known historical change. Regional factors such as coastal upwelling, changes in discharge rates from rivers and glaciers, sea ice loss, and urbanization have created "ocean acidification hotspots" where changes are occurring at even faster rates.

The acidification of the oceans has already caused a suppression of carbonate ion concentrations that are critical for marine calcifying animals such as corals, zooplankton, and shellfish. Many of these animals form the foundation of the marine food web. Today, more than a billion people worldwide rely on food from the ocean as their primary source of protein. Ocean acidification puts this important resource at risk.

Observations have shown that the northeastern Pacific Ocean, including the Arctic and sub-Arctic seas, is particularly susceptible to significant shifts in pH and calcium carbonate saturation levels. Recent analyses show that large areas of the oceans along the U.S. west coast, the Bering Sea, and the western Arctic Ocean, will become difficult for calcifying animals within the next 50 years. In particular, animals that form calcium carbonate shells, including corals, crabs, clams, oysters, and tiny free-swimming snails called pteropods, could be particularly vulnerable, especially during the larval stage.

Projections indicate that in higher emissions pathways, current pH could be reduced from the current level of 8.1 to as low as 7.8 by the end of the century. Such large changes in ocean pH have probably not been experienced on the planet for the past 100 million years, and it is unclear whether and how quickly ocean life could adapt to such rapid acidification.

CAUSES OF CLIMATE CHANGE

Earth's Temperature Is a Balancing Act

Earth's temperature depends on the balance between energy entering and leaving the planet's system. When incoming energy from the sun is absorbed by the Earth system, Earth warms. When the sun's energy is reflected back into space, Earth avoids warming. When energy is released back into space, Earth cools. Many factors, both natural and human, can cause changes in Earth's energy balance, including:

- Changes in the greenhouse effect, which affects the amount of heat retained by Earth's atmosphere
- Variations in the sun's energy reaching Earth
- Changes in the reflectivity of Earth's atmosphere and surface

These factors have caused Earth's climate to change many times.

Scientists have pieced together a picture of Earth's climate, dating back hundreds of thousands of years, by analyzing a number of indirect measures of climate such as ice cores, tree rings, glacier lengths, pollen remains, and ocean sediments, and by studying changes in Earth's orbit around the sun.

The historical record shows that the climate system varies naturally over a wide range of time scales. In general, climate changes prior to the Industrial Revolution in the 1700s can be explained by natural causes, such as changes in solar energy, volcanic eruptions, and natural changes in greenhouse gas (GHG) concentrations.

Recent climate changes, however, cannot be explained by natural causes alone. Research indicates that natural causes are very unlikely to explain most observed warming, especially warming since the mid-twentieth century. Rather, human activities can very likely explain most of that warming.

The Greenhouse Effect

When sunlight reaches Earth's surface, it can either be reflected back into space or absorbed by Earth. Once absorbed, the planet releases some of the energy back into the atmosphere as heat (also called infrared radiation). Greenhouse gases (GHGs) like water vapor (H_2O), carbon dioxide (CO_2), and methane (CH_4) absorb energy, slowing or preventing the loss of heat to space. In this way, GHGs act like a blanket, making Earth warmer than it would otherwise be. This process is commonly known as the "greenhouse effect."

The Role of the Greenhouse Effect in the Past

In the distant past (prior to about 10,000 years ago), CO_2 levels tended to track the glacial cycles. During warm 'interglacial' periods, CO_2 levels have been higher. During cool 'glacial' periods, CO_2 levels have been lower. This is because the heating or cooling of Earth's surface can cause changes in greenhouse gas concentrations. These changes often act as a positive feedback, amplifying existing temperature changes.

The Recent Role of the Greenhouse Effect

Since the Industrial Revolution began around 1750, human activities have contributed substantially to climate change by adding CO_2 and other heat-trapping gases to the atmosphere. These greenhouse gas emissions have increased the greenhouse effect and caused Earth's surface temperature to rise. The primary human activity affecting the amount and rate of climate change is greenhouse gas emissions from the burning of fossil fuels.

The Main Greenhouse Gases

The most important GHGs directly emitted by humans include CO_2, CH_4, nitrous oxide (N_2O), and several others. The sources and recent trends of these gases are detailed below.

Carbon Dioxide. Carbon dioxide (CO_2) is the primary greenhouse gas emitted through human activities. In 2012, CO_2 accounted for about 82 percent of all U.S. greenhouse gas emissions from human activities. Carbon dioxide is naturally present in the atmosphere as part of the Earth's carbon cycle (the natural circulation of carbon among the atmosphere, oceans, soil, plants, and animals). Human activities are altering the carbon cycle—both by adding more CO_2 to the atmosphere and by influencing the ability of natural sinks, like forests, to remove CO_2 from the atmosphere. While CO_2 emissions come from a variety of natural sources, human-related emissions are responsible for the increase that has occurred in the atmosphere since the industrial revolution.

The main human activity that emits CO_2 is the combustion of fossil fuels (coal, natural gas, and oil) for energy and transportation, although certain industrial processes and land-use changes also emit CO_2. The main sources of CO_2 emissions in the United States are described below.

- **Electricity**. Electricity is a significant source of energy in the United States and is used to power homes, business, and industry. The combustion of fossil fuels to generate electricity is the largest single source of CO_2 emissions in the nation, accounting for about 38 percent of total US CO_2 emissions and 31 percent of total US greenhouse gas emissions in 2012. The type of fossil fuel used to generate electricity will emit different amounts of CO_2. To produce a given amount of electricity, burning coal will produce more CO_2 than oil or natural gas.
- **Transportation**. The combustion of fossil fuels such as gasoline and diesel to transport people and goods is the second largest source of CO_2 emissions, accounting for about 32 percent of total US CO_2 emissions and 27 percent of total US greenhouse gas emissions in 2012. This category includes transportation sources such as highway vehicles, air travel, marine transportation, and rail.
- **Industry**. Many industrial processes emit CO_2 through fossil fuel combustion. Several processes also produce CO_2 emissions through chemical reactions that do not involve combustion, for example, the production and consumption of mineral products such as cement, the production of metals such as iron and steel, and the production of

chemicals. Fossil fuel combustion from various industrial processes accounted for about 14 percent of total US CO_2 emissions and 12 percent of total US greenhouse gas emissions in 2012. Note that many industrial processes also use electricity and therefore indirectly cause the emissions from the electricity production.

Carbon dioxide is constantly being exchanged among the atmosphere, ocean, and land surface as it is both produced and absorbed by many microorganisms, plants, and animals. However, emissions and removal of CO_2 by these natural processes tend to balance. Since the Industrial Revolution began around 1750, human activities have contributed substantially to climate change by adding CO_2 and other heat-trapping gases to the atmosphere.

In the United States, since 1990, the management of forests and nonagricultural land has acted as a net sink of CO_2, which means that more CO_2 is removed from the atmosphere, and stored in plants and trees, than is emitted. This sink offset about 15 percent of total emissions in 2012.

CO_2 emissions in the United States increased by about 5 percent between 1990 and 2012. Since the combustion of fossil fuel is the largest source of greenhouse gas emissions in the United States, changes in emissions from fossil fuel combustion have historically been the dominant factor affecting total U.S. emission trends. Changes in CO_2 emissions from fossil fuel combustion are influenced by many long-term and short-term factors, including population growth, economic growth, changing energy prices, new technologies, changing behavior, and seasonal temperatures. Between 1990 and 2012, the increase in CO_2 emissions corresponded with increased energy use by an expanding economy and population, and an overall growth in emissions from electricity generation. Transportation emissions also contributed to the 5 percent increase, largely due to an increase in miles traveled by motor vehicles. Going forward, CO_2 emissions in the United States are projected to grow by about 1.5 percent between 2005 and 2020.

Carbon dioxide's lifetime is poorly defined because the gas is not destroyed over time, but instead moves among different parts of the ocean–atmosphere–land system. Some of the excess carbon dioxide will be absorbed quickly (for example, by the ocean surface), but some will remain in the atmosphere for thousands of years, due in part to the very slow process by which carbon is transferred to ocean sediments.

The most effective way to reduce carbon dioxide (CO_2) emissions is to reduce fossil fuel consumption. Many strategies for reducing CO_2 emissions from energy are cross-cutting and apply to homes, businesses, industry, and transportation.

Methane. Methane is the second most prevalent greenhouse gas emitted in the United States from human activities. In 2012, CH_4 accounted for about 9 percent of all US greenhouse gas emissions from human activities. Methane is emitted by natural sources such as wetlands, as well as human activities such as leakage from natural gas systems and the raising of livestock. Natural processes in soil and chemical reactions in the atmosphere help remove CH_4 from the atmosphere. Methane's lifetime in the atmosphere is much shorter than carbon dioxide (CO_2), but CH_4 is more efficient at trapping radiation than CO_2. Pound for pound, the comparative impact of CH_4 on climate change is over 20 times greater than CO_2 over a 100-year period.

Globally, over 60 percent of total CH_4 emissions come from human activities. Methane is emitted from industry, agriculture, and waste management activities, described below.

- **Industry**. Natural gas and petroleum systems are the largest source of CH_4 emissions from industry in the United States. Methane is the primary component of natural gas. Some CH_4 is emitted to the atmosphere during the production, processing, storage, transmission, and distribution of natural gas. Because gas is often found alongside petroleum, the production, refinement, transportation, and storage of crude oil is also a source of CH_4 emissions.
- **Agriculture**. Domestic livestock such as cattle, buffalo, sheep, goats, and camels produce large amounts of CH_4 as part of their normal digestive process. Also, when animals' manure is stored or managed in lagoons or holding tanks, CH_4 is produced. Because humans raise these animals for food, the emissions are considered human-related. Globally, the Agriculture sector is the primary source of CH_4 emissions.
- **Waste from Homes and Businesses**. Methane is generated in landfills as waste decomposes and in the treatment of wastewater. Landfills are the third largest source of CH_4 emissions in the United States.

Methane is also emitted from a number of natural sources. Wetlands are the largest source, emitting CH_4 from bacteria that decompose organic materials in the absence of oxygen. Smaller sources include termites, oceans, sediments, volcanoes, and wildfires.

Methane emissions in the United States decreased by almost 11 percent between 1990 and 2012. During this time period, emissions increased from sources associated with agricultural activities, while emissions decreased from sources associated with the exploration and production of natural gas and petroleum products.

Nitrous Oxide. In 2012, nitrous oxide (N_2O) accounted for about 6 percent of all US greenhouse gas emissions from human activities. Nitrous oxide is naturally present in the atmosphere as part of the Earth's nitrogen cycle, and has a variety of natural sources. However, human activities such as agriculture, fossil fuel combustion, wastewater management, and industrial processes are increasing the amount of N_2O in the atmosphere. Nitrous oxide molecules stay in the atmosphere for an average of 120 years before being removed by a sink or destroyed through chemical reactions. The impact of 1 pound of N_2O on warming the atmosphere is over 300 times that of 1 pound of carbon dioxide.

Globally, about 40 percent of total N_2O emissions come from human activities. Nitrous oxide is emitted from agriculture, transportation, and industry activities, described below.

- **Agriculture**. Nitrous oxide is emitted when people add nitrogen to the soil through the use of synthetic fertilizers. Agricultural soil management is the largest source of N_2O emissions in the United States, accounting for about 75 percent of total US N_2O emissions in 2012. Nitrous oxide is also emitted during the breakdown of nitrogen in livestock manure and urine, which contributed to 4 percent of N_2O emissions in 2012.
- **Transportation**. Nitrous oxide is emitted when transportation fuels are burned. Motor vehicles, including passenger cars and trucks, are the primary source of N_2O emissions from transportation. The amount of N_2O emitted from transportation depends on the type of fuel and vehicle technology, maintenance, and operating practices.
- **Industry**. Nitrous oxide is generated as a byproduct during the production of nitric acid, which is used to make synthetic commercial fertilizer, and in the production of adipic acid, which is used to make fibers, like nylon, and other synthetic products.

Nitrous oxide emissions occur naturally through many sources associated with the nitrogen cycle, which is the natural circulation of nitrogen among the atmosphere, plants, animals, and microorganisms that live in soil and water. Nitrogen takes on a variety of chemical forms throughout the nitrogen cycle, including N_2O. Natural emissions of N_2O are mainly from bacteria breaking down nitrogen in soils and the oceans. Nitrous oxide is removed from the atmosphere when it is absorbed by certain types of bacteria or destroyed by ultraviolet radiation or chemical reactions.

Nitrous oxide (N_2O) emissions in the United States have increased by about 3 percent between 1990 and 2012. This increase in emissions is due in part to annual variation in agricultural soil emissions, and an increase in emissions from the electric power sector. Nitrous oxide emissions from agricultural soils have varied during this period and were about 9 percent higher in 2012 than in 1990.

Going forward, N_2O emissions are projected to increase by 5 percent between 2005 and 2020, driven largely by increases in emissions from agricultural activities.

Other Greenhouse Gases

Water vapor is the most abundant greenhouse gas and also the most important in terms of its contribution to the natural greenhouse effect, despite having a short atmospheric lifetime. Some human activities can influence local water vapor levels. However, on a global scale, the concentration of water vapor is controlled by temperature, which influences overall rates of evaporation and precipitation. Therefore, the global concentration of water vapor is not substantially affected by direct human emissions.

Tropospheric ozone (O_3), which also has a short atmospheric lifetime, is a potent greenhouse gas. Chemical reactions create ozone from emissions of nitrogen oxides and volatile organic compounds from automobiles, power plants, and other industrial and commercial sources in the presence of sunlight. In addition to trapping heat, ozone is a pollutant that can cause respiratory health problems and damage crops and ecosystems.

Chlorofluorocarbons (CFCs), hydrochlorofluorocarbons (HCFCs), hydrofluorocarbons (HFCs), perfluorocarbons (PFCs), and sulfur hexafluoride (SF_6), together called F-gases, are often used in coolants, foaming agents, fire extinguishers, solvents, pesticides, and aerosol propellants. Unlike water vapor and ozone, these F-gases have a long atmospheric lifetime, and some of these emissions will affect the climate for many decades or centuries.

Other Climate Forcers

Black carbon (BC) is a solid particle or aerosol, not a gas, but it also contributes to warming of the atmosphere. Unlike GHGs, BC can directly absorb incoming and reflected sunlight in addition to absorbing infrared radiation. BC can also deposit on and darken snow and ice, increasing the snow's absorption of sunlight and accelerating melt.

Sulfates, organic carbon, and other aerosols can cause cooling by reflecting sunlight.

Warming and cooling aerosols can interact with clouds, changing a number of cloud attributes such as their formation, dissipation, reflectivity, and precipitation rates. Clouds can contribute both to cooling, by reflecting sunlight, and warming, by trapping outgoing heat.

Changes in the Sun's Energy

Climate is influenced by natural changes that affect how much solar energy reaches Earth. These changes include changes within the sun and changes in Earth's orbit.

Changes occurring in the sun itself can affect the intensity of the sunlight that reaches Earth's surface. The intensity of the sunlight can cause either warming (during periods of stronger solar intensity) or cooling (during periods of weaker solar intensity). The sun follows a natural 11-year cycle of small ups and downs in intensity, but the effect on Earth's climate is small.

Changes in the shape of Earth's orbit as well as the tilt and position of Earth's axis can also affect the amount of sunlight reaching Earth's surface.

The Role of the Sun's Energy in the Past

Changes in the sun's intensity have influenced Earth's climate in the past. For example, the so-called "Little Ice Age" between the seventeenth and nineteenth centuries may have been partially caused by a low solar activity phase from 1645 to 1715, which coincided with cooler temperatures. The "Little Ice Age" refers to a slight cooling of North America, Europe, and probably other areas around the globe.

Changes in Earth's orbit have had a big impact on climate over tens of thousands of years. In fact, the amount of summer sunshine on the Northern Hemisphere, which is affected by changes in the planet's orbit, appears to control the advance and retreat of ice sheets. These changes appear to be the primary cause of past cycles of ice ages, in which Earth has experienced long periods of cold temperatures (ice ages), as well as shorter interglacial periods (periods between ice ages) of relatively warmer temperatures.

The Recent Role of the Sun's Energy

Changes in solar energy continue to affect climate. However, solar activity has been relatively constant, aside from the 11-year cycle, since the mid-20th century and therefore does not explain the recent warming of Earth. Similarly, changes in the shape of Earth's orbit as well as the tilt and position of Earth's axis affect temperature on relatively long timescales (tens of thousands of years), and therefore cannot explain the recent warming.

Changes in Reflectivity

When sunlight reaches Earth, it can be reflected or absorbed. The amount that is reflected or absorbed depends on Earth's surface and atmosphere. Light-colored objects and surfaces, like snow and clouds, tend to reflect most sunlight, while darker objects and surfaces, like the ocean, forests, or soil, tend to absorb more sunlight.

The term albedo refers to the amount of solar radiation reflected from an object or surface, often expressed as a percentage. Earth as a whole has an albedo of about 30 percent, meaning that 70 percent of the sunlight that reaches the planet is absorbed. Absorbed sunlight warms Earth's land, water, and atmosphere.

Reflectivity is also affected by aerosols. Aerosols are small particles or liquid droplets in the atmosphere that can absorb or reflect sunlight. Unlike greenhouse gases (GHGs), the climate effects of aerosols vary depending on what they are made of and where they are emitted. Those aerosols that reflect sunlight, such as particles from volcanic eruptions or sulfur emissions from burning coal, have a cooling effect. Those that absorb sunlight, such as black carbon (a part of soot), have a warming effect.

The Role of Reflectivity in the Past

Natural changes in reflectivity, like the melting of sea ice or increases in cloud cover, have contributed to climate change in the past, often acting as feedbacks to other processes.

Volcanoes have played a noticeable role in climate. Volcanic particles that reach the upper atmosphere can reflect enough sunlight back to space to cool the surface of the planet by a few tenths of a degree for several years. These particles are an example of cooling aerosols. Volcanic particles from a single eruption do not produce long-term change because they remain in the atmosphere for a much shorter time than GHGs.

The Recent Role of Reflectivity

Human changes in land use and land cover have changed Earth's reflectivity. Processes such as deforestation, reforestation, desertification, and urbanization often contribute to changes in climate in the places they occur. These effects may be significant regionally, but are smaller when averaged over the entire globe.

In addition, human activities have generally increased the number of aerosol particles in the atmosphere. Overall, human-generated aerosols have a net cooling effect offsetting about one-third of the total warming effect associated with human greenhouse gas emissions. Reductions in overall aerosol emissions can therefore lead to more warming. However, targeted reductions in black carbon emissions can reduce warming.

FUTURE CLIMATE CHANGE

Increasing Greenhouse Gas Concentrations

Greenhouse gas concentrations in the atmosphere will continue to increase unless the billions of tons of our annual emissions decrease substantially. Increased concentrations are expected to:

- Increase Earth's average temperature
- Influence the patterns and amounts of precipitation
- Reduce ice and snow cover, as well as permafrost
- Raise sea level
- Increase the acidity of the oceans

These changes will impact our food supply, water resources, infrastructure, ecosystems, and even our own health.

Factors Affecting Future Changes

The magnitude and rate of future climate change will primarily depend on the following factors:

- The rate at which levels of greenhouse gas concentrations in our atmosphere continue to increase

- How strongly features of the climate (e.g., temperature, precipitation, and sea level) respond to the expected increase in greenhouse gas concentrations
- Natural influences on climate (e.g., from volcanic activity and changes in the sun's intensity) and natural processes within the climate system (e.g., changes in ocean circulation patterns)

Scientists use computer models of the climate system to better understand these issues and project future climate changes.

Long-Term Affect of Greenhouse Gases

Many greenhouse gases stay in the atmosphere for long periods of time. As a result, even if emissions stopped increasing, atmospheric greenhouse gas concentrations would continue to increase and remain elevated for hundreds of years. Moreover, if we stabilized concentrations and the composition of today's atmosphere remained steady (which would require a dramatic reduction in current greenhouse gas emissions), surface air temperatures would continue to warm. This is because the oceans, which store heat, take many decades to fully respond to higher greenhouse gas concentrations. The ocean's response to higher greenhouse gas concentrations and higher temperatures will continue to impact climate over the next several decades to hundreds of years.

Because it is difficult to project far-off future emissions and other human factors that influence climate, scientists use a range of scenarios using various assumptions about future economic, social, technological, and environmental conditions.

Future Temperature Changes

We have already observed global warming over the last several decades. Future temperatures are expected to change further. Climate models project the following key temperature-related changes.

Key Global Projections

- Average global temperatures are expected to increase by 2°F to 11.5°F by 2100, depending on the level of future greenhouse gas emissions, and the outcomes from various climate models.

- By 2100, global average temperature is expected to warm at least twice as much as it has during the last 100 years.
- Ground-level air temperatures are expected to continue to warm more rapidly over land than oceans.
- Some parts of the world are projected to see larger temperature increases than the global average.

Key US Projections

- By 2100, the average U.S. temperature is projected to increase by about 4°F to 11°F, depending on emissions scenario and climate model.
- An increase in average temperatures worldwide implies more frequent and intense extreme heat events, or heat waves. The number of days with high temperatures above 90°F is expected to increase throughout the United States, especially in areas that already experience heat waves. For example, areas of the Southeast and Southwest currently experience an average of 60 days per year with a high temperature above 90°F. These areas are projected to experience 150 or more days a year above 90°F by the end of the century, under a higher emissions scenario. In addition to occurring more frequently, these very hot days are projected to be about 10°F hotter at the end of this century than they are today, under a higher emissions scenario.

Future Precipitation and Storm Events

Patterns of precipitation and storm events, including both rain and snowfall are also likely to change. However, some of these changes are less certain than the changes associated with temperature. Projections show that future precipitation and storm changes will vary by season and region. Some regions may have less precipitation, some may have more precipitation, and some may have little or no change. The amount of rain falling in heavy precipitation events is likely to increase in most regions, while storm tracks are projected to shift poleward. Climate models project the following precipitation and storm changes.

Key Global Projections

- Global average annual precipitation through the end of the century is expected to increase, although changes in the amount and intensity of precipitation will vary by region.

- The intensity of precipitation events will likely increase on average. This will be particularly pronounced in tropical and high-latitude regions, which are also expected to experience overall increases in precipitation.
- The strength of the winds associated with tropical storms is likely to increase. The amount of precipitation falling in tropical storms is also likely to increase.
- Annual average precipitation is projected to increase in some areas and decrease in others. The figure to the right shows projected regional differences in precipitation for summer and winter.

Key US Projections
- Northern areas are projected to become wetter, especially in the winter and spring. Southern areas, especially in the West, are projected to become drier.
- Heavy precipitation events will likely be more frequent. Heavy downpours that currently occur about once every 20 years are projected to occur about every four to 15 years by 2100, depending on location.
- More precipitation is expected to fall as rain rather than snow, particularly in some northern areas.
- The intensity of Atlantic hurricanes is likely to increase as the ocean warms. Climate models project that for each 1.8°F increase in tropical sea surface temperatures the rainfall rates of hurricanes could increase by 6-18 percent and the wind speeds of the strongest hurricanes could increase by about 1-8 percent. There is less confidence in projections of the frequency of hurricanes, but the global frequency of tropical hurricanes is likely to decrease or remain essentially unchanged.
- Cold-season storm tracks are expected to continue to shift northward. The strongest cold-season storms are projected to become stronger and more frequent.

Future Ice, Snowpack, and Permafrost

Arctic sea ice is already declining. The area of snow cover in the Northern Hemisphere has decreased since about 1970. Permafrost temperature has increased over the last century.

Over the next century, it is expected that sea ice will continue to decline, glaciers will continue to shrink, snow cover will continue to decrease, and permafrost will continue to thaw. Potential changes to ice, snow, and permafrost are described below.

Key Global Projections

- For every 2°F of warming, models project about a 15 percent decrease in the extent of annually averaged sea ice and a 25 percent decrease in September Arctic sea ice.
- The coastal sections of the Greenland and Antarctic ice sheets are expected to continue to melt or slide into the ocean. If the rate of this ice melting increases in the twenty-first century, the ice sheets could add significantly to global sea level rise.
- Glaciers are expected to continue to decrease in size. The rate of melting is expected to continue to increase, which will contribute to sea level rise.

Key US Projections

- Northern Hemisphere snow cover is expected to decrease by approximately 15 percent by 2100.
- Models project the snow season will continue to shorten, with snow accumulation beginning later and melting starting earlier. Snowpack is expected to decrease in many regions.
- Permafrost is expected to continue to thaw in northern latitudes. This would have large impacts in Alaska.

Future Sea Level Change

Warming temperatures contribute to sea level rise by: expanding ocean water; melting mountain glaciers and ice caps; and causing portions of the Greenland and Antarctic ice sheets to melt or flow into the ocean.

Since 1870, global sea level has risen by about eight inches. Estimates of future sea level rise vary for different regions, but global sea level for the next century is expected to rise at a greater rate than during the past 50 years.

The contribution of thermal expansion, ice caps, and small glaciers to sea level rise is relatively well-studied, but the impacts of climate change on ice sheets are less understood and represent an active area of research. Thus it is more difficult to predict how much changes in ice sheets will contribute to sea level rise.

Ice loss from the Greenland and Antarctic ice sheets could contribute an additional one foot of sea level rise, depending on how the ice sheets respond.

Regional and local factors will influence future relative sea level rise for specific coastlines around the world. For example, relative sea level rise depends on land elevation changes that occur as a result of subsidence (sinking) or uplift (rising). Assuming that these historical geological forces continue, a two-foot rise in global sea level by 2100 would result in the following relative sea level rise:

- 2.3 feet at New York City
- 2.9 feet at Hampton Roads, Virginia
- 3.5 feet at Galveston, Texas
- one foot at Neah Bay in Washington

Relative sea level rise also depends on local changes in currents, winds, salinity, and water temperatures, as well as proximity to thinning ice sheets.

Future Ocean Acidification

Oceans become more acidic as carbon dioxide (CO_2) emissions in the atmosphere dissolve in the ocean. This change is measured on the pH scale, with lower values being more acidic. The pH level of the oceans has decreased by approximately 0.1 pH units since pre-industrial times, which is equivalent to a 25 percent increase in acidity. The pH level of the oceans is projected to decrease even more by the end of the century as CO_2 concentrations are expected to increase for the foreseeable future.

Ocean acidification adversely affects many marine species, including plankton, mollusks, shellfish, and corals. As ocean acidification increases, the availability of calcium carbonate will decline. Calcium carbonate is a key building block for the shells and skeletons of many marine organisms. If atmospheric CO_2 concentrations double, coral calcification rates are projected to decline by more than 30 percent. If CO_2 concentrations continue to rise at their current rate, corals could become rare on tropical and subtropical reefs by 2050.

RESPONSE OPTIONS

As the impacts of climate change become more prevalent, Americans face decisions about how to plan and respond. Using scientific information to prepare for climate change can create economic opportunities, and proactively managing the risks can reduce impacts and costs over time.

Actions to prepare for and adjust to changing climate conditions (thereby reducing harm or taking advantage of new opportunities) are known as "adaptation." The other major category of response options is known as mitigation, and involves efforts to reduce the amount and speed of future climate change by limiting emissions or removing carbon dioxide from the atmosphere. Adaptation and mitigation actions are linked in multiple ways, including that effective mitigation reduces the need for adaptation in the future.

Preparing for both climate variability and climate change can reduce impacts while also facilitating a more rapid and efficient response to changes as they happen. Such efforts are accelerating at the Federal, regional, state, tribal, and local levels, and in the corporate and non-governmental sectors. Actions to reduce emissions, increase carbon uptake, adapt to changing climate, and increase resilience to impacts can improve public health, economic development, ecosystem protection, and quality of life.

SOURCE MATERIAL

US Environmental Protection Agency. "Causes of Climate Change." http://www.epa.gov/climatechange/science/causes.html.
———. "Future Climate Change." http://www.epa.gov/climatechange /science/future.html.
———. "Overview of Greenhouse Gases." http://www.epa.gov/climatechange /ghgemissions/gases.html
US Global Change Research Program. "Climate Change: Response Options," http://www.globalchange.gov/climate-change/response-options.
———. US National Climate Assessment. October 2014 [May 2014]. http:// nca2014.globalchange.gov/report.

FURTHER READING

Intergovernmental Panel on Climate Change. *Climate Change 2013: The Physical Science Basis*. Cambridge and New York: Cambridge University Press, 2013. http://www.ipcc.ch/pdf/assessment-report/ar5/wg1/WG1AR5_ALL _FINAL.pdf.

National Aeronautics and Space Administration. "Global Climate Change: Vital Signs of the Planet." http://climate.nasa.gov.

National Oceanic and Atmospheric Administration. "Climate.gov: Science & Information for a Climate-Smart Nation." https://www.climate.gov.

National Research Council. *Advancing the Science of Climate Change*. Washington, DC: The National Academies Press, 2010. http:// nas-sites.org /americasclimatechoices/sample-page/panel-reports/87-2/.

———. *Climate Stabilization Targets: Emissions, Concentrations, and Impacts over Decades to Millennia*. Washington, DC: The National Academies Press, 2011. http://nas-sites.org/americasclimatechoices/other-reports-on -climate-change/2011-2/climate-stabilization-targets/.

US Department of State. "Global Climate Change." http://www.state.gov/e /oes/climate/.

US Environmental Protection Agency. *US Greenhouse Gas Inventory Report: 1990-2013*. Washington, DC: US Environmental Protection Agency, April 15, 2015. http://www.epa.gov/climatechange/ghgemissions /usinventoryreport.html.

2

Clean Air

This chapter presents information on common air pollutants and the regulations put in place to reduce them, especially the Clean Air Act. It ends with a discussion of acid rain and its effects on the environment and human health. Information in this chapter is from the US Environmental Protection Agency.

THE PLAIN ENGLISH GUIDE TO THE CLEAN AIR ACT

Why Should You Be Concerned About Air Pollution?

You could go days without food and hours without water, but you would last only a few minutes without air. On average, each of us breathes over 3,000 gallons of air each day. You must have air to live. However, did you know that breathing polluted air can make you sick?

Air pollution can damage trees, crops, other plants, lakes, and animals. In addition to damaging the natural environment, air pollution also damages buildings, monuments, and statues. It not only reduces how far you can see in national parks and cities, it even interferes with aviation.

In 1970, Congress created the Environmental Protection Agency (EPA) and passed the Clean Air Act, giving the federal government authority to clean up air pollution in this country. Since then, EPA and states, tribes, local governments, industry, and environmental groups have worked to establish a variety of programs to reduce air pollution levels across America.

The Clean Air Act has helped change the way many of us work or do business. In some cases, it has even changed the way we live. This guide provides a brief introduction to the programs, philosophies, and policies in the Clean Air Act.

Air Pollution and Your Health

Breathing polluted air can make your eyes and nose burn. It can irritate your throat and make breathing difficult. In fact, pollutants like tiny airborne particles and ground-level ozone can trigger respiratory problems, especially for people with asthma. Today, nearly 30 million adults and children in the United States have been diagnosed with asthma. Asthma sufferers can be severely affected by air pollution. Air pollution can also aggravate health problems for the elderly and others with heart or respiratory diseases.

Some toxic chemicals released in the air such as benzene or vinyl chloride are highly toxic and can cause cancer, birth defects, long term injury to the lungs, as well as brain and nerve damage. And in some cases, breathing these chemicals can even cause death.

Other pollutants make their way up into the upper atmosphere, causing a thinning of the protective ozone layer. This has led to changes in the environment and dramatic increases in skin cancers and cataracts (eye damage).

Air Pollution and the Environment

Air pollution isn't just a threat to our health, it also damages our environment. Toxic air pollutants and the chemicals that form acid rain and ground-level ozone can damage trees, crops, wildlife, lakes and other bodies of water. Those pollutants can also harm fish and other aquatic life.

Air Pollution and the Economy

The health, environmental, and economic impacts of air pollution are significant. Each day, air pollution causes thousands of illnesses leading to lost days at work and school. Air pollution also reduces agricultural crop and commercial forest yields by billions of dollars each year.

Understanding the Clean Air Act

Brief History of the Clean Air Act

In October 1948, a thick cloud of air pollution formed above the industrial town of Donora, Pennsylvania. The cloud which lingered for five days, killed 20 people and caused sickness in 6,000 of the town's 14,000 people. In 1952, over 3,000 people died in what became known as London's "Killer Fog." The smog was so thick that buses could not run without guides walking ahead of them carrying lanterns.

Events like these alerted us to the dangers that air pollution poses to public health. Several federal and state laws were passed, including the original Clean Air Act of 1963, which established funding for the study and the cleanup of air pollution. But there was no comprehensive federal response to address air pollution until Congress passed a much stronger Clean Air Act in 1970. That same year Congress created the EPA and gave it the primary role in carrying out the law. Since 1970, EPA has been responsible for a variety of Clean Air Act programs to reduce air pollution nationwide.

In 1990, Congress dramatically revised and expanded the Clean Air Act, providing EPA even broader authority to implement and enforce regulations reducing air pollutant emissions. The 1990 Amendments also placed an increased emphasis on more cost-effective approaches to reduce air pollution.

Clean Air Act Roles and Responsibilities

The Clean Air Act is a federal law covering the entire country. However, states, tribes and local governments do a lot of the work to meet the Act's requirements. For example, representatives from these agencies work with companies to reduce air pollution. They also review and approve permit applications for industries or chemical processes.

EPA's Role

Under the Clean Air Act, EPA sets limits on certain air pollutants, including setting limits on how much can be in the air anywhere in the United States. This helps to ensure basic health and environmental protection from air pollution for all Americans. The Clean Air Act also gives EPA the authority to limit emissions of air pollutants coming from sources like chemical plants, utilities, and steel mills. Individual states or tribes may have stronger air pollution laws, but they may not have weaker pollution limits than those set by EPA.

EPA must approve state, tribal, and local agency plans for reducing air pollution. If a plan does not meet the necessary requirements, EPA can issue sanctions against the state and, if necessary, take over enforcing the Clean Air Act in that area.

EPA assists state, tribal, and local agencies by providing research, expert studies, engineering designs, and funding to support clean air progress. Since 1970, Congress and the EPA have provided several billion dollars to the states, local agencies, and tribal nations to accomplish this.

State and Local Governments' Role

It makes sense for state and local air pollution agencies to take the lead in carrying out the Clean Air Act. They are able to develop solutions for pollution problems that require special understanding of local industries, geography, housing, and travel patterns, as well as other factors.

State, local, and tribal governments also monitor air quality, inspect facilities under their jurisdictions and enforce Clean Air Act regulations.

States have to develop State Implementation Plans (SIPs) that outline how each state will control air pollution under the Clean Air Act. A SIP is a collection of the regulations, programs and policies that a state will use to clean up polluted areas. The states must involve the public and industries through hearings and opportunities to comment on the development of each state plan.

Tribal Nations' Role

In its 1990 revision of the Clean Air Act, Congress recognized that Indian Tribes have the authority to implement air pollution control programs.

EPA's Tribal Authority Rule gives Tribes the ability to develop air quality management programs, write rules to reduce air pollution and implement and enforce their rules in Indian Country. While state and local agencies are responsible for all Clean Air Act requirements, Tribes may develop and implement only those parts of the Clean Air Act that are appropriate for their lands.

Key Elements of the Clean Air Act

EPA's mission is to protect human health and the environment. To achieve this mission, EPA implements a variety of programs under the Clean Air Act that focus on:

- reducing outdoor, or ambient, concentrations of air pollutants that cause smog, haze, acid rain, and other problems;
- reducing emissions of toxic air pollutants that are known to, or are suspected of, causing cancer or other serious health effects; and
- phasing out production and use of chemicals that destroy stratospheric ozone.

These pollutants come from stationary sources (like chemical plants, gas stations, and powerplants) and mobile sources (like cars, trucks, and planes).

Cleaning Up Commonly Found Air Pollutants

Six common air pollutants (also known as "criteria pollutants") are found all over the United States. They are particle pollution (often referred to as particulate matter), ground-level ozone, carbon monoxide, sulfur oxides, nitrogen oxides, and lead. These pollutants can harm your health and the environment, and cause property damage. Of the six pollutants, particle pollution and ground-level ozone are the most widespread health threats. Details about these two pollutants are discussed below.

EPA calls these pollutants "criteria" air pollutants because it regulates them by developing human health-based and/or environmentally-based criteria (science-based guidelines) for setting permissible levels. The set of limits based on human health is called primary standards. Another set of limits intended to prevent environmental and property damage is called secondary standards. A geographic area with air quality that is cleaner than the primary standard is called an "attainment" area; areas that do not meet the primary standard are called "nonattainment" areas.

EPA has been developing programs to cut emissions of these commonly found air pollutants since the Clean Air Act was passed in 1970. It's a big job, and although a great deal of progress has been made, it will take time to make the air healthy throughout the country. There are still several areas of the country, including many large cities, that are classified as nonattainment for at least one of the six common pollutants. Despite continued improvements in air quality, millions of people live in areas with monitoring data measuring unhealthy levels of pollution.

Particle Pollution. Particle pollution, also known as particulate matter (PM), includes the very fine dust, soot, smoke, and droplets that are formed from chemical reactions, and produced when fuels such as coal, wood, or oil are burned. For example, sulfur dioxide and nitrogen oxide gases from motor vehicles, electric power generation, and industrial facilities react with sunlight and water vapor to form particles. Particles may also come from fireplaces, wood stoves, unpaved roads, crushing and grinding operations, and may be blown into the air by the wind.

EPA scientists and other health experts are concerned about particle pollution because very small or "fine" particles can get deep into the lungs. These fine particles, by themselves, or in combination with other air pollutants, can cause increased emergency room visits and hospital admissions for respiratory illnesses, and tens of thousands of deaths each year. They can aggravate asthma, cause acute respiratory symptoms such as coughing, reduce lung function resulting in shortness of breath, and cause chronic bronchitis.

The elderly, children, and asthmatics are particularly susceptible to health problems caused by breathing fine particles. Individuals with pre-existing heart or lung disease are also at an increased risk of health problems due to particle pollution.

Particles also cause haze reducing visibility in places like national parks and wilderness areas that are known for their scenic vistas. These are places where we expect to see clearly for long distances. In many parts of the United States, pollution has reduced the distance and clarity of what we see by 70 percent.

Fine particles can remain suspended in the air and travel long distances with the wind. For example, over 20 percent of the particles that form haze in the Rocky Mountains National Park have been estimated to come from hundreds of miles away.

Particles also make buildings, statues and other outdoor structures dirty. Trinity Church in downtown New York City was black until a few years ago, when cleaning off almost 200 years worth of soot brought the church's stone walls back to their original light pink color.

Before the 1990 Clean Air Act went into effect, EPA set limits on airborne particles smaller than 10 micrometers in diameter called PM10. These are tiny particles (seven of these particles lined up next to each other would cover a distance no wider than a human hair). Research has shown that even smaller particles (1/4 the size of a PM10 particle) are more likely to harm our health. So in 1997, EPA published limits for fine particles, called PM2.5. To reduce particle levels, additional controls are being required on a variety of sources including power plants and diesel trucks.

Ground-level Ozone. Ground-level ozone is a primary component of smog. Ground-level ozone can cause human health problems and damage forests and agricultural crops. Repeated exposure to ozone can make people more susceptible to respiratory infections and lung inflammation. It also can aggravate pre-existing respiratory diseases, such as asthma. Children are at risk from ozone pollution because they are outside, playing and exercising, during the summer days when ozone levels are at their highest. They also can be more susceptible because their lungs are still developing. People with asthma and even active healthy adults, such as construction workers, can experience a reduction in lung function and an increase in respiratory symptoms (chest pain and coughing) when exposed to low levels of ozone during periods of moderate exertion.

The two types of chemicals that are the main ingredients in forming ground-level ozone are called volatile organic compounds (VOCs) and nitrogen oxides (NOx). VOCs are released by cars burning gasoline, petroleum refineries, chemical manufacturing plants, and other industrial facilities. The solvents used in paints and other consumer and business products contain VOCs. The 1990 Clean Air Act has resulted in changes in product formulas to reduce the VOC content of those products. Nitrogen oxides (NOx) are produced when cars and other sources like power plants and industrial boilers burn fuels such as gasoline, coal, or oil. The reddish-brown color you sometimes see when it is smoggy comes from the nitrogen oxides.

The pollutants that react to form ground-level ozone literally cook in the sky during the hot summertime season. It takes time for smog to form—several hours from the time pollutants get into the air until the ground-level ozone reaches unhealthy levels.

Weather and the lay of the land (for example, hills around a valley, high mountains between a big industrial city and suburban or rural areas) help determine where ground-level ozone goes and how bad it gets. When temperature inversions occur (warm air stays trapped near the ground by a layer of cooler air) and winds are calm, high concentrations of ground- level ozone may persist for days at a time. As traffic and other sources add more ozone-forming pollutants to the air, the ground-level ozone gets worse.

How the Clean Air Act Reduces Air Pollution Such as Particle Pollution and Ground-level Ozone. First, EPA works with state governors and tribal government leaders to identify "nonattainment" areas where the air does not meet allowable limits for a common air pollutant. States and tribes usually do much of the planning for cleaning up common air pollutants. They develop plans, called State/Tribal Implementation Plans, to reduce air pollutants to allowable levels. Then they use a permit system as part of their plan to make sure power plants, factories, and other pollution sources meet their goals to clean up the air.

The Clean Air Act requirements are comprehensive and cover many different pollution sources and a variety of clean-up methods to reduce common air pollutants. Many of the clean-up requirements for particle pollution and ground-level ozone involve large industrial sources (power plants, chemical producers, and petroleum refineries), as well as motor vehicles (cars, trucks, and buses). Also, in nonattainment areas, controls are generally required for smaller pollution sources, such as gasoline stations and paint shops.

Cars, Trucks, Buses, and "Nonroad" Equipment

Today, motor vehicles are responsible for nearly one- half of smog-forming volatile organic compounds (VOCs), more than half of the nitrogen oxide (NOx) emissions, and about half of the toxic air pollutant emissions in the United States. Motor vehicles, including nonroad vehicles, now account for 75 percent of carbon monoxide emissions nationwide.

The total vehicle miles people travel in the United States increased 178 percent between 1970 and 2005 and continues to increase at a rate of two to three percent each year. In the United States, there are more than 210 million cars and light-duty trucks on the road. In addition, the types of cars people drive have changed greatly since 1970. Beginning in the late 1980s, Americans began driving more vans, sport utility vehicles (SUVs), and pickup trucks as personal vehicles. By the year 2000, these "light-duty trucks" accounted for about half of the new passenger car sales. These bigger vehicles typically consume more gasoline per mile and many of them pollute three to five times more than cars.

The Clean Air Act takes a comprehensive approach to reducing pollution from these sources by requiring manufacturers to build cleaner engines; refiners to produce cleaner fuels; and certain areas with air pollution problems to adopt and run passenger vehicle inspection and maintenance programs. EPA has issued a series of regulations affecting passenger cars, diesel trucks and buses, and so-called "nonroad" equipment (recreational vehicles, lawn and garden equipment, etc.) that will dramatically reduce emissions as people buy new vehicles and equipment.

Cleaner Cars. The Clean Air Act required EPA to issue a series of rules to reduce pollution from vehicle exhaust, refueling emissions and evaporating gasoline. As a result, emissions from a new car purchased today are well over 90 percent cleaner than a new vehicle purchased in 1970. This applies to SUVs and pickup trucks, as well. Beginning in 2004, all new passenger vehicles—including SUVs, minivans, vans and pick-up trucks—must meet more stringent tailpipe emission standards. This marks the first time that light-duty trucks, including SUVs, pickups, and minivans are subject to the same national pollution standards as cars. As more of these cleaner vehicles enter the national fleet, harmful emissions will drop dramatically.

These reductions would not be possible without cleaner, very low sulfur gasoline and diesel fuel. In addition to their direct emissions benefits, cleaner fuels enable sophisticated emission control devices to effectively control pollution. Congress recognized the importance of cleaner fuels to reducing motor vehicle emissions and gave EPA authority to regulate fuels in the Clean Air Act.

Lead and Other Toxic Pollutants. One of EPA's earliest accomplishments was the elimination of lead from gasoline. Elevated levels of lead can damage organs and the brain and nervous system, and affect the heart and blood. Adverse health effects range from behavior disorders and anemia to mental retardation and permanent nerve damage. Children are especially susceptible to lead's toxic effects on the nervous system, which can result in learning deficits and lowered IQ. In the mid-1970s, EPA
began its lead phase-out effort by proposing to limit the amount of lead that could be used in gasoline. By the summer of 1974, unleaded gasoline was widely available around the country, improving public health and providing protection for the catalytic converters that manufacturers began to install on all new vehicles. This effort was followed by even stronger restrictions on the use of lead in gasoline in the 1980s. In 1996, leaded gasoline was finally banned as a result of the Clean Air Act.

Under the Clean Air Act, EPA has also put into place standards to reduce toxic air emissions from mobile sources. These standards will cut toxic emissions from gasoline, vehicles, and even gas containers.

Reformulated Gasoline. The Clean Air Act requires certain metropolitan areas with the worst ground-level ozone pollution to use gasoline that has been reformulated to reduce air pollution. Other areas, including the District of Columbia and 17 states, with ground-level ozone levels exceeding the public health standards, have voluntarily chosen to use reformulated gasoline. Reformulated gasoline reduces emissions of toxic air pollutants, such as benzene, as well as pollutants that contribute to smog.

Low Sulfur Fuels. Beginning in 2006, refiners have been supplying gasoline with sulfur levels much lower than in the past, reducing the sulfur levels in gasoline by 90 percent. Sulfur in gasoline inhibits a vehicle's catalytic converter from effectively cleaning up the exhaust. The advanced vehicle emission control systems in passenger cars and light trucks are even more sensitive to sulfur, so reducing the sulfur content of gasoline will ensure that vehicle emission control devices are effective in reducing pollution. In addition to cutting emissions from new vehicles, lower sulfur fuel will result in lower emissions from vehicles currently on the road.

Since 2006, refiners have begun supplying diesel fuel with very low sulfur levels for highway diesel vehicles. As with gasoline vehicles, efficient new emission controls on diesel engines require this "Ultra- Low Sulfur Diesel" (ULSD) fuel to function properly. Highway diesel fuel sulfur levels are 97 percent cleaner than diesel prior to 2006. In 2007, refiners began reducing sulfur in diesel fuel used for nonroad diesel engines, such as construction equipment.

Alternative Fuels. The Clean Air Act encourages development and sale of alternative fuels. Alternative fuels are transportation fuels other than gasoline and diesel, including natural gas, propane, methanol, ethanol, electricity, and biodiesel. These fuels can be cleaner than gasoline or diesel and can reduce emissions of harmful pollutants. Renewable alternative fuels are made from biomass materials like wood, waste paper, grasses, vegetable oils, and corn. They are biodegradable and reduce carbon dioxide emissions. In addition, most alternative fuels are produced domestically, which
is better for our economy, energy security and helps offset the cost of imported oil.

The Clean Air Act also requires EPA to establish a national renewable fuel (RF) program. This program is designed to significantly increase the volume of renewable fuel that is blended into gasoline and diesel.

Cleaner Trucks, Buses and "Nonroad" Equipment. Diesel engines are more durable and are more fuel efficient than gasoline engines, but can pollute significantly more. Heavy-duty trucks and buses account for about one-third of nitrogen oxides emissions and one-quarter of particle pollution emissions from transportation sources. In some large cities, the contribution is even greater. Similarly, nonroad diesel engines such as construction and agricultural equipment emit large quantities of harmful particle pollution and nitrogen oxides, which contribute to ground-level ozone and other pervasive air quality problems.

EPA has issued rules to cut emissions from onroad and nonroad vehicles by more than 90 percent by combining stringent emissions standards for diesel engines and clean, ultra-low sulfur diesel fuel. Under the Clean Air Act, EPA is also addressing pollution from a range of nonroad sources, including locomotives and marine vessels, recreational vehicles, and lawn and garden equipment. Together these sources comprise a significant portion of emissions from the transportation sector.

Transportation Policies. Congress required "conformity" in the Clean Air Act Amendments of 1990. In other words, transportation projects such as construction of highways and transit rail lines cannot be federally funded or approved unless they are consistent with state air quality goals. In addition, transportation projects must not cause or contribute to new violations of the air quality standards, worsen existing violations, or delay attainment of air quality standards.

The conformity provisions require areas that have poor air quality now, or had it in the past, to examine the long-term air quality impacts of their transportation system and ensure that it is compatible with the area's clean air goals. In doing so, those areas must assess the impacts of growth on air pollution and decide how to manage growth. State and local agencies must work together to either change the transportation plan and/or the state air plan to achieve the necessary emission reductions.

Inspection and Maintenance Programs. Proper maintenance of a car's engine and pollution control equipment is critical to reduce excessive air pollution. To help ensure that such maintenance occurs, the Clean Air Act requires certain areas with air pollution problems to run inspection and maintenance (I/M) programs. The 1990 Act also established the requirement that passenger vehicles be equipped with on board diagnostics. The diagnostics system is designed to trigger a dashboard "check engine" light alerting the driver of a possible pollution control device malfunction. To help ensure that motorists respond to the "check engine" light in a timely manner, the Act requires that I/M programs include an inspection of the on board diagnostic system.

Interstate and International Air Pollution

Air pollution does not recognize state or international boundaries. Pollutants can be carried long distances by the wind. Dirty air even turns up in places where you least expect it, like national parks or wilderness areas in remote parts of the United States.

Taller smokestacks can lift pollutants high above a local community but help pollutants get into wind currents that can carry them hundreds, even thousands, of miles. For example, emissions from power plants and industrial boilers can travel hundreds of miles and contribute to smog, haze, and air pollution in downwind states. One family of pollutants, nitrogen oxides, also reacts with other chemicals, sunlight and heat to form ground-level ozone. The nitrogen oxides and the ozone itself can be transported with the weather to help cause unhealthy air in cities and towns far downwind.

States and tribes seeking to clean up air pollution are sometimes unable to meet EPA's national standards because of pollution blowing in from other areas. The Clean Air Act has a number of programs designed to reduce long-range transport of pollution from one area to another. The Act has provisions designed to ensure that emissions from one state are not contributing to public health problems in downwind states.It does this, in part, by requiring that each state's implementation plan contain provisions to prevent the emissions from the facilities or sources within its borders from contributing significantly to air pollution problems "downwind"—specifically in those areas that fail to meet EPA's national air quality standards. If a state or tribe has not developed the necessary plan to address this downwind pollution, EPA can require the state to do so. If the state still does not take the necessary action, EPA can implement a federal plan to achieve the necessary emission reductions.

Also, the Act gives any state or tribe the authority to ask EPA to set emission limits for specific sources of pollution in other (upwind) areas that significantly contribute to its air quality problems. States and tribes can petition EPA to require the upwind areas to reduce air pollution.

The Act provides for interstate commissions to develop regional strategies for cleaning up air pollution. For instance, state and tribal governments from Maine to Virginia, the government of the District of Columbia, and EPA are working together through the Ozone Transport Commission (OTC) to reduce ground-level ozone along the east coast.

The Clean Air Act also requires EPA to work with states to reduce the regional haze that affects visibility in 156 national parks and wilderness areas, including the Grand Canyon, Yosemite, the Great Smokies, and Shenandoah National Parks. During much of the year in these areas, a veil of white or brown haze hangs in the air blurring the view. Most of this haze is not natural. It is air pollution, carried by the wind often many hundreds of miles from where it originated. Under the regional haze provisions of the Clean Air Act, the states and tribes, in coordination with the EPA, the National Park Service, U.S. Fish and Wildlife Service, the U.S. Forest Service, and others, develop and implement air quality protection plans to reduce the pollution that causes visibility impairment. EPA has worked with states and tribes across the country to form Regional Planning Organizations to develop plans to reduce pollutants that cause haze.

Reducing Acid Rain

You have probably heard of "acid rain." But you may not have heard of other forms of acid precipitation such as acid snow, acid fog or mist, or dry forms of acidic pollution such as acid gas and acid dust. All of these can be formed in the atmosphere and fall to Earth causing human health problems, hazy skies, environmental problems and property damage. Acid precipitation is produced when certain types of air pollutants mix with the moisture in the air to form an acid. These acids then fall to Earth as rain, snow, or fog. Even when the weather is dry, acid pollutants may fall to Earth in gases or particles.

Sulfur dioxide (SO_2) and nitrogen oxides (NO_x) are the principal pollutants that cause acid precipitation. SO_2 and NO_x emissions released to the air react with water vapor and other chemicals to form acids that fall back to Earth. Power plants burning coal and heavy oil produce over two-thirds of the annual SO_2 emissions in the United States. The majority of NO_x (about 50 percent) comes from cars, buses, trucks, and other forms of transportation. About 40 percent of NO_x emissions are from power plants. The rest is emitted from various sources like industrial and commercial boilers.

Heavy rainstorms and melting snow can cause temporary increases in acidity in lakes and streams, primarily in the eastern United States. The temporary increases may last for days or even weeks, causing harm to fish and other aquatic life.

The air pollutants that cause acid rain can do more than damage the environment—they can damage our health. High levels of SO_2 in the air aggravate various lung problems in people with asthma and can cause breathing difficulties in children and the elderly. In some instances, breathing high levels of SO_2 can even damage lung tissue and cause premature death.

Acid lakes and streams have been found all over the country. For instance, lakes in Acadia National Park on Maine's Mt. Desert Island have become acidic due to pollution from the midwest and the east coast. Streams in Maryland and West Virginia, as well as lakes in the Upper Peninsula of Michigan, have been damaged by acid rain. Since the wind can carry pollutants across the country, the effects of acid rain can be seen far from the original source of the acid- forming pollutant.

Acid rain has damaged trees in the mountains of Vermont and other states. Red spruce trees at high altitudes appear to be especially sensitive to acid rain. The pollutants that cause acid rain can make the air hazy or foggy; this occurs in the eastern United States in areas like the Great Smokies and Shenandoah National Park, areas where vacationers go to enjoy the beautiful scenery and awe-inspiring views. In addition to damaging the natural environment, acid rain can damage manmade objects such as stone statues, buildings, and monuments.

The 1990 changes to the Clean Air Act introduced a nationwide approach to reducing acid pollution. The law is designed to reduce acid rain and improve public health by dramatically reducing emissions of sulfur dioxide (SO_2) and oxides of nitrogen (NO_x). Using a market-based cap and trade approach, the program sets a permanent cap on the total amount of SO_2 that may be emitted by electric power plants nationwide. As of 2005, emission reductions were more than 7 million tons from power plants, or 41 percent below 1980 levels.

The initial phase of EPA's Acid Rain Program went into effect in 1995. The law required the highest emitting units at 110 power plants in 21 Midwest, Appalachian, and Northeastern states to reduce emissions of SO_2. The second phase of the program went into effect in 2000, further reducing SO_2 emissions from big coal-burning power plants. Some smaller plants were also included in the second phase of the program. Total SO_2 releases for the nation's power plants are permanently limited to the level set by the 1990 Clean Air Act—about 50 percent of the levels emitted in 1980.

Each allowance is worth one ton of SO_2 emissions released from the plant's smokestack. Plants may only release the amount of SO_2 equal to the allowances they have been issued. If a plant expects to release more SO_2 than it has allowances, it has to purchase more allowances or use technology and other methods to control emissions. A plant can buy allowances from another power plant that has more allowances than it needs to cover its emissions.

There is an allowances market that operates like the stock market, in which brokers or anyone who wants to take part in buying or selling allowances can participate. Allowances are traded and sold nationwide.

EPA's Acid Rain Program has provided bonus allowances to power plants for installing clean coal technology that reduces SO_2 releases, using renewable energy sources (solar, wind, etc.), or encouraging energy conservation by customers so that less power needs to be produced. EPA has also awarded allowances to industrial sources voluntarily entering the Acid Rain Program.

The 1990 Clean Air Act has stiff monetary penalties for plants that release more pollutants than are covered by their allowances. All power plants covered by the Acid Rain Program have to install continuous emission monitoring systems, and instruments that keep track of how much SO_2 and NO_x the plant's individual units are releasing. Power plant operators keep track of this information hourly and report it electronically to EPA four times each year. EPA uses this information to make sure that the plant is not releasing quantities of pollutants exceeding the plant's allowances. A power plant's program for meeting its SO2 and NOx limits will appear on the plant's permit, which is filed with the state and EPA and is available for public review.

Market Approaches and Economic Incentives. Besides the ground-breaking features in the Acid Rain Program, the 1990 Clean Air Act encouraged other innovative approaches that spur technology. These approaches allow businesses greater flexibility in how they comply with the law, and thus clean-up air pollution as efficiently and inexpensively as possible. For example:

EPA's new cleaner vehicle standards include an averaging system that allows manufacturers to choose how to produce a mix of more- or less-polluting vehicles, as long as the overall fleet average is lower.

Gasoline refiners can receive credits if they produce cleaner gasoline than required, and they use those credits when their gasoline does not quite meet the clean-up requirements.

Reducing Toxic Air Pollutants

Toxic air pollutants, or air toxics, are known to cause or are suspected of causing cancer, birth defects, reproduction problems, and other serious illnesses. Exposure to certain levels of some toxic air pollutants can cause difficulty in breathing, nausea or other illnesses. Exposure to certain toxic pollutants can even cause death.

Some toxic air pollutants are of concern because they degrade slowly or not at all, as in the case of metals such as mercury or lead. These persistent air toxics can remain in the environment for a long time and can be transported great distances. Toxic air pollutants, like mercury or polychlorinated biphenyls, deposited onto soil or into lakes and streams persist and bioaccumulate in the environment. They can affect living systems and food chains, and eventually affect people when they eat contaminated food. This can be particularly important for American Indians or other communities where cultural practices or subsistence life styles are prevalent.

The majority of air toxics come from manmade sources, such as factory smokestack emissions and motor vehicle exhaust.

Gasoline also contains air toxics. When you put fuel in your car, gases escape and form a vapor. You can smell these vapors when you refuel your vehicle.

When cars and trucks burn gasoline, toxic air pollutants are emitted from the tailpipe. Those air toxics are combustion products—chemicals that are produced when gasoline is burned. EPA is working with industries to develop cleaner-burning fuels and more efficient engines, and is taking steps to make sure that pollution control devices installed in motor vehicles work properly. EPA has issued requirements that are leading to cleaner-burning diesel engines, reducing releases of particle pollution and air toxics.

Air toxics are also released from industrial sources, such as chemical factories, refineries, and incinerators, and even from small industrial and commercial sources, such as dry cleaners and printing shops. Under the 1990 Clean Air Act, EPA has regulated both large and small sources of air toxics, but has mainly focused efforts on larger sources.

Before the 1990 Clean Air Act Amendments, EPA regulated air toxics one chemical at a time. This approach did not work well. Between 1970 and 1990, EPA established regulations for only seven pollutants. The 1990 Clean Air Act Amendments took a completely different approach to reducing toxic air pollutants. The Amendments required EPA to identify categories of industrial sources for 187 listed toxic air pollutants and to take steps to reduce pollution by requiring sources to install controls or change production processes. It makes good sense to regulate by categories of industries rather than one pollutant at a time, since many individual sources release more than one toxic chemical. Developing controls and process changes for industrial source categories can result in major reductions in releases of multiple pollutants at one time.

EPA has published regulations covering a wide range of industrial categories, including chemical plants, incinerators, dry cleaners, and manufacturers of wood furniture. Harmful air toxics from large industrial sources, such as chemical plants, petroleum refineries, and paper mills, have been reduced by nearly 70 percent. These regulations mostly apply to large, so-called "major" sources and also to some smaller sources known as "area" sources. In most cases, EPA does not prescribe a specific control technology, but sets a performance level based on a technology or other practices already used by the better-controlled and lower emitting sources in an industry. EPA works to develop regulations that give companies as much flexibility as possible in deciding how they reduce their toxic air emissions—as long as the companies meet the levels required in the regulations.

The 1990 Clean Air Act requires EPA to first set regulations using a technology-based or performance-based approach to reduce toxic emissions from industrial sources. After EPA sets the technology-based regulations, the Act requires EPA to evaluate any remaining ("residual") risks, and decide whether it is necessary to control the source further. That assessment of remaining risk was initiated in the year 2000 for some of the industries covered by the technology-based standards.

Air Toxics and Risk. The Clean Air Act requires a number of studies to help EPA better characterize risks to human health and the environment from air toxics. Those studies provide information for rulemaking and support national and local efforts to address risks through pollution prevention and other voluntary programs. Among these risk reduction initiatives are:

The Integrated Urban Air Toxics Strategy includes local and community-based initiatives to reduce local toxic air emissions. The primary goal of the strategy is to reduce public health risks from both indoor and outdoor sources of toxic air pollutants.

The Great Waters Program incorporates activities to investigate and reduce the deposition of toxic air pollutants to the "Great Waters," which include the Chesapeake Bay, Lake Champlain, the Great Lakes, National Estuary Program areas, and National Estuarine Research Reserves.

Initiatives targeting emission reductions of persistent bioaccumulative toxics (PBTs) like mercury, DDT (a pesticide banned in the United States), and dioxins.

Protecting the Stratospheric Ozone Layer

Ozone can be good or bad depending on where it is located. Close to the Earth's surface, ground-level ozone is a harmful air pollutant. Ozone in the stratosphere, high above the Earth, protects human health and the environment from the sun's harmful ultraviolet radiation. This natural shield has been gradually depleted by manmade chemicals. So in 1990, Congress added provisions to the Clean Air Act for protecting the stratospheric ozone layer. Ozone in the stratosphere, a layer of the atmosphere located 10 to 30 miles above the Earth, serves as a shield, protecting people and the environment from the sun's harmful ultraviolet radiation. The stratospheric ozone layer filters out harmful sun rays, including a type of sunlight called ultraviolet B. Exposure to ultraviolet B (UVB) has been linked to cataracts (eye damage) and skin cancer. Scientists have also linked increased UVB exposures to crop injury and damage to ocean plant life.

In the mid-1970s, scientists became concerned that chlorofluorocarbons (CFCs) could destroy stratospheric ozone. At that time, CFCs were widely used as aerosol propellants in consumer products such as hairsprays and deodorants, and as coolants in refrigerators and air conditioners. In 1978, the U.S. government banned CFCs as propellants in most aerosol uses.

Scientists have been monitoring the stratospheric ozone layer since the 1970s. In the 1980s, scientists began accumulating evidence that the ozone layer was being depleted. The ozone hole in the region of the South Pole, which has appeared each year during the Antarctic winter (our summer), often is bigger than the continental United States. Between 1978 and 1997, scientists have measured a 5 percent loss of stratospheric ozone—a significant amount.

Over 190 countries, including the major industrialized nations such as the United States, have signed the 1987 Montreal Protocol, which calls for elimination of chemicals that destroy stratospheric ozone. Countries that signed the Protocol are committed to limiting the production and use of those chemicals.

The 1990 Clean Air Act required EPA to set up a program for phasing out production and use of ozone-destroying chemicals. In 1996, U.S. production ended for many of the chemicals capable of doing the most serious harm such as CFCs, halons, and methyl chloroform.

Unfortunately, it will be about 60 years before the stratospheric ozone layer heals. Because of the ozone-destroying chemicals already in the stratosphere and those that will arrive within the next few years, stratospheric ozone destruction will likely continue throughout the decade. September 24, 2006, tied for the largest ozone hole on record at 29 million square kilometers (11.4 million square miles). The year 2006 also saw the second largest sustained ozone hole.

The Clean Air Act includes other steps to protect the ozone layer. The Act encourages the development of "ozone-friendly" substitutes for ozone-destroying chemicals. Many products and processes have been reformulated to be more "ozone-friendly." For instance, refrigerators no longer use CFCs.

Sometimes it isn't easy to phase out an ozone-destroying chemical. For instance, substitutes have not been found for CFCs used in certain medical applications. The limit on the production of methyl bromide, a pesticide, was extended because farmers did not yet have an effective alternative. Despite the inevitable delays because of technical and economic concerns, ozone-destroying chemicals are being phased out, and, with continued work, over time the protective ozone layer will be repaired.

Permits

One of the major initiatives Congress added to the Clean Air Act in 1990 is an operating permit program for larger industrial and commercial sources that release pollutants into the air. Operating permits include information on which pollutants are being released, how much may be released, and what kinds of steps the source's owner or operator is required to take to reduce the pollution. Permits must include plans to measure and report the air pollution emitted. States and tribes issue operating permits. If those governments do not do a satisfactory job of carrying out the Clean Air Act permitting requirements, EPA can take over issuing permits.

Operating permits are especially useful for businesses covered by more than one part of the Clean Air Act and additional state or local requirements, since information about all of a source's air pollution is in one place. The permit program simplifies and clarifies businesses' obligations for cleaning up air pollution and can reduce paperwork. For instance, an electric power plant may be covered by the acid rain, toxic air pollutant, and smog (ground-level ozone) sections of the Clean Air Act. The detailed information required by those separate sections is consolidated into one place in an operating permit.

Thousands of operating permits that have been issued across the United States are available to the public. Contact your state or regional air pollution control agency or EPA for information on access to those documents.

Businesses seeking permits have to pay permit fees, much like car owners paying for car registrations. These fees pay for the air pollution control activities related to operating permits.

Enforcement

The Clean Air Act gives EPA important enforcement powers. In the past, it was difficult for EPA to penalize a company for violating the Clean Air Act—the Agency had to go to court for even minor violations. The 1990 Amendments strengthened EPA's power to enforce the Act, increasing the range of civil and criminal sanctions available. In general, when EPA finds that a violation has occurred, the agency can issue an order requiring the violator to comply, issue an administrative penalty order (use EPA administrative authority to force payment of a penalty), or bring a civil judicial action (sue the violator in court).

Public Participation

Public participation is a very important part of the 1990 Clean Air Act. Throughout the Act, different provisions give the public opportunities to take part in determining how the law is carried out.

Often, when EPA is working on a major rule, the Agency will hold hearings in various cities across the country, at which the public can comment.

You can also submit written comments directly to EPA for inclusion in the public record associated with that rule. Or, for instance, you can participate in development of a state or tribal implementation plan. Commenting on a state or tribal plan could be worthwhile since approaches for cleaning up pollution could have direct effects on the way you and your family live.

The 1990 Clean Air Act gives you opportunities to take direct action to get pollution cleaned up in your community. You can get involved in reviewing air pollution permits for industrial sources in your area. You also can ask EPA, your state or tribe to take action against a polluter, and, in some cases, you may be able to take legal action against a source's owner or operator.

Reports required by the 1990 Clean Air Act are usually available to the public. Those reports include a great deal of information on how much pollution is being released by industrial and commercial sources. Monitoring data collected by EPA, states and tribes that measure the level of selected pollutants in a community's air are also available to the public.

How the Clean Air Act Is Working

There are several ways you can tell how well the Clean Air Act is working. Over time, the Clean Air Act will continue to reduce air pollution, but it will take time for some of the Act's provisions to have their full impact.

In general, when EPA or state, local, and tribal governments require sources of pollution to adopt control measures, you will see results right away. For instance, when large industrial facilities are required to install pollution control equipment, releases of pollutants should drop when the equipment is installed. On the other hand, in the case of cars and trucks, it may take several years for old vehicles to be retired from the road before the full effects of cleaning up cars and trucks will be seen.

You can also check on how individual facilities are meeting their clean-up requirements. Air pollutant releases at individual facilities such as power plants are set out in the facility's permit, which you can review.

Monitoring air quality is the best way to tell if the air is getting cleaner, because the monitors accurately report how much of a pollutant is in the air. You can request EPA, state, local, or tribal monitoring reports that show changes over time. It is updated frequently, so you can get recent information on what's happening to the air in your community.

The "Air Quality Index" (AQI) is a "public-friendly" way of using actual monitoring data to help us assess how clean our air is. Americans are familiar with many radio, TV, and newspaper weather forecasters talking about the

AQI—telling you that the air is so polluted that a "Code Orange" or "Code Red" air quality condition is in effect. The AQI tracks pollution for your local area. The color codes, which range from green to purple, correspond to specific pollution levels. As clean-up programs are implemented for the air pollutants tracked by the AQI, we hope to see a reduction in the number of Code Orange and Code Red air quality days.

SIX COMMON AIR POLLUTANTS

The Clean Air Act requires EPA to set National Ambient Air Quality Standards for six common air pollutants. These commonly found air pollutants (also known as "criteria pollutants") are found all over the United States. They are ground-level ozone, particle pollution (often referred to as particulate matter), carbon monoxide, nitrogen oxides, sulfur oxides, and lead. These pollutants can harm your health and the environment, and cause property damage. Of the six pollutants, particle pollution and ground-level ozone are the most widespread health threats. EPA calls these pollutants "criteria" air pollutants because it regulates them by developing human health-based and/or environmentally-based criteria (science-based guidelines) for setting permissible levels. The set of limits based on human health is called primary standards. Another set of limits intended to prevent environmental and property damage is called secondary standards.

Ozone

Ozone is found in two regions of the Earth's atmosphere – at ground level and in the upper regions of the atmosphere. Both types of ozone have the same chemical composition (O_3). While upper atmospheric ozone protects the earth from the sun's harmful rays, ground level ozone is the main component of smog.

Tropospheric, or ground level ozone, is not emitted directly into the air, but is created by chemical reactions between oxides of nitrogen (NOx) and volatile organic compounds (VOC). Ozone is likely to reach unhealthy levels on hot sunny days in urban environments. Ozone can also be transported long distances by wind. For this reason, even rural areas can experience high ozone levels.

High ozone concentrations have also been observed in cold months, where a few high elevation areas in the Western U.S. with high levels of local

VOC and NOx emissions have formed ozone when snow is on the ground and temperatures are near or below freezing. Ozone contributes to what we typically experience as "smog" or haze, which still occurs most frequently in the summertime, but can occur throughout the year in some southern and mountain regions.

Ground level ozone—what we breathe—can harm our health. Even relatively low levels of ozone can cause health effects. People with lung disease, children, older adults, and people who are active outdoors may be particularly sensitive to ozone.

Children are at greatest risk from exposure to ozone because their lungs are still developing and they are more likely to be active outdoors when ozone levels are high, which increases their exposure. Children are also more likely than adults to have asthma.

Ozone also affects sensitive vegetation and ecosystems, including forests, parks, wildlife refuges and wilderness areas. In particular, ozone harms sensitive vegetation, including trees and plants during the growing season.

Emissions from industrial facilities and electric utilities, motor vehicle exhaust, gasoline vapors, and chemical solvents are some of the major sources of NOx and VOC.

Under the Clean Air Act, EPA has established health and environmentally protective standards for ozone in the air we breathe. EPA and others have instituted a variety of multi-faceted programs to meet these standards.

Throughout the country, additional programs are being put into place to cut NOx and VOC emissions from vehicles, industrial facilities, and electric utilities. Programs are also aimed at reducing pollution by reformulating fuels and consumer/commercial products, such as paints and chemical solvents that contain VOC.

Voluntary and innovative programs encourage communities to adopt practices, such as carpooling, to reduce harmful emissions.

Health Effects

Ozone in the air we breathe can harm our health—typically on hot, sunny days when ozone can reach unhealthy levels. Even relatively low levels of ozone can cause health effects. Children, people with lung disease, older adults, and people who are active outdoors, including outdoor workers, may be particularly sensitive to ozone.

Children are at greatest risk from exposure to ozone because their lungs are still developing and they are more likely to be active outdoors when ozone levels are high, which increases their exposure. Children are also more likely than adults to have asthma.

Breathing ozone can trigger a variety of health problems including chest pain, coughing, throat irritation, and congestion. It can worsen bronchitis, emphysema, and asthma. Ground level ozone also can reduce lung function and inflame the linings of the lungs. Repeated exposure may permanently scar lung tissue.

Ozone can:

- Make it more difficult to breathe deeply and vigorously.
- Cause shortness of breath and pain when taking a deep breath.
- Cause coughing and sore or scratchy throat.
- Inflame and damage the airways.
- Aggravate lung diseases such as asthma, emphysema, and chronic bronchitis.
- Increase the frequency of asthma attacks.
- Make the lungs more susceptible to infection.
- Continue to damage the lungs even when the symptoms have disappeared.

These effects may lead to increased school absences, medication use, visits to doctors and emergency rooms, and hospital admissions. Research also indicates that ozone exposure may increase the risk of premature death from heart or lung disease.

Ozone is particularly likely to reach unhealthy levels on hot sunny days in urban environments. It is a major part of urban smog. Ozone can also be transported long distances by wind. For this reason, even rural areas can experience high ozone levels. And, in some cases, ozone can occur throughout the year in some southern and mountain regions.

Environmental Effects

Ozone also affects sensitive vegetation and ecosystems, including forests, parks, wildlife refuges and wilderness areas. In particular, ozone harms sensitive vegetation, including trees and plants during the growing season.

Plant species that are sensitive to ozone and potentially at an increased risk from exposure include trees such as black cherry, quaking aspen, ponderosa pine and cottonwood. These trees are found in many areas of the country.

Ground level ozone can have harmful effects on sensitive vegetation and ecosystems. When sufficient ozone enters the leaves of a plant, it can:

- Interfere with the ability of sensitive plants to produce and store food.
- Visibly damage the leaves of trees and other plants, harming the appearance of vegetation in urban areas, national parks, and recreation areas

In addition to reduced tree growth and visible injury to leaves, continued ozone exposure over time can lead to increased susceptibility of sensitive plant species to disease, damage from insects, effects of other pollutants, competition, and harm from severe weather. These effects can also have adverse impacts on ecosystems, including loss of species diversity and changes to habitat quality and water and nutrient cycles.

Particulate Matter

Particle pollution (also called particulate matter or PM) is the term for a mixture of solid particles and liquid droplets found in the air. Some particles, such as dust, dirt, soot, or smoke, are large or dark enough to be seen with the naked eye. Others are so small they can only be detected using an electron microscope.

Particle pollution includes "inhalable coarse particles," with diameters larger than 2.5 micrometers and smaller than 10 micrometers and "fine particles," with diameters that are 2.5 micrometers and smaller. How small is 2.5 micrometers? Think about a single hair from your head. The average human hair is about 70 micrometers in diameter – making it 30 times larger than the largest fine particle.

These particles come in many sizes and shapes and can be made up of hundreds of different chemicals. Some particles, known as primary particles are emitted directly from a source, such as construction sites, unpaved roads, fields, smokestacks or fires. Others form in complicated reactions in the atmosphere of chemicals such as sulfur dioxides and nitrogen oxides that are emitted from power plants, industries and automobiles. These particles, known as secondary particles, make up most of the fine particle pollution in the country.

EPA regulates inhalable particles (fine and coarse). Particles larger than 10 micrometers (sand and large dust) are not regulated by EPA.

Health: Particle pollution contains microscopic solids or liquid droplets that are so small that they can get deep into the lungs and cause serious health problems. The size of particles is directly linked to their potential for causing health problems. Small particles less than 10 micrometers in diameter pose the greatest problems, because they can get deep into your lungs, and some may even get into your bloodstream.

Visibility: Fine particles (PM2.5) are the main cause of reduced visibility (haze) in parts of the United States, including many of our treasured national parks and wilderness areas.

Reducing particle pollution: EPA's national and regional rules to reduce emissions of pollutants that form particle pollution will help state and local governments meet the Agency's national air quality standards.

Health Effects

The size of particles is directly linked to their potential for causing health problems. Small particles less than 10 micrometers in diameter pose the greatest problems, because they can get deep into your lungs, and some may even get into your bloodstream.

Exposure to such particles can affect both your lungs and your heart. Small particles of concern include "inhalable coarse particles" (such as those found near roadways and dusty industries), which are larger than 2.5 micrometers and smaller than 10 micrometers in diameter; and "fine particles" (such as those found in smoke and haze), which are 2.5 micrometers in diameter and smaller.

The Clean Air Act requires EPA to set air quality standards to protect both public health and the public welfare (e.g. visibility, crops and vegetation). Particle pollution affects both.

Particle pollution - especially fine particles - contains microscopic solids or liquid droplets that are so small that they can get deep into the lungs and cause serious health problems. Numerous scientific studies have linked particle pollution exposure to a variety of problems, including:

- premature death in people with heart or lung disease,
- nonfatal heart attacks,
- irregular heartbeat,
- aggravated asthma,
- decreased lung function, and
- increased respiratory symptoms, such as irritation of the airways, coughing or difficulty breathing.

People with heart or lung diseases, children and older adults are the most likely to be affected by particle pollution exposure. However, even if you are healthy, you may experience temporary symptoms from exposure to elevated levels of particle pollution.

Environmental Effects

Visibility Impairment. Fine particles (PM2.5) are the main cause of reduced visibility (haze) in parts of the United States, including many of our treasured national parks and wilderness areas. For more information about visibility, visit www.epa.gov/visibility.

Environmental Damage. Particles can be carried over long distances by wind and then settle on ground or water. The effects of this settling include: making lakes and streams acidic; changing the nutrient balance in coastal waters and large river basins; depleting the nutrients in soil; damaging sensitive forests and farm crops; and affecting the diversity of ecosystems. More information about the effects of particle pollution and acid rain.

Aesthetic Damage. Particle pollution can stain and damage stone and other materials, including culturally important objects such as statues and monuments. More information about the effects of particle pollution and acid rain.

Carbon Monoxide

Carbon monoxide (CO) is a colorless, odorless gas emitted from combustion processes. Nationally and, particularly in urban areas, the majority of CO emissions to ambient air come from mobile sources. CO can cause harmful health effects by reducing oxygen delivery to the body's organs (like the heart and brain) and tissues. At extremely high levels, CO can cause death.

EPA first set air quality standards for CO in 1971. For protection of both public health and welfare, EPA set a 8-hour primary standard at 9 parts per million (ppm) and a 1-hour primary standard at 35 ppm.

In a review of the standards completed in 1985, EPA revoked the secondary standards (for public welfare) due to a lack of evidence of adverse effects on public welfare at or near ambient concentrations.

The last review of the CO NAAQS was completed in 1994 and the Agency chose not to revise the standards at that time.

Everywhere in the country has air quality that meets the current CO standards. Most sites have measured concentrations below the national standards since the early 1990s, since which time, improvements in motor vehicle emissions controls have contributed to significant reductions in ambient concentrations.

CO can cause harmful health effects by reducing oxygen delivery to the body's organs (like the heart and brain) and tissues. At extremely high levels, CO can cause death.

Exposure to CO can reduce the oxygen-carrying capacity of the blood. People with several types of heart disease already have a reduced capacity for pumping oxygenated blood to the heart, which can cause them to experience myocardial ischemia (reduced oxygen to the heart), often accompanied by chest pain (angina), when exercising or under increased stress. For these people, short-term CO exposure further affects their body's already compromised ability to respond to the increased oxygen demands of exercise or exertion.

Nitrogen Oxides

Nitrogen dioxide (NO_2) is one of a group of highly reactive gasses known as "oxides of nitrogen," or "nitrogen oxides (NO_x)." Other nitrogen oxides include nitrous acid and nitric acid. EPA's National Ambient Air Quality Standard uses NO_2 as the indicator for the larger group of nitrogen oxides. NO_2 forms quickly from emissions from cars, trucks and buses, power plants, and off-road equipment. In addition to contributing to the formation of ground-level ozone, and fine particle pollution, NO_2 is linked with a number of adverse effects on the respiratory system.

EPA first set standards for NO_2 in 1971, setting both a primary standard (to protect health) and a secondary standard (to protect the public welfare) at 0.053 parts per million (53 ppb), averaged annually. The Agency has reviewed the standards twice since that time, but chose not to revise the annual standards at the conclusion of each review. In January 2010, EPA established an additional primary standard at 100 ppb, averaged over one hour. Together the primary standards protect public health, including the health of sensitive populations - people with asthma, children, and the elderly. No area of the country has been found to be out of compliance with the current NO_2 standards.

All areas presently meet the current (1971) NO_2 NAAQS, with annual NO_2 concentrations measured at area-wide monitors well below the level of the standard (53 ppb). Annual average ambient NO2 concentrations, as measured at area-wide monitors, have decreased by more than 40 percent since 1980. Currently, the annual average NO2 concentrations range from approximately 10-20 ppb.

EPA expects NO2 concentrations will continue to decrease in the future as a result of a number of mobile source regulations that are taking effect. Tier 2 standards for light-duty vehicles began phasing in during 2004, and new NOx standards for heavy-duty engines are phasing in between 2007 and 2010 model years. Current air quality monitoring data reflects only a few years of vehicles entering the fleet that meet these strict NOx standards.

Current scientific evidence links short-term NO2 exposures, ranging from 30 minutes to 24 hours, with adverse respiratory effects including airway inflammation in healthy people and increased respiratory symptoms in people with asthma.

Also, studies show a connection between breathing elevated short-term NO2 concentrations, and increased visits to emergency departments and hospital admissions for respiratory issues, especially asthma.

NO2 concentrations in vehicles and near roadways are appreciably higher than those measured at monitors in the current network. In fact, in-vehicle concentrations can be 2-3 times higher than measured at nearby area-wide monitors. Near-roadway (within about 50 meters) concentrations of NO2 have been measured to be approximately 30 to 100 percent higher than concentrations away from roadways.

Individuals who spend time on or near major roadways can experience short-term NO2 exposures considerably higher than measured by the current network. Approximately 16 percent of U.S housing units are located within 300 ft of a major highway, railroad, or airport (approximately 48 million people). This population likely includes a higher proportion of nonwhite and economically-disadvantaged people.

NO2 exposure concentrations near roadways are of particular concern for susceptible individuals, including people with asthma asthmatics, children, and the elderly

The sum of nitric oxide (NO) and NO2 is commonly called nitrogen oxides or NOx. Other oxides of nitrogen including nitrous acid and nitric acid are part of the nitrogen oxide family. While EPA's National Ambient Air Quality Standard (NAAQS) covers this entire family, NO2 is the component of greatest interest and the indicator for the larger group of nitrogen oxides.

NOx react with ammonia, moisture, and other compounds to form small particles. These small particles penetrate deeply into sensitive parts of the lungs and can cause or worsen respiratory disease, such as emphysema and bronchitis, and can aggravate existing heart disease, leading to increased hospital admissions and premature death.

Ozone is formed when NOx and volatile organic compounds react in the presence of heat and sunlight. Children, the elderly, people with lung diseases such as asthma, and people who work or exercise outside are at risk for adverse effects from ozone. These include reduction in lung function and increased respiratory symptoms as well as respiratory-related emergency department visits, hospital admissions, and possibly premature deaths.

Emissions that lead to the formation of NO2 generally also lead to the formation of other NOx. Emissions control measures leading to reductions in NO2 can generally be expected to reduce population exposures to all gaseous NOx. This may have the important co-benefit of reducing the formation of ozone and fine particles both of which pose significant public health threats.

Sulfur Dioxide

Sulfur dioxide (SO2) is one of a group of highly reactive gasses known as "oxides of sulfur." The largest sources of SO2 emissions are from fossil fuel combustion at power plants (73 percent) and other industrial facilities (20 percent). Smaller sources of SO2 emissions include industrial processes such as extracting metal from ore, and the burning of high sulfur containing fuels by locomotives, large ships, and non-road equipment. SO2 is linked with a number of adverse effects on the respiratory system.

EPA first set standards for SO2 in 1971. EPA set a 24-hour primary standard at 140 ppb and an annual average standard at 30 ppb (to protect health). EPA also set a 3-hour average secondary standard at 500 ppb (to protect the public welfare). In 1996, EPA reviewed the SO2 NAAQS and chose not to revise the standards.

In 2010, EPA revised the primary SO2 NAAQS by establishing a new 1-hour standard at a level of 75 parts per billion (ppb). EPA revoked the two existing primary standards because they would not provide additional public health protection given a 1-hour standard at 75 ppb.

EPA first set standards for SO2 in 1971. EPA set a 24-hour primary standard at 140 parts per billion (ppb) and an annual average standard at 30 ppb (to protect health). EPA also set a 3-hour average secondary standard at 500 ppb (to protect the public welfare). In 1996, EPA reviewed the SO2 NAAQS and chose not to revise the standards.

In 2010, EPA revised the primary SO_2 standards by establishing a new 1-hour standard at a level of 75 ppb. EPA revoked the two existing primary standards because they would not provide additional public health protection given a 1-hour standard at 75 ppb.

In 2012, EPA took final action to retain the current secondary standard for SO_2 of 500 ppb averaged over three hours, not to be exceeded more than once per year

Current scientific evidence links short-term exposures to SO_2, ranging from 5 minutes to 24 hours, with an array of adverse respiratory effects including bronchoconstriction and increased asthma symptoms. These effects are particularly important for asthmatics at elevated ventilation rates (e.g., while exercising or playing.)

Studies also show a connection between short-term exposure and increased visits to emergency departments and hospital admissions for respiratory illnesses, particularly in at-risk populations including children, the elderly, and asthmatics.

EPA's National Ambient Air Quality Standard for SO_2 is designed to protect against exposure to the entire group of sulfur oxides (SOx). SO_2 is the component of greatest concern and is used as the indicator for the larger group of gaseous sulfur oxides (SOx). Other gaseous sulfur oxides (e.g. SO_3) are found in the atmosphere at concentrations much lower than SO_2.

Emissions that lead to high concentrations of SO_2 generally also lead to the formation of other SOx. Control measures that reduce SO_2 can generally be expected to reduce people's exposures to all gaseous SOx. This may have the important co-benefit of reducing the formation of fine sulfate particles, which pose significant public health threats.

SOx can react with other compounds in the atmosphere to form small particles. These particles penetrate deeply into sensitive parts of the lungs and can cause or worsen respiratory disease, such as emphysema and bronchitis, and can aggravate existing heart disease, leading to increased hospital admissions and premature death. EPA's NAAQS for particulate matter (PM) are designed to provide protection against these health effects.

Lead

Lead (Pb) is a metal found naturally in the environment as well as in manufactured products. The major sources of lead emissions have historically been from fuels in on-road motor vehicles (such as cars and trucks) and industrial sources. As a result of EPA's regulatory efforts to remove lead from on-road motor vehicle gasoline, emissions of lead from the transportation sector dramatically declined by 95 percent between 1980 and 1999, and levels of lead in the air decreased by 94 percent between 1980 and 1999. Today, the highest levels of lead in air are usually found near lead smelters. The major sources of lead emissions to the air today are ore and metals processing and piston-engine aircraft operating on leaded aviation gasoline.

In the past, motor vehicles were the major contributor of lead emissions to the air. As a result of EPA's regulatory efforts to reduce lead in on-road motor vehicle gasoline, air emissions of lead from the transportation sector, and particularly the automotive sector, have greatly declined over the past two decades. Major sources of lead emissions to the air today are ore and metals processing and piston-engine aircraft operating on leaded aviation gasoline. The highest air concentrations of lead are usually found near lead smelters. Other stationary sources are waste incinerators, utilities, and lead-acid battery manufacturers.

In addition to exposure to lead in air, other major exposure pathways include ingestion of lead in drinking water and lead-contaminated food as well as incidental ingestion of lead-contaminated soil and dust. Lead-based paint remains a major exposure pathway in older homes.

Once taken into the body, lead distributes throughout the body in the blood and is accumulated in the bones. Depending on the level of exposure, lead can adversely affect the nervous system, kidney function, immune system, reproductive and developmental systems and the cardiovascular system. Lead exposure also affects the oxygen carrying capacity of the blood. The lead effects most commonly encountered in current populations are neurological effects in children and cardiovascular effects (e.g., high blood pressure and heart disease) in adults. Infants and young children are especially sensitive to even low levels of lead, which may contribute to behavioral problems, learning deficits and lowered IQ.

Lead is persistent in the environment and accumulates in soils and sediments through deposition from air sources, direct discharge of waste streams to water bodies, mining, and erosion. Ecosystems near point sources of lead demonstrate a wide range of adverse effects including losses in biodiversity, changes in community composition, decreased growth and reproductive rates in plants and animals, and neurological effects in vertebrates.

ACID RAIN

"Acid rain" is a broad term referring to a mixture of wet and dry deposition (deposited material) from the atmosphere containing higher than normal amounts of nitric and sulfuric acids. The precursors, or chemical forerunners, of acid rain formation result from both natural sources, such as volcanoes and decaying vegetation, and man-made sources, primarily emissions of sulfur dioxide (SO_2) and nitrogen oxides (NOx) resulting from fossil fuel combustion. In the United States, roughly two-thirds of all SO_2 and one quarter of all NOx come from electric power generation that relies on burning fossil fuels, like coal. Acid rain occurs when these gases react in the atmosphere with water, oxygen, and other chemicals to form various acidic compounds. The result is a mild solution of sulfuric acid and nitric acid. When sulfur dioxide and nitrogen oxides are released from power plants and other sources, prevailing winds blow these compounds across state and national borders, sometimes over hundreds of miles.

Wet deposition refers to acidic rain, fog, and snow. If the acid chemicals in the air are blown into areas where the weather is wet, the acids can fall to the ground in the form of rain, snow, fog, or mist. As this acidic water flows over and through the ground, it affects a variety of plants and animals. The strength of the effects depends on several factors, including how acidic the water is; the chemistry and buffering capacity of the soils involved; and the types of fish, trees, and other living things that rely on the water.

In areas where the weather is dry, the acid chemicals may become incorporated into dust or smoke and fall to the ground through dry deposition, sticking to the ground, buildings, homes, cars, and trees. Dry deposited gases and particles can be washed from these surfaces by rainstorms, leading to increased runoff. This runoff water makes the resulting mixture more acidic. About half of the acidity in the atmosphere falls back to earth through dry deposition.

Acid rain causes acidification of lakes and streams and contributes to the damage of trees at high elevations (for example, red spruce trees above 2,000 feet) and many sensitive forest soils. In addition, acid rain accelerates the decay of building materials and paints, including irreplaceable buildings, statues, and sculptures that are part of our nation's cultural heritage. Prior to falling to the earth, sulfur dioxide (SO_2) and nitrogen oxide (NOx) gases and their particulate matter derivatives—sulfates and nitrates—contribute to visibility degradation and harm public health.

Surface Waters and Aquatic Animals

The ecological effects of acid rain are most clearly seen in the aquatic, or water, environments, such as streams, lakes, and marshes. Acid rain flows into streams, lakes, and marshes after falling on forests, fields, buildings, and roads. Acid rain also falls directly on aquatic habitats. Most lakes and streams have a pH between 6 and 8, although some lakes are naturally acidic even without the effects of acid rain. Acid rain primarily affects sensitive bodies of water, which are located in watersheds whose soils have a limited ability to neutralize acidic compounds (called "buffering capacity"). Lakes and streams become acidic (i.e., the pH value goes down) when the water itself and its surrounding soil cannot buffer the acid rain enough to neutralize it. In areas where buffering capacity is low, acid rain releases aluminum from soils into lakes and streams; aluminum is highly toxic to many species of aquatic organisms.

Lakes and Streams

Many lakes and streams examined in a National Surface Water Survey (NSWS) suffer from chronic acidity, a condition in which water has a constant low pH level. The survey investigated the effects of acidic deposition in over 1,000 lakes larger than 10 acres and in thousands of miles of streams believed to be sensitive to acidification. Of the lakes and streams surveyed, acid rain caused acidity in 75 percent of the acidic lakes and about 50 percent of the acidic streams. Several regions in the United States. were identified as containing many of the surface waters sensitive to acidification. They include the Adirondacks and Catskill Mountains in New York, the mid-Appalachian highlands along the east coast, the upper Midwest, and mountainous areas of the Western United States. In areas like the Northeastern United States, where soil-buffering capacity is poor, some lakes now have a pH value of less than 5. One of the most acidic lakes reported is Little Echo Pond in Franklin, New York. Little Echo Pond has a pH of 4.2.

Acidification is also a problem in lakes that were not surveyed in federal research projects. For example, although lakes smaller than 10 acres were not included in the NSWS, there are from one to four times as many of these small lakes as there are larger lakes. In the Adirondacks, the percentage of acidic lakes is significantly higher when it includes smaller lakes.

Streams flowing over soil with low buffering capacity are as susceptible to damage from acid rain as lakes. Approximately 580 of the streams in the Mid-Atlantic Coastal Plain are acidic primarily due to acidic deposition. In the New Jersey Pine Barrens, for example, over 90 percent of the streams are acidic, which is the highest rate of acidic streams in the nation. Over 1,350 of the streams in the Mid-Atlantic Highlands (mid-Appalachia) are acidic, primarily due to acidic deposition.

The acidification problem in both the United States and Canada grows in magnitude if "episodic acidification" is taken into account. Episodic acidification refers to brief periods during which pH levels decrease due to runoff from melting snow or heavy downpours. Lakes and streams in many areas throughout the U.S. are sensitive to episodic acidification. In the Mid-Appalachians, the Mid-Atlantic Coastal Plain, and the Adirondack Mountains, many additional lakes and streams become temporarily acidic during storms and spring snowmelt. For example, approximately 70 percent of sensitive lakes in the Adirondacks are at risk of episodic acidification. This amount is over three times the amount of chronically acidic lakes. In the mid-Appalachians, approximately 30 percent of sensitive streams are likely to become acidic during an episode. This level is seven times the number of chronically acidic streams in that area. Episodic acidification can cause "fish kills."

Emissions from U.S. sources also contribute to acidic deposition in eastern Canada, where the soil is very similar to the soil of the Adirondack Mountains, and the lakes are consequently extremely vulnerable to chronic acidification problems. The Canadian government has estimated that 14,000 lakes in eastern Canada are acidic.

Fish and Other Aquatic Organisms

Acid rain causes a cascade of effects that harm or kill individual fish, reduce fish population numbers, completely eliminate fish species from a waterbody, and decrease biodiversity. As acid rain flows through soils in a watershed, aluminum is released from soils into the lakes and streams located in that watershed. So, as pH in a lake or stream decreases, aluminum levels increase. Both low pH and increased aluminum levels are directly toxic to fish. In addition, low pH and increased aluminum levels cause chronic stress that may not kill individual fish, but leads to lower body weight and smaller size and makes fish less able to compete for food and habitat.

Some types of plants and animals are able to tolerate acidic waters. Others, however, are acid-sensitive and will be lost as the pH declines. Generally, the young of most species are more sensitive to environmental conditions than adults. At pH 5, most fish eggs cannot hatch. At lower pH levels, some adult fish die. Some acid lakes have no fish. The chart below shows that not all fish, shellfish, or the insects that they eat can tolerate the same amount of acid; for example, frogs can tolerate water that is more acidic (i.e., has a lower pH) than trout.

Ecosystems

Together, biological organisms and the environment in which they live are called an ecosystem. The plants and animals living within an ecosystem are highly interdependent. For example, frogs may tolerate relatively high levels of acidity, but if they eat insects like the mayfly, they may be affected because part of their food supply may disappear. Because of the connections between the many fish, plants, and other organisms living in an aquatic ecosystem, changes in pH or aluminum levels affect biodiversity as well. Thus, as lakes and streams become more acidic, the numbers and types of fish and other aquatic plants and animals that live in these waters decrease.

The Role of Nitrogen

The impact of nitrogen on surface waters is also critical. Nitrogen plays a significant role in episodic acidification and new research recognizes the importance of nitrogen in long-term chronic acidification as well. Furthermore, the adverse impact of atmospheric nitrogen deposition on estuaries and near-coastal water bodies is significant. Scientists estimate that 10 to 45 percent of the nitrogen produced by various human activities that reaches estuaries and coastal ecosystems is transported and deposited via the atmosphere. For example, about 30 percent of the nitrogen in the Chesapeake Bay comes from atmospheric deposition. Nitrogen is an important factor in causing eutrophication (oxygen depletion) of water bodies. The symptoms of eutrophication include blooms of algae (both toxic and non-toxic), declines in the health of fish and shellfish, loss of seagrass beds and coral reefs, and ecological changes in food webs. According to the National Oceanic and Atmospheric Administration (NOAA), these conditions are common in many of our nation's coastal ecosystems. These ecological changes impact human populations by changing the availability of seafood and creating a risk of consuming contaminated fish or shellfish, reducing our ability to use and enjoy our coastal ecosystems, and causing economic impact on people who rely on healthy coastal ecosystems, such as fishermen and those who cater to tourists.

EPA's Acid Rain Program

Acid rain control will produce significant benefits in terms of lowered surface water acidity. If acidic deposition levels were to remain constant over the next 50 years (the time frame used for projection models), the acidification rate of lakes in the Adirondack Mountains that are larger than 10 acres would rise by 50 percent or more. Scientists predict, however, that the decrease in SO2 emissions required by the Acid Rain Program will significantly reduce acidification due to atmospheric sulfur. Without the reductions in SO2 emissions, the proportions of acidic aquatic ecosystems would remain high or dramatically worsen.

Forests

Over the years, scientists, foresters, and others have noted a slowed growth of some forests. Leaves and needles turn brown and fall off when they should be green and healthy. In extreme cases, individual trees or entire areas of the forest simply die off without an obvious reason.

After much analysis, researchers now know that acid rain causes slower growth, injury, or death of forests. Acid rain has been implicated in forest and soil degradation in many areas of the eastern U.S., particularly high elevation forests of the Appalachian Mountains from Maine to Georgia that include areas such as the Shenandoah and Great Smoky Mountain National Parks. Of course, acid rain is not the only cause of such conditions. Other factors contribute to the overall stress of these areas, including air pollutants, insects, disease, drought, or very cold weather. In most cases, in fact, the impacts of acid rain on trees are due to the combined effects of acid rain and these other environmental stressors. After many years of collecting information on the chemistry and biology of forests, researchers are beginning to understand how acid rain works on the forest soil, trees, and other plants.

The Forest Floor

A spring shower in the forest washes leaves and falls through the trees to the forest floor below. Some trickles over the ground and runs into streams, rivers, or lakes, and some of the water soaks into the soil. That soil may neutralize some or all of the acidity of the acid rainwater. This ability is called buffering capacity, and without it, soils become more acidic. Differences in soil buffering capacity are an important reason why some areas that receive acid rain show a lot of damage, while other areas that receive about the same amount of acid rain do not appear to be harmed at all. The ability of forest soils to resist, or buffer, acidity depends on the thickness and composition of the soil, as well as the type of bedrock beneath the forest floor. Midwestern states like Nebraska and Indiana have soils that are well buffered. Places in the mountainous northeast, like New York's Adirondack and Catskill Mountains, have thin soils with low buffering capacity.

Trees

Acid rain does not usually kill trees directly. Instead, it is more likely to weaken trees by damaging their leaves, limiting the nutrients available to them, or exposing them to toxic substances slowly released from the soil. Quite often, injury or death of trees is a result of these effects of acid rain in combination with one or more additional threats.

Scientists know that acidic water dissolves the nutrients and helpful minerals in the soil and then washes them away before trees and other plants can use them to grow. At the same time, acid rain causes the release of substances that are toxic to trees and plants, such as aluminum, into the soil. Scientists believe that this combination of loss of soil nutrients and increase of toxic aluminum may be one way that acid rain harms trees. Such substances also wash away in the runoff and are carried into streams, rivers, and lakes. More of these substances are released from the soil when the rainfall is more acidic.

However, trees can be damaged by acid rain even if the soil is well buffered. Forests in high mountain regions often are exposed to greater amounts of acid than other forests because they tend to be surrounded by acidic clouds and fog that are more acidic than rainfall. Scientists believe that when leaves are frequently bathed in this acid fog, essential nutrients in their leaves and needles are stripped away. This loss of nutrients in their foliage makes trees more susceptible to damage by other environmental factors, particularly cold winter weather.

Other Plants

Acid rain can harm other plants in the same way it harms trees. Although damaged by other air pollutants such as ground level ozone, food crops are not usually seriously affected because farmers frequently add fertilizers to the soil to replace nutrients that have washed away. They may also add crushed limestone to the soil. Limestone is an alkaline material and increases the ability of the soil to act as a buffer against acidity.

Automotive Coatings

Over the past two decades, there have been numerous reports of damage to automotive paints and other coatings. The reported damage typically occurs on horizontal surfaces and appears as irregularly shaped, permanently etched areas. The damage can best be detected under fluorescent lamps, can be most easily observed on dark colored vehicles, and appears to occur after evaporation of a moisture droplet. In addition, some evidence suggests damage occurs most frequently on freshly painted vehicles. Usually the damage is permanent; once it has occurred, the only solution is to repaint.

The general consensus within the auto industry is that some form of environmental fallout causes the damage. "Environmental fallout"—a term widely used in the auto and coatings industries—refers to damage caused by air pollution (e.g., acid rain), decaying insects, bird droppings, pollen, and tree sap. The results of laboratory experiments and at least one field study have demonstrated that acid rain can scar automotive coatings. Furthermore, chemical analyses of the damaged areas of some exposed test panels indicate elevated levels of sulfate, implicating acid rain.

The popular term "acid rain" refers to both wet and dry deposition of acidic pollutants that may damage material surfaces, including auto finishes. These pollutants, which are released when coal and other fossil fuels are burned, react with water vapor and oxidants in the atmosphere and are chemically transformed into sulfuric and nitric acids. The acidic compounds then may fall to earth as rain, snow, fog, or may join dry particles and fall as dry deposition. All forms of acid rain, including dry deposition, especially when dry acidic deposition is mixed with dew or rain, may damage automotive coatings. However, it has been difficult to quantify the specific contribution of acid rain to paint finish damage relative to damage caused by other forms of environmental fallout, by the improper application of paint or by deficient paint formulations. According to coating experts, trained specialists can differentiate between the various forms of damage, but the best way of determining the cause of chemically induced damage is to conduct a detailed, chemical analysis of the damaged area.

Because evaporation of acidic moisture appears to be a key element in the damage, any steps taken to eliminate its occurrence on freshly painted vehicles may alleviate the problem. These steps include frequent washing followed by hand drying, covering the vehicle during precipitation events, and use of one of the protective coatings currently on the market that claim to protect the original finish. However, data on the performance of these coatings are not yet sufficient.

The auto and coatings industries are fully aware of the potential damage and are actively pursuing the development of coatings that are more resistant to environmental fallout, including acid rain. The problem is not a universal one—it does not affect all coatings or all vehicles even in geographic areas known to be subject to acid rain—which suggests that technology exists to protect against this damage. Until that technology is implemented to protect all vehicles or until acid deposition is adequately reduced, frequent washing and drying and covering of the vehicle appear to be the best methods for consumers who wish to minimize acid rain damage.

Materials

Acid rain and the dry deposition of acidic particles contribute to the corrosion of metals (such as bronze) and the deterioration of paint and stone (such as marble and limestone). These effects significantly reduce the societal value of buildings, bridges, cultural objects (such as statues, monuments, and tombstones), and cars.

Dry deposition of acidic compounds can also dirty buildings and other structures, leading to increased maintenance costs. To reduce damage to automotive paint caused by acid rain and acidic dry deposition, some manufacturers use acid-resistant paints, at an average cost of $5 for each new vehicle (or a total of $61 million per year for all new cars and trucks sold in the United States). EPA's Acid Rain Program will reduce damage to materials by limiting SO_2 emissions. The benefits of EPA's Acid Rain Program are measured, in part, by the costs now paid to repair or prevent damage—the costs of repairing buildings and bridges, using acid-resistant paints on new vehicles, plus the value that society places on the details of a statue lost forever to acid rain.

Visibility

Sulfates and nitrates that form in the atmosphere from sulfur dioxide (SO_2) and nitrogen oxides (NO_x) emissions contribute to visibility impairment, meaning we cannot see as far or as clearly through the air. Sulfate particles account for 50 to 70 percent of the visibility reduction in the eastern part of the United States, affecting our enjoyment of national parks, such as the Shenandoah and the Great Smoky Mountains. The Acid Rain Program is expected to improve the visual range in the eastern United States by 30 percent. Based on a study of the value national park visitors place on visibility, the visual range improvements expected at national parks of the eastern United States due to the Acid Rain Program's SO2 reductions will be worth over a billion dollars annually by the year 2010. In the western part of the United States, nitrates and carbon also play roles, but sulfates have been implicated as an important source of visibility impairment in many of the Colorado River Plateau national parks, including the Grand Canyon, Canyonlands, and Bryce Canyon.

Human Health

Acid rain looks, feels, and tastes just like clean rain. The harm to people from acid rain is not direct. Walking in acid rain, or even swimming in an acid lake, is no more dangerous than walking or swimming in clean water. However, the pollutants that cause acid rain—sulfur dioxide (SO2) and nitrogen oxides (NOx)—do damage human health. These gases interact in the atmosphere to form fine sulfate and nitrate particles that can be transported long distances by winds and inhaled deep into people's lungs. Fine particles can also penetrate indoors. Many scientific studies have identified a relationship between elevated levels of fine particles and increased illness and premature death from heart and lung disorders, such as asthma and bronchitis.

Based on health concerns, SO2 and NOx have historically been regulated under the Clean Air Act, including the Acid Rain Program. In the eastern United States, sulfate aerosols make up about 25 percent of fine particles. By lowering SO2 and NOx emissions from power generation, the Acid Rain Program will reduce the levels of fine sulfate and nitrate particles and so reduce the incidence and the severity of these health problems. When fully implemented by the year 2010, the public health benefits of the Acid Rain Program are estimated to be valued at $50 billion annually, due to decreased mortality, hospital admissions, and emergency room visits.

SOURCE MATERIAL

US Environmental Protection Agency. "Carbon Monoxide." http://www.epa .gov/airquality/carbonmonoxide/.
———. "Effects of Acid Rain." http://www.epa.gov/acidrain/effects/index .html.

———. "Ground-Level Ozone." http://www.epa.gov/air/ozonepollution/basic.html.

———. "Lead in Air." http://www.epa.gov/air/lead/.

———. "Nitrogen Dioxide." http://www.epa.gov/air/nitrogenoxides/.

———. "Particulate Matter (PM)." http://www.epa.gov/air/particlepollution/.

———. *The Plain English Guide to the Clean Air Act*. Research Triangle Park, NC: Office of Air Quality Planning and Standards, 2007. Publication No.EPA-456/K-07-001. http://www.epa.gov /air/caa/peg/pdfs/peg.pdf.

———. "Six Common Air Pollutants." http://www.epa.gov/airquality /urbanair/.

———. "Sulfur Dioxide." http://www.epa.gov/air/sulfurdioxide/.

———. "What is Acid Rain." http://www.epa.gov/acidrain/what/index.html.

FURTHER READING

National Atmospheric Deposition Program. "Acid Rain." http://nadp.sws.uiuc.edu/educ/acidrain.aspx

Natural Resources Defense Council. "Air." http://www.nrdc.org/air/.

US Environmental Protection Agency. "Air Pollutants." http://www.epa.gov /air/airpollutants.html.

———. "Summary of the Clean Air Act." http://www2.epa.gov/laws-regulations/summary-clean-air-act.

World Health Organization. "Air Pollution." http://www.who.int/topics/air_pollution/en/.

3

Clean Water

This chapter presents information on clean water, safe drinking water, and water pollution from the US Environmental Protection Agency and the White House Council on Environmental Quality.

We take our water supplies for granted, yet they are limited. Only one percent of all the world's water can be used for drinking. Nearly 97 percent of the world's water is salty or otherwise undrinkable, and the other two percent is locked away in ice caps and glaciers. There is no "new" water: whether our source water is a stream, river, lake, spring, or well, we are using the same water the dinosaurs used millions of years ago.

The average American uses about 90 gallons of water each day in the home, and each American household uses approximately 107,000 gallons of water each year. For the most part, we use water treated to meet drinking water standards to flush toilets, water lawns, and wash dishes, clothes, and cars. In fact, 50-70 percent of home water is used for watering lawns and gardens. Nearly 14 percent of the water a typical homeowner pays for is never even used—it leaks down the drain.

The United States enjoys one of the best supplies of drinking water in the world. Nevertheless, many of us who once gave little or no thought to the water that comes from our taps are now asking the question: "Is my water safe to drink?" While tap water that meets federal and state standards is generally safe to drink, threats to drinking water are increasing. Short-term disease outbreaks and water restrictions during droughts have demonstrated that we can no longer take our drinking water for granted.

Some people may also be more vulnerable to contaminants in drinking water than the general population. People undergoing chemotherapy or living with HIV/AIDS, transplant patients, children and infants, the frail elderly, and pregnant women and their fetuses can be particularly at risk for infections.

Congress passed the Safe Drinking Water Act (SDWA) in 1974 to protect public health by regulating the nation's public drinking water supply and protecting sources of drinking water. SDWA is administered by the U.S. Environmental Protection Agency (EPA) and its state partners.

The highlights of the act were:

- Authorizes EPA to set enforceable health standards for contaminants in drinking water
- Requires public notification of water systems violations and annual reports (Consumer Confidence Reports) to customers on contaminants found in their drinking water
- Establishes a federal-state partnership for regulation enforcement
- Includes provisions specifically designed to protect underground sources of drinking water
- Requires disinfection of surface water supplies, except those with pristine, protected sources
- Establishes a multi-billion-dollar state revolving loan fund for water system upgrades
- Requires an assessment of the vulnerability of all drinking water sources to contamination

The Safe Drinking Water Act (SDWA) defines a public water system (PWS) as one that serves piped water to at least 25 persons or 15 service connections for at least 60 days each year. There are approximately 161,000 public water systems in the United States. Such systems may be publicly or privately owned. Community water systems (CWSs) are public water systems that serve people year-round in their homes. Most people in the U.S. (268 million) get their water from a community water system. EPA also regulates other kinds of public water systems, such as those at schools, campgrounds, factories, and restaurants. Private water supplies, such as household wells that serve one or a few homes, are not regulated by EPA.

Much of the existing water infrastructure (underground pipes, treatment plants, and other facilities) was built many years ago. In 1999, EPA conducted the second Drinking Water Infrastructure Needs Survey, and found that drinking water systems will need to invest $150 billion over a 20-year period to ensure clean and safe drinking water.

Nationwide, drinking water systems have spent hundreds of billions of dollars to build drinking water treatment and distribution systems. From 1995 to 2000, more than $50 billion was spent on capital investments to fund water quality improvements.

With the aging of the nation's infrastructure, the clean water and drinking water industries face a significant challenge to sustain and advance their achievements in protecting public health. EPA's Clean Water & Drinking Water Infrastructure Gap Analysis has found that if present levels of spending do not increase, there will be a significant funding gap by the year 2019.

Since 1999, water suppliers have been required to provide local annual Consumer Confidence Reports to their customers. These reports are due by July 1 each year, and contain information on contaminants found in the drinking water, possible health effects, and the water's source.

Systems will inform customers about violations of less immediate concern in the first water bill sent after the violation, in a Consumer Confidence Report, or by mail within a year. In 1998, states began compiling information on individual systems, so you can evaluate the overall quality of drinking water in your state. Additionally, EPA must compile and summarize the state reports into an annual report on the condition of the nation's drinking water. To view the most recent annual report, see www.epa.gov/safewater/annual.

Actual events of drinking water contamination are rare, and typically do not occur at levels likely to pose health concerns. However, as development in our modern society increases, there are growing numbers of activities that can contaminate our drinking water. Improperly disposed-of chemicals, animal and human wastes, wastes injected underground, and naturally occurring substances have the potential to contaminate drinking water. Likewise, drinking water that is not properly treated or disinfected, or that travels through an improperly maintained distribution system, may also pose a health risk. Greater vigilance by you the consumer, your water supplier, and your government can help prevent such events in your water supply.

Contaminants can enter water supplies either as a result of human and animal activities, or because they occur naturally in the environment.

Threats to your drinking water may exist in your neighborhood, or may occur many miles away. Some typical examples are microbial contamination, chemical contamination from fertilizers, and lead contamination.

The potential for health problems from microbial-contaminated drinking water is demonstrated by localized outbreaks of waterborne disease. Many of these outbreaks have been linked to contamination by bacteria or viruses, probably from human or animal wastes. Certain pathogens (disease-causing microorganisms), such as Cryptosporidium, may occasionally pass through water filtration and disinfection processes in numbers high enough to cause health problems, particularly in vulnerable members of the population. Cryptosporidium causes the gastrointestinal disease, cryptosporidiosis, and can cause serious, sometimes fatal, symptoms, especially among sensitive members of the population.

A serious outbreak of cryptosporidiosis occurred in 1993 in Milwaukee, Wisconsin, causing more than 400,000 persons to be infected with the disease, and resulting in at least 50 deaths. This was the largest recorded outbreak of waterborne disease in United States history.

Nitrate, a chemical most commonly used as a fertilizer, poses an immediate threat to infants when it is found in drinking water at levels above the national standard. Nitrates are converted to nitrites in the intestines. Once absorbed into the bloodstream, nitrites prevent hemoglobin from transporting oxygen. (Older children have an enzyme that restores hemoglobin.) Excessive levels can cause "blue baby syndrome," which can be fatal without immediate medical attention. Infants most at risk for blue baby syndrome are those who are already sick, and while they are sick, consume food that is high in nitrates or drink water or formula mixed with water that is high in nitrates. Avoid using water with high nitrate levels for drinking. This is especially important for infants and young children, nursing mothers, pregnant women and certain elderly people.

Lead, a metal found in natural deposits, is commonly used in household plumbing materials and water service lines. The greatest exposure to lead is swallowing lead paint chips or breathing in lead dust. But lead in drinking water can also cause a variety of adverse health effects. In babies and children, exposure to lead in drinking water above the action level of lead (0.015 milligram per liter) can result in delays in physical and mental development, along with slight deficits in attention span and learning abilities. Adults who drink this water over many years could develop kidney problems or high blood pressure. Lead is rarely found in source water, but enters tap water through corrosion of plumbing materials. Very old and poorly maintained homes may be more likely to have lead pipes, joints, and solder. However, new homes are also at risk: pipes legally considered to be "lead-free" may contain up to eight percent lead. These pipes can leach significant amounts of lead in the water for the first several months after their installation.

WATER TREATMENT

Your drinking water comes from surface water or ground water. The water that systems pump and treat from sources open to the atmosphere, such as rivers, lakes, and reservoirs is known as surface water. Water pumped from wells drilled into underground aquifers, geologic formations containing water, is called ground water. The quantity of water produced by a well depends on the nature of the rock, sand, or soil in the aquifer from which the water is drawn. Drinking water wells may be shallow (50 feet or less) or deep (more than 1,000 feet). More water systems have ground water than surface water as a source (approximately 147,000 v. 14,500), but more people drink from a surface water system (195 million v. 101,400). Large-scale water supply systems tend to rely on surface water resources, while smaller water systems tend to use ground water. Your water utility or public works department can tell you the source of your public water supply. An underground network of pipes typically delivers drinking water to the homes and businesses served by the water system. Small systems serving just a handful of households may be relatively simple, while large metropolitan systems can be extremely complex—sometimes consisting of thousands of miles of pipes serving millions of people. Drinking water must meet required health standards when it leaves the treatment plant. After treated water leaves the plant, it is monitored within the distribution system to identify and remedy any problems such as water main breaks, pressure variations, or growth of microorganisms.

Water utilities treat nearly 34 billion gallons of water every day. The amount and type of treatment applied varies with the source and quality of the water. Generally, surface water systems require more treatment than ground water systems because they are directly exposed to the atmosphere and runoff from rain and melting snow.

Water suppliers use a variety of treatment processes to remove contaminants from drinking water. These individual processes can be arranged in a "treatment train" (a series of processes applied in a sequence). The most commonly used processes include coagulation (flocculation and sedimentation), filtration, and disinfection. Some water systems also use ion exchange and adsorption. Water utilities select the treatment combination most appropriate to treat the contaminants found in the source water of that particular system.

- Flocculation: This step removes dirt and other particles suspended in the water. Alum and iron salts or synthetic organic polymers are added to the water to form tiny sticky particles called "floc," which attract the dirt particles.
- Sedimentation: The flocculated particles then settle naturally out of the water.

Many water treatment facilities use filtration to remove all particles from the water. Those particles include clays and silts, natural organic matter, precipitates from other treatment processes in the facility, iron and manganese, and microorganisms. Filtration clarifies the water and enhances the effectiveness of disinfection.

Disinfection of drinking water is considered to be one of the major public health advances of the twentieth century. Water is often disinfected before it enters the distribution system to ensure that dangerous microbial contaminants are killed. Chlorine, chlorinates, or chlorine dioxides are most often used because they are very effective disinfectants, and residual concentrations can be maintained in the water system.

WATER CONSERVATION

Americans use much more water each day than individuals in both developed and undeveloped countries: For example, the average European uses 53 gallons; the average Sub-Saharan citizen, three to five gallons.

Water efficiency plays an important role in protecting water sources and improving water quality. By using water wisely, we can save money and help the environment. Water efficiency means using less water to provide the same benefit. Using water-saving techniques could save you hundreds of dollars each year, while also reducing the amount of pollutants entering our waterways.

The national average cost of water is $2.00 per 1,000 gallons. The average American family spends about $474 each year on water and sewage charges.5 American households spend an additional $230 per year on water heating costs. By replacing appliances such as the dishwasher and inefficient fixtures such as toilets and showerheads, you can save a substantial amount each year in water, sewage, and energy costs. There are many ways to save water in and around your home.

The industrial and commercial sectors can conserve water through recycling and waste reduction. Industry has implemented conservation measures to comply with state and federal water pollution controls. Evaluation of industrial plant data may show that a particular process or manufacturing step uses the most water or causes the greatest contamination. Such areas can be targeted for water conservation. Also, water that is contaminated by one process may be usable in other plant processes that do not require high-quality water.

PRIVATE WELLS

EPA regulates public water systems; it does not have the authority to regulate private wells. Approximately 15 percent of Americans rely on their own private drinking water supplies (Drinking Water from Household Wells, 2002 [105]), and these supplies are not subject to EPA standards. Unlike public drinking water systems serving many people, they do not have experts regularly checking the water's source and its quality before it is sent to the tap. These households must take special precautions to ensure the protection and maintenance of their drinking water supplies.

The risk of having problems depends on how good your well is—how well it was built and located, and how well you maintain it. It also depends on your local environment. That includes the quality of the aquifer from which your water is drawn and the human activities going on in your area that can affect your well.

Several sources of pollution are easy to spot by sight, taste, or smell. However, many serious problems can be found only by testing your water. Knowing the possible threats in your area will help you decide the kind of tests you may need.

There are six basic steps you can take to help protect your private drinking water supply:

1. Identify potential problem sources.
2. Talk with local experts.
3. Have your water tested periodically.
4. Have the test results interpreted and explained clearly.
5. Set and follow a regular maintenance schedule for your well, and keep up-to-date records.

6. Immediately remedy any problems.

Understanding and spotting possible pollution sources is the first step to safeguarding your drinking water. If your drinking water comes from a well, you may also have a septic system. Septic systems and other on-site wastewater disposal systems are major potential sources of contamination of private water supplies if they are poorly maintained or located improperly, or if they are used for disposal of toxic chemicals.

Ground water conditions vary greatly from place to place, and local experts can give you the best information about your drinking water supply. Some examples are your health department's "sanitarian," local water-well contractors, public water system officials, county extension agents of the Natural Resources Conservation Service (NRCS), local or county planning commissions, and your local library.

Test your water every year for total coliform bacteria, nitrates, total dissolved solids, and pH levels. If you suspect other contaminants, test for these as well. As the tests can be expensive, limit them to possible problems specific to your situation. Local experts can help you identify these contaminants. You should also test your water after replacing or repairing any part of the system, or if you notice any change in your water's look, taste, or smell. Often, county health departments perform tests for bacteria and nitrates. For other substances, health departments, environmental offices, or county governments should have a list of state-certified laboratories. Your State Laboratory Certification Officer can also provide you with this list. Call the Safe Drinking Water Hotline for the name and number of your state's certification officer. Any laboratory you use should be certified to do drinking water testing.

Compare your well's test results to federal and state drinking water standards. You may need to consult experts to aid you in understanding your results, such as the state agency that licenses water well contractors, your local health department, or your state's drinking water program.

Proper well and septic system construction and continued maintenance are keys to the safety of your water supply. Your state water well and septic system contractor licensing agency, local health department, or local public water system professional can provide information on well construction. Make certain your contractors are licensed by the state, if required, or certified by the National Ground Water Association.

Maintain your well, fixing problems before they reach crisis levels, and keep up-to-date records of well installation and repairs, as well as plumbing and water costs. Protect your own well area from contamination.

Wetlands

Wetlands are part of the foundation of our nation's water resources and are vital to the health of waterways and communities that are downstream. Wetlands feed downstream waters, trap floodwaters, recharge groundwater supplies, remove pollution, and provide fish and wildlife habitat. Wetlands are also economic drivers because of their key role in fishing, hunting, agriculture and recreation.

Generally, wetlands are lands where saturation with water is the dominant factor determining the nature of soil development and the types of plant and animal communities living in the soil and on its surface. Wetlands vary widely because of regional and local differences in soils, topography, climate, hydrology, water chemistry, vegetation, and other factors, including human disturbance. Indeed, wetlands are found from the tundra to the tropics and on every continent except Antarctica.

For regulatory purposes under the Clean Water Act, the term wetlands means "those areas that are inundated or saturated by surface or groundwater at a frequency and duration sufficient to support, and that under normal circumstances do support, a prevalence of vegetation typically adapted for life in saturated soil conditions. Wetlands generally include swamps, marshes, bogs and similar areas."

Wetlands include swamps, marshes and bogs. Wetlands vary widely because of differences in soils, topography, climate, hydrology, water chemistry, vegetation, and other factors.

Wetlands are often found alongside waterways and in flood plains. However, some wetlands have no apparent connection to surface water like rivers, lakes or the ocean, but have critical groundwater connections.

Wetlands are recognized as important features in the landscape that provide numerous beneficial services for people and for fish and wildlife. Some of these services, or functions, include protecting and improving water quality, providing fish and wildlife habitats, storing floodwaters, and maintaining surface water flow during dry periods. These beneficial services, considered valuable to societies worldwide, are the result of the inherent and unique natural characteristics of wetlands.

Economics

Wetlands contribute to the national and local economies by producing resources, enabling recreational activities and providing other benefits, such as pollution control and flood protection. While it can be difficult to calculate the economic value provided by a single wetland, it is possible to evaluate the range of services provided by all wetlands and assign a dollar value. These amounts can be impressive. According to one assessment of natural ecosystems, "the dollar value of wetlands worldwide was estimated to be $14.9 trillion" (Costanza et al. 1997).

Wetlands improve water quality in nearby rivers and streams, and thus have considerable value as filters for future drinking water. When water enters a wet- land, it slows down and moves around wetland plants. Much of the suspended sediment drops out and settles to the wetland floor. Plant roots and microorganisms on plant stems and in the soil absorb excess nutrients in the water from fertilizers, manure, leaking septic tanks and municipal sewage. While a certain level of nutrients is necessary in water ecosystems, excess nutrients can cause algae growth that's harmful to fish and other aquatic life. A wetland's natural filtration process can remove excess nutrients before water leaves a wetland, making it healthier for drinking, swimming and sup- porting plants and animals. For example, the Congaree Bottomland Hardwood Swamp in South Carolina removes a quantity of pollutants from the watershed equivalent to that which would be removed by a $5 million treatment plant.

Flood damages in the U.S. average $2 billion each year, causing significant loss of life and property, according to NOAA. Wetlands can play a role in reducing the frequency and intensity of floods by acting as natural buffers, soaking up and storing a significant amount of floodwater. A wetland can typically store about three-acre feet of water, or one million gallons. An acre-foot is one acre of land, about three-quarters the size of a football field, covered one foot deep in water. Three acre-feet describes the same area of land covered by three feet of water.

Coastal wetlands serve as storm surge protectors when hurricanes or tropical storms come ashore. In the Gulf coast area, barrier islands, shoals, marshes, forested wetlands and other features of the coastal landscape can provide a significant and potentially sustainable buffer from wind wave action and storm surge generated by tropical storms and hurricanes, according to the Working Group for Post-Hurricane Planning for the Louisiana Coast. After peak flood flows have passed, wetlands slowly release the stored waters, reducing property damage downstream or inland. One reason floods have become more costly is that over half of the wetlands in the United States have been drained or filled. The loss of more than 64 million acres of wetlands in the Upper Mississippi Basin since the 1780s contributed to high floodwaters during the Great Flood of 1993 that caused billions of dollars in damage. The damage sustained by the Gulf Coast during Hurricane Katrina could have been less severe if more wetlands along the coast and Mississippi delta had been in place.

Because natural wetlands are so effective at removing pollutants from water that flows through them, engineers and scientists construct systems that replicate some of the functions of natural wetlands. These constructed treatment wetlands use natural processes involving wetland vegetation, soils and their associated microbial life to improve water quality. They are often less expensive to build than traditional wastewater and storm water treatment options, have low operating and maintenance expenses and can handle fluctuating water levels. For example, in 1990 city managers in Phoenix, Arizona, needed to improve the performance of a wastewater treatment plant to meet new state water quality standards. After learning that upgrading the plant might cost as much as $635 million, the managers started to look for a more cost-effective way to provide final treatment to the plant's wastewater discharge into the Salt River. A preliminary study suggested that a constructed wetland system would sufficiently clean the discharge water while supporting high-quality wetland habitat for birds, including endangered species, and protecting downstream residents from flooding. All these benefits would be achieved at a lower cost than retrofitting the existing treatment plant. As a result, the 12-acre Tres Rios Demonstration Project began in 1993 with assistance from the Corps of Engineers, the Bureau of Reclamation and EPA's Environmental Technology Initiative and now receives about two million gallons of wastewater per day. This project is still flourishing, serving as a home for thousands of birds and other wildlife. There are hundreds of wastewater treatment wetlands operating in the United States today.

The Nation's wetlands are vital to fish health and thus to the Nation's multibillion dollar fishing industry. Wetlands provide an essential link in the life cycle of 75 percent of the fish and shellfish commercially harvested in the U.S., and up to 90 percent of the recreational fish catch. Wetlands pro- vide a consistent food supply, shelter and nursery grounds for both marine and freshwater species. Landings of crab, shrimp and salmon were valued at $1,167 billion in 2004. These species are dependent on wetlands for at least part of their life cycles. In 2004 the dockside value of fin fish and shellfish landed in the United States was $3.7 billion and was the basis for the $7.2 billion fishery processing business. U.S. consumers spent an estimated $54.4 billion for fishery products in 2000, according to the U. S. Fish and Wildlife Service (USFWS).

Recreation Wetlands are often inviting places for popular recreational activities including hiking, fishing, bird watching, photography and hunting.

More than 82 million Americans took part in these activities in 2001, spending more than $108 billion on these pursuits said Ducks Unlimited [111]. For example, over 34 million people went fishing in 2001, spending an average of $1,046 and 16 days each on the water. Anglers spent $14.7 billion in 2001 for fishing trips, $17 billion on equipment and $4 billion for licenses, stamps, tags, land leasing and ownership, membership dues, contributions and magazines. The overall economic impact of recreational fishing is estimated at $116 billion, according to the American Sportfishing Association [112], and wetlands play a crucial role in the life cycle of up to 90 percent of the fish caught recreationally. In 2001, approximately 3 million people hunted migratory birds, and 6.5 million small mammals that are often found in wetlands. They spent more than $2.2 billion, including $111 million paid by migratory bird and large game hunters to lease hunting areas and blinds, often located on private property with wetlands said the U. S. Fish and Wildlife Service.

Each year nearly $200 million in hunters' federal excise taxes are distributed to state agencies to support wildlife management programs, the purchase of lands open to hunters and hunter education and safety classes. Proceeds from the federal Duck Stamp, a required purchase of migratory water fowl hunters, have purchased more than five million acres of habitat for the refuge system. Just watching the wildlife, many of which depend on wetlands, has become a popular pastime. More than 66 million people 16 years old and older—31 percent of all Americans—fed, photographed and observed wildlife in 2001 and spent $40 billion on their activities said the U. S. Fish and Wildlife Service.

Many industries, in addition to the fishing industry, derive benefits or produce products dependent on wetlands. Part of this economic value lies in the variety of commercial products they provide, such as food and energy sources. Rice can be grown in a wetland during part of the year, and the same area can serve as a wildlife habitat for the rest of the year. Some wetland plant species, such as wild rice and various reeds, can be harvested for or used to produce specialty foods, medicines, cosmetics and decorative items. In many coastal and river delta wetlands, haying of wetland vegetation is important to livestock producers. In Europe, reed-growing for building materials is undergoing a revival in some countries as people realize the full potential of reeds as a roofing material. Aesthetically pleasing, thatched roofs are superior insulators to conventional tile roofs, and they have a life span of 25-40 years. Fur-bearing animals, such as mink, muskrat and beaver, use wetlands during some part of their life cycle. Income can be derived from trapping these furbearers, either by direct sale of their pelts or by leasing wetlands for the fur harvest. The nation's harvest of muskrat pelts alone was worth $124 million in 2004. Wetlands also provide employment opportunities, including such positions as surveyor or park ranger. The production of raw materials from wetlands provides jobs to those employed in the commercial fishing, specialty food and cosmetic industries. These are billion dollar industries that depend in part on wetlands to flourish. In addition to the many ways wetlands provide economic benefits, they offer numerous less tangible benefits as well. These include providing aesthetic value to residential communities, reducing streambank erosion and providing educational opportunities as an ideal "outdoor classroom." By nearly any measure used, it pays to save wetlands.

Fish and Wildlife

More than one-third of the United States' threatened and endangered species live only in wetlands, and nearly half use wetlands at some point in their lives. Many other animals and plants depend on wetlands for survival. Estuarine and marine fish and shellfish, various birds, and certain mammals must have coastal wetlands to survive. Most commercial and game fish breed and raise their young in coastal marshes and estuaries. Menhaden, flounder, sea trout, spot, croaker, and striped bass are among the more familiar fish that depend on coastal wetlands. Shrimp, oysters, clams, and blue and Dungeness crabs likewise need these wetlands for food, shelter, and breeding grounds. For many animals and plants, like wood ducks, muskrat, cattails, and swamp rose, inland wetlands are the only places they can live. Beaver may actually create their own wetlands. For others, such as striped bass, peregrine falcon, otter, black bear, raccoon, and deer, wetlands provide important food, water, or shelter. Many of the U.S. breeding bird populations—including ducks, geese, woodpeckers, hawks, wading birds, and many songbirds—feed, nest, and raise their young in wetlands. Migratory waterfowl use coastal and inland wetlands as resting, feeding, breeding, or nesting grounds for at least part of the year. Indeed, an international agreement to protect wetlands of international importance was developed because some species of migratory birds are completely dependent on certain wetlands and would become extinct if those wetlands were destroyed.

CLEAN OCEANS

The importance of ocean, coastal, and Great Lakes ecosystems cannot be overstated; simply put, we need them to survive. It is clear that these invaluable and life-sustaining assets are vulnerable to human activities and, at the same time, human communities are rendered more vulnerable when these resources are degraded, yet ocean, coastal, and Great Lakes ecosystems are experiencing an unprecedented rate of change due to human activities. We are only now beginning to understand the full extent of the direct and indirect consequences of our actions on these systems.

Climate change is impacting the ocean, our coasts, and the Great Lakes. Increasing water temperatures are altering habitats, migratory patterns, and ecosystem structure and function. Coastal communities are facing sea-level rise, inundation, increased threats from storms, erosion, and significant loss of coastal wetlands. The ocean's ability to absorb carbon dioxide from the atmosphere buffers the impacts of climate change, but also causes the ocean to become more acidic, threatening not only the survival of individual species of marine life, but also entire marine ecosystems. The ocean buffers increased global temperatures by absorbing heat, but increasing temperatures are causing sea levels to rise by expanding seawater volume and melting land-based ice. Increased temperatures may eventually reduce the ocean's ability to absorb carbon dioxide. Conversely, climate change is predicted to lower the water levels of the Great Lakes, thereby altering water cycles, habitats, and economic uses of the lakes.

Along many areas of our coasts and within the Great Lakes, biological diversity is in decline due to overfishing, introduction of invasive species, and loss and degradation of essential habitats from coastal development and associated human activities. The introduction of non-native species can carry significant ecological and economic costs. Human and marine ecosystem health are threatened by a range of challenges, including increased levels of exposure to toxins from harmful algal blooms and other sources, and greater contact with infectious agents. Areas in numerous bays, estuaries, gulfs, and the Great Lakes are now consistently low in or lacking oxygen, creating dead zones along our bays and coasts. Unsustainable fishing (e.g., overfishing) remains a serious concern with consequences for marine ecosystems and human communities. In the Arctic, environmental changes are revealing the vulnerability of its ecosystems. These changes are increasing stressors and impacts on the ecosystems, people, and communities in the region and are presenting new domestic and international management challenges.

Many of these concerns are attributable not only to activities within ocean, coastal, and Great Lakes ecosystems, but also to actions that take place in our Nation's interior. For example, our industries, agricultural and transportation operations, cities, and suburbs generate various forms of pollution. Industrial operations emit pollutants, such as nitrogen and mercury, into the atmosphere that often find their way into the ocean and Great Lakes. Rain washes residues, chemicals, and oily runoff from our roadways into our estuaries and coastal waters. Heavy rainfall events can wash sediment, pesticides, debris, and nutrients from our fields, lawns, and agricultural operations into our waters. Urban and suburban development, including the construction of roads, highways, and other infrastructure, as well as modification to rivers and streams, can adversely affect the habitats of aquatic and terrestrial species.

Demands on the ocean, our coasts, and the Great Lakes are intensifying, spurred by population growth, migration to coastal areas, and economic activities. Human uses of the ocean, coasts, and the Great Lakes are expanding at a rate that challenges our ability to plan and manage them under the current sector-by-sector approach. New and expanding uses—including energy development, shipping, aquaculture, and emerging security requirements—are expected to place increasing demands on our ocean, coastal, and Great Lakes ecosystems. There is also increasing demand for access to these places for recreational, cultural, and other societal pursuits. As these demands increase, overlapping uses and differing views about which activities should occur where can generate conflicts and misunderstandings. At the same time, there is an overarching need to sustain and preserve abundant marine resources and healthy ecosystems that are critical to the well-being and continued prosperity of our Nation.

In order to better meet our Nation's stewardship responsibilities for the ocean, our coasts, and the Great Lakes, President Obama established the Interagency Ocean Policy Task Force on June 12, 2009. The Task Force is composed of 24 senior-level officials from executive departments, agencies, and offices across the Federal government and led by the Chair of the Council on Environmental Quality (CEQ). The President charged the Task Force with developing recommendations to enhance our ability to maintain healthy, resilient, and sustainable ocean, coasts, and Great Lakes resources for the benefit of present and future generations.

The Deepwater Horizon-BP oil spill in the Gulf of Mexico [116] and resulting environmental crisis is a stark reminder of how vulnerable our marine environments are, and how much communities and our Nation rely on healthy and resilient ocean and coastal ecosystems. The ocean, our coasts, and the Great Lakes deeply impact the lives of all Americans, whether we live and work in the country's heartland or along its shores. America's rich and productive coastal regions and waters support tens of millions of jobs and contribute trillions of dollars to the national economy each year. They also host a growing number of important activities, including recreation, science, commerce, transportation, energy development, and national security and they provide a wealth of natural resources and ecological benefits.

Nearly half of the country's population lives in coastal counties, and millions of visitors enjoy our Nation's seashores each year. The ocean, our coasts, and the Great Lakes are vital places for recreation, including boating, fishing, and swimming, nature watching, and diving. These activities not only help fuel our economy, but also are critical to the social and cultural fabric of our country. In addition, coastal ecosystems provide essential ecological services. Barrier islands, coral reefs, mangroves, and coastal wetlands help to protect our coastal communities from damaging floods and storms. Coastal wetlands shelter recreational and commercial fish species, provide critical habitat for migratory birds and mammals, and serve as a natural filter to help keep our waters clean.

Despite the critical importance of these areas to our health and well-being, the ocean, coasts and Great Lakes face a wide range of threats from human activities. Overfishing, pollution, coastal development and the impacts of climate change are altering ecosystems, reducing biological diversity, and placing more stress on wildlife and natural resources, as well as on people and coastal communities. Compounding these threats, human uses of the ocean, coasts, and Great Lakes are expanding at a rate that challenges our ability to plan and manage significant and often competing demands. Demands for energy development, shipping, aquaculture, emerging security requirements and other new and existing uses are expected to grow. Overlapping uses and differing views about which activities should occur where can generate conflicts and misunderstandings. As we work to accommodate these multiple uses, we must also ensure continued public access for recreation and other pursuits, and sustain and preserve the abundant marine resources and healthy ecosystems that are critical to the well-being and prosperity of our Nation.

The challenges we face in the stewardship of the ocean, our coasts, and the Great Lakes lie not only within the ecosystems themselves, but also in the laws, authorities, and governance structures intended to manage our use and conservation of them. United States governance and management of these areas span hundreds of domestic policies, laws, and regulations covering international, Federal, State, tribal, and local interests. Challenges and gaps arise from the complexity and structure of this regime.

The time has come for a comprehensive national policy for the steward-ship of the ocean, our coasts, and the Great Lakes. Today, as never before, we better comprehend the links among land, air, fresh water, ocean, ice, and human activities. Advances in science and technology provide better and timelier information to guide decision-making. By applying the principles of ecosystem-based management (which integrates ecological, social, economic, commerce, health, and security goals, and which recognizes both that hu-mans are key components of ecosystems and also that healthy ecosystems are essential to human welfare) and of adaptive management (which calls for routine reassessment of management actions to allow for better informed and improved future decisions) in a coordinated and collaborative approach, the Nation will more effectively address the challenges facing the ocean, our coasts, and the Great Lakes and ensure their continued health for this and future generations.

FINAL RECOMMENDATIONS OF THE TASK FORCE

To develop its recommendations, the Task Force reviewed Federal, State, and foreign policies and models, past and pending legislation, the recom-mendations contained in the two earlier Ocean Commissions' reports, and public comments.

The Task Force also initiated a robust public engagement process to re-ceive input from a diversity of voices across the country. On behalf of the Task Force, CEQ hosted 38 expert roundtables to hear from a broad range of stakeholder groups. The Task Force also hosted six regional public meet-ings, and created a website to accept public comments through CEQ. The Task Force received more than 5,000 public comments, with many of the groups commenting representing constituencies of hundreds or thousands of members.

The Task Force recommendations set a new direction for improved stew-ardship of the ocean, our coasts, and the Great Lakes. They provide: (1) our Nation's first ever National Policy for the Stewardship of the Ocean, Our Coasts, and the Great Lakes (National Policy); (2) a strengthened governance structure to provide sustained, high-level, and coordinated attention to ocean, coastal, and Great Lakes issues; (3) a targeted implementation strat-egy that identifies and prioritizes nine categories for action that the United States should pursue; and (4) a framework for effective coastal and marine spatial planning (CMSP) that establishes a comprehensive, integrated, ecosystem-based approach to address conservation, economic activity, user conflict, and sustainable use of ocean, coastal, and Great Lakes resources.

The recommended National Policy establishes a comprehensive national approach to uphold our stewardship responsibilities; ensures accountability for our actions; and serves as a model of balanced, productive, efficient, sustainable, and informed ocean, coastal, and Great Lakes use, management, and conservation within the global community. The National Policy recognizes that America's stewardship of the ocean, our coasts, and the Great Lakes is intrinsically and intimately linked to environmental sustainability, human health and well-being, national prosperity, adaptation to climate and other environmental change, social justice, foreign policy, and national and homeland security. It sets forth overarching guiding principles for United States management decisions and actions affecting the ocean, our coasts, and the Great Lakes.

Policy Coordination Framework

No single agency can successfully resolve the complex and pressing problems facing the ocean, our coasts, and the Great Lakes. Successful stewardship will require an effective governance structure with sustained leadership and broad interagency coordination to effectively manage the many uses of these resources. A coordinated Federal effort, proactively guided by a senior-level interagency body, will ensure that the hundreds of domestic policies, laws, and regulations governing the management of the ocean, our coasts, and the Great Lakes are implemented in a meaningful way.

The Task Force recommends a combination of modifications to the structure of the existing Committee on Ocean Policy1, a stronger mandate and direction, and renewed and sustained high-level engagement. Subject to later refinements, the Task Force recommends:

1. Establishing a new National Ocean Council (NOC) which consolidates and strengthens the Principal- and Deputy-level components of the existing Committee on Ocean Policy within a single structure;
2. Strengthening the decision-making and dispute-resolution processes by defining clear roles for the NOC and the NOC leadership;
3. Formally engaging with State, tribal, and local authorities to address relevant issues through the creation of a new committee composed of their designated representatives;

4. Strengthening the link between science and management through a new NOC Steering Committee; and

5. Strengthening coordination between the NOC, the National Security Council, the National Economic Council, the Office of Energy and Climate Change, the Council on Environmental Quality, the Office of Science and Technology Policy, the Office of Management and Budget, and other White House entities.

It is the Policy of the United States to:

- Protect, maintain, and restore the health and biological diversity of ocean, coastal, and Great Lakes ecosystems and resources;
- Improve the resiliency of ocean, coastal, and Great Lakes ecosystems, communities, and economies;
- Bolster the conservation and sustainable uses of land in ways that will improve the health of ocean, coastal, and Great Lakes ecosystems;
- Use the best available science and knowledge to inform decisions affecting the ocean, our coasts, and the Great Lakes, and enhance humanity's capacity to understand, respond, and adapt to a changing global environment;
- Support sustainable, safe, secure, and productive access to, and uses of the ocean, our coasts, and the Great Lakes;
- Respect and preserve our Nation's maritime heritage, including our social, cultural, recreational, and historical values;
- Exercise rights and jurisdiction and perform duties in accordance with applicable international law, including respect for and preservation of navigational rights and freedoms, which are essential for the global economy and international peace and security;
- Increase scientific understanding of ocean, coastal, and Great Lakes ecosystems as part of the global interconnected systems of air, land, ice, and water, including their relationships to humans and their activities;
- Improve our understanding and awareness of changing environmental conditions, trends, and their causes, and of human activities taking place in ocean, coastal, and Great Lakes waters; and
- Foster a public understanding of the value of the ocean, our coasts, and the Great Lakes to build a foundation for improved stewardship.

These recommendations establish high-level direction and policy guidance from a clearly designated and identifiable authority. They also call for more consistent and sustained senior-level participation and attention on ocean-related issues from all member agencies and departments essential to effective management. The Task Force is confident that this combination of improvements provides a framework for more successful policy coordination to improve the stewardship of the ocean, our coasts, and the Great Lakes.

The Task Force recommends an implementation strategy that identifies nine priority objectives (i.e., categories for action) that our Nation should pursue. These priority objectives provide a bridge between policy and specific actions, but do not prescribe in detail how individual entities will undertake their responsibilities, leaving those details to be determined through the development of strategic action plans. The Task Force recommends the following nine priority objectives:

1. Ecosystem-based management: Adopt ecosystem-based management as a foundational principle for the comprehensive management of the ocean, our coasts, and the Great Lakes.
2. Coastal and marine spatial Planning: Implement comprehensive, integrated, ecosystem-based coastal and marine spatial planning and management in the United States.
3. Inform decisions and improve understanding: Increase knowledge to continually inform and improve management and policy decisions and the capacity to respond to change and challenges. Better educate the public through formal and informal programs about the ocean, our coasts, and the Great Lakes.
4. Coordinate and support: Better coordinate and support Federal, State, tribal, local, and regional management of the ocean, our coasts, and the Great Lakes. Improve coordination and integration across the Federal Government, and as appropriate, engage with the international community.
5. Resiliency and adaptation to climate change and ocean acidification: Strengthen resiliency of coastal communities and marine and Great Lakes environments and their abilities to adapt to climate change impacts and ocean acidification.
6. Regional ecosystem Protection and restoration: Establish and implement an integrated ecosystem protection and restoration strategy that is science-based and aligns conservation and restoration goals at the Federal, State, tribal, local, and regional levels.
7. Water Quality and sustainable Practices on land: Enhance water quality in the ocean, along our coasts, and in the Great Lakes by promoting and implementing sustainable practices on land.

8. Changing conditions in the arctic: Address environmental stewardship needs in the Arctic Ocean and adjacent coastal areas in the face of climate-induced and other environmental changes.
9. Ocean, coastal, and Great lakes observations, mapping, and infrastructure: Strengthen and integrate Federal and non-Federal ocean observing systems, sensors, data collection platforms, data management, and mapping capabilities into a national system, and integrate that system into international observation efforts.

The NOC will develop strategic action plans for each of the priority objectives, focusing on key areas identified by the Task Force. Each strategic action plan will identify specific and measurable near-term, mid-term, and long-term actions, with appropriate milestones, performance measures, and outcomes to meet each objective. In addition, each plan will explicitly identify key lead and participating agencies; gaps and needs in science and technology; potential resource requirements and efficiencies; and steps for integrating or coordinating current and out-year budgets. This strategy will allow adequate time to fully consider the necessary details for implementation, and, as appropriate, to coordinate and collaborate with States, tribal, and local authorities, regional governance structures, academic institutions, nongovernmental organizations, recreational users, and private enterprise.

The National Goals of Coastal and Marine Spatial Planning

1. Support sustainable, safe, secure, efficient, and productive uses of the ocean, our coasts, and the Great Lakes, including those that contribute to the economy, commerce, recreation, conservation, homeland and national security, human health, safety, and welfare;
2. Protect, maintain, and restore the Nation's ocean, coastal, and Great Lakes resources and ensure resilient ecosystems and their ability to provide sustained delivery of ecosystem services;
3. Provide for and maintain public access to the ocean, coasts, and Great Lakes;
4. Promote compatibility among uses and reduce user conflicts and environmental impacts;
5. Improve the rigor, coherence, and consistency of decision-making and regulatory processes;
6. Increase certainty and predictability in planning for and implementing new investments for ocean, coastal, and Great Lakes uses; and

7. Enhance interagency, intergovernmental, and international communication and collaboration.

COASTAL WATERSHED PROTECTION

The coastal watershed has several parts. It starts up at the beginning headwaters of the streams and rivers that ultimately drain down to the coastal areas. Headwaters often include wetlands, and wetlands often are adjacent to the flowing waters of rivers or streams. As the streams and rivers flow to coastal waters, they are influenced by many land and water uses. They pass through upland areas used for a variety of purposes such as farming, housing, businesses, recreation, and conservation. Upon reaching the coastal areas, the rivers empty into estuaries, which provide a unique habitat for a diverse group of organisms. Among other habitat functions, rivers and estuaries provide breeding and feeding grounds for a variety of aquatic and terrestrial animals. Nearshore waters, the areas directly offshore from the beach, are part of the coastal watershed because they are influenced by the activities going on along the shoreline and by pollutants coming from the land. Farther offshore are coral reefs (in tropical areas) and other offshore habitats that are part of the coastal watershed as well.

If a river or stream flows through an agricultural area, it can pick up fertilizer, manure, and pesticides from farming operations that run off the land after a rainstorm. As it passes urbanized and suburbanized areas, it might gather fertilizers that wash off lawns, untreated sewage from failing septic tanks, wastewater discharges from industrial facilities, sediment from construction sites, and runoff from impervious surfaces like parking lots.

Coastal Watershed Pollutants

Soil (loose dirt) from construction sites, farms, and areas where dirt is exposed can wash off into streams and rivers when it rains and flow to lakes, estuaries, and oceans. The result can be muddy waters that smother organisms living on the bottom, decrease the amount of light reaching the sea grass beds, and clog fish gills. Some kinds of pollutants can bind to sediment and flow with it to coastal waters.

Excess nutrients can also wash off the land when it rains and end up in coastal waters. Sources of excess nutrients include lawn fertilizers, pet and farm animal waste, decaying plant material, failing septic tanks, atmospheric deposition, and inefficient sewage treatment plants. The loss of wetlands in many watersheds has reduced the ability of nature to process these nutrients before they enter rivers, streams, and ultimately estuaries. These nutrients can cause an excessive amount of algae (microscopic plants) to grow in the water, blocking the light reaching sea grass. When the algae die off, the decaying process uses up the oxygen in the water, leaving little, if any, for fish and other aquatic organisms. In addition, some of these algae and related organisms (including Pfiesteria piscicida) release toxins that can kill fish or shellfish, and can be harmful, or even fatal, to humans.

Toxic substances, such as pesticides from lawns, gardens, and farms, and lead, oils, and greases deposited on roads from cars and trucks, can all run off the land with rainfall and snowmelt. Industrial plants and municipal wastewater treatment plants can also contribute to the amount of toxic substances entering streams and rivers and ultimately lakes, estuaries, and coastal waters. Fish kills and loss of the recreational uses of an area can occur.

Pathogens are microscopic organisms like bacteria and viruses. They come from untreated or poorly treated sewage, pet and farm animal waste, and improperly handled medical waste. Pathogens in the water in unsafe amounts result in beach closures, shellfish bed closures, fish kills, and human health problems.

Resource Impacts

Activities in the watershed can adversely affect a variety of resources.

- *Beaches*—Overloading of pollutants such as sewage and debris can result in beach closings.
- *Bays and estuaries*—Pollutants in and structural alterations to bays and estuaries can lead to loss of breeding and feeding grounds of fish, other aquatic animals, and birds, as well as loss of recreational areas.
- *Nearshore waters*—Along with bays and estuaries, nearshore waters are collection places for pollutants that flow from the watershed.
- *Coral reefs and other offshore areas*—Marine debris and pollutants such as nutrients and pesticides can flow offshore and affect coral reefs and other offshore habitats.

It is important to think of the watershed as a whole system that is tied together. What happens in one part of the watershed can affect another part, sometimes hundreds of miles away.

In recent years, EPA has invested considerable effort in streamlining program requirements that hinder watershed approaches and in developing useful watershed tools and services. For example, EPA has:

- Increased efforts to assist states in assessing the quality of their watersheds through a variety of programs.
- Applied watershed planning tools to the wetland permitting process to identify areas that are suitable or unsuitable for development.
- Provided financial assistance to states, territories, and tribes to promote watershed planning and management.
- Developed the "Surf Your Watershed" web site, which provides watershed-specific information to the public through the Internet and has increased public awareness of watersheds.
- Implemented the National Estuary Program to protect specific coastal watersheds and foster citizen and local government involvement in coastal watershed protection.

EPA also works with state, local, and community organizations to help them initiate grassroots efforts for protecting watersheds.

National Estuary Program

The National Estuary Program (NEP) was established under Section 320 of the 1987 Clean Water Act (CWA) Amendments as a U.S. Environmental Protection Agency (EPA) place-based program to protect and restore the water quality and ecological integrity of estuaries of national significance. Section 320 of the CWA calls for each NEP to develop and implement a Comprehensive Conservation and Management Plan (CCMP). The CCMP is a long-term plan that contains specific targeted actions designed to address water quality, habitat, and living resources challenges in its estuarine watershed.

Each NEP has a Management Conference (MC) made up of diverse stakeholders including citizens, local, state, and Federal agencies, as well as with non-profit and private sector entities. Using a consensus-building approach and collaborative decision-making process, each MC works closely together to implement the CCMP. The MC ensures that the CCMP is uniquely tailored to the local environmental conditions, is based on local input, and supports local priorities.

Currently there are 28 estuaries located along the Atlantic, Gulf, and Pacific coasts and in Puerto Rico that have been designated as estuaries of national significance. Each NEP focuses it work within a particular place or boundary called a study area which includes the estuary, and surrounding watershed.

Estuaries face a host of common challenges. Because we love and depend on the water, more than half of the people in the United States live within 100 miles of the coast, including on the shores of estuaries. And more and more people are moving to these areas. Coastal communities are growing three times faster than counties elsewhere in the country.

MARINE POLLUTION

Significant environmental impacts to coastal and ocean ecosystems occur via direct pollution from vessels, and as a vector for the invasion of non-indigenous species. Pollution from recreational, commercial, and military vessels emanates from a variety of sources, and include: gray water (water from sinks and sewers), bilgewater, black water (sewage), ballast water, antifouling paints (and their leachate), hazardous materials, and municipal and commercial garbage and other wastes.

Ocean Dumping/Dredging

In 1972, Congress enacted the Marine Protection, Research, and Sanctuaries Act (MPRSA, also known as the Ocean Dumping Act) to prohibit the dumping of material into the ocean that would unreasonably degrade or endanger human health or the marine environment. Virtually all material ocean dumped today is dredged material (sediments) removed from the bottom of waterbodies in order to maintain navigation channels and berthing areas. Other materials that are currently ocean disposed include fish wastes, human remains, and vessels.

Ocean dumping cannot occur unless a permit is issued under the MPRSA. In the case of dredged material, the decision to issue a permit is made by the U.S. Army Corps of Engineers, using EPA's environmental criteria and subject to EPA's concurrence. For all other materials, EPA is the permitting agency. EPA is also responsible for designating recommended ocean dumping sites for all types of materials.

Hypoxia

Hypoxia means low oxygen and is primarily a problem for estuaries and coastal waters. Hypoxic waters have dissolved oxygen concentrations of less than 2-3 ppm. Hypoxia can be caused by a variety of factors, including excess nutrients, primarily nitrogen and phosphorus, and waterbody stratification due to saline or temperature gradients. These excess nutrients, eutrophication, promote algal growth. As dead algae decompose, oxygen is consumed in the process, resulting in low levels of oxygen in the water.

Nutrients can come from many sources, including any of the following:

- Fertilizers from agriculture, golf courses, and suburban lawns
- Erosion of soil full of nutrients
- Discharges from sewage treatment plants
- Deposition of atmospheric nitrogen

The hypoxic zone in the Gulf of Mexico forms every summer and is a result of excess nutrients from the Mississippi River and seasonal stratification (layering) of waters in the Gulf. Nutrient-laden freshwater from the Mississippi River flows into the Gulf of Mexico. This freshwater is less dense and remains above the more dense saline Gulf water. In addition to the saline gradient caused where the freshwater and saline water meet, the freshwater is warmer than the deeper ocean water, further contributing to the stratification. This stratification prevents the mixing of oxygen-rich surface water with oxygen-poor water on the bottom of the Gulf. Without mixing, oxygen in the bottom water is limited and the hypoxic condition remains.

Direct effects of hypoxia include fish kills, which deplete valuable fisheries and disrupt ecosystems. Mobile animals (e.g., adult fish) can typically survive a hypoxic event by moving to waters with more oxygen. Less mobile or immobile animals, such as mussels or crabs, cannot move to waters with more oxygen and are often killed during hypoxic events. Ultimately, hypoxia causes a severe decrease in the amount of life in hypoxia zones. Hypoxia also affects the ability of young fish or shellfish to find the food and habitat necessary to become adults. As a result, fish and shellfish stocks may be reduced or become less stable because less young reach adulthood. Hypoxia can also affect species that rely on fish for food. Such species might have to leave an area to find the necessary food to survive.

Marine Debris

Marine debris is a problem along shorelines, and in coastal waters, estuaries, and oceans throughout the world. Marine debris is any man-made, solid material that enters our waterways either directly or indirectly. Marine debris enters our oceans and coasts from a number of land- and ocean-based sources. More people move near our Nation's coasts each year, and the production of trash and the potential for marine debris continues to increase. We need to better control the disposal of trash and other wastes, or we will continue to find marine debris in our rivers, streams, and oceans.

Trash and litter along our coasts and in our waterways can be harmful to our health, the environment, and the economy. Most trash that ends up in the water begins its journey on land.

When trash is not recycled or properly thrown away on land, it can become marine debris. For example, trash in the streets can wash into sewers, storm drains, or inland rivers and streams when it rains and can be carried to oceans and coastal waters. People who go to the beach sometimes leave behind trash.

Recreational and commercial fishermen sometimes lose or discard large fishing nets and lines in the ocean. Ships and recreational boats at sea sometimes intentionally or accidentally dump trash directly into the ocean. Trash from boats may be thrown, dropped, or blown overboard.

EPA and other stakeholders support the annual International Coastal Cleanup (ICC), implemented by Ocean Conservancy. The ICC currently involves 50 US states and territories and 104 countries from around the world. The ICC is the largest volunteer environmental data-gathering effort and cleanup of coastal and underwater areas in the world. Thousands of participants learn the value of preventing and controlling marine debris. The ICC takes place on the third Saturday in September every year.

Ocean Conservancy with support from EPA recently completed the National Marine Debris Monitoring Program (NMDMP). The NMDMP was developed to standardize marine debris data collection and assess marine debris sources and trends in the U.S. NMDMP used trained volunteers to conduct monthly marine debris surveys on designated beaches over a five-year period. The NMDMP Report indicates that approximately 49 percent of the marine debris items collected nationally during the study originated from land-based sources, 18 percent from ocean-based sources, and 33 percent from general sources (i.e., items that originate on land or at sea).

SOURCE MATERIAL

US Environmental Protection Agency. *Water on Tap: What You Need to Know.* Washington, DC: US Environmental Protection Agency, 2009. http://www.epa.gov/ogwdw/wot/pdfs/book_waterontap_full.pdf.

The White House. "Final Recommendations of the Interagency Ocean Policy Task Force." The White House Council on Environmental Quality. July 19, 2010. https://www.whitehouse.gov/files/documents/OPTF _FinalRecs.pdf

FURTHER READING

Centers for Disease Control and Prevention. "Drinking Water." http://www .cdc.gov/healthywater/drinking/.

US Environmental Protection Agency. "Water." http://water.epa.gov/index .cfm.

US Geological Survey. "Water Resources of the United States." http://www .usgs.gov/water/.

The White House. "Commitment to Clean Water." The White House Council on Environmental Quality. https://www.whitehouse.gov /administration/eop/ceq /initiatives/clean-water.

———. *Clean Water: Foundation of Healthy Communities and a Healthy Environment.* April 27, 2011. https://www.whitehouse.gov/sites/default/files /microsites/ceq/clean_water_framework.pdf.

World Health Organization. "Drinking Water." http://www.who.int/topics /drinking_water/en/.

4

Renewable Energy

This chapter presents current information on various renewable energy technologies from the National Renewable Energy Laboratory and the Department of Energy's Office of Energy Efficiency and Renewable Energy.

The United States currently relies heavily on coal, oil, and natural gas for its energy. Fossil fuels are nonrenewable, that is, they draw on finite resources that will eventually dwindle, becoming too expensive or too environmentally damaging to retrieve. In contrast, renewable energy resources—such as wind and solar energy—are constantly replenished and will never run out.

Renewable energy technologies produce sustainable, clean energy from sources such as the sun, the wind, plants, and water. According to the Energy Information Administration, in 2007, renewable sources of energy accounted for about seven percent of total energy consumption and 9.4 percent of total electricity generation in the United States. Renewable energy technologies have the potential to strengthen our nation's energy security, improve environmental quality, and contribute to a strong energy economy.

SOLAR

Solar is the Latin word for sun—a powerful source of energy that can be used to heat, cool, and light our homes and businesses. That's because more energy from the sun falls on the earth in one hour than is used by everyone in the world in one year. A variety of technologies convert sunlight to usable energy for buildings. The most commonly used solar technologies for homes and businesses are solar water heating, passive solar design for space heating and cooling, and solar photovoltaics for electricity.

Businesses and industry also use these technologies to diversify their energy sources, improve efficiency, and save money. Solar photovoltaic and concentrating solar power technologies are also being used by developers and utilities to produce electricity on a massive scale to power cities and small towns.

Solar Photovoltaic Technology

Photovoltaic (PV) materials and devices convert sunlight into electrical energy, and PV cells are commonly known as solar cells. Photovoltaics can literally be translated as light-electricity.

First used in about 1890, "photovoltaic" has two parts: photo, derived from the Greek word for light, and volt, relating to electricity pioneer Alessandro Volta. And this is what photovoltaic materials and devices do—they convert light energy into electrical energy, as French physicist Edmond Becquerel discovered as early as 1839.

Becquerel discovered the process of using sunlight to produce an electric current in a solid material. But it took more than another century to truly understand this process. Scientists eventually learned that the photoelectric or photovoltaic effect caused certain materials to convert light energy into electrical energy at the atomic level.

PV systems are already an important part of our daily lives. Simple PV systems provide power for small consumer items such as calculators and wristwatches. More complicated systems provide power for communications satellites, water pumps, and the lights, appliances, and machines in some homes and workplaces. Many road and traffic signs also are now powered by PV. In many cases, PV power is the least expensive form of electricity for these tasks.

Photovoltaic Cells

Photovoltaic (PV) cells, or solar cells, take advantage of the photoelectric effect to produce electricity. PV cells are the building blocks of all PV systems because they are the devices that convert sunlight to electricity.

Commonly known as solar cells, individual PV cells are electricity-producing devices made of semiconductor materials. PV cells come in many sizes and shapes, from smaller than a postage stamp to several inches across. They are often connected together to form PV modules that may be up to several feet long and a few feet wide.

Modules, in turn, can be combined and connected to form PV arrays of different sizes and power output. The modules of the array make up the major part of a PV system, which can also include electrical connections, mounting hardware, power-conditioning equipment, and batteries that store solar energy for use when the sun is not shining.

When light shines on a PV cell, it may be reflected, absorbed, or pass right through. But only the absorbed light generates electricity. The energy of the absorbed light is transferred to electrons in the atoms of the PV cell semiconductor material. With their newfound energy, these electrons escape from their normal positions in the atoms and become part of the electrical flow, or current, in an electrical circuit. A special electrical property of the PV cell—what is called a "built-in electric field"—provides the force, or voltage, needed to drive the current through an external load, such as a light bulb.

Photovoltaic Systems

A photovoltaic (PV), or solar electric system, is made up of several photovoltaic solar cells. An individual PV cell is usually small, typically producing about 1 or 2 watts of power. To boost the power output of PV cells, they are connected together to form larger units called modules. Modules, in turn, can be connected to form even larger units called arrays, which can be interconnected to produce more power, and so on. In this way, PV systems can be built to meet almost any electric power need, small or large.

By themselves, modules or arrays do not represent an entire PV system. Systems also include structures that point them toward the sun and components that take the direct-current electricity produced by modules and "condition" that electricity, usually by converting it to alternate-current electricity. PV systems may also include batteries. These items are referred to as the balance of system (BOS) components.

- Combining modules with BOS components creates an entire PV system. This system is usually everything needed to meet a particular energy demand, such as powering a water pump, the appliances and lights in a home, or—if the PV system is large enough—all the electrical requirements of a community.

Flat-Plate Systems. The most common photovoltaic (PV) array design uses flat-plate PV modules or panels. These panels can be fixed in place or allowed to track the movement of the sun. They respond to sunlight that is direct or diffuse. Even in clear skies, the diffuse component of sunlight accounts for between 10 percent and 20 percent of the total solar radiation on a horizontal surface. On partly sunny days, up to 50 percent of that radiation is diffuse, and on cloudy days, 100 percent of the radiation is diffuse.

> The simplest PV array consists of flat-plate PV panels in a fixed position. The advantages of fixed arrays are that they lack moving parts, there is virtually no need for extra equipment, and they are relatively lightweight. These features make them suitable for many locations, including most residential roofs. But because the panels are fixed in place, their orientation to the sun is usually at an angle that is less than optimal. Therefore, fixed arrays collect less energy per unit area of array than tracking arrays. However, this drawback must be balanced against the higher cost of the tracking system.

Concentrator Systems. Concentrator photovoltaic (PV) systems use less solar cell material than other PV systems. PV cells are the most expensive components of a PV system, on a per-area basis. A concentrator makes use of relatively inexpensive materials such as plastic lenses and metal housings to capture the solar energy shining on a fairly large area and focus that energy onto a smaller area—the solar cell. One measure of the effectiveness of this approach is the concentration ratio—in other words, how much concentration the cell is receiving.

Concentrator PV systems have several advantages over flat-plate systems. First, concentrator systems reduce the size or number of cells needed and allows certain designs to use more expensive semiconductor materials which would otherwise be cost prohibitive. Second, a solar cell's efficiency increases under concentrated light. How much that efficiency increases depends largely on the design of the solar cell and the material used to make it. Third, a concentrator can be made of small individual cells. This is an advantage because it is harder to produce large-area, high-efficiency solar cells than it is to produce small-area cells.

However, challenges exist for concentrators. First, the required concentrating optics are significantly more expensive than the simple covers needed for flat-plate solar systems, and most concentrators must track the sun throughout the day and year to be effective. Thus, achieving higher concentration ratios means using not only expensive tracking mechanisms but also more precise controls. Both reflectors and lenses have been used to concentrate light for PV systems.

The most promising lens for PV applications is the Fresnel lens, which uses a miniature sawtooth design to focus incoming light. When the teeth run in straight rows, the lenses act as line-focusing concentrators. When the teeth are arranged in concentric circles, light is focused at a central point. However, no lens can transmit 100 percent of the incident light. The best that lenses can transmit is 90 percent to 95 percent, and in practice, most transmit less. Furthermore, concentrators cannot focus diffuse sunlight, which makes up about 30 percent of the solar radiation available on a clear day.

High concentration ratios also introduce a heat problem. When solar radiation is concentrated, so is the amount of heat produced. Cell efficiencies decrease as temperatures increase, and higher temperatures also threaten the long-term stability of solar cells. Therefore, the solar cells must be kept cool in a concentrator system, requiring sophisticated heat sync cooling designs.

One of the most important design goals of concentrator systems is to minimize electrical resistance where the electrical contacts on the cell carry off the current generated by the cell. A pattern using wide grid lines, known as fingers, in the contacting grid on top of the cell are ideal for low resistance, but they block too much light from reaching the cell because of their shadow. One solution to the problems of resistance and shadowing is prismatic covers. These special covers act like a prism and direct incoming light to parts of the cell's surface that are between the metal fingers of the electrical contact grid. Another solution is a back-contact cell, which differs from conventional cells in that both the positive and negative electrical contacts are on the back. Placing all the electrical contacts on the back of the cell eliminates power losses from shadowing, but it also requires exceptionally good-quality silicon material.

Concentrating Solar Power

Concentrating solar power (CSP) technologies use mirrors to reflect and concentrate sunlight onto receivers that collect solar energy and convert it to heat. This thermal energy can then be used to produce electricity via a steam turbine or heat engine that drives a generator.

Concentrating solar power offers a utility-scale, firm, dispatchable renewable energy option that can help meet our nation's demand for electricity. CSP plants produce power by first using mirrors to focus sunlight to heat a working fluid. Ultimately, this high-temperature fluid is used to spin a turbine or power an engine that drives a generator. The final product is electricity.

Smaller CSP systems can be located directly where power is needed. For example, single dish/engine systems can produce 3 to 25 kilowatts of power and are well suited for distributed applications.

There are several varieties of CSP systems.

Linear Concentrator Systems

Linear concentrating solar power (CSP) collectors capture the sun's energy with large mirrors that reflect and focus the sunlight onto a linear receiver tube. The receiver contains a fluid that is heated by the sunlight and then used to create superheated steam that spins a turbine that drives a generator to produce electricity. Alternatively, steam can be generated directly in the solar field, which eliminates the need for costly heat exchangers.

Linear concentrating collector fields consist of a large number of collectors in parallel rows that are typically aligned in a north-south orientation to maximize annual and summer energy collection. With a single-axis sun-tracking system, this configuration enables the mirrors to track the sun from east to west during the day, which ensures that the sun reflects continuously onto the receiver tubes.

Parabolic Trough Systems. The most common CSP system in the United States is a linear concentrator that uses parabolic trough collectors. In such a system, the receiver tube is positioned along the focal line of each parabola-shaped reflector. The tube is fixed to the mirror structure, and the heated fluid—either a heat-transfer fluid or water/steam—flows through and out of the field of solar mirrors to where it is used to create steam (or, in the case of a water/steam receiver, it is sent directly to the turbine).

The largest individual trough systems generate 80 megawatts of electricity. However, individual systems being developed will generate 250 megawatts. In addition, individual systems can be co-located in power parks. Their capacity would be constrained only by the transmission capacity of nearby power lines and the availability of contiguous land.

Trough designs may incorporate thermal storage. In these systems, the collector field is oversized to heat a storage system during the day that can be used in the evening or during cloudy weather to generate additional steam to produce electricity. Parabolic trough plants can also be designed as hybrids, meaning that they use fossil fuel to supplement the solar output during periods of low solar radiation. In such a design, a natural gas-fired heater or gas-steam boiler/reheater is used. In the future, troughs may be integrated with existing or new combined-cycle natural-gas- and coal-fired plants.

Linear Fresnel Reflector Systems. A second linear concentrator technology is the linear Fresnel reflector system. Flat or slightly curved mirrors mounted on trackers on the ground are configured to reflect sunlight onto a receiver tube fixed in space above the mirrors. A small parabolic mirror is sometimes added atop the receiver to further focus the sunlight.

Dish/Engine Systems

The dish/engine system is a concentrating solar power (CSP) technology that produces relatively small amounts of electricity compared to other CSP technologies—typically in the range of 3 to 25 kilowatts. Dish/engine systems use a parabolic dish of mirrors to direct and concentrate sunlight onto a central engine that produces electricity. The two major parts of the system are the solar concentrator and the power conversion unit.

Solar Concentrator. The solar concentrator, or dish, gathers the solar energy coming directly from the sun. The resulting beam of concentrated sunlight is reflected onto a thermal receiver that collects the solar heat. The dish is mounted on a structure that tracks the sun continuously throughout the day to reflect the highest percentage of sunlight possible onto the thermal receiver.

Power Conversion Unit. The power conversion unit includes the thermal receiver and the engine/generator. The thermal receiver is the interface between the dish and the engine/generator. It absorbs the concentrated beams of solar energy, converts them to heat, and transfers the heat to the engine/generator. A thermal receiver can be a bank of tubes with a cooling fluid—usually hydrogen or helium—that typically is the heat-transfer medium and also the working fluid for an engine. Alternate thermal receivers are heat pipes, where the boiling and condensing of an intermediate fluid transfers the heat to the engine.

The engine/generator system is the subsystem that takes the heat from the thermal receiver and uses it to produce electricity. The most common type of heat engine used in dish/engine systems is the Stirling engine. A Stirling engine uses the heated fluid to move pistons and create mechanical power. The mechanical work, in the form of the rotation of the engine's crankshaft, drives a generator and produces electrical power.

Power Tower Systems

In power tower concentrating solar power systems, numerous large, flat, sun-tracking mirrors, known as heliostats, focus sunlight onto a receiver at the top of a tall tower. A heat-transfer fluid heated in the receiver is used to generate steam, which, in turn, is used in a conventional turbine generator to produce electricity. Some power towers use water/steam as the heat-transfer fluid. Other advanced designs are experimenting with molten nitrate salt because of its superior heat-transfer and energy-storage capabilities. Individual commercial plants can be sized to produce up to 200 megawatts of electricity.

Two large-scale power tower demonstration projects have been deployed in the United States. During its operation from 1982 to 1988, the 10-megawatt Solar One plant near Barstow, California, demonstrated the viability of power towers by producing more than 38 million kilowatt-hours of electricity.

The Solar Two plant was a retrofit of Solar One to demonstrate the advantages of molten salt for heat transfer and thermal storage. Using its highly efficient molten-salt energy storage system, Solar Two successfully demonstrated efficient collection of solar energy and dispatch of electricity. It also demonstrated the ability to routinely produce electricity during cloudy weather and at night. In one demonstration, Solar Two delivered power to the grid 24 hours a day for almost seven consecutive days before cloudy weather interrupted operation.

Spain has several power tower systems. Planta Solar 10 and Planta Solar 20 are water/steam systems with capacities of 11 and 20 megawatts, respectively. Solar Tres will produce some 15 megawatts of electricity and have the capacity for molten-salt thermal storage.

Thermal Storage Systems

One challenge facing the widespread use of solar energy is reduced or curtailed energy production when the sun sets or is blocked by clouds. Thermal energy storage provides a workable solution to this challenge.

In a concentrating solar power (CSP) system, the sun's rays are reflected onto a receiver, which creates heat that is used to generate electricity. If the receiver contains oil or molten salt as the heat-transfer medium, then the thermal energy can be stored for later use. This enables CSP systems to be cost-competitive options for providing clean, renewable energy.

Several thermal energy storage technologies have been tested and implemented since 1985. These include the two-tank direct system, two-tank indirect system, and single-tank thermocline system.

Two-Tank Direct System. Solar thermal energy in this system is stored in the same fluid used to collect it. The fluid is stored in two tanks—one at high temperature and the other at low temperature. Fluid from the low-temperature tank flows through the solar collector or receiver, where solar energy heats it to a high temperature, and it then flows to the high-temperature tank for storage. Fluid from the high-temperature tank flows through a heat exchanger, where it generates steam for electricity production. The fluid exits the heat exchanger at a low temperature and returns to the low-temperature tank.

Two-tank direct storage was used in early parabolic trough power plants (such as Solar Electric Generating Station I) and at the Solar Two power tower in California. The trough plants used mineral oil as the heat-transfer and storage fluid; Solar Two used molten salt.

Two-Tank Indirect System. Two-tank indirect systems function in the same way as two-tank direct systems, except different fluids are used as the heat-transfer and storage fluids. This system is used in plants in which the heat-transfer fluid is too expensive or not suited for use as the storage fluid.

The storage fluid from the low-temperature tank flows through an extra heat exchanger, where it is heated by the high-temperature heat-transfer fluid. The high-temperature storage fluid then flows back to the high-temperature storage tank. The fluid exits this heat exchanger at a low temperature and returns to the solar collector or receiver, where it is heated back to a high temperature. Storage fluid from the high-temperature tank is used to generate steam in the same manner as the two-tank direct system. The indirect system requires an extra heat exchanger, which adds cost to the system.

This system will be used in many of the parabolic power plants in Spain and has also been proposed for several U.S. parabolic plants. The plants will use organic oil as the heat-transfer fluid and molten salt as the storage fluid.

Single-Tank Thermocline System. Single-tank thermocline systems store thermal energy in a solid medium—most commonly, silica sand—located in a single tank. At any time during operation, a portion of the medium is at high temperature, and a portion is at low temperature. The hot- and cold-temperature regions are separated by a temperature gradient or thermocline. High-temperature heat-transfer fluid flows into the top of the thermocline and exits the bottom at low temperature. This process moves the thermocline downward and adds thermal energy to the system for storage. Reversing the flow moves the thermocline upward and removes thermal energy from the system to generate steam and electricity. Buoyancy effects create thermal stratification of the fluid within the tank, which helps to stabilize and maintain the thermocline.

Using a solid storage medium and only needing one tank reduces the cost of this system relative to two-tank systems. This system was demonstrated at the Solar One power tower, where steam was used as the heat-transfer fluid and mineral oil was used as the storage fluid.

Solar Process Heat Basics

Commercial and industrial buildings may use the same solar technologies—photovoltaics, passive heating, daylighting, and water heating—that are used for residential buildings. These nonresidential buildings can also use solar energy technologies that would be impractical for a home. These technologies include ventilation air preheating, solar process heating, and solar cooling.

Space Heating

Many large buildings need ventilated air to maintain indoor air quality. In cold climates, heating this air can use large amounts of energy. But a solar ventilation system can preheat the air, saving both energy and money. This type of system typically uses a transpired collector, which consists of a thin, black metal panel mounted on a south-facing wall to absorb the sun's heat. Air passes through the many small holes in the panel. A space behind the perforated wall allows the air streams from the holes to mix together. The heated air is then sucked out from the top of the space into the ventilation system.

Water Heating

Solar water-heating systems are designed to provide large quantities of hot water for nonresidential buildings. A typical system includes solar collectors that work along with a pump, heat exchanger, and/or one or more large storage tanks. The two main types of solar collectors used for nonresidential buildings—an evacuated-tube collector and a linear concentrator—can operate at high temperatures with high efficiency. An evacuated-tube collector is a set of many double-walled, glass tubes and reflectors to heat the fluid inside the tubes. A vacuum between the two walls insulates the inner tube, retaining the heat. Linear concentrators use long, rectangular, curved (U-shaped) mirrors tilted to focus sunlight on tubes that run along the length of the mirrors. The concentrated sunlight heats the fluid within the tubes.

Space Cooling

Space cooling can be accomplished using thermally activated cooling systems (TACS) driven by solar energy. Because of a high initial cost, TACS are not widespread. The two systems currently in operation are solar absorption systems and solar desiccant systems. Solar absorption systems use thermal energy to evaporate a refrigerant fluid to cool the air. In contrast, solar desiccant systems use thermal energy to regenerate desiccants that dry the air, thereby cooling the air. These systems also work well with evaporative coolers (also called "swamp coolers") in more humid climates.

HYDROPOWER

Hydropower, or hydroelectric power, is the most common and least expensive source of renewable electricity in the United States today. According to the Energy Information Administration, more than six percent of the country's electricity was produced from hydropower resources in 2008, and about 70 percent of all renewable electricity generated in the United States came from hydropower resources.

Hydropower technologies have a long history of use because of their many benefits, including high availability and lack of emissions.

Hydropower technologies use flowing water to create energy that can be captured and turned into electricity. Both large and small-scale power producers can use hydropower technologies to produce clean electricity.

Large-Scale Hydropower

Large-scale hydropower plants are generally developed to produce electricity for government or electric utility projects. These plants are more than 30 megawatts (MW) in size, and there is more than 80,000 MW of installed generation capacity in the United States today.

Most large-scale hydropower projects use a dam and a reservoir to retain water from a river. When the stored water is released, it passes through and rotates turbines, which spin generators to produce electricity. Water stored in a reservoir can be accessed quickly for use during times when the demand for electricity is high.

Dammed hydropower projects can also be built as power storage facilities. During periods of peak electricity demand, these facilities operate much like a traditional hydropower plant—water released from the upper reservoir passes through turbines, which spins generators to produce electricity. However, during periods of low electricity use, electricity from the grid is used to spin the turbines backward, which causes the turbines to pump water from a river or lower reservoir to an upper reservoir, where the water can be stored until the demand for electricity is high again.

A third type of hydropower project, called run of the river, does not require large impoundment dams (although it may require a small, less obtrusive dam). Instead, a portion of a river's water is diverted into a canal or pipe to spin turbines.

Many large-scale dam projects have been criticized for altering wildlife habitats, impeding fish migration, and affecting water quality and flow patterns. As a result of increased environmental regulation, the National Hydropower Association forecasts a decline in large-scale hydropower use through 2020. Research and development efforts have succeeded in reducing many of these environmental impacts through the use of fish ladders (to aid fish migration), fish screens, new turbine designs, and reservoir aeration.

Microhydropower

Microhydropower systems are small hydroelectric power systems of less than 100 kilowatts (kW) used to produce mechanical energy or electricity for farms, ranches, homes, and villages.

How a Microhydropower System Works

All hydropower systems use the energy of flowing water to produce electricity or mechanical energy. Although there are several ways to harness moving water to produce energy, "run-of-the-river systems," which do not require large storage reservoirs, are most often used for microhydropower systems.

For run-of-the-river microhydropower systems, a portion of a river's water is diverted to a water conveyance—a channel, pipeline, or pressurized pipeline (called a penstock)—that delivers it to a turbine or waterwheel. The moving water rotates the wheel or turbine, which spins a shaft. The motion of the shaft can be used for mechanical processes, such as pumping water, or it can be used to power an alternator or generator to generate electricity.

Microhydropower System Components

Run-of-the-river microhydropower systems consist of:

- A water conveyance, which is a channel, pipeline, or pressurized pipeline (penstock) that delivers the water
- A turbine, pump, or waterwheel, which transforms the energy of flowing water into rotational energy
- An alternator or generator, which transforms the rotational energy into electricity
- A regulator, which controls the generator
- Wiring, which delivers the electricity

Many systems also use an inverter to convert the low-voltage direct current (DC) electricity produced by the system into 120 or 240 V of alternating current (AC) electricity.

Commercially available turbines and generators are usually sold as a package. Do-it-yourself systems require careful matching of a generator with the turbine horsepower and speed.

Whether a microhydropower system will be grid-connected or stand-alone will determine its final balance of system components. For example, some stand-alone systems use batteries to store the electricity generated by the system. However, because hydropower resources tend to be more seasonal in nature than wind or solar resources, batteries may not always be practical. If batteries are used, they should be located as close to the turbine as possible because it is difficult to transmit low-voltage power over long distances.

Dams or diversion structures are rarely used in microhydropower projects. They are an added expense and require professional assistance from a civil engineer. In addition, dams increase the potential for environmental and maintenance problems.

WIND

We have been harnessing the wind's energy for hundreds of years. From old Holland to farms in the United States, windmills have been used for pumping water or grinding grain. Today, the windmill's modern equivalent—a wind turbine—can use the wind's energy to generate electricity.

Wind turbines, like windmills, are mounted on a tower to capture the most energy. At 100 feet (30 meters) or more aboveground, they can take advantage of the faster and less turbulent wind. Turbines catch the wind's energy with their propeller-like blades. Usually, two or three blades are mounted on a shaft to form a rotor.

A blade acts much like an airplane wing. When the wind blows, a pocket of low-pressure air forms on the downwind side of the blade. The low-pressure air pocket then pulls the blade toward it, causing the rotor to turn. This is called lift. The force of the lift is actually much stronger than the wind's force against the front side of the blade, which is called drag. The combination of lift and drag causes the rotor to spin like a propeller, and the turning shaft spins a generator to make electricity.

Most wind energy technologies can be used as stand-alone applications, connected to a utility power grid, or even combined with a photovoltaic system. For utility-scale sources of wind energy, a large number of turbines are usually built close together to form a wind farm that provides grid power. Several electricity providers use wind farms to supply power to their customers.

Stand-alone turbines are typically used for water pumping or communications. However, homeowners and farmers in windy areas can also use small wind systems to generate electricity.

Although all wind turbines operate on similar principles, several varieties are in use today. These include horizontal axis turbines and vertical axis turbines.

Horizontal Axis Turbines

Horizontal axis turbines are the most common turbine configuration used today. They consist of a tall tower, atop which sits a fan-like rotor that faces into or away from the wind, a generator, a controller, and other components. Most horizontal axis turbines built today are two- or three-bladed.

Horizontal axis turbines sit high atop towers to take advantage of the stronger and less turbulent wind at 100 feet (30 meters) or more aboveground. Each blade acts like an airplane wing, so when wind blows, a pocket of low-pressure air forms on the downwind side of the blade. The low-pressure air pocket then pulls the blade toward it, which causes the rotor to turn. This is called lift. The force of the lift is actually much stronger than the wind's force against the front side of the blade, which is called drag. The combination of lift and drag causes the rotor to spin like a propeller, and the turning shaft spins a generator to make electricity.

Vertical Axis Turbines

Vertical axis turbines are of two types: Savonius and Darrieus. Neither type is in wide use.

The Darrieus turbine was invented in France in the 1920s. Often described as looking like an eggbeater, it has vertical blades that rotate into and out of the wind. Using aerodynamic lift, it can capture more energy than drag devices. The Giromill and cycloturbine are variants on the Darrieus turbine.

The Savonius turbine is S-shaped if viewed from above. This drag-type turbine turns relatively slowly but yields a high torque. It is useful for grinding grain, pumping water, and many other tasks, but its slow rotational speeds are not good for generating electricity.

In addition, windmills are still used for a variety of purposes. Windmills have been used by humans since at least 200 B.C. for grinding grain and pumping water. By the 1900s, windmills were used on farms and ranches in the United States to pump water and, later, to produce electricity. Windmills have more blades than modern wind turbines, and they rely on drag to rotate the blades.

BIOMASS

There are many types of biomass—organic matter such as plants, residue from agriculture and forestry, and the organic component of municipal and industrial wastes—that can now be used to produce fuels, chemicals, and power. Wood has been used to provide heat for thousands of years. This flexibility has resulted in increased use of biomass technologies. According to the Energy Information Administration, 53 percent of all renewable energy consumed in the United States was biomass-based in 2007.

Biomass technologies break down organic matter to release stored energy from the sun. The process used depends on the type of biomass and its intended end-use.

Biofuels

Biofuels are liquid or gaseous fuels produced from biomass. Most biofuels are used for transportation, but some are used as fuels to produce electricity. The expanded use of biofuels offers an array of benefits for our energy security, economic growth, and environment.

Current biofuels research focuses on new forms of biofuels such as ethanol and biodiesel, and on biofuels conversion processes.

Ethanol

Ethanol—an alcohol—is made primarily from the starch in corn grain. It is most commonly used as an additive to petroleum-based fuels to reduce toxic air emissions and increase octane. Today, roughly half of the gasoline sold in the United States includes five percent-10 percent ethanol.

Biodiesel

Biodiesel use is relatively small, but its benefits to air quality are dramatic. Biodiesel is produced through a process that combines organically-derived oils with alcohol (ethanol or methanol) in the presence of a catalyst to form ethyl or methyl ester. The biomass-derived ethyl or methyl esters can be blended with conventional diesel fuel or used as a neat fuel (100 percent biodiesel).

Biofuel Conversion

The conversion of biomass solids into liquid or gaseous biofuels is a complex process. Today, the most common conversion processes are biochemical- and thermochemical-based. However, researchers are also exploring photobiological conversion processes.

Biochemical Conversion Processes. In biochemical conversion processes, enzymes and microorganisms are used as biocatalysts to convert biomass or biomass-derived compounds into desirable products. Cellulase and hemicellulase enzymes break down the carbohydrate fractions of biomass to five- and six-carbon sugars in a process known as hydrolysis. Yeast and bacteria then ferment the sugars into products such as ethanol. Biotechnology advances are expected to lead to dramatic biochemical conversion improvements.

Thermochemical Conversion Processes. Heat energy and chemical catalysts can be used to break down biomass into intermediate compounds or products. In gasification, biomass is heated in an oxygen-starved environment to produce a gas composed primarily of hydrogen and carbon monoxide.

In pyrolysis, biomass is exposed to high temperatures in the absence of air, causing it to decompose. Solvents, acids, and bases can be used to fractionate biomass into an array of products including sugars, cellulosic fibers, and lignin.

Photobiological Conversion Processes. Photobiological conversion processes use the natural photosynthetic activity of organisms to produce biofuels directly from sunlight. For example, the photosynthetic activities of bacteria and green algae have been used to produce hydrogen from water and sunlight.

Biopower

Biopower is the production of electricity or heat from biomass resources. With 10 gigawatts of installed capacity, biopower technologies are proven options in the United States today.

Biopower technologies include direct combustion, co-firing, and anaerobic digestion.

Direct Combustion

Most electricity generated from biomass is produced by direct combustion using conventional boilers. These boilers primarily burn waste wood products from the agriculture and wood-processing industries. When burned, the wood produces steam, which spins a turbine. The spinning turbine then activates a generator that produces electricity.

Co-Firing

Co-firing involves replacing a portion of the petroleum-based fuel in high-efficiency coal-fired boilers with biomass. Co-firing has been successfully demonstrated in most boiler technologies, including pulverized coal, cyclone, fluidized bed, and spreader stoker units. Co-firing biomass can significantly reduce the sulfur dioxide emissions of coal-fired power plants and is a least-cost renewable energy option for many power producers.

Anaerobic Digestion

Anaerobic digestion, or methane recovery, is a common technology used to convert organic waste to electricity or heat. In anaerobic digestion, organic matter is decomposed by bacteria in the absence of oxygen to produce methane and other byproducts that form a renewable natural gas.

Bio-Based Products

Almost all of the products we currently make from fossil fuels can also be made from biomass. These bioproducts, or bio-based products, are not only made from renewable sources, but they also often require less energy to produce than petroleum-based ones.

Researchers have discovered that the process for making biofuels also can be used to make antifreeze, plastics, glues, artificial sweeteners, and gel for toothpaste.

Other important building blocks for bio-based products are carbon monoxide and hydrogen. When biomass is heated with a small amount of oxygen, these two gases are produced in abundance. Scientists call this mixture biosynthesis gas. Biosynthesis gas can be used to make plastics and acids, which can then be used to make photographic films, textiles, and synthetic fabrics.

When biomass is heated in the absence of oxygen, it forms pyrolysis oil. A chemical called phenol can be extracted from pyrolysis oil, and it is used to make wood adhesives, molded plastic, and foam insulation.

In the future, you may see biorefineries—much like petroleum refineries—producing not only biofuels but also a variety of bioproducts. These biorefineries could also generate electricity for their own use and for possible sale as well as their own process heat.

GEOTHERMAL

Geothermal technologies use the clean, sustainable heat from the Earth. Geothermal resources include the heat retained in shallow ground, hot water and rock found a few miles beneath the Earth's surface, and extremely high-temperature molten rock called magma located deep in the Earth.

Many technologies have been developed to take advantage of geothermal energy. This heat can be drawn from several sources: hot water or steam reservoirs deep in the earth that are accessed by drilling; geothermal reservoirs located near the earth's surface, mostly located in the western U.S., Alaska, and Hawaii; and the shallow ground near the Earth's surface that maintains a relatively constant temperature of 50°–60°F.

This variety of geothermal resources allows them to be used on both large and small scales. A utility can use the hot water and steam from reservoirs to drive generators and produce electricity for its customers. Other applications apply the heat produced from geothermal directly to various uses in buildings, roads, agriculture, and industrial plants. Still others use the heat directly from the ground to provide heating and cooling in homes and other buildings.

Electricity Production

Heat from the earth—geothermal energy—heats water that has seeped into underground reservoirs. These reservoirs can be tapped for a variety of uses, depending on the temperature of the water. The energy from high-temperature reservoirs (225°-600°F) can be used to produce electricity.

In the United States, geothermal energy has been used to generate electricity on a large scale since 1960. Through research and development, geothermal power is becoming more cost-effective and competitive with fossil fuels.

There are currently three types of geothermal power plants:

Dry Steam

Dry steam plants use steam from underground wells to rotate a turbine, which activates a generator to produce electricity. There are only two known underground resources of steam in the United States: The Geysers in northern California and Old Faithful in Yellowstone National Park. Because Yellowstone is protected from development, the power plants at The Geysers are the only dry steam plants in the country.

Flash Steam

The most common type of geothermal power plant, flash steam plants use water at temperatures of more than 360°F. As this hot water flows up through wells in the ground, the decrease in pressure causes some of the water to boil into steam. The steam is then used to power a generator, and any leftover water and condensed steam is returned to the reservoir.

Binary Cycle

Binary cycle plants use the heat from lower-temperature reservoirs (225°-360°F) to boil a working fluid, which is then vaporized in a heat exchanger and used to power a generator. The water, which never comes into direct contact with the working fluid, is then injected back into the ground to be reheated.

Heat Pumps

Geothermal heat pumps use the constant temperature of the earth as an exchange medium for heat. Although many parts of the country experience seasonal temperature extremes—from scorching heat in the summer to sub-zero cold in the winter—the ground a few feet below the earth's surface remains at a relatively constant temperature.

Depending on the latitude, ground temperatures range from 45°F (7°C) to 75°F (21°C). So, like a cave's, the ground's temperature is warmer than the air above it during winter and cooler than the air above it in summer. Geothermal heat pumps take advantage of this by exchanging heat with the earth through a ground heat exchanger.

Geothermal heat pumps are able to heat, cool, and, if so equipped, supply homes and buildings with hot water. A geothermal heat pump system consists of a heat pump, an air delivery system (ductwork), and a heat exchanger—a system of pipes buried in shallow ground. In the winter, the heat pump removes heat from the heat exchanger and pumps it into the indoor air delivery system. In the summer, the process is reversed, and the heat pump moves heat from the indoor air into the heat exchanger. The heat removed from the indoor air during the summer can also be used to provide a free source of hot water.

There are four types of geothermal heat pump systems. Three of these—horizontal, vertical, and pond/lake—are closed-loop systems. The fourth type is open-loop. Which is best depends on the climate, soil conditions, available land, and local installation costs at a particular site. All of these approaches can be used for residential and commercial building applications.

Closed-Loop Systems

Horizontal. This type of geothermal heat pump is generally most cost-effective for residential installations, particularly for new construction where sufficient land is available. It requires trenches at least 4 feet deep. The most common layouts use two pipes, one buried at 6 feet and the other at 4 feet, or two pipes placed side-by-side at 5 feet in the ground in a 2-foot-wide trench. The Slinky™ method of looping pipe allows more pipe in a shorter trench, which cuts installation costs and makes horizontal installation possible in areas that would not be viable for conventional horizontal applications.

Vertical. Large commercial buildings and schools often use vertical systems because the land area required for horizontal loops is prohibitive. Vertical loops are also used where the soil is too shallow for trenching, and they minimize the disturbance to existing landscaping. For a vertical system, holes (approximately 4 inches in diameter) are drilled about 20 feet apart and 100–400 feet deep. Into these holes go two pipes that are connected at the bottom with a U-bend to form a loop. The vertical loops are connected with horizontal pipe (i.e., manifold), placed in trenches, and connected to the heat pump in the building.

Ponds or Lakes. If a site has an adequate body of water, a water-source heat pump may be the lowest-cost option. A supply line pipe is run underground from the building to the water and coiled into circles at least 8 feet under the surface to prevent freezing. The coils should be placed only in a water source that meets minimum volume, depth, and quality criteria.

Open-Loop System

This type of system uses well or surface body water as the heat exchange fluid that circulates directly through the heat pump system. Once it has circulated through the system, the water returns to the ground through the well, a recharge well, or surface discharge. This option is practical only where there is an adequate supply of relatively clean water and all local codes and regulations regarding groundwater discharge are met.

HYDROGEN

Hydrogen is the simplest element on Earth. A hydrogen atom consists of only one proton and one electron. It is also the most plentiful element in the universe.

Despite its simplicity and abundance, hydrogen doesn't occur naturally as a gas on Earth. It is always combined with other elements. Water, for example, is a combination of hydrogen and oxygen. Hydrogen is also found in many organic compounds, notably the "hydrocarbons" that make up fuels such as gasoline, natural gas, methanol, and propane.

Hydrogen Fuel

Hydrogen is a clean fuel that, when consumed, produces only water. Hydrogen can be produced from a variety of domestic sources, such as coal, natural gas, nuclear power, and renewable power. These qualities make it an attractive fuel option for transportation and electricity generation applications.

Hydrogen is an energy carrier that can be used to store, move, and deliver energy produced from other sources. The energy in hydrogen fuel is derived from the fuels and processes used to produce the hydrogen.

Today, hydrogen fuel can be produced through several methods. The most common methods are thermal, electrolytic, and photolytic processes.

Thermal Processes

Thermal processes for hydrogen production typically involve steam reforming, a high-temperature process in which steam reacts with a hydrocarbon fuel to produce hydrogen. Many hydrocarbon fuels can be reformed to produce hydrogen, including natural gas, diesel, renewable liquid fuels, gasified coal, or gasified biomass. Today, about 95 percent of all hydrogen is produced from steam reforming of natural gas.

Electrolytic Processes

Water can be separated into oxygen and hydrogen through a process called electrolysis. Electrolytic processes take place in an electrolyzer, which functions much like a fuel cell in reverse.

Photolytic Processes

Photolytic processes use light as the agent for hydrogen production. Photobiological processes use the natural photosynthetic activity of bacteria and green algae to produce hydrogen. Photoelectrochemical processes use specialized semiconductors to separate water into hydrogen and oxygen.

Fuel Cells

Fuel cells are an emerging technology that can provide heat and electricity for buildings and electrical power for vehicles and electronic devices.

How Fuel Cells Work

Fuel cells work like batteries, but they do not run down or need recharging. They produce electricity and heat as long as fuel is supplied. A fuel cell consists of two electrodes—a negative electrode (or anode) and a positive electrode (or cathode)—sandwiched around an electrolyte. A fuel, such as hydrogen, is fed to the anode, and air is fed to the cathode. Activated by a catalyst, hydrogen atoms separate into protons and electrons, which take different paths to the cathode. The electrons go through an external circuit, creating a flow of electricity. The protons migrate through the electrolyte to the cathode, where they reunite with oxygen and the electrons to produce water and heat.

Learn more about fuel cell operation by viewing the Fuel Cell Technologies Office's fuel cell animation.

Types of Fuel Cells

Although the basic operations of all fuel cells are the same, numerous varieties have been developed to take advantage of different electrolytes and serve different application needs.

Polymer Electrolyte Membrane Fuel Cells. Polymer electrolyte membrane (PEM) fuel cells, also called proton exchange membrane fuel cells, use a polymer membrane as the electrolyte. These cells operate at relatively low temperatures and can quickly vary their output to meet shifting power demands. PEM fuel cells are the best candidates for powering automobiles. They can also be used for stationary power production.

Direct-Methanol Fuel Cells. The direct-methanol fuel cell (DMFC) is similar to the PEM cell in that it uses a polymer membrane as an electrolyte. However, DMFCs use methanol directly on the anode, which eliminates the need for a fuel reformer. DMFCs are of interest for powering portable electronic devices, such as laptop computers and battery rechargers.

Alkaline Fuel Cells. Alkaline fuel cells use an alkaline electrolyte such as potassium hydroxide or an alkaline membrane. Originally used by NASA on space missions, alkaline fuel cells are now finding new applications, such as in portable power.

Phosphoric Acid Fuel Cells. Phosphoric acid fuel cells use a phosphoric acid electrolyte held inside a porous matrix, and operate at about 200°C. They are typically used in modules of 400 kW or greater and are being used for stationary power production in hotels, hospitals, grocery stores, and office buildings, where waste heat can also be used. Phosphoric acid can also be immobilized in polymer membranes, and fuel cells using these membranes are of interest for a variety of stationary power applications.

Molten Carbonate Fuel Cells. Molten carbonate fuel cells use a molten carbonate salt immobilized in a porous matrix as their electrolyte. They are already being used in a variety of medium-to-large-scale stationary applications, where their high efficiency produces net energy savings. Their high-temperature operation (approximately 600°C) enables them to internally reform fuels such as natural gas and biogas.

Solid Oxide Fuel Cells. Solid oxide fuel cells use a thin layer of ceramic as a solid electrolyte. They are being developed for use in a variety of stationary power applications, as well as in auxiliary power devices for heavy-duty trucks. Operating at 700 – 1000°C with zirconia-based electrolytes, and as low as 500°C with ceria-based electrolytes, these fuel cells can internally reform natural gas and biogas, and can be combined with a gas turbine to produce electrical efficiencies as high as 75 percent.

Combined Heat and Power. In addition to electricity, fuel cells produce heat. This heat can be used to fulfill heating needs, including hot water and space heating. Combined heat and power fuel cells are of interest for powering houses and buildings, where total efficiency as high as 90 percent is achievable. This high efficiency operation saves money, saves energy, and reduces greenhouse gas emissions.

Regenerative or Reversible Fuel Cells. This special class of fuel cells produces electricity from hydrogen and oxygen, but can be reversed and powered with electricity to produce hydrogen and oxygen. This emerging technology could provide storage of excess energy produced by intermittent renewable energy sources, such as wind and solar power stations, releasing this energy during times of low power production.

OCEAN

Oceans cover more than 70 percent of the Earth's surface. As the world's largest solar collectors, oceans contain thermal energy from the sun and produce mechanical energy from tides and waves. Even though the sun affects all ocean activity, the gravitational pull of the moon primarily drives tides, and wind powers ocean waves.

Ocean Thermal Energy Conversion

A process called <i>ocean thermal energy conversion</i> (OTEC) uses the heat energy stored in the Earth's oceans to generate electricity.

OTEC works best when the temperature difference between the warmer, top layer of the ocean and the colder, deep ocean water is about 36°F (20°C). These conditions exist in tropical coastal areas, roughly between the Tropic of Capricorn and the Tropic of Cancer. To bring the cold water to the surface, ocean thermal energy conversion plants require an expensive, large-diameter intake pipe, which is submerged a mile or more into the ocean's depths.

Some energy experts believe that if ocean thermal energy conversion can become cost-competitive with conventional power technologies, it could be used to produce billions of watts of electrical power.

History

OTEC technology is not new. In 1881, Jacques Arsene d'Arsonval, a French physicist, proposed tapping the thermal energy of the ocean. But it was d'Arsonval's student, Georges Claude, who in 1930 built the first OTEC plant in Cuba. The system produced 22 kilowatts of electricity with a low-pressure turbine. In 1935, Claude constructed another plant aboard a 10,000-ton cargo vessel moored off the coast of Brazil. However, weather and waves destroyed both plants before they became net power generators. (Net power is the amount of power generated after subtracting power needed to run the system.)

In 1956, French scientists designed another 3-megawatt OTEC plant for Abidjan, Ivory Coast, West Africa. The plant was never completed, however, because it was too expensive.

The United States became involved in OTEC research in 1974 with the establishment of the Natural Energy Laboratory of Hawaii Authority. The laboratory has become one of the world's leading test facilities for OTEC technology.

Ocean Thermal Energy Conversion Technologies

There are three kinds of OTEC systems: closed-cycle, open-cycle, and hybrid.

Closed Cycle. Closed-cycle systems use fluids with a low boiling point, such as ammonia, to rotate a turbine to generate electricity. Warm surface seawater is pumped through a heat exchanger, where the low-boiling-point fluid is vaporized. The expanding vapor turns the turbo-generator. Cold deep seawater—which is pumped through a second heat exchanger—then condenses the vapor back into a liquid that is then recycled through the system.

In 1979, the Natural Energy Laboratory and several private-sector partners developed the mini OTEC experiment, which achieved the first successful at-sea production of net electrical power from closed-cycle OTEC. The mini OTEC vessel was moored 1.5 miles (2.4 km) off the Hawaiian coast and produced enough net electricity to illuminate the ship's light bulbs and run its computers and televisions.

In 1999, the Natural Energy Laboratory tested a 250-kW pilot OTEC closed-cycle plant, the largest such plant ever put into operation.

Open-Cycle. Open-cycle systems use the tropical oceans' warm surface water to make electricity. When warm seawater is placed in a low-pressure container, it boils. The expanding steam drives a low-pressure turbine attached to an electrical generator. The steam, which has left its salt behind in the low-pressure container, is almost pure, fresh water. It is condensed back into a liquid by exposure to cold temperatures from deep-ocean water.

In 1984, the Solar Energy Research Institute (now the National Renewable Energy Laboratory) developed a vertical-spout evaporator to convert warm seawater into low-pressure steam for open-cycle plants. Energy conversion efficiencies as high as 97 percent were achieved. In May 1993, an open-cycle OTEC plant at Keahole Point, Hawaii, produced 50,000 watts of electricity during a net power-producing experiment.

Hybrid. Hybrid systems combine the features of closed- and open-cycle systems. In a hybrid system, warm seawater enters a vacuum chamber, where it is flash-evaporated into steam, similar to the open-cycle evaporation process. The steam vaporizes a low-boiling-point fluid (in a closed-cycle loop) that drives a turbine to produce electricity.

Complementary Technologies

OTEC has potential benefits beyond power production. For example, spent cold seawater from an OTEC plant can chill fresh water in a heat exchanger or flow directly into a cooling system. Simple systems of this type have air-conditioned buildings at the Natural Energy Laboratory for several years.

OTEC technology also supports chilled-soil agriculture. When cold seawater flows through underground pipes, it chills the surrounding soil. The temperature difference between plant roots in the cool soil and plant leaves in the warm air allows many plants that evolved in temperate climates to be grown in the subtropics. The Natural Energy Laboratory maintains a demonstration garden near its OTEC plant with more than 100 fruits and vegetables, many of which would not normally survive in Hawaii.

Aquaculture is perhaps the most well-known byproduct of OTEC. Cold-water delicacies, such as salmon and lobster, thrive in the nutrient-rich, deep seawater culled from the OTEC process. Microalgae such as Spirulina, a health food supplement, also can be cultivated in the deep-ocean water.

Finally, an advantage of open or hybrid-cycle OTEC plants is the production of fresh water from seawater. Theoretically, an OTEC plant that generates two megawatts of net electricity could produce about 14,118.3 cubic feet (4,300 cubic meters) of desalinated water each day.

Environmental and Economic Challenges

In general, careful site selection is key to keeping the environmental effects of OTEC minimal. OTEC experts believe that appropriate spacing of plants throughout tropical oceans can nearly eliminate any potential negative effects on ocean temperatures and marine life.

OTEC power plants require substantial capital investment upfront. OTEC researchers believe private sector firms probably will be unwilling to make the enormous initial investment required to build large-scale plants until the price of fossil fuels increases dramatically or national governments provide financial incentives. Another factor hindering the commercialization of OTEC is that there are only a few hundred land-based sites in the tropics where deep-ocean water is close enough to shore to make OTEC plants feasible.

Tidal Energy

Some of the oldest ocean energy technologies use tidal power. All coastal areas experience two high tides and two low tides over a period of slightly more than 24 hours. For those tidal differences to be harnessed into electricity, the difference between high and low tides must be more than 16 feet (or at least 5 meters). However, there are only about 40 sites on Earth with tidal ranges of this magnitude.

Currently, there are no tidal power plants in the United States, but conditions are good for tidal power generation in the Pacific Northwest and the Atlantic Northeast regions.

Tidal Energy Technologies

Tidal energy technologies include barrages or dams, tidal fences, and tidal turbines.

Barrages or Dams. A barrage or dam is typically used to convert tidal energy into electricity by forcing water through turbines, which activate a generator. Gates and turbines are installed along the dam. When the tides produce an adequate difference in the level of water on opposite sides of the dam, the gates are opened. The water then flows through the turbines. The turbines turn an electric generator to produce electricity.

Tidal Fences. Tidal fences look like giant turnstiles. They can reach across channels between small islands or across straits between the mainland and an island. The turnstiles spin via tidal currents typical of coastal waters. Some of these currents run at 5–8 knots (5.6–9 miles per hour) and generate as much energy as winds of much higher velocity. Because seawater has a much higher density than air, ocean currents carry significantly more energy than air currents (wind).

Tidal Turbines. Tidal turbines look like wind turbines. They are arrayed underwater in rows, as in some wind farms. The turbines function best where coastal currents run between 3.6 and 4.9 knots (4 and 5.5 mph). In currents of that speed, a 49.2-foot (15-meter) diameter tidal turbine can generate as much energy as a 197-foot (60-meter) diameter wind turbine. Ideal locations for tidal turbine farms are close to shore in water 65.5–98.5 feet (20–30 meters) deep.

Environmental and Economic Challenges

Tidal power plants that dam estuaries can impede sea life migration, and silt build-ups behind such facilities can affect local ecosystems. Tidal fences may also disturb sea life migration. Newly developed tidal turbines ultimately may prove to be the least environmentally damaging of the tidal power technologies because they do not block migratory paths.

It does not cost much to operate tidal power plants, but their construction costs are high, which lengthens payback periods. As a result, the cost per kilowatt-hour of tidal power is not competitive with conventional fossil fuel power.

Wave Energy

Wave energy technologies extract energy directly from surface waves or from pressure fluctuations below the surface. Renewable energy analysts believe there is enough energy in ocean waves to provide up to 2 terawatts of electricity. (A terawatt is equal to a trillion watts.)

However, wave energy cannot be harnessed everywhere. Wave power-rich areas of the world include the western coasts of Scotland, northern Canada, southern Africa, and Australia as well as the northeastern and northwestern coasts of the United States. In the Pacific Northwest alone, it is feasible that wave energy could produce 40–70 kilowatts (kW) per 3.3 feet (1 meter) of western coastline.

Wave Energy Technologies

Wave energy can be converted into electricity by offshore or onshore systems.

Offshore Systems. Offshore systems are situated in deep water, typically of more than 131 feet (40 meters). Sophisticated mechanisms—such as the Salter Duck—use the bobbing motion of the waves to power a pump that creates electricity. Other offshore devices use hoses connected to floats that ride the waves. The rise and fall of the float stretches and relaxes the hose, which pressurizes the water, which, in turn, rotates a turbine.

Specially built seagoing vessels can also capture the energy of offshore waves. These floating platforms create electricity by funneling waves through internal turbines and then back into the sea.

Onshore Systems. Built along shorelines, onshore wave power systems extract the energy of breaking waves. Onshore system technologies include:

Oscillating Water Columns: Oscillating water columns consist of a partially submerged concrete or steel structure that has an opening to the sea below the waterline. It encloses a column of air above a column of water. As waves enter the air column, they cause the water column to rise and fall. This alternately compresses and depressurizes the air column. As the wave retreats, the air is drawn back through the turbine as a result of the reduced air pressure on the ocean side of the turbine.

Tapchans: Tapchans, or tapered channel systems, consist of a tapered channel that feeds into a reservoir constructed on cliffs above sea level. The narrowing of the channel causes the waves to increase in height as they move toward the cliff face. The waves spill over the walls of the channel into the reservoir, and the stored water is then fed through a turbine.

Pendulor Devices: Pendulor wave-power devices consist of a rectangular box that is open to the sea at one end. A flap is hinged over the opening, and the action of the waves causes the flap to swing back and forth. The motion powers a hydraulic pump and a generator.

Environmental and Economic Challenges

Careful site selection is the key to keeping the environmental effects of wave power systems to a minimum. Wave energy system planners can choose sites that preserve scenic shorefronts and avoid areas where wave energy systems can significantly alter flow patterns of sediment on the ocean floor.

Economically, wave power systems have a hard time competing with traditional power sources. However, the costs to produce wave energy are coming down. Some European experts predict that wave power devices will find lucrative niche markets. Once built, they have low operation and maintenance costs because their fuel—seawater—is free.

FUTURE OF RENEWABLE ENERGY

The National Renewable Energy Laboratory's "Renewable Energy Futures" study assesses the extent to which future US electricity demand could be supplied by commercially available renewable generation technologies under a range of assumptions for generation technology improvement, electric system operational constraints, and electricity demand. That study estimates that by 2050, 80 percent of US electricity demand could be generated from renewable energy technologies. The analysis shows that realizing this significant transformation of the electricity sector would require:

- Sustained build-up of many renewable resources in all regions of the United States
- Deployment of an appropriate mix of renewable technologies from the abundant and diverse US renewable resource supply in a way that accommodates institutional or operational constraints to the electricity system, including constraints to transmission expansion, system flexibility, and resource accessibility
- Establishment of mechanisms to ensure adequate contribution to planning and operating reserves from conventional generators, dispatchable renewable generators, storage, and demand-side technologies
- Increasing the flexibility of the electric system through the adoption of some combination of storage technologies, demand-side options, ramping of conventional generation, more flexible dispatch of conventional generators, energy curtailment, and transmission
- Expansion of transmission infrastructure to enable access to diverse and remote resources and greater reserve sharing and balancing over larger geographic areas.

These general requirements indicate that many aspects of the electric system may need to evolve substantially for high levels of renewable electricity to be deployed.

SOURCE MATERIAL

US Department of Energy. "Renewable Energy." http://www.energy.gov /science-innovation/energy-sources/renewable-energy.

————. "Renewable Electricity Generation." Office of Energy Efficiency and Renewable Energy. http://energy.gov/eere/renewables.
National Renewable Energy Laboratory. "Science and Technology Highlights." http://www.nrel.gov/research/highlights.html.

FURTHER READING

Natural Resources Defense Council. "Renewable Energy for America: Harvesting the Benefits of Homegrown, Renewable Energy." http://www.nrdc.org/energy/renewables/.
Union of Concerned Scientists. "Renewable Energy." http://www.ucsusa.org/our-work/energy/our-energy-choices/our-energy-choices-renewable-energy#.VYmyzs6XISQ.
US Environmental Protection Agency. "Clean Energy." http://www.epa.gov/cleanenergy/.

Appendix A: Timeline

1828   Carl Sprengel formulated the Law of the Minimum stating that economic growth is limited not by the total of resources available, but by the scarcest resource.

1845   First use of the term "carrying capacity" in a report by the U.S. Secretary of State to the Senate.

1849   Establishment of the US Department of the Interior.

1851   Henry David Thoreau delivers an address to the Concord (Massachusetts) Lyceum declaring that "in Wildness is the preservation of the World." In 1863, this address is published posthumously as the essay "Walking" in Thoreau's *Excursions*.

1854   Henry David Thoreau publishes *Walden; or, Life in the Woods.*

1860   Henry David Thoreau delivers an address to the Middlesex (Massachusetts) Agricultural Society, entitled "The Succession of Forest Trees," in which he analyzes aspects of what later came to be understood as forest ecology and urges farmers to plant trees in natural patterns of succession.

1862   John Ruskin publishes *Unto This Last*, which contains a proto-environmental indictment of the effects of unrestricted industrial expansion on both human beings and the natural world.

The book influenced Mahatma Gandhi, William Morris and Patrick Geddes.

1864   George Perkins Marsh publishes *Man and Nature; or, Physical Geography as Modified by Human Action* (revised 1874 as *The Earth as Modified by Human Action*), the first systematic analysis of humanity's destructive impact on the natural environment and a work which becomes (in Lewis Mumford's words) "the fountainhead of the conservation movement."

1866   The term "ecology" is coined (in German as *Oekologie* by Ernst Heinrich Philipp August Haeckel (1834–1919) in his *Generelle Morphologie der Organismen.*

The American Society for the Prevention of Cruelty to Animals is founded.

1869   Samuel Bowles publishes Our New West. Records of Travel between the Mississippi River and the Pacific Ocean, an influential traveller's account of the wilds and peoples of the West, in which he advocates preservation of other scenic areas such as Niagara Falls and the Adirondacks.

1872   The term "acid rain" is coined by Robert Angus Smith in the book Air and Rain.

World's first national park, Yellowstone National Park.

Arbor Day was founded by J. Sterling Morton of Nebraska City, Nebraska.

1873   International Meteorological Organization is formed.

1874   Charles Hallock establishes Forest and Stream magazine sparking a U.S. national debate about ethics and hunting.

German graduate student Othmar Zeidler first synthesises DDT, later to be used as an insecticide.

1876   British River Pollution Control Act makes it illegal to dump sewage into a stream.

1879   U.S. Geological Survey formed. John Wesley Powell, explorer of
            the Colorado River a decade earlier, will become its head in
            March 1881.

1890   Yosemite National Park Bill, established the Yosemite and Se-
            quoia National Parks in California.

1892   John Muir, (1838–1914), founded the Sierra Club.

1895   Sewage cleanup in London means the return of some fish spe-
            cies (grilse, whitebait, flounder, and eel, smelt) to the River
            Thames.

1902   George Washington Carver writes How to Build Up Worn Out
            Soils.

1903   March 14, US President Theodore Roosevelt creates first Na-
            tional Bird Preserve, (the beginning of the Wildlife Refuge sys-
            tem), on Pelican Island, Florida.

            7300 hectares of land in the Lake District of the Andes foothills
            in Patagonia are donated by Francisco Moreno as the first park,
            Nahuel Huapi National Park, in what eventually becomes the
            National Park System of Argentina.

1905   The term "smog" is coined by Henry Antoine Des Voeux in a
            London meeting to express concern over air pollution.

            The National Audubon Society is founded.

1906   Antiquities Act, passed by US Congress which authorized the
            president to set aside national monument sites.

1908   Muir Woods National Monument was established on January 9
            and now governed by the National Park Service.

            The National Conservation Commission, appointed in June by
            President Roosevelt.

1909   US President Theodore Roosevelt convenes the North Ameri-
            can Conservation Conference, held in Washington, D.C. and

attended by representatives of Canada, Newfoundland, Mexico, and the United States.

1913   US Congress enacts law which destroyed the Hetch Hetchy Valley.

1916   US Congress created the National Park Service.

1918   The Save-the-Redwoods League founded to protect the remaining Coast Redwood trees.

Congress approves the Migratory Bird Treaty Act of 1918, which implements a 1916 Convention (between the U.S. and Britain, acting for Canada) for the Protection of Migratory birds, and establishes responsibility for international migratory bird protection.

1919   The National Parks Conservation Association is founded.

1924   The death of English textile worker Nellie Kershaw from asbestosis was the first account of disease attributed to occupational asbestos exposure.

1927   Great Mississippi Flood.

1928   Thomas Midgley, Jr. develops chlorofluorocarbons (CFC's) as a non-toxic refrigerant.

1929   the Swann Chemical Company develops polychlorinated biphenyls (PCBs) for transformer coolant use. They were banned from production in the US in 1976.

1930-1940   The Dust Bowl, widespread land degradation due to drought in the North American prairie.

1934   Fish and Wildlife Coordination Act.

1935   Soil Conservation and Domestic Allotment Act.

The Wilderness Society is founded.

1936   The National Wildlife Federation is founded.

1939   Insecticidal properties of DDT discovered by Paul Hermann
            Müller.

1948   International Union for Conservation of Nature and Natural
            Resources (IUCN) founded.

1949   First known dioxin exposure incident, in a West Virginia herbi-
            cide production plant..

1951   The Nature Conservancy founded.

            World Meteorological Organization (WMO) established by the
            United Nations.

            Drinking water fluoridation becomes an official policy of the
            U.S. Public Health Service to reduce tooth decay.

1954   The first nuclear power plant to generate electricity opened in
            Soviet Union.

            Watershed Protection and Flood Prevention Act

1955   Air Pollution Control Act

1956   Fish and Wildlife Act.

1958   Mauna Loa Observatory starts monitoring of atmospheric car-
            bon dioxide levels.

1960   Federal Water Pollution Control Act

1961   World Wildlife Fund (WWF) founded.

1962   Rachel Carson publishes Silent Spring.

            The first White House Conservation Conference takes place.

1963   The Partial Nuclear Test Ban Treaty is signed by the U.S., the
            U.K. and the U.S.S.R.

            Clean Air Act

1964   Wilderness Act.

1965   In the Storm King case, a judge rules that aesthetic impacts could be considered in deciding whether Consolidated Edison could demolish a mountain, a landmark case in environmental law.

Water Quality Act, Solid Waste Disposal Act, Amendments to the Clean Air Act

1966   National Wildlife Refuge System Act, Fur Seal Act, National Historic Preservation Act

1967   Environmental Defense Fund founded.

Torrey Canyon oil spill

Amendments to the Clean Air Act.

1968   National Trails System Act, Wild and Scenic Rivers Act.

1969   National Environmental Policy Act including the first requirements on Environmental impact assessment.

Friends of the Earth founded.

1970   First Earth Day celebrated in United States

US Environmental Protection Agency established.

Center for Science in the Public Interest founded.

Environmental Action founded.

Natural Resources Defense Council founded.

Norman Borlaug, the father of the Green Revolution, wins the Nobel Peace Prize.

Occupational Safety and Health Act

1971   Greenpeace founded in Vancouver, Canada.

1972   The Conference on the Human Environment, held in Stockholm, Sweden.

United Nations Environment Programme founded as a result of the Stockholm conference.

Oslo Convention on dumping waste at sea, later merged with the Paris Convention on land-based sources of marine pollution into the Convention for the Protection of the Marine Environment of the North-East Atlantic.

Marine Mammal Protection Act, Marine Protection, Research, and Sanctuaries Act (also known as Ocean Dumping Act), Noise Control Act, Clean Water Act, Coastal Zone Management Act.

DDT banned.

The Trust for Public Land founded.

1973	Convention on International Trade in Endangered Species of Wild Fauna and Flora (CITES), Endangered Species Preservation Act.
1974	National Reserves Management Act.
1975	Energy Policy and Conservation Act.
1976	Resource Conservation and Recovery Act (RCRA)
1977	Surface Mining Control and Reclamation Act, Soil and Water Resources Conservation Act.
1979	Convention on Long-Range Transboundary Air Pollution.
	Three Mile Island accident
1980	Global 2000 Report to the President
	Alaska National Interest Lands Conservation Act, Low Level Radioactive Waste Policy Act
1982	Coastal Barrier Resources Act.
	United Nations Convention on the Law of the Sea (UNCLOS), Nuclear Waste Policy Act

1984   Bhopal disaster in Indian

1985   Rainforest Action Network founded.

Antarctic ozone hole discovered.

1986   Chernobyl, world's worst nuclear power accident occurs at a plant in Ukraine.

Emergency Wetlands Resources Act, National Appliance Energy Conservation Act

1988   Ocean Dumping Ban Act.

Intergovernmental Panel on Climate Change (IPCC) established

1989   Exxon Valdez oil spill.

Montreal Protocol enacted on substances that deplete the ozone layer

1990   National Environmental Education Act.

Clean Air Act—major amendment

Dolphin safe label introduced.

1991   Protocol on Environmental Protection to the Antarctic Treaty signed

1992   Earth Summit held in Rio de Janeiro

1994   United Nations Convention to Combat Desertification.

First genetically modified food crop released to the market.

1997   U.S. Senate unanimously passed by a 95–0 vote the Byrd-Hagel Resolution, which stated that the U.S. should not be a signatory to any protocol that did not include binding targets and timetables for developing as well as industrialized nations.

The Kyoto Protocol agreed.

2001   U.S. rejects Kyoto Protocol.

            IPCC Third Assessment Report.

2004   Earthquake causes tsunamis in the Indian Ocean, killing nearly
            a quarter of a million people.

2005   Hurricanes Katrina, Rita, and Wilma cause widespread destruc-
            tion and environmental harm

2006   Former US vice president Al Gore releases *An Inconvenient
            Truth*.

2007   IPCC Fourth Assessment Report.

2014   IPCC Fifth Assessment Report.

Appendix B: Glossary

TERMS

Abandoned Well: A well whose use has been permanently discontinued or which is in a state of such disrepair that it cannot be used for its intended purpose.

Abatement: Reducing the degree or intensity of, or eliminating, pollution.

Abatement Debris: Waste from remediation activities.

Absorbed Dose: In exposure assessment, the amount of a substance that penetrates an exposed organism's absorption barriers (e.g. skin, lung tissue, gastrointestinal tract) through physical or biological processes. The term is synonymous with internal dose.

Absorption: The uptake of water , other fluids, or dissolved chemicals by a cell or an organism (as tree roots absorb dissolved nutrients in soil.)

Absorption Barrier: Any of the exchange sites of the body that permit uptake of various substances at different rates (e.g. skin, lung tissue, and gastrointestinal-tract wall)

Accident Site: The location of an unexpected occurrence, failure or loss, either at a plant or along a transportation route, resulting in a release of hazardous materials.

Acclimatization: The physiological and behavioral adjustments of an organism to changes in its environment.

Acid: A corrosive solution with a pH less than 7.

Acid Aerosol: Acidic liquid or solid particles small enough to become airborne. High concentrations can irritate the lungs and have been associated with respiratory diseases like asthma.

Acid Deposition: A complex chemical and atmospheric phenomenon that occurs when emissions of sulfur and nitrogen compounds and other substances are transformed by chemical processes in the atmosphere, often far from the original sources, and then deposited on earth in either wet or dry form. The wet forms, popularly called "acid rain," can fall to earth as rain, snow, or fog. The dry forms are acidic gases or particulates.

Acid Mine Drainage: Drainage of water from areas that have been mined for coal or other mineral ores. The water has a low pH because of its contact with sulfur-bearing material and is harmful to aquatic organisms.

Acid Neutralizing Capacity: Measure of ability of a base (e.g. water or soil) to resist changes in pH.

Acid Rain: (See: acid deposition.)

Acidic: The condition of water or soil that contains a sufficient amount of acid substances to lower the pH below 7.0.

Action Levels: 1. Regulatory levels recommended by EPA for enforcement by FDA and USDA when pesticide residues occur in food or feed commodities for reasons other than the direct application of the pesticide. As opposed to "tolerances" which are established for residues occurring as a direct result of proper usage, action levels are set for inadvertent residues resulting from previous legal use or accidental contamination. 2. In the Superfund program, the existence of a contaminant concentration in the environment high enough to warrant action or trigger a response under SARA and the National Oil and Hazardous Substances Contingency Plan. The term is also used in other regulatory programs. (See: tolerances.)

Activated Carbon: A highly adsorbent form of carbon used to remove odors and toxic substances from liquid or gaseous emissions. In waste treatment, it is used to remove dissolved organic matter from waste drinking water. It is also used in motor vehicle evaporative control systems.

Activated Sludge: Product that results when primary effluent is mixed with bacteria-laden sludge and then agitated and aerated to promote biological treatment, speeding the breakdown of organic matter in raw sewage undergoing secondary waste treatment.

Activator: A chemical added to a pesticide to increase its activity.

Active Ingredient: In any pesticide product, the component that kills, or otherwise controls, target pests. Pesticides are regulated primarily on the basis of active ingredients.

Activity Plans: Written procedures in a school's asbestos-management plan that detail the steps a Local Education Agency (LEA) will follow in performing the initial and additional cleaning, operation and maintenance-program tasks; periodic surveillance; and reinspection required by the Asbestos Hazard Emergency Response Act (AHERA).

Acute Effect: An adverse effect on any living organism which results in severe symptoms that develop rapidly; symptoms often subside after the exposure stops.

Acute Exposure: A single exposure to a toxic substance which may result in severe biological harm or death. Acute exposures are usually characterized as lasting no longer than a day, as compared to longer, continuing exposure over a period of time.

Acute Toxicity: The ability of a substance to cause severe biological harm or death soon after a single exposure or dose. Also, any poisonous effect resulting from a single short-term exposure to a toxic substance. (See: chronic toxicity, toxicity.)

Adaptation: Changes in an organism's physiological structure or function or habits that allow it to survive in new surroundings.

Add-on Control Device: An air pollution control device such as carbon absorber or incinerator that reduces the pollution in an exhaust gas. The control device usually does not affect the process being controlled and thus is "add-on" technology, as opposed to a scheme to control pollution through altering the basic process itself.

Adequately Wet: Asbestos containing material that is sufficiently mixed or penetrated with liquid to prevent the release of particulates.

Administered Dose: In exposure assessment, the amount of a substance given to a test subject (human or animal) to determine dose-response relationships. Since exposure to chemicals is usually inadvertent, this quantity is often called potential dose.

Administrative Order: A legal document signed by EPA directing an individual, business, or other entity to take corrective action or refrain from an activity. It describes the violations and actions to be taken, and can be enforced in court. Such orders may be issued, for example, as a result of an administrative complaint whereby the respondent is ordered to pay a penalty for violations of a statute.

Administrative Order On Consent: A legal agreement signed by EPA and an individual, business, or other entity through which the violator agrees to pay for correction of violations, take the required corrective or cleanup actions, or refrain from an activity. It describes the actions to be taken, may be subject to a comment period, applies to civil actions, and can be enforced in court.

Administrative Procedures Act: A law that spells out procedures and requirements related to the promulgation of regulations.

Administrative Record: All documents which EPA considered or relied on in selecting the response action at a Superfund site, culminating in the record of decision for remedial action or, an action memorandum for removal actions.

Adsorption: Removal of a pollutant from air or water by collecting the pollutant on the surface of a solid material; e.g., an advanced method of treating waste in which activated carbon removes organic matter from waste-water.

Adulterants: Chemical impurities or substances that by law do not belong in a food, or pesticide.

Adulterated: 1. Any pesticide whose strength or purity falls below the quality stated on its label. 2. A food, feed, or product that contains illegal pesticide residues.

Advanced Treatment: A level of wastewater treatment more stringent than secondary treatment; requires an 85-percent reduction in conventional pollutant concentration or a significant reduction in non-conventional pollutants. Sometimes called tertiary treatment.

Advanced Wastewater Treatment: Any treatment of sewage that goes beyond the secondary or biological water treatment stage and includes the removal of nutrients such as phosphorus and nitrogen and a high percentage of suspended solids. (See primary, secondary treatment.)

Adverse Effects Data: FIFRA requires a pesticide registrant to submit data to EPA on any studies or other information regarding unreasonable adverse effects of a pesticide at any time after its registration.

Advisory: A non-regulatory document that communicates risk information to those who may have to make risk management decisions.

Aerated Lagoon: A holding and/or treatment pond that speeds up the natural process of biological decomposition of organic waste by stimulating the growth and activity of bacteria that degrade organic waste.

Aeration: A process which promotes biological degradation of organic matter in water. The process may be passive (as when waste is exposed to air), or active (as when a mixing or bubbling device introduces the air).

Aeration Tank: A chamber used to inject air into water.

Aerobic: Life or processes that require, or are not destroyed by, the presence of oxygen. (See: anaerobic.)

Aerobic Treatment: Process by which microbes decompose complex organic compounds in the presence of oxygen and use the liberated energy for reproduction and growth. (Such processes include extended aeration, trickling filtration, and rotating biological contactors.)

Aerosol: 1. Small droplets or particles suspended in the atmosphere, typically containing sulfur. They are usually emitted naturally (e.g. in volcanic eruptions) and as the result of anthropogenic (human) activities such as burning fossil fuels. 2. The pressurized gas used to propel substances out of a container.

Aerosol: A finely divided material suspended in air or other gaseous environment.

Affected Landfill: Under the Clean Air Act, landfills that meet criteria for capacity, age, and emissions rates set by the EPA. They are required to collect and combust their gas emissions.

Affected Public: 1.The people who live and/or work near a hazardous waste site. 2. The human population adversely impacted following exposure to a toxic pollutant in food, water, air, or soil.

Afterburner: In incinerator technology, a burner located so that the combustion gases are made to pass through its flame in order to remove smoke and odors. It may be attached to or be separated from the incinerator proper.

Age Tank: A tank used to store a chemical solution of known concentration for feed to a chemical feeder. Also called a day tank.

Agent: Any physical, chemical, or biological entity that can be harmful to an organism (synonymous with stressors.)

Agent Orange: A toxic herbicide and defoliant used in the Vietnam conflict, containing 2,4,5-trichlorophen-oxyacetic acid (2,4,5-T) and 2-4 dichlorophenoxyacetic acid (2,4-D) with trace amounts of dioxin.

Agricultural Pollution: Farming wastes, including runoff and leaching of pesticides and fertilizers; erosion and dust from plowing; improper disposal of animal manure and carcasses; crop residues, and debris.

Agricultural Waste: Poultry and livestock manure, and residual materials in liquid or solid form generated from the production and marketing of poultry, livestock or fur-bearing animals; also includes grain, vegetable, and fruit harvest residue.

Agroecosystem: Land used for crops, pasture, and livestock; the adjacent uncultivated land that supports other vegetation and wildlife; and the associated atmosphere, the underlying soils, groundwater, and drainage networks.

AHERA Designated Person (ADP): A person designated by a Local Education Agency to ensure that the AHERA requirements for asbestos management and abatement are properly implemented.

Air Binding: Situation where air enters the filter media and harms both the filtration and backwash processes.

Air Changes Per Hour (ACH): The movement of a volume of air in a given period of time; if a house has one air change per hour, it means that the air in the house will be replaced in a one-hour period.

Air Cleaning: Indoor-air quality-control strategy to remove various airborne particulates and/or gases from the air. Most common methods are particulate filtration, electrostatic precipitation, and gas sorption.

Air Contaminant: Any particulate matter, gas, or combination thereof, other than water vapor. (See: air pollutant.)

Air Curtain: A method of containing oil spills. Air bubbling through a perforated pipe causes an upward water flow that slows the spread of oil. It can also be used to stop fish from entering polluted water.

Air Exchange Rate: The rate at which outside air replaces indoor air in a given space.

Air Gap: Open vertical gap or empty space that separates drinking water supply to be protected from another water system in a treatment plant or other location. The open gap protects the drinking water from contamination by backflow or back siphonage.

Air Handling Unit: Equipment that includes a fan or blower, heating and/or cooling coils, regulator controls, condensate drain pans, and air filters.

Air Mass: A large volume of air with certain meteorological or polluted characteristics--e.g., a heat inversion or smogginess--while in one location. The characteristics can change as the air mass moves away.

Air Monitoring: (See: monitoring.)

Air/Oil Table: The surface between the vadose zone and ambient oil; the pressure of oil in the porous medium is equal to atmospheric pressure.

Air Padding: Pumping dry air into a container to assist with the withdrawal of liquid or to force a liquefied gas such as chlorine out of the container.

Air Permeability: Permeability of soil with respect to air. Important to the design of soil-gas surveys. Measured in darcys or centimeters-per-second.

Air Plenum: Any space used to convey air in a building, furnace, or structure. The space above a suspended ceiling is often used as an air plenum.

Air Pollutant: Any substance in air that could, in high enough concentration, harm man, other animals, vegetation, or material. Pollutants may include almost any natural or artificial composition of airborne matter capable of being airborne. They may be in the form of solid particles, liquid droplets, gases, or in combination thereof. Generally, they fall into two main groups: (1) those emitted directly from identifiable sources and (2) those produced in the air by interaction between two or more primary pollutants, or by reaction with normal atmospheric constituents, with or without photoactivation. Exclusive of pollen, fog, and dust, which are of natural origin, about 100 contaminants have been identified. Air pollutants are often grouped in categories for ease in classification; some of he categories are: solids, sulfur compounds, volatile organic chemicals, particulate matter, nitrogen compounds, oxygen compounds, halogen compounds, radioactive compound, and odors.

Air Pollution: The presence of contaminants or pollutant substances in the air that interfere with human health or welfare, or produce other harmful environmental effects.

Air Pollution Control Device: Mechanism or equipment that cleans emissions generated by a source (e.g. an incinerator, industrial smokestack, or an automobile exhaust system) by removing pollutants that would otherwise be released to the atmosphere.

Air Pollution Episode: A period of abnormally high concentration of air pollutants, often due to low winds and temperature inversion, that can cause illness and death. (See: episode, pollution.)

Air Quality Control Region:

Air Quality Criteria: The levels of pollution and lengths of exposure above which adverse health and welfare effects may occur.

Air Quality Standards: The level of pollutants prescribed by regulations that are not be exceeded during a given time in a defined area.

Air Sparging: Injecting air or oxygen into an aquifer to strip or flush volatile contaminants as air bubbles up through The ground water and is captured by a vapor extraction system.

Air Stripping: A treatment system that removes volatile organic compounds (VOCs) from contaminated ground water or surface water by forcing an airstream through the water and causing the compounds to evaporate.

Air Toxics: Any air pollutant for which a national ambient air quality standard (NAAQS) does not exist (i.e. excluding ozone, carbon monoxide, PM-10, sulfur dioxide, nitrogen oxide) that may reasonably be anticipated to cause cancer; respiratory, cardiovascular, or developmental effects; reproductive dysfunctions, neurological disorders, heritable gene mutations, or other serious or irreversible chronic or acute health effects in humans.

Airborne Particulates: Total suspended particulate matter found in the atmosphere as solid particles or liquid droplets. Chemical composition of particulates varies widely, depending on location and time of year. Sources of airborne particulates include: dust, emissions from industrial processes, combustion products from the burning of wood and coal, combustion products associated with motor vehicle or non-road engine exhausts, and reactions to gases in the atmosphere.

Airborne Release: Release of any pollutant into the air.

Alachlor: A herbicide, marketed under the trade name Lasso, used mainly to control weeds in corn and soybean fields.

Alar: Trade name for daminozide, a pesticide that makes apples redder, firmer, and less likely to drop off trees before growers are ready to pick them. It is also used to a lesser extent on peanuts, tart cherries, concord grapes, and other fruits.

Aldicarb: An insecticide sold under the trade name Temik. It is made from ethyl isocyanate.

Algae: Simple rootless plants that grow in sunlit waters in proportion to the amount of available nutrients. They can affect water quality adversely by lowering the dissolved oxygen in the water. They are food for fish and small aquatic animals.

Algal Blooms: Sudden spurts of algal growth, which can affect water quality adversely and indicate potentially hazardous changes in local water chemistry.

Algicide: Substance or chemical used specifically to kill or control algae.

Aliquot: A measured portion of a sample taken for analysis. One or more aliquots make up a sample. (See: duplicate.)

Alkaline: The condition of water or soil which contains a sufficient amount of alkali substance to raise the pH above 7.0.

Alkalinity: The capacity of bases to neutralize acids. An example is lime added to lakes to decrease acidity.

Allergen: A substance that causes an allergic reaction in individuals sensitive to it.

Alluvial: Relating to and/or sand deposited by flowing water.

Alternate Method: Any method of sampling and analyzing for an air or water pollutant that is not a reference or equivalent method but that has been demonstrated in specific cases-to EPA's satisfaction-to produce results adequate for compliance monitoring.

Alternative Compliance: A policy that allows facilities to choose among methods for achieving emission-reduction or risk-reduction instead of command-and control regulations that specify standards and how to meet them. Use of a theoretical emissions bubble over a facility to cap the amount of pollution emitted while allowing the company to choose where and how (within the facility) it complies.(See: bubble, emissions trading.)

Alternative Fuels: Substitutes for traditional liquid, oil-derived motor vehicle fuels like gasoline and diesel. Includes mixtures of alcohol-based fuels with gasoline, methanol, ethanol, compressed natural gas, and others.

Alternative Remedial Contract Strategy Contractors: Government contractors who provide project management and technical services to support remedial response activities at National Priorities List sites.

Ambient Air: Any unconfined portion of the atmosphere: open air, surrounding air.

Ambient Air Quality Standards: (See: Criteria Pollutants and National Ambient Air Quality Standards.)

Ambient Measurement: A measurement of the concentration of a substance or pollutant within the immediate environs of an organism; taken to relate it to the amount of possible exposure.

Ambient Medium: Material surrounding or contacting an organism (e.g. outdoor air, indoor air, water, or soil, through which chemicals or pollutants can reach the organism. (See: biological medium, environmental medium.)

Ambient Temperature: Temperature of the surrounding air or other medium.

Amprometric Titration: A way of measuring concentrations of certain substances in water using an electric current that flows during a chemical reaction.

Anaerobic: A life or process that occurs in, or is not destroyed by, the absence of oxygen.

Anaerobic Decomposition: Reduction of the net energy level and change in chemical composition of organic matter caused by microorganisms in an oxygen-free environment.

Animal Dander: Tiny scales of animal skin, a common indoor air pollutant.

Animal Studies: Investigations using animals as surrogates for humans with the expectation that the results are pertinent to humans.

Anisotropy: In hydrology, the conditions under which one or more hydraulic properties of an aquifer vary from a reference point.

Annular Space, Annulus: The space between two concentric tubes or casings, or between the casing and the borehole wall.

Antagonism: Interference or inhibition of the effect of one chemical by the action of another.

Antarctic "Ozone Hole": Refers to the seasonal depletion of ozone in the upper atmosphere above a large area of Antarctica. (See: Ozone Hole.)

Anti-Degradation Clause: Part of federal air quality and water quality requirements prohibiting deterioration where pollution levels are above the legal limit.

Anti-Microbial: An agent that kills microbes.

Applicable or Relevant and Appropriate Requirements (ARARs): Any state or federal statute that pertains to protection of human life and the environment in addressing specific conditions or use of a particular cleanup technology at a Superfund site,

Applied Dose: In exposure assessment, the amount of a substance in contact with the primary absorption boundaries of an organism (e.g. skin, lung tissue, gastrointestinal track) and available for absorption.

Aqueous: Something made up of water.

Aqueous Solubility: The maximum concentration of a chemical that will dissolve in pure water at a reference temperature.

Aquifer: An underground geological formation, or group of formations, containing water. Are sources of groundwater for wells and springs.

Aquifer Test: A test to determine hydraulic properties of an aquifer.

Aquitard: Geological formation that may contain groundwater but is not capable of transmitting significant quantities of it under normal hydraulic gradients. May function as confining bed.

Architectural Coatings: Coverings such as paint and roof tar that are used on exteriors of buildings.

Area of Review: In the UIC program, the area surrounding an injection well that is reviewed during the permitting process to determine if flow between aquifers will be induced by the injection operation.

Area Source: Any source of air pollution that is released over a relatively small area but which cannot be classified as a point source. Such sources may include vehicles and other small engines, small businesses and household activities, or biogenic sources such as a forest that releases hydrocarbons.

Aromatics: A type of hydrocarbon, such as benzene or toluene, with a specific type of ring structure. Aromatics are sometimes added to gasoline in order to increase octane. Some aromatics are toxic.

Arsenicals: Pesticides containing arsenic.

Artesian (Aquifer or Well): Water held under pressure in porous rock or soil confined by impermeable geological formations.

Asbestos: A mineral fiber that can pollute air or water and cause cancer or asbestosis when inhaled. EPA has banned or severely restricted its use in manufacturing and construction.

Asbestos Abatement: Procedures to control fiber release from asbestos-containing materials in a building or to remove them entirely, including removal, encapsulation, repair, enclosure, encasement, and operations and maintenance programs.

Asbestos Assessment: In the asbestos-in-schools program, the evaluation of the physical condition and potential for damage of all friable asbestos containing materials and thermal insulation systems.

Asbestos Program Manager: A building owner or designated representative who supervises all aspects of the facility asbestos management and control program.

Asbestos-Containing Waste Materials (ACWM): Mill tailings or any waste that contains commercial asbestos and is generated by a source covered by the Clean Air Act Asbestos NESHAPS.

Asbestosis: A disease associated with inhalation of asbestos fibers. The disease makes breathing progressively more difficult and can be fatal.

Ash: The mineral content of a product remaining after complete combustion.

Assay: A test for a specific chemical, microbe, or effect.

Assessment Endpoint: In ecological risk assessment, an explicit expression of the environmental value to be protected; includes both an ecological entity and specific attributed thereof. entity (e.g. salmon are a valued ecological entity; reproduction and population maintenance--the attribute--form an assessment endpoint.)

Assimilation: The ability of a body of water to purify itself of pollutants.

Assimilative Capacity: The capacity of a natural body of water to receive wastewaters or toxic materials without deleterious effects and without damage to aquatic life or humans who consume the water.

Association of Boards of Certification: An international organization representing boards which certify the operators of waterworks and wastewater facilities.

Attainment Area: An area considered to have air quality as good as or better than the national ambient air quality standards as defined in the Clean Air Act. An area may be an attainment area for one pollutant and a non-attainment area for others.

Attenuation: The process by which a compound is reduced in concentration over time, through absorption, adsorption, degradation, dilution, and/or transformation. an also be the decrease with distance of sight caused by attenuation of light by particulate pollution.

Attractant: A chemical or agent that lures insects or other pests by stimulating their sense of smell.

Attrition: Wearing or grinding down of a substance by friction. Dust from such processes contributes to air pollution.

Availability Session: Informal meeting at a public location where interested citizens can talk with EPA and state officials on a one-to-one basis.

Available Chlorine: A measure of the amount of chlorine available in chlorinated lime, hypochlorite compounds, and other materials used as a source of chlorine when compared with that of liquid or gaseous chlorines.

Avoided Cost: The cost a utility would incur to generate the next increment of electric capacity using its own resources; many landfill gas projects' buy back rates are based on avoided costs.

A-Scale Sound Level: A measurement of sound approximating the sensitivity of the human ear, used to note the intensity or annoyance level of sounds.

Back Pressure: A pressure that can cause water to backflow into the water supply when a user's waste water system is at a higher pressure than the public system.

Backflow/Back Siphonage: A reverse flow condition created by a difference in water pressures that causes water to flow back into the distribution pipes of a drinking water supply from any source other than the intended one.

Background Level: 1. The concentration of a substance in an environmental media (air, water, or soil) that occurs naturally or is not the result of human activities. 2. In exposure assessment the concentration of a substance in a defined control area, during a fixed period of time before, during, or after a data-gathering operation..

Backwashing: Reversing the flow of water back through the filter media to remove entrapped solids.

Backyard Composting: Diversion of organic food waste and yard trimmings from the municipal waste stream by composting hem in one's yard through controlled decomposition of organic matter by bacteria and fungi into a humus-like product. It is considered source reduction, not recycling, because the composted materials never enter the municipal waste stream.

Barrel Sampler: Open-ended steel tube used to collect soil samples.

BACT—Best Available Control Technology: An emission limitation based on the maximum degree of emission reduction (considering energy, environmental, and economic impacts) achievable through application of production processes and available methods, systems, and techniques. BACT does not permit emissions in excess of those allowed under any applicable Clean Air Act provisions. Use of the BACT concept is allowable on a case by case basis for major new or modified emissions sources in attainment areas and applies to each regulated pollutant.

Bacteria: (Singular: bacterium) Microscopic living organisms that can aid in pollution control by metabolizing organic matter in sewage, oil spills or other pollutants. However, bacteria in soil, water or air can also cause human, animal and plant health problems.

Bactericide: A pesticide used to control or destroy bacteria, typically in the home, schools, or hospitals.

Baffle: A flat board or plate, deflector, guide, or similar device constructed or placed in flowing water or slurry systems to cause more uniform flow velocities to absorb energy and to divert, guide, or agitate liquids.

Baffle Chamber: In incinerator design, a chamber designed to promote the settling of fly ash and coarse particulate matter by changing the direction and/or reducing the velocity of the gases produced by the combustion of the refuse or sludge.

Baghouse Filter: Large fabric bag, usually made of glass fibers, used to eliminate intermediate and large (greater than 20 PM in diameter) particles. This device operates like the bag of an electric vacuum cleaner, passing the air and smaller particles while entrapping the larger ones.

Bailer: A pipe with a valve at the lower end, used to remove slurry from the bottom or side of a well as it is being drilled, or to collect groundwater samples from wells or open boreholes. 2. A tube of varying length.

Baling: Compacting solid waste into blocks to reduce volume and simplify handling.

Ballistic Separator: A machine that sorts organic from inorganic matter for composting.

Band Application: The spreading of chemicals over, or next to, each row of plants in a field.

Banking: A system for recording qualified air emission reductions for later use in bubble, offset, or netting transactions. (See: emissions trading.)

Bar Screen: In wastewater treatment, a device used to remove large solids.

Barrier Coating(s): A layer of a material that obstructs or prevents passage of something through a surface that is to be protected; e.g., grout, caulk, or various sealing compounds; sometimes used with polyurethane membranes to prevent corrosion or oxidation of metal surfaces, chemical impacts on various materials, or, for example, to prevent radon infiltration through walls, cracks, or joints in a house.

Basal Application: In pesticides, the application of a chemical on plant stems or tree trunks just above the soil line.

Basalt: Consistent year-round energy use of a facility; also refers to the minimum amount of electricity supplied continually to a facility.

Bean Sheet: Common term for a pesticide data package record.

Bed Load: Sediment particles resting on or near the channel bottom that are pushed or rolled along by the flow of water.

BEN: EPA's computer model for analyzing a violator's economic gain from not complying with the law.

Bench-scale Tests: Laboratory testing of potential cleanup technologies (See: treatability studies.)

Benefit-Cost Analysis: An economic method for assessing the benefits and costs of achieving alternative health-based standards at given levels of health protection.

Benthic/Benthos: An organism that feeds on the sediment at the bottom of a water body such as an ocean, lake, or river.

Bentonite: A colloidal clay, expansible when moist, commonly used to provide a tight seal around a well casing.

Beryllium: An metal hazardous to human health when inhaled as an airborne pollutant. It is discharged by machine shops, ceramic and propellant plants, and foundries.

Best Available Control Measures (BACM): A term used to refer to the most effective measures (according to EPA guidance) for controlling small or dispersed particulates and other emissions from sources such as roadway dust, soot and ash from woodstoves and open burning of rush, timber, grasslands, or trash.

Best Available Control Technology (BACT): For any specific source, the currently available technology producing the greatest reduction of air pollutant emissions, taking into account energy, environmental, economic, and other costs.

Best Available Control Technology (BACT): The most stringent technology available for controlling emissions; major sources are required to use BACT, unless it can be demonstrated that it is not feasible for energy, environmental, or economic reasons.

Best Demonstrated Available Technology (BDAT): As identified by EPA, the most effective commercially available means of treating specific types of hazardous waste. The BDATs may change with advances in treatment technologies.

Best Management Practice (BMP): Methods that have been determined to be the most effective, practical means of preventing or reducing pollution from non-point sources.

Bimetal: Beverage containers with steel bodies and aluminum tops; handled differently from pure aluminum in recycling.

Bioaccumulants: Substances that increase in concentration in living organisms as they take in contaminated air, water, or food because the substances are very slowly metabolized or excreted. (See: biological magnification.)

Bioassay: A test to determine te relative strength of a substance by comparing its effect on a test organism with that of a standard preparation.

Bioavailabiliity: Degree of ability to be absorbed and ready to interact in organism metabolism.

Biochemical Oxygen Demand (BOD): A measure of the amount of oxygen consumed in the biological processes that break down organic matter in water. The greater the BOD, the greater the degree of pollution.

Bioconcentration: The accumulation of a chemical in tissues of a fish or other organism to levels greater than in the surrounding medium.

Biodegradable: Capable of decomposing under natural conditions.

Biodiversity: Refers to the variety and variability among living organisms and the ecological complexes in which they occur. Diversity can be defined as the number of different items and their relative frequencies. For biological diversity, these items are organized at many levels, ranging from complete ecosystems to the biochemical structures that are the molecular basis of heredity. Thus, the term encompasses different ecosystems, species, and genes.

Biological Contaminants: Living organisms or derivates (e.g. viruses, bacteria, fungi, and mammal and bird antigens) that can cause harmful health effects when inhaled, swallowed, or otherwise taken into the body.

Biological Control: In pest control, the use of animals and organisms that eat or otherwise kill or out-compete pests.

Biological Integrity: The ability to support and maintain balanced, integrated, functionality in the natural habitat of a given region. Concept is applied primarily in drinking water management.

Biological Magnification: Refers to the process whereby certain substances such as pesticides or heavy metals move up the food chain, work their way into rivers or lakes, and are eaten by aquatic organisms such as fish, which in turn are eaten by large birds, animals or humans. The substances become concentrated in tissues or internal organs as they move up the chain. (See: bioaccumulants.)

Biological Measurement: A measurement taken in a biological medium. For exposure assessment, it is related to the measurement is taken to related it to the established internal dose of a compound.

Biological Medium: One of the major component of an organism; e.g. blood, fatty tissue, lymph nodes or breath, in which chemicals can be stored or transformed. (See: ambient medium, environmental medium.)

Biological Oxidation: Decomposition of complex organic materials by microorganisms. Occurs in self-purification of water bodies and in activated sludge wastewater treatment.

Biological Oxygen Demand (BOD): An indirect measure of the concentration of biologically degradable material present in organic wastes. It usually reflects the amount of oxygen consumed in five days by biological processes breaking down organic waste.

Biological pesticides: Certain microorganism, including bacteria, fungi, viruses, and protozoa that are effective in controlling pests. These agents usually do not have toxic effects on animals and people and do not leave toxic or persistent chemical residues in the environment.

Biological Stressors: Organisms accidentally or intentionally dropped into habitats in which they do not evolve naturally; e.g. gypsy moths, Dutch elm disease, certain types of algae, and bacteria.

Biological Treatment: A treatment technology that uses bacteria to consume organic waste.

Biologically Effective Dose: The amount of a deposited or absorbed compound reaching the cells or target sites where adverse effect occur, or where the chemical interacts with a membrane.

Biologicals: Vaccines, cultures and other preparations made from living organisms and their products, intended for use in diagnosing, immunizing, or treating humans or animals, or in related research.

Biomass: All of the living material in a given area; often refers to vegetation.

Biome: Entire community of living organisms in a single major ecological area. (See: biotic community.)

Biomonitoring: 1. The use of living organisms to test the suitability of effluents for discharge into receiving waters and to test the quality of such waters downstream from the discharge. 2. Analysis of blood, urine, tissues, etc. to measure chemical exposure in humans.

Bioremediation: Use of living organisms to clean up oil spills or remove other pollutants from soil, water, or wastewater; use of organisms such as non-harmful insects to remove agricultural pests or counteract diseases of trees, plants, and garden soil.

Biosensor: Analytical device comprising a biological recognition element (e.g. enzyme, receptor, DNA, antibody, or microorganism) in intimate contact with an electrochemical, optical, thermal, or acoustic signal transducer that together permit analyses of chemical properties or quantities. Shows potential development in some areas, including environmental monitoring.

Biosphere: The portion of Earth and its atmosphere that can support life.

Biostabilizer: A machine that converts solid waste into compost by grinding and aeration.

Biota: The animal and plant life of a given region.

Biotechnology: Techniques that use living organisms or parts of organisms to produce a variety of products (from medicines to industrial enzymes) to improve plants or animals or to develop microorganisms to remove toxics from bodies of water, or act as pesticides.

Biotic Community: A naturally occurring assemblage of plants and animals that live in the same environment and are mutually sustaining and interdependent. (See: biome.)

Biotransformation: Conversion of a substance into other compounds by organisms; includes biodegredation.

Blackwater: Water that contains animal, human, or food waste.

Blood Products: Any product derived from human blood, including but not limited to blood plasma, platelets, red or white corpuscles, and derived licensed products such as interferon.

Bloom: A proliferation of algae and/or higher aquatic plants in a body of water; often related to pollution, especially when pollutants accelerate growth.

BOD5: The amount of dissolved oxygen consumed in five days by biological processes breaking down organic matter.

Body Burden: The amount of a chemical stored in the body at a given time, especially a potential toxin in the body as the result of exposure.

Bog: A type of wetland that accumulates appreciable peat deposits. Bogs depend primarily on precipitation for their water source, and are usually acidic and rich in plant residue with a conspicuous mat of living green moss.

Boiler: A vessel designed to transfer heat produced by combustion or electric resistance to water. Boilers may provide hot water or steam.

Boom: 1. A floating device used to contain oil on a body of water. 2. A piece of equipment used to apply pesticides from a tractor or truck.

Borehole: Hole made with drilling equipment.

Botanical Pesticide: A pesticide whose active ingredient is a plant-produced chemical such as nicotine or strychnine. Also called a plant-derived pesticide.

Bottle Bill: Proposed or enacted legislation which requires a returnable deposit on beer or soda containers and provides for retail store or other redemption. Such legislation is designed to discourage use of throw-away containers.

Bottom Ash: The non-airborne combustion residue from burning pulverized coal in a boiler; the material which falls to the bottom of the boiler and is removed mechanically; a concentration of non-combustible materials, which may include toxics.

Bottom Land Hardwoods: Forested freshwater wetlands adjacent to rivers in the southeastern United States, especially valuable for wildlife breeding, nesting and habitat.

Bounding Estimate: An estimate of exposure, dose, or risk that is higher than that incurred by the person in the population with the currently highest exposure, dose, or risk. Bounding estimates are useful in developing statements that exposures, doses, or risks are not greater than an estimated value.

Brackish: Mixed fresh and salt water.

Breakpoint Chlorination: Addition of chlorine to water until the chlorine demand has been satisfied.

Breakthrough: A crack or break in a filter bed that allows the passage of floc or particulate matter through a filter; will cause an increase in filter effluent turbidity.

Breathing Zone: Area of air in which an organism inhales.

Brine Mud: Waste material, often associated with well-drilling or mining, composed of mineral salts or other inorganic compounds.

British Thermal Unit: Unit of heat energy equal to the amount of heat required to raise the temperature of one pound of water by one degree Fahrenheit at sea level.

Broadcast Application: The spreading of pesticides over an entire area.

Brownfields: Abandoned, idled, or under used industrial and commercial facilities/sites where expansion or redevelopment is complicated by real or perceived environmental contamination. They can be in urban, suburban, or rural areas. EPA's Brownfields initiative helps communities mitigate potential health risks and restore the economic viability of such areas or properties.

Bubble: A system under which existing emissions sources can propose alternate means to comply with a set of emissions limitations; under the bubble concept, sources can control more than required at one emission point where control costs are relatively low in return for a comparable relaxation of controls at a second emission point where costs are higher.

Bubble Policy: (See: emissions trading.)

Buffer: A solution or liquid whose chemical makeup is such that it minimizes changes in pH when acids or bases are added to it.

Buffer Strips: Strips of grass or other erosion-resisting vegetation between or below cultivated strips or fields.

Building Cooling Load: The hourly amount of heat that must be removed from a building to maintain indoor comfort (measured in British thermal units (Btus).

Building Envelope: The exterior surface of a building's construction--the walls, windows, floors, roof, and floor. Also called building shell.

Building Related Illness: Diagnosable illness whose cause and symptoms can be directly attributed to a specific pollutant source within a building (e.g. Legionnaire's disease, hypersensitivity, pneumonitis.) (See: sick building syndrome.)

Bulk Sample: A small portion (usually thumbnail size) of a suspect asbestos-containing building material collected by an asbestos inspector for laboratory analysis to determine asbestos content.

Bulky Waste: Large items of waste materials, such as appliances, furniture, large auto parts, trees, stumps.

Burial Ground (Graveyard): A disposal site for radioactive waste materials that uses earth or water as a shield.

Buy-Back Center: Facility where individuals or groups bring reyclables in return for payment.

By-product: Material, other than the principal product, generated as a consequence of an industrial process or as a breakdown product in a living system.

Cadmium (Cd): A heavy metal that accumulates in the environment.

Cancellation: Refers to Section 6 (b) of the Federal Insecticide, Fungicide and Rodenticide Act (FIFRA) which authorizes cancellation of a pesticide registration if unreasonable adverse effects to the environment and public health develop when a product is used according to widespread and commonly recognized practice, or if its labeling or other material required to be submitted does not comply with FIFRA provisions.

Cap: A layer of clay, or other impermeable material installed over the top of a closed landfill to prevent entry of rainwater and minimize leachate.

Capacity Assurance Plan: A statewide plan which supports a state's ability to manage the hazardous waste generated within its boundaries over a twenty year period.

Capillary Action: Movement of water through very small spaces due to molecular forces called capillary forces.

Capillary Fringe: The porous material just above the water table which may hold water by capillarity (a property of surface tension that draws water upwards) in the smaller void spaces.

Capillary Fringe: The zone above he water table within which the porous medium is saturated by water under less than atmospheric pressure.

Capture Efficiency: The fraction of organic vapors generated by a process that are directed to an abatement or recovery device.

Carbon Absorber: An add-on control device that uses activated carbon to absorb volatile organic compounds from a gas stream. (The VOCs are later recovered from the carbon.)

Carbon Adsorption: A treatment system that removes contaminants from ground water or surface water by forcing it through tanks containing activated carbon treated to attract the contaminants.

Carbon Monoxide (CO): A colorless, odorless, poisonous gas produced by incomplete fossil fuel combustion.

Carbon Tetrachloride (CC14): Compound consisting of one carbon atom ad four chlorine atoms, once widely used as a industrial raw material, as a solvent, and in the production of CFCs. Use as a solvent ended when it was discovered to be carcinogenic.

Carboxyhemoglobin: Hemoglobin in which the iron is bound to carbon monoxide(CO) instead of oxygen.

Carcinogen: Any substance that can cause or aggravate cancer.

Carrier: 1.The inert liquid or solid material in a pesticide product that serves as a delivery vehicle for the active ingredient. Carriers do not have toxic properties of their own. 2. Any material or system that can facilitate the movement of a pollutant into the body or cells.

Carrying Capacity: 1. In recreation management, the amount of use a recreation area can sustain without loss of quality. 2. In wildlife management, the maximum number of animals an area can support during a given period.

CAS Registration Number: A number assigned by the Chemical Abstract Service to identify a chemical.

Case Study: A brief fact sheet providing risk, cost, and performance information on alternative methods and other pollution prevention ideas, compliance initiatives, voluntary efforts, etc.

Cask: A thick-walled container (usually lead) used to transport radioactive material. Also called a coffin.

Catalyst: A substance that changes the speed or yield of a chemical reaction without being consumed or chemically changed by the chemical reaction.

Catalytic Converter: An air pollution abatement device that removes pollutants from motor vehicle exhaust, either by oxidizing them into carbon dioxide and water or reducing them to nitrogen.

Catalytic Incinerator: A control device that oxidizes volatile organic compounds (VOCs) by using a catalyst to promote the combustion process. Catalytic incinerators require lower temperatures than conventional thermal incinerators, thus saving fuel and other costs.

Categorical Exclusion: A class of actions which either individually or cumulatively would not have a significant effect on the human environment and therefore would not require preparation of an environmental assessment or environmental impact statement under the National Environmental Policy Act (NEPA).

Categorical Pretreatment Standard: A technology-based effluent limitation for an industrial facility discharging into a municipal sewer system. Analogous in stringency to Best Availability Technology (BAT) for direct dischargers.

Cathodic Protection: A technique to prevent corrosion of a metal surface by making it the cathode of an electrochemical cell.

Cavitation: The formation and collapse of gas pockets or bubbles on the blade of an impeller or the gate of a valve; collapse of these pockets or bubbles drives water with such force that it can cause pitting of the gate or valve surface.

Cells: 1. In solid waste disposal, holes where waste is dumped, compacted, and covered with layers of dirt on a daily basis. 2. The smallest structural part of living matter capable of functioning as an independent unit.

Cementitious: Densely packed and nonfibrous friable materials.

Central Collection Point: Location were a generator of regulated medical waste consolidates wastes originally generated at various locations in his facility. The wastes are gathered together for treatment on-site or for transportation elsewhere for treatment and/or disposal. This term could also apply to community hazardous waste collections, industrial and other waste management systems.

Centrifugal Collector: A mechanical system using centrifugal force to remove aerosols from a gas stream or to remove water from sludge.

CERCLIS: The federal Comprehensive Environmental Response, Compensation, and Liability Information System is a database that includes all sites which have been nominated for investigation by the Superfund program.

Channelization: Straightening and deepening streams so water will move faster, a marsh-drainage tactic that can interfere with waste assimilation capacity, disturb fish and wildlife habitats, and aggravate flooding.

Characteristic: Any one of the four categories used in defining hazardous waste: ignitability, corrosivity, reactivity, and toxicity.

Characterization of Ecological Effects: Part of ecological risk assessment that evaluates ability of a stressor to cause adverse effects under given circumstances.

Characterization of Exposure: Portion of an ecological risk assessment that evaluates interaction of a stressor with one or more ecological entities.

Check-Valve Tubing Pump: Water sampling tool also referred to as a water Pump.

Chemical Case: For purposes of review and regulation, the grouping of chemically similar pesticide active ingredients (e.g. salts and esters of the same chemical) into chemical cases.

Chemical Compound: A distinct and pure substance formed by the union or two or more elements in definite proportion by weight.

Chemical Element: A fundamental substance comprising one kind of atom; the simplest form of matter.

Chemical Oxygen Demand (COD): A measure of the oxygen required to oxidize all compounds, both organic and inorganic, in water.

Chemical Stressors: Chemicals released to the environment through industrial waste, auto emissions, pesticides, and other human activity that can cause illnesses and even death in plants and animals.

Chemical Treatment: Any one of a variety of technologies that use chemicals or a variety of chemical processes to treat waste.

Chemnet: Mutual aid network of chemical shippers and contractors that assigns a contracted emergency response company to provide technical support if a representative of the firm whose chemicals are involved in an incident is not readily available.

Chemosterilant: A chemical that controls pests by preventing reproduction.

Chemtrec: The industry-sponsored Chemical Transportation Emergency Center; provides information and/or emergency assistance to emergency responders.

Child Resistant Packaging (CRP): Packaging that protects children or adults from injury or illness resulting from accidental contact with or ingestion of residential pesticides that meet or exceed specific toxicity levels. Required by FIFRA regulations. Term is also used for protective packaging of medicines.

Chiller: A device that generates a cold liquid that is circulated through an air-handling unit's cooling coil to cool the air supplied to the building.

Chilling Effect: The lowering of the Earth's temperature because of increased particles in the air blocking the sun's rays. (See: greenhouse effect.)

Chisel Plowing: Preparing croplands by using a special implement that avoids complete inversion of the soil as in conventional plowing. Chisel plowing can leave a protective cover or crops residues on the soil surface to help prevent erosion and improve filtration.

Chlorinated Hydrocarbons: 1. Chemicals containing only chlorine, carbon, and hydrogen. These include a class of persistent, broad-spectrum insecticides that linger in the environment and accumulate in the food chain. Among them are DDT, aldrin, dieldrin, heptachlor, chlordane, lindane, endrin, Mirex, hexachloride, and toxaphene. Other examples include TCE, used as an industrial solvent. 2. Any chlorinated organic compounds including chlorinated solvents such as dichloromethane, trichloromethylene, chloroform.

Chlorinated Solvent: An organic solvent containing chlorine atoms(e.g. methylene chloride and 1,1,1-trichloromethane). Uses of chlorinated solvents are include aerosol spray containers, in highway paint, and dry cleaning fluids.

Chlorination: The application of chlorine to drinking water, sewage, or industrial waste to disinfect or to oxidize undesirable compounds.

Chlorinator: A device that adds chlorine, in gas or liquid form, to water or sewage to kill infectious bacteria.

Chlorine-Contact Chamber: That part of a water treatment plant where effluent is disinfected by chlorine.

Chlorofluorocarbons (CFCs): A family of inert, nontoxic, and easily liquefied chemicals used in refrigeration, air conditioning, packaging, insulation, or as solvents and aerosol propellants. Because CFCs are not destroyed in the lower atmosphere they drift into the upper atmosphere where their chlorine components destroy ozone. (See: fluorocarbons.)

Chlorophenoxy: A class of herbicides that may be found in domestic water supplies and cause adverse health effects.

Chlorosis: Discoloration of normally green plant parts caused by disease, lack of nutrients, or various air pollutants.

Cholinesterase: An enzyme found in animals that regulates nerve impulses by the inhibition of acetylcholine. Cholinesterase inhibition is associated with a variety of acute symptoms such as nausea, vomiting, blurred vision, stomach cramps, and rapid heart rate.

Chromium: (See: heavy metals.)

Chronic Effect: An adverse effect on a human or animal in which symptoms recur frequently or develop slowly over a long period of time.

Chronic Exposure: Multiple exposures occurring over an extended period of time or over a significant fraction of an animal's or human's lifetime (Usually seven years to a lifetime.)

Chronic Toxicity: The capacity of a substance to cause long-term poisonous health effects in humans, animals, fish, and other organisms. (See: acute toxicity.)

Circle of Influence: The circular outer edge of a depression produced in the water table by the pumping of water from a well. (See: cone of depression.)

Cistern: Small tank or storage facility used to store water for a home or farm; often used to store rain water.

Clarification: Clearing action that occurs during wastewater treatment when solids settle out. This is often aided by centrifugal action and chemically induced coagulation in wastewater.

Clarifier: A tank in which solids settle to the bottom and are subsequently removed as sludge.

Class I Area: Under the Clean Air Act. a Class I area is one in which visibility is protected more stringently than under the national ambient air quality standards; includes national parks, wilderness areas, monuments, and other areas of special national and cultural significance.

Class I Substance: One of several groups of chemicals with an ozone depletion potential of 0.2 or higher, including CFCS, Halons, Carbon Tetrachloride, and Methyl Chloroform (listed in the Clean Air Act), and HBFCs and Ethyl Bromide (added by EPA regulations). (See: Global warming potential.)

Class II Substance: A substance with an ozone depletion potential of less than 0.2. All HCFCs are currently included in this classification. (See: Global warming potential.)

Clay Soil: Soil material containing more than 40 percent clay, less than 45 percent sand, and less than 40 percent silt.

Clean Coal Technology: Any technology not in widespread use prior to the Clean Air Act Amendments of 1990. This Act will achieve significant reductions in pollutants associated with the burning of coal.

Clean Fuels: Blends or substitutes for gasoline fuels, including compressed natural gas, methanol, ethanol, and liquified petroleum gas.

Cleaner Technologies Substitutes Assessment: A document that systematically evaluates the relative risk, performance, and cost trade-offs of technological alternatives; serves as a repository for all the technical data (including methodology and results) developed by a DfE or other pollution prevention or education project.

Cleanup: Actions taken to deal with a release or threat of release of a hazardous substance that could affect humans and/or the environment. The term "cleanup" is sometimes used interchangeably with the terms remedial action, removal action, response action, or corrective action.

Clear Cut: Harvesting all the trees in one area at one time, a practice that can encourage fast rainfall or snowmelt runoff, erosion, sedimentation of streams and lakes, and flooding, and destroys vital habitat.

Clear Well: A reservoir for storing filtered water of sufficient quantity to prevent the need to vary the filtration rate with variations in demand. Also used to provide chlorine contact time for disinfection.

Climate Change (also referred to as 'global climate change'): The term 'climate change' is sometimes used to refer to all forms of climatic inconsistency, but because the Earth's climate is never static, the term is more properly used to imply a significant change from one climatic condition to another. In some cases, 'climate change' has been used synonymously with the term, 'global warming'; scientists however, tend to use the term in the wider sense to also include natural changes in climate. (See: global warming.)

Cloning: In biotechnology, obtaining a group of genetically identical cells from a single cell; making identical copies of a gene.

Closed-Loop Recycling: Reclaiming or reusing wastewater for non-potable purposes in an enclosed process.

Closure: The procedure a landfill operator must follow when a landfill reaches its legal capacity for solid ceasing acceptance of solid waste and placing a cap on the landfill site.

Co-fire: Burning of two fuels in the same combustion unit; e.g., coal and natural gas, or oil and coal.

Coagulation: Clumping of particles in wastewater to settle out impurities, often induced by chemicals such as lime, alum, and iron salts.

Coal Cleaning Technology: A precombustion process by which coal is physically or chemically treated to remove some of its sulfur so as to reduce sulfur dioxide emissions.

Coal Gasification: Conversion of coal to a gaseous product by one of several available technologies.

Coastal Zone: Lands and waters adjacent to the coast that exert an influence on the uses of the sea and its ecology, or whose uses and ecology are affected by the sea.

Code of Federal Regulations (CFR): Document that codifies all rules of the executive departments and agencies of the federal government. It is divided into fifty volumes, known as titles. Title 40 of the CFR (referenced as 40 CFR) lists all environmental regulations.

Coefficient of Haze (COH): A measurement of visibility interference in the atmosphere.

Cogeneration: The consecutive generation of useful thermal and electric energy from the same fuel source.

Coke Oven: An industrial process which converts coal into coke, one of the basic materials used in blast furnaces for the conversion of iron ore into iron.

Cold Temperature CO: A standard for automobile emissions of carbon monoxide (CO) emissions to be met at a low temperature (i.e. 20 degrees Fahrenheit). Conventional automobile catalytic converters are not efficient in cold weather until they warm up.

Coliform Index: A rating of the purity of water based on a count of fecal bacteria.

Coliform Organism: Microorganisms found in the intestinal tract of humans and animals. Their presence in water indicates fecal pollution and potentially adverse contamination by pathogens.

Collector: Public or private hauler that collects nonhazardous waste and recyclable materials from residential, commercial, institutional and industrial sources. (See: hauler.)

Collector Sewers: Pipes used to collect and carry wastewater from individual sources to an interceptor sewer that will carry it to a treatment facility.

Colloids: Very small, finely divided solids (that do not dissolve) that remain dispersed in a liquid for a long time due to their small size and electrical charge.

Combined Sewer Overflows: Discharge of a mixture of storm water and domestic waste when the flow capacity of a sewer system is exceeded during rainstorms.

Combined Sewers: A sewer system that carries both sewage and storm-water runoff. Normally, its entire flow goes to a waste treatment plant, but during a heavy storm, the volume of water may be so great as to cause overflows of untreated mixtures of storm water and sewage into receiving waters. Storm-water runoff may also carry toxic chemicals from industrial areas or streets into the sewer system.

Combustion: 1. Burning, or rapid oxidation, accompanied by release of energy in the form of heat and light. 2. Refers to controlled burning of waste, in which heat chemically alters organic compounds, converting into stable inorganics such as carbon dioxide and water.

Combustion Chamber: The actual compartment where waste is burned in an incinerator.

Combustion Product: Substance produced during the burning or oxidation of a material.

Command Post: Facility located at a safe distance upwind from an accident site, where the on-scene coordinator, responders, and technical representatives make response decisions, deploy manpower and equipment, maintain liaison with news media, and handle communications.

Command-and-Control Regulations: Specific requirements prescribing how to comply with specific standards defining acceptable levels of pollution.

Comment Period: Time provided for the public to review and comment on a proposed EPA action or rulemaking after publication in the Federal Register.

Commercial Waste: All solid waste emanating from business establishments such as stores, markets, office buildings, restaurants, shopping centers, and theaters.

Commercial Waste Management Facility: A treatment, storage, disposal, or transfer facility which accepts waste from a variety of sources, as compared to a private facility which normally manages a limited waste stream generated by its own operations.

Commingled Recyclables: Mixed recyclables that are collected together.

Comminuter: A machine that shreds or pulverizes solids to make waste treatment easier.

Comminution: Mechanical shredding or pulverizing of waste. Used in both solid waste management and wastewater treatment.

Common Sense Initiative: Voluntary program to simplify environmental regulation to achieve cleaner, cheaper, smarter results, starting with six major industry sectors.

Community: In ecology, an assemblage of populations of different species within a specified location in space and time. Sometimes, a particular subgrouping may be specified, such as the fish community in a lake or the soil arthropod community in a forest.

Community Relations: The EPA effort to establish two-way communication with the public to create understanding of EPA programs and related actions, to ensure public input into decision-making processes related to affected communities, and to make certain that the Agency is aware of and responsive to public concerns. Specific community relations activities are required in relation to Superfund remedial actions.

Community Water System: A public water system which serves at least 15 service connections used by year-round residents or regularly serves at least 25 year-round residents.

Compact Fluorescent Lamp (CFL): Small fluorescent lamps used as more efficient alternatives to incandescent lighting. Also called PL, CFL, Twin-Tube, or BIAX lamps.

Compaction: Reduction of the bulk of solid waste by rolling and tamping.

Comparative Risk Assessment: Process that generally uses the judgement of experts to predict effects and set priorities among a wide range of environmental problems.

Complete Treatment: A method of treating water that consists of the addition of coagulant chemicals, flash mixing, coagulation-flocculation, sedimentation, and filtration. Also called conventional filtration.

Compliance Coal: Any coal that emits less than 1.2 pounds of sulfur dioxide per million Btu when burned. Also known as low sulfur coal.

Compliance Coating: A coating whose volatile organic compound content does not exceed that allowed by regulation.

Compliance Cycle: The 9-year calendar year cycle, beginning January 1, 1993, during which public water systems must monitor. Each cycle consists of three 3-year compliance periods.

Compliance Monitoring: Collection and evaluation of data, including self-monitoring reports, and verification to show whether pollutant concentrations and loads contained in permitted discharges are in compliance with the limits and conditions specified in the permit.

Compliance Schedule: A negotiated agreement between a pollution source and a government agency that specifies dates and procedures by which a source will reduce emissions and, thereby, comply with a regulation.

Composite Sample: A series of water samples taken over a given period of time and weighted by flow rate.

Compost: A humus or soil-like material created from aerobic, microbial decomposition of organic materials such as food scraps, yard trimmings, and manure

Composting: The controlled biological decomposition of organic material in the presence of air to form a humus-like material. Controlled methods of composting include mechanical mixing and aerating, ventilating the materials by dropping them through a vertical series of aerated chambers, or placing the compost in piles out in the open air and mixing it or turning it periodically.

Composting Facilities: 1. An offsite facility where the organic component of municipal solid waste is decomposed under controlled conditions; 2.an aerobic process in which organic materials are ground or shredded and then decomposed to humus in windrow piles or in mechanical digesters, drums, or similar enclosures.

Compressed Natural Gas (CNG): An alternative fuel for motor vehicles; considered one of the cleanest because of low hydrocarbon emissions and its vapors are relatively non-ozone producing. However, vehicles fueled with CNG do emit a significant quantity of nitrogen oxides.

Concentration: The relative amount of a substance mixed with another substance. An example is five ppm of carbon monoxide in air or 1 mg/l of iron in water.

Condensate: 1.Liquid formed when warm landfill gas cools as it travels through a collection system. 2. Water created by cooling steam or water vapor.

Condensate Return System: System that returns the heated water condensing within steam piping to the boiler and thus saves energy.

Conditional Registration: Under special circumstances, the Federal Insecticide, Fungicide, and Rodenticide Act (FIFRA) permits registration of pesticide products that is "conditional" upon the submission of additional data. These special circumstances include a finding by the EPA Administrator that a new product or use of an existing pesticide will not significantly increase the risk of unreasonable adverse effects. A product containing a new (previously unregistered) active ingredient may be conditionally registered only if the Administrator finds that such conditional registration is in the public interest, that a reasonable time for conducting the additional studies has not elapsed, and the use of the pesticide for the period of conditional registration will not present an unreasonable risk.

Conditionally Exempt Generators (CE): Persons or enterprises which produce less than 220 pounds of hazardous waste per month. Exempt from most regulation, they are required merely to determine whether their waste is hazardous, notify appropriate state or local agencies, and ship it by an authorized transporter to a permitted facility for proper disposal. (See : small quantity generator.)

Conductance: A rapid method of estimating the dissolved solids content of water supply by determining the capacity of a water sample to carry an electrical current. Conductivity is a measure of the ability of a solution to carry and electrical current.

Conductivity: A measure of the ability of a solution to carry an electrical current.

Cone of Depression: A depression in the water table that develops around a pumped well.

Cone of Influence: The depression, roughly conical in shape, produced in a water table by the pumping of water from a well.

Cone Penterometer Testing (CPT): A direct push system used to measure lithology based on soil penetration resistance. Sensors in the tip of the cone of the DP rod measure tip resistance and side-wall friction, transmitting electrical signals to digital processing equipment on the ground surface. (See: direct push.)

Confidential Business Information (CBI): Material that contains trade secrets or commercial or financial information that has been claimed as confidential by its source (e.g. a pesticide or new chemical formulation registrant). EPA has special procedures for handling such information.

Confidential Statement of Formula (CSF): A list of the ingredients in a new pesticide or chemical formulation. The list is submitted at the time for application for registration or change in formulation.

Confined Aquifer: An aquifer in which ground water is confined under pressure which is significantly greater than atmospheric pressure.

Confluent Growth: A continuous bacterial growth covering all or part of the filtration area of a membrane filter in which the bacteria colonies are not discrete.

Consent Decree: A legal document, approved by a judge, that formalizes an agreement reached between EPA and potentially responsible parties (PRPs) through which PRPs will conduct all or part of a cleanup action at a Superfund site; cease or correct actions or processes that are polluting the environment; or otherwise comply with EPA initiated regulatory enforcement actions to resolve the contamination at the Superfund site involved. The consent decree describes the actions PRPs will take and may be subject to a public comment period.

Conservation: Preserving and renewing, when possible, human and natural resources. The use, protection, and improvement of natural resources according to principles that will ensure their highest economic or social benefits.

Conservation Easement: Easement restricting a landowner to land uses that that are compatible with long-term conservation and environmental values.

Constituent(s) of Concern: Specific chemicals that are identified for evaluation in the site assessment process

Construction and Demolition Waste: Waste building materials, dredging materials, tree stumps, and rubble resulting from construction, remodeling, repair, and demolition of homes, commercial buildings and other structures and pavements. May contain lead, asbestos, or other hazardous substances.

Construction Ban: If, under the Clean Air Act, EPA disapproves an area's planning requirements for correcting nonattainment, EPA can ban the construction or modification of any major stationary source of the pollutant for which the area is in nonattainment.

Consumptive Water Use: Water removed from available supplies without return to a water resources system, e.g. water used in manufacturing, agriculture, and food preparation.

Contact Pesticide: A chemical that kills pests when it touches them, instead of by ingestion. Also, soil that contains the minute skeletons of certain algae that scratch and dehydrate waxy-coated insects.

Contaminant: Any physical, chemical, biological, or radiological substance or matter that has an adverse effect on air, water, or soil.

Contamination: Introduction into water, air, and soil of microorganisms, chemicals, toxic substances, wastes, or wastewater in a concentration that makes the medium unfit for its next intended use. Also applies to surfaces of objects, buildings, and various household and agricultural use products.

Contamination Source Inventory: An inventory of contaminant sources within delineated State Water-Protection Areas. Targets likely sources for further investigation.

Contingency Plan: A document setting out an organized, planned, and coordinated course of action to be followed in case of a fire, explosion, or other accident that releases toxic chemicals, hazardous waste, or radioactive materials that threaten human health or the environment. (See: National Oil and Hazardous Substances Contingency Plan.)

Continuous Discharge: A routine release to the environment that occurs without interruption, except for infrequent shutdowns for maintenance, process changes, etc.

Continuous Sample: A flow of water, waste or other material from a particular place in a plant to the location where samples are collected for testing. May be used to obtain grab or composite samples.

Contour Plowing: Soil tilling method that follows the shape of the land to discourage erosion.

Contour Strip Farming: A kind of contour farming in which row crops are planted in strips, between alternating strips of close-growing, erosion-resistant forage crops.

Contract Labs: Laboratories under contract to EPA, which analyze samples taken from waste, soil, air, and water or carry out research projects.

Control Technique Guidelines (CTG): EPA documents designed to assist state and local pollution authorities to achieve and maintain air quality standards for certain sources (e.g. organic emissions from solvent metal cleaning known as degreasing) through reasonably available control technologies (RACT).

Controlled Reaction: A chemical reaction under temperature and pressure conditions maintained within safe limits to produce a desired product or process.

Conventional Filtration: (See: complete treatment.)

Conventional Pollutants: Statutorily listed pollutants understood well by scientists. These may be in the form of organic waste, sediment, acid, bacteria, viruses, nutrients, oil and grease, or heat.

Conventional Site Assessment: Assessment in which most of the sample analysis and interpretation of data is completed off-site; process usually requires repeated mobilization of equipment and staff in order to fully determine the extent of contamination.

Conventional Systems: Systems that have been traditionally used to collect municipal wastewater in gravity sewers and convey it to a central primary or secondary treatment plant prior to discharge to surface waters.

Conventional Tilling: Tillage operations considered standard for a specific location and crop and that tend to bury the crop residues; usually considered as a base for determining the cost effectiveness of control practices.

Conveyance Loss: Water loss in pipes, channels, conduits, ditches by leakage or evaporation.

Cooling Electricity Use: Amount of electricity used to meet the building cooling load. (See: building cooling load.)

Cooling Tower: A structure that helps remove heat from water used as a coolant; e.g., in electric power generating plants.

Cooling Tower: Device which dissipates the heat from water-cooled systems by spraying the water through streams of rapidly moving air.

Cooperative Agreement: An assistance agreement whereby EPA transfers money, property, services or anything of value to a state, university, non-profit, or not-for-profit organization for the accomplishment of authorized activities or tasks.

Core: The uranium-containing heart of a nuclear reactor, where energy is released.

Core Program Cooperative Agreement: An assistance agreement whereby EPA supports states or tribal governments with funds to help defray the cost of non-item-specific administrative and training activities.

Corrective Action: EPA can require treatment, storage and disposal (TSDF) facilities handling hazardous waste to undertake corrective actions to clean up spills resulting from failure to follow hazardous waste management procedures or other mistakes. The process includes cleanup procedures designed to guide TSDFs toward in spills.

Corrosion: The dissolution and wearing away of metal caused by a chemical reaction such as between water and the pipes, chemicals touching a metal surface, or contact between two metals.

Corrosive: A chemical agent that reacts with the surface of a material causing it to deteriorate or wear away.

Cost/Benefit Analysis: A quantitative evaluation of the costs which would have incurred by implementing an environmental regulation versus the overall benefits to society of the proposed action.

Cost Recovery: A legal process by which potentially responsible parties who contributed to contamination at a Superfund site can be required to reimburse the Trust Fund for money spent during any cleanup actions by the federal government.

Cost Sharing: A publicly financed program through which society, as a beneficiary of environmental protection, shares part of the cost of pollution control with those who must actually install the controls. In Superfund, for example, the government may pay part of the cost of a cleanup action with those responsible for the pollution paying the major share.

Cost-Effective Alternative: An alternative control or corrective method identified after analysis as being the best available in terms of reliability, performance, and cost. Although costs are one important consideration, regulatory and compliance analysis does not require EPA to choose the least expensive alternative. For example, when selecting or approving a method for cleaning up a Superfund site, the Agency balances costs with the long-term effectiveness of the methods proposed and the potential danger posed by the site.

Cover Crop: A crop that provides temporary protection for delicate seedlings and/or provides a cover canopy for seasonal soil protection and improvement between normal crop production periods.

Cover Material: Soil used to cover compacted solid waste in a sanitary landfill.

Cradle-to-Grave or Manifest System: A procedure in which hazardous materials are identified and followed as they are produced, treated, transported, and disposed of by a series of permanent, linkable, descriptive documents (e.g. manifests). Commonly referred to as the cradle-to-grave system.

Criteria: Descriptive factors taken into account by EPA in setting standards for various pollutants. These factors are used to determine limits on allowable concentration levels, and to limit the number of violations per year. When issued by EPA, the criteria provide guidance to the states on how to establish their standards.

Criteria Pollutants: The 1970 amendments to the Clean Air Act required EPA to set National Ambient Air Quality Standards for certain pollutants known to be hazardous to human health. EPA has identified and set standards to protect human health and welfare for six pollutants:

ozone, carbon monoxide, total suspended particulates, sulfur dioxide, lead, and nitrogen oxide. The term, "criteria pollutants" derives from the requirement that EPA must describe the characteristics and potential health and welfare effects of these pollutants. It is on the basis of these criteria that standards are set or revised.

Critical Effect: The first adverse effect, or its known precursor, that occurs as a dose rate increases. Designation is based on evaluation of overall database.

Crop Consumptive Use: The amount of water transpired during plant growth plus what evaporated from the soil surface and foliage in the crop area.

Crop Rotation: Planting a succession of different crops on the same land rea as opposed to planting the same crop time after time.

Cross Contamination: The movement of underground contaminants from one level or area to another due to invasive subsurface activities.

Cross-Connection: Any actual or potential connection between a drinking water system and an unapproved water supply or other source of contamination.

Crumb Rubber: Ground rubber fragments the size of sand or silt used in rubber or plastic products, or processed further into reclaimed rubber or asphalt products.

Cryptosporidium: A protozoan microbe associated with the disease cryptosporidiosis in man. The disease can be transmitted through ingestion of drinking water, person-to-person contact, or other pathways, and can cause acute diarrhea, abdominal pain, vomiting, fever, and can be fatal as it was in the Milwaukee episode.

Cubic Feet Per Minute (CFM): A measure of the volume of a substance flowing through air within a fixed period of time. With regard to indoor air, refers to the amount of air, in cubic feet, that is exchanged with outdoor air in a minute's time; i.e. the air exchange rate.

Cullet: Crushed glass.

Cultural Eutrophication: Increasing rate at which water bodies "die" by pollution from human activities.

Cultures and Stocks: Infectious agents and associated biologicals including cultures from medical and pathological laboratories; cultures and stocks of infectious agents from research and industrial laboratories; waste from the production of biologicals; discarded live and attenuated vaccines; and culture dishes and devices used to transfer, inoculate, and mix cultures. (See: regulated medical waste.)

Cumulative Ecological Risk Assessment: Consideration of the total ecological risk from multiple stressors to a given eco-zone.

Cumulative Exposure: The sum of exposures of an organism to a pollutant over a period of time.

Cumulative Working Level Months (CWLM): The sum of lifetime exposure to radon working levels expressed in total working level months.

Curb Stop: A water service shutoff valve located in a water service pipe near the curb and between the water main and the building.

Curbside Collection: Method of collecting recyclable materials at homes, community districts or businesses.

Cutie-Pie: An instrument used to measure radiation levels.

Cuttings: Spoils left by conventional drilling with hollow stem auger or rotary drilling equipment.

Cyclone Collector: A device that uses centrifugal force to remove large particles from polluted air.

Data Call-In: A part of the Office of Pesticide Programs (OPP) process of developing key required test data, especially on the long-term, chronic effects of existing pesticides, in advance of scheduled Registration Standard reviews. Data Call-In from manufacturers is an adjunct of the Registration Standards program intended to expedite re-registration.

Data Quality Objectives (DQOs): Qualitative and quantitative statements of the overall level of uncertainty that a decision-maker will accept in results or decisions based on environmental data. They provide the statistical framework for planning and managing environmental data operations consistent with user's needs.

Day Tank: Another name for deaerating tank. (See: age tank.)

DDT: The first chlorinated hydrocarbon insecticide chemical name: Dichloro-Diphenyl-Trichloroethane. It has a half-life of 15 years and can collect in fatty tissues of certain animals. EPA banned registration and interstate sale of DDT for virtually all but emergency uses in the United States in 1972 because of its persistence in the environment and accumulation in the food chain.

Dead End: The end of a water main which is not connected to other parts of the distribution system.

Deadmen: Anchors drilled or cemented into the ground to provide additional reactive mass for DP sampling rigs.

Decant: To draw off the upper layer of liquid after the heaviest material (a solid or another liquid) has settled.

Decay Products: Degraded radioactive materials, often referred to as "daughters" or "progeny"; radon decay products of most concern from a public health standpoint are polonium-214 and polonium-218.

Dechlorination: Removal of chlorine from a substance.

Decomposition: The breakdown of matter by bacteria and fungi, changing the chemical makeup and physical appearance of materials.

Decontamination: Removal of harmful substances such as noxious chemicals, harmful bacteria or other organisms, or radioactive material from exposed individuals, rooms and furnishings in buildings, or the exterior environment.

Deep-Well Injection: Deposition of raw or treated, filtered hazardous waste by pumping it into deep wells, where it is contained in the pores of permeable subsurface rock.

Deflocculating Agent: A material added to a suspension to prevent settling.

Defluoridation: The removal of excess flouride in drinking water to prevent the staining of teeth.

Defoliant: An herbicide that removes leaves from trees and growing plants.

Degasification: A water treatment that removes dissolved gases from the water.

Degree-Day: A rough measure used to estimate the amount of heating required in a given area; is defined as the difference between the mean daily temperature and 65 degrees Fahrenheit. Degree-days are also calculated to estimate cooling requirements.

Delegated State: A state (or other governmental entity such as a tribal government) that has received authority to administer an environmental regulatory program in lieu of a federal counterpart. As used in connection with NPDES, UIC, and PWS programs, the term does not connote any transfer of federal authority to a state.

Delist: Use of the petition process to have a facility's toxic designation rescinded.

Demand-side Waste Management: Prices whereby consumers use purchasing decisions to communicate to product manufacturers that they prefer environmentally sound products packaged with the least amount of waste, made from recycled or recyclable materials, and containing no hazardous substances.

Demineralization: A treatment process that removes dissolved minerals from water.

Denitrification: The biological reduction of nitrate to nitrogen gas by denitrifying bacteria in soil.

Dense Non-Aqueous Phase Liquid (DNAPL): Non-aqueous phase liquids such as chlorinated hydrocarbon solvents or petroleum fractions with a specific gravity greater than 1.0 that sink through the water column until they reach a confining layer. Because they are at the bottom of aquifers instead of floating on the water table, typical monitoring wells do not indicate their presence.

Density: A measure of how heavy a specific volume of a solid, liquid, or gas is in comparison to water. depending on the chemical.

Depletion Curve: In hydraulics, a graphical representation of water depletion from storage-stream channels, surface soil, and groundwater. A depletion curve can be drawn for base flow, direct runoff, or total flow.

Depressurization: A condition that occurs when the air pressure inside a structure is lower that the air pressure outdoors. Depressurization can occur when household appliances such as fireplaces or furnaces, that consume or exhaust house air, are not supplied with enough makeup air. Radon may be drawn into a house more rapidly under depressurized conditions.

Dermal Absorption/Penetration: Process by which a chemical penetrates the skin and enters the body as an internal dose.

Dermal Exposure: Contact between a chemical and the skin.

Dermal Toxicity: The ability of a pesticide or toxic chemical to poison people or animals by contact with the skin. (See: contact pesticide.)

DES: A synthetic estrogen, diethylstilbestrol is used as a growth stimulant in food animals. Residues in meat are thought to be carcinogenic.

Desalination: [Desalinization] (1) Removing salts from ocean or brackish water by using various technologies. (2) Removal of salts from soil by artificial means, usually leaching.

Desiccant: A chemical agent that absorbs moisture; some desiccants are capable of drying out plants or insects, causing death.

Design Capacity: The average daily flow that a treatment plant or other facility is designed to accommodate.

Design Value: The monitored reading used by EPA to determine an area's air quality status; e.g., for ozone, the fourth highest reading measured over the most recent three years is the design value.

Designated Pollutant: An air pollutant which is neither a criteria nor hazardous pollutant, as described in the Clean Air Act, but for which new source performance standards exist. The Clean Air Act does require states to control these pollutants, which include acid mist, total reduced sulfur (TRS), and fluorides.

Designated Uses: Those water uses identified in state water quality standards that must be achieved and maintained as required under the Clean Water Act. Uses can include cold water fisheries, public water supply, and irrigation.

Designer Bugs: Popular term for microbes developed through biotechnology that can degrade specific toxic chemicals at their source in toxic waste dumps or in ground water.

Destination Facility: The facility to which regulated medical waste is shipped for treatment and destruction, incineration, and/or disposal.

Destratification: Vertical mixing within a lake or reservoir to totally or partially eliminate separate layers of temperature, plant, or animal life.

Destroyed Medical Waste: Regulated medical waste that has been ruined, torn apart, or mutilated through thermal treatment, melting, shredding, grinding, tearing, or breaking, so that it is no longer generally recognized as medical waste, but has not yet been treated (excludes compacted regulated medical waste).

Destruction and Removal Efficiency (DRE): A percentage that represents the number of molecules of a compound removed or destroyed in an incinerator relative to the number of molecules entering the system (e.g. a DRE of 99.99 percent means that 9,999 molecules are destroyed for every 10,000 that enter; 99.99 percent is known as "four nines." For some pollutants, the RCRA removal requirement may be as stringent as "six nines").

Destruction Facility: A facility that destroys regulated medical waste.

Desulfurization: Removal of sulfur from fossil fuels to reduce pollution.

Detectable Leak Rate: The smallest leak (from a storage tank), expressed in terms of gallons- or liters-per-hour, that a test can reliably discern with a certain probability of detection or false alarm.

Detection Criterion: A predetermined rule to ascertain whether a tank is leaking or not. Most volumetric tests use a threshold value as the detection criterion. (See: volumetric tank tests.)

Detection Limit: The lowest concentration of a chemical that can reliably be distinguished from a zero concentration.

Detention Time: 1. The theoretical calculated time required for a small amount of water to pass through a tank at a given rate of flow. 2. The actual time that a small amount of water is in a settling basin, flocculating basin, or rapid-mix chamber. 3. In storage reservoirs, the length of time water will be held before being used.

Detergent: Synthetic washing agent that helps to remove dirt and oil. Some contain compounds which kill useful bacteria and encourage algae growth when they are in wastewater that reaches receiving waters.

Development Effects: Adverse effects such as altered growth, structural abnormality, functional deficiency, or death observed in a developing organism.

Dewater: 1. Remove or separate a portion of the water in a sludge or slurry to dry the sludge so it can be handled and disposed of. 2. Remove or drain the water from a tank or trench.

Diatomaceous Earth (Diatomite): A chalk-like material (fossilized diatoms) used to filter out solid waste in wastewater treatment plants; also used as an active ingredient in some powdered pesticides.

Diazinon: An insecticide. In 1986, EPA banned its use on open areas such as sod farms and golf courses because it posed a danger to migratory birds. The ban did not apply to agricultural, home lawn or commercial establishment uses.

Dibenzofurans: A group of organic compounds, some of which are toxic.

Dicofol: A pesticide used on citrus fruits.

Diffused Air: A type of aeration that forces oxygen into sewage by pumping air through perforated pipes inside a holding tank.

Diffusion: The movement of suspended or dissolved particles (or molecules) from a more concentrated to a less concentrated area. The process tends to distribute the particles or molecules more uniformly.

Digester: In wastewater treatment, a closed tank; in solid-waste conversion, a unit in which bacterial action is induced and accelerated in order to break down organic matter and establish the proper carbon to nitrogen ratio.

Digestion: The biochemical decomposition of organic matter, resulting in partial gasification, liquefaction, and mineralization of pollutants.

Dike: A low wall that can act as a barrier to prevent a spill from spreading.

Diluent: Any liquid or solid material used to dilute or carry an active ingredient.

Dilution Ratio: The relationship between the volume of water in a stream and the volume of incoming water. It affects the ability of the stream to assimilate waste.

Dimictic: Lakes and reservoirs that freeze over and normally go through two stratifications and two mixing cycles a year.

Dinocap: A fungicide used primarily by apple growers to control summer diseases. EPA proposed restrictions on its use in 1986 when laboratory tests found it caused birth defects in rabbits.

Dinoseb: A herbicide that is also used as a fungicide and insecticide. It was banned by EPA in 1986 because it posed the risk of birth defects and sterility.

Dioxin: Any of a family of compounds known chemically as dibenzo-p-dioxins. Concern about them arises from their potential toxicity as contaminants in commercial products. Tests on laboratory animals indicate that it is one of the more toxic anthropogenic (man-made) compounds.

Direct Discharger: A municipal or industrial facility which introduces pollution through a defined conveyance or system such as outlet pipes; a point source.

Direct Filtration: A method of treating water which consists of the addition of coagulent chemicals, flash mixing, coagulation, minimal flocculation, and filtration. Sedimentation is not uses.

Direct Push: Technology used for performing subsurface investigations by driving, pushing, and/or vibrating small-diameter hollow steel rods into the ground/ Also known as direct drive, drive point, or push technology.

Direct Runoff: Water that flows over the ground surface or through the ground directly into streams, rivers, and lakes.

Discharge: Flow of surface water in a stream or canal or the outflow of ground water from a flowing artesian well, ditch, or spring. Can also apply tp discharge of liquid effluent from a facility or to chemical emissions into the air through designated venting mechanisms.

Disinfectant: A chemical or physical process that kills pathogenic organisms in water, air, or on surfaces. Chlorine is often used to disinfect sewage treatment effluent, water supplies, wells, and swimming pools.

Disinfectant By-Product: A compound formed by the reaction of a disinfecctant such as chlorine with organic material in the water supply; a chemical byproduct of the disinfection process..

Disinfectant Time: The time it takes water to move from the point of disinfectant application (or the previous point of residual disinfectant measurement) to a point before or at the point where the residual disinfectant is measured. In pipelines, the time is calculated by dividing the internal volume of the pipe by he maximum hourly flow rate; within mixing basins and storage reservoirs it is determined by tracer studies of an equivalent demonstration.

Dispersant: A chemical agent used to break up concentrations of organic material such as spilled oil.

Displacement Savings: Saving realized by displacing purchases of natural gas or electricity from a local utility by using landfill gas for power and heat.

Disposables: Consumer products, other items, and packaging used once or a few times and discarded.

Disposal: Final placement or destruction of toxic, radioactive, or other wastes; surplus or banned pesticides or other chemicals; polluted soils; and drums containing hazardous materials from removal actions or accidental releases. Disposal may be accomplished through use of approved secure landfills, surface impoundments, land farming, deep-well injection, ocean dumping, or incineration.

Disposal Facilities: Repositories for solid waste, including landfills and combustors intended for permanent containment or destruction of waste materials. Excludes transfer stations and composting facilities.

Dissolved Oxygen (DO): The oxygen freely available in water, vital to fish and other aquatic life and for the prevention of odors. DO levels are considered a most important indicator of a water body's ability to support desirable aquatic life. Secondary and advanced waste treatment are generally designed to ensure adequate DO in waste-receiving waters.

Dissolved Solids: Disintegrated organic and inorganic material in water. Excessive amounts make water unfit to drink or use in industrial processes.

Distillation: The act of purifying liquids through boiling, so that the steam or gaseous vapors condense to a pure liquid. Pollutants and contaminants may remain in a concentrated residue.

Disturbance: Any event or series of events that disrupt ecosystem, community, or population structure and alters the physical environment.

Diversion: 1. Use of part of a stream flow as water supply. 2. A channel with a supporting ridge on the lower side constructed across a slope to divert water at a non-erosive velocity to sites where it can be used and disposed of.

Diversion Rate: The percentage of waste materials diverted from traditional disposal such as landfilling or incineration to be recycled, composted, or re-used.

DNA Hybridization: Use of a segment of DNA, called a DNA probe, to identify its complementary DNA; used to detect specific genes.

Dobson Unit (DU): Units of ozone level measurement. measurement of ozone levels. If, for example, 100 DU of ozone were brought to the earth's surface they would form a layer one millimeter thick. Ozone levels vary geographically, even in the absence of ozone depletion.

Domestic Application: Pesticide application in and around houses, office buildings, motels, and other living or working areas.(See: residential use.)

Dosage/Dose: 1. The actual quantity of a chemical administered to an organism or to which it is exposed. 2. The amount of a substance that reaches a specific tissue (e.g. the liver). 3. The amount of a substance available for interaction with metabolic processes after crossing the outer boundary of an organism. (See: absorbed dose, administered dose, applied dose, potential dose.)

Dose Equivalent: The product of the absorbed dose from ionizing radiation and such factors as account for biological differences due to the type of radiation and its distribution in the body in the body.

Dose Rate: In exposure assessment, dose per time unit (e.g. mg/day), sometimes also called dosage.

Dose Response: Shifts in toxicological responses of an individual (such as alterations in severity) or populations (such as alterations in incidence) that are related to changes in the dose of any given substance.

Dose Response Curve: Graphical representation of the relationship between the dose of a stressor and the biological response thereto.

Dose-Response Assessment: 1. Estimating the potency of a chemical. 2. In exposure assessment, the process of determining the relationship between the dose of a stressor and a specific biological response. 3. Evaluating the quantitative relationship between dose and toxicological responses.

Dose-Response Relationship: The quantitative relationship between the amount of exposure to a substance and the extent of toxic injury or disease produced.

Dosimeter: An instrument to measure dosage; many so-called dosimeters actually measure exposure rather than dosage. Dosimetry is the process or technology of measuring and/or estimating dosage.

DOT Reportable Quantity: The quantity of a substance specified in a U.S. Department of Transportation regulation that triggers labeling, packaging and other requirements related to shipping such substances.

Downgradient: The direction that groundwater flows; similar to "downstream" for surface water.

Downstream Processors: Industries dependent on crop production (e.g. canneries and food processors).

DP Hole: Hole in the ground made with DP equipment. (See: direct push.)

Draft: 1. The act of drawing or removing water from a tank or reservoir. 2. The water which is drawn or removed.

Draft Permit: A preliminary permit drafted and published by EPA; subject to public review and comment before final action on the application.

Drainage: Improving the productivity of agricultural land by removing excess water from the soil by such means as ditches or subsurface drainage tiles.

Drainage Basin: The area of land that drains water, sediment, and dissolved materials to a common outlet at some point along a stream channel.

Drainage Well: A well drilled to carry excess water off agricultural fields. Because they act as a funnel from the surface to the groundwater below. Drainage wells can contribute to groundwater pollution.

Drawdown: 1. The drop in the water table or level of water in the ground when water is being pumped from a well. 2. The amount of water used from a tank or reservoir. 3. The drop in the water level of a tank or reservoir.

Dredging: Removal of mud from the bottom of water bodies. This can disturb the ecosystem and causes silting that kills aquatic life. Dredging of contaminated muds can expose biota to heavy metals and other toxics. Dredging activities may be subject to regulation under Section 404 of the Clean Water Act.

Drilling Fluid: Fluid used to lubricate the bit and convey drill cuttings to the surface with rotary drilling equipment. Usually composed of bentonite slurry or muddy water. Can become contaminated, leading to cross contamination, and may require special disposal. Not used with DP methods

Drinking Water Equivalent Level: Protective level of exposure related to potentially non-carcinogenic effects of chemicals that are also known to cause cancer.

Drinking Water State Revolving Fund: The Fund provides capitalization grants to states to develop drinking water revolving loan funds to help finance system infrastructure improvements, assure source-water protection, enhance operation and management of drinking-water systems, and otherwise promote local water-system compliance and protection of public health.

Drive Casing: Heavy duty steel casing driven along with the sampling tool in cased DP systems. Keeps the hole open between sampling runs and is not removed until last sample has been collected.

Drive Point Profiler: An exposed groundwater DP system used to collect multiple depth-discrete groundwater samples. Ports in the tip of the probe connect to an internal stainless steel or teflon tube that extends to the surface. Samples are collected via suction or airlift methods.

Deionized water is pumped down through the ports to prevent plugging while driving the tool to the next sampling depth.

Drop-off: Recyclable materials collection method in which individuals bring them to a designated collection site.

Dual-Phase Extraction: Active withdrawal of both liquid and gas phases from a well usually involving the use of a vacuum pump.

Dump: A site used to dispose of solid waste without environmental controls.

Duplicate: A second aliquot or sample that is treated the same as the original sample in order to determine the precision of the analytical method. (See: aliquot.)

Dustfall Jar: An open container used to collect large particles from the air for measurement and analysis.

Dynamometer. A device used to place a load on an engine and measure its performance.

Dystrophic Lakes: Acidic, shallow bodies of water that contain much humus and/or other organic matter; contain many plants but few fish.

Ecological Entity: In ecological risk assessment, a general term referring to a species, a group of species, an ecosystem function or characteristic, or a specific habitat or biome.

Ecological/Environmental Sustainability: Maintenance of ecosystem components and functions for future generations.

Ecological Exposure: Exposure of a non-human organism to a stressor.

Ecological Impact: The effect that a man-caused or natural activity has on living organisms and their non-living (abiotic) environment.

Ecological Indicator: A characteristic of an ecosystem that is related to, or derived from, a measure of biotic or abiotic variable, that can provide quantitative information on ecological structure and function. An indicator can contribute to a measure of integrity and sustainability.

Ecological Integrity: A living system exhibits integrity if, when subjected to disturbance, it sustains and organizes self-correcting ability to recover toward a biomass end-state that is normal for that system. End-states other than the pristine or naturally whole may be accepted as normal and good.

Ecological Risk Assessment: The application of a formal framework, analytical process, or model to estimate the effects of human actions(s) on a natural resource and to interpret the significance of those effects in light of the uncertainties identified in each component of the assessment process. Such analysis includes initial hazard identification, exposure and dose-response assessments, and risk characterization.

Ecology: The relationship of living things to one another and their environment, or the study of such relationships.

Economic Poisons: Chemicals used to control pests and to defoliate cash crops such as cotton.

Ecosphere: The "bio-bubble" that contains life on earth, in surface waters, and in the air. (See: biosphere.)

Ecosystem: The interacting system of a biological community and its non-living environmental surroundings.

Ecosystem Structure: Attributes related to the instantaneous physical state of an ecosystem; examples include species population density, species richness or evenness, and standing crop biomass.

Ecotone: A habitat created by the juxtaposition of distinctly different habitats; an edge habitat; or an ecological zone or boundary where two or more ecosystems meet.

Effluent: Wastewater--treated or untreated--that flows out of a treatment plant, sewer, or industrial outfall. Generally refers to wastes discharged into surface waters.

Effluent Guidelines: Technical EPA documents which set effluent limitations for given industries and pollutants.

Effluent Limitation: Restrictions established by a state or EPA on quantities, rates, and concentrations in wastewater discharges.

Effluent Standard: (See: effluent limitation.)

Ejector: A device used to disperse a chemical solution into water being treated.

Electrodialysis: A process that uses electrical current applied to permeable membranes to remove minerals from water. Often used to desalinize salty or brackish water.

Electromagnetic Geophysical Methods: Ways to measure subsurface conductivity via low-frequency electromagnetic induction.

Electrostatic Precipitator (ESP): A device that removes particles from a gas stream (smoke) after combustion occurs. The ESP imparts an electrical charge to the particles, causing them to adhere to metal plates inside the precipitator. Rapping on the plates causes the particles to fall into a hopper for disposal.

Eligible Costs: The construction costs for wastewater treatment works upon which EPA grants are based.

EMAP Data: Environmental monitoring data collected under the auspices of the Environmental Monitoring and Assessment Program. All EMAP data share the common attribute of being of known quality, having been collected in the context of explicit data quality objectives (DQOs) and a consistent quality assurance program.

Emergency and Hazardous Chemical Inventory: An annual report by facilities having one or more extremely hazardous substances or hazardous chemicals above certain weight limits.

Emergency (Chemical): A situation created by an accidental release or spill of hazardous chemicals that poses a threat to the safety of workers, residents, the environment, or property.

Emergency Episode: (See: air pollution episode.)

Emergency Exemption: Provision in FIFRA under which EPA can grant temporary exemption to a state or another federal agency to allow the use of a pesticide product not registered for that particular use. Such actions involve unanticipated and/or severe pest problems where there is not time or interest by a manufacturer to register the product for that use. (Registrants cannot apply for such exemptions.)

Emergency Removal Action: 1. Steps take to remove contaminated materials that pose imminent threats to local residents (e.g. removal of leaking drums or the excavation of explosive waste.) 2. The state record of such removals.

Emergency Response Values: Concentrations of chemicals, published by various groups, defining acceptable levels for short-term exposures in emergencies.

Emergency Suspension: Suspension of a pesticide product registration due to an imminent hazard. The action immediately halts distribution, sale, and sometimes actual use of the pesticide involved.

Emission: Pollution discharged into the atmosphere from smokestacks, other vents, and surface areas of commercial or industrial facilities; from residential chimneys; and from motor vehicle, locomotive, or aircraft exhausts.

Emission Cap: A limit designed to prevent projected growth in emissions from existing and future stationary sources from eroding any mandated reductions. Generally, such provisions require that any emission growth from facilities under the restrictions be offset by equivalent reductions at other facilities under the same cap. (See: emissions trading.)

Emission Factor: The relationship between the amount of pollution produced and the amount of raw material processed. For example, an emission factor for a blast furnace making iron would be the number of pounds of particulates per ton of raw materials.

Emission Inventory: A listing, by source, of the amount of air pollutants discharged into the atmosphere of a community; used to establish emission standards.

Emission Standard: The maximum amount of air polluting discharge legally allowed from a single source, mobile or stationary.

Emissions Trading: The creation of surplus emission reductions at certain stacks, vents or similar emissions sources and the use of this surplus to meet or redefine pollution requirements applicable to other emissions sources. This allows one source to increase emissions when another source reduces them, maintaining an overall constant emission level. Facilities that reduce emissions substantially may "bank" their "credits" or sell them to other facilities or industries.

Emulsifier: A chemical that aids in suspending one liquid in another. Usually an organic chemical in an aqueous solution.

Encapsulation: The treatment of asbestos-containing material with a liquid that covers the surface with a protective coating or embeds fibers in an adhesive matrix to prevent their release into the air.

Enclosure: Putting an airtight, impermeable, permanent barrier around asbestos-containing materials to prevent the release of asbestos fibers into the air.

End User: Consumer of products for the purpose of recycling. Excludes products for re-use or combustion for energy recovery.

End-of-the-pipe: Technologies such as scrubbers on smokestacks and catalytic convertors on automobile tailpipes that reduce emissions of pollutants after they have formed.

End-use Product: A pesticide formulation for field or other end use. The label has instructions for use or application to control pests or regulate plant growth. The term excludes products used to formulate other pesticide products.

Endangered Species: Animals, birds, fish, plants, or other living organisms threatened with extinction by anthropogenic (man-caused) or other natural changes in their environment. Requirements for declaring a species endangered are contained in the Endangered Species Act.

Endangerment Assessment: A study to determine the nature and extent of contamination at a site on the National Priorities List and the risks posed to public health or the environment. EPA or the state conducts the study when a legal action is to be taken to direct potentially responsible parties to clean up a site or pay for it. An endangerment assessment supplements a remedial investigation.

Endrin: A pesticide toxic to freshwater and marine aquatic life that produces adverse health effects in domestic water supplies.

Energy Management System: A control system capable of monitoring environmental and system loads and adjusting HVAC operations accordingly in order to conserve energy while maintaining comfort.

Energy Recovery: Obtaining energy from waste through a variety of processes (e.g. combustion).

Enforceable Requirements: Conditions or limitations in permits issued under the Clean Water Act Section 402 or 404 that, if violated, could result in the issuance of a compliance order or initiation of a civil or criminal action under federal or applicable state laws. If a permit has not been issued, the term includes any requirement which, in the Regional Administrator's judgement, would be included in the permit when issued. Where no permit applies, the term includes any requirement which the RA determines is necessary for the best practical waste treatment technology to meet applicable criteria.

Enforcement: EPA, state, or local legal actions to obtain compliance with environmental laws, rules, regulations, or agreements and/or obtain penalties or criminal sanctions for violations. Enforcement procedures may vary, depending on the requirements of different environmental laws and related implementing regulations. Under CERCLA, for example, EPA will seek to require potentially responsible parties to clean up a Superfund site, or pay for the cleanup, whereas under the Clean Air Act the Agency may invoke sanctions against cities failing to meet ambient air quality standards that could prevent certain types of construction or federal funding. In other situations, if investigations by EPA and state agencies uncover willful violations, criminal trials and penalties are sought.

Enforcement Decision Document (EDD): A document that provides an explanation to the public of EPA's selection of the cleanup alternative at enforcement sites on the National Priorities List. Similar to a Record of Decision.

Engineered Controls: Method of managing environmental and health risks by placing a barrier between the contamination and the rest of the site, thus limiting exposure pathways.

Enhanced Inspection and Maintenance (I&M): An improved automobile inspection and maintenance program--aimed at reducing automobile emissions---that contains, at a minimum, more vehicle types and model years, tighter inspection, and better management practices. It may also include annual computerized or centralized inspections, under-the-hood inspection--for signs of tampering with pollution control equipment--and increased repair waiver cost.

Enrichment: The addition of nutrients (e.g. nitrogen, phosphorus, carbon compounds) from sewage effluent or agricultural runoff to surface water, greatly increases the growth potential for algae and other aquatic plants.

Entrain: To trap bubbles in water either mechanically through turbulence or chemically through a reaction.

Environment: The sum of all external conditions affecting the life, development and survival of an organism.

Environmental Assessment: An environmental analysis prepared pursuant to the National Environmental Policy Act to determine whether a federal action would significantly affect the environment and thus require a more detailed environmental impact statement.

Environmental Audit: An independent assessment of the current status of a party's compliance with applicable environmental requirements or of a party's environmental compliance policies, practices, and controls.

Environmental/Ecological Risk: The potential for adverse effects on living organisms associated with pollution of the environment by effluents, emissions, wastes, or accidental chemical releases; energy use; or the depletion of natural resources.

Environmental Equity/Justice: Equal protection from environmental hazards for individuals, groups, or communities regardless of race, ethnicity, or economic status. This applies to the development, implementation, and enforcement of environmental laws, regulations, and policies, and implies that no population of people should be forced to shoulder a disproportionate share of negative environmental impacts of pollution or environmental hazard due to a lack of political or economic strength levels.

Environmental Exposure: Human exposure to pollutants originating from facility emissions. Threshold levels are not necessarily surpassed, but low-level chronic pollutant exposure is one of the most common forms of environmental exposure (See: threshold level).

Environmental Fate: The destiny of a chemical or biological pollutant after release into the environment.

Environmental Fate Data: Data that characterize a pesticide's fate in the ecosystem, considering factors that foster its degradation (light, water, microbes), pathways and resultant products.

Environmental Impact Statement: A document required of federal agencies by the National Environmental Policy Act for major projects or legislative proposals significantly affecting the environment. A tool for decision making, it describes the positive and negative effects of the undertaking and cites alternative actions.

Environmental Indicator: A measurement, statistic or value that provides a proximate gauge or evidence of the effects of environmental management programs or of the state or condition of the environment.

Environmental Justice: The fair treatment of people of all races, cultures, incomes, and educational levels with respect to the development and enforcement of environmental laws, regulations, and policies.

Environmental Lien: A charge, security, or encumbrance on a property's title to secure payment of cost or debt arising from response actions, cleanup, or other remediation of hazardous substances or petroleum products.

Environmental Medium: A major environmental category that surrounds or contacts humans, animals, plants, and other organisms (e.g. surface water, ground water, soil or air) and through which chemicals or pollutants move. (See: ambient medium, biological medium.)

Environmental Monitoring for Public Access and Community Tracking: Joint EPA, NOAA, and USGS program to provide timely and effective communication of environmental data and information through improved and updated technology solutions that support timely environmental monitoring reporting, interpreting, and use of the information for the benefit of the public. (See: real-time monitoring.)

Environmental Response Team: EPA experts located in Edison, N.J., and Cincinnati, OH, who can provide around-the-clock technical assistance to EPA regional offices and states during all types of hazardous waste site emergencies and spills of hazardous substances.

Environmental Site Assessment: The process of determining whether contamination is present on a parcel of real property.

Environmental Sustainability: Long-term maintenance of ecosystem components and functions for future generations.

Environmental Tobacco Smoke: Mixture of smoke from the burning end of a cigarette, pipe, or cigar and smoke exhaled by the smoker. (See: passive smoking/secondhand smoke.)

Epidemiology: Study of the distribution of disease, or other health-related states and events in human populations, as related to age, sex, occupation, ethnicity, and economic status in order to identify and alleviate health problems and promote better health.

Epilimnion: Upper waters of a thermally stratified lake subject to wind action.

Episode (Pollution): An air pollution incident in a given area caused by a concentration of atmospheric pollutants under meteorological conditions that may result in a significant increase in illnesses or deaths. May also describe water pollution events or hazardous material spills.

Equilibrium: In relation to radiation, the state at which the radioactivity of consecutive elements within a radioactive series is neither increasing nor decreasing.

Equivalent Method: Any method of sampling and analyzing for air pollution which has been demonstrated to the EPA Administrator's satisfaction to be, under specific conditions, an acceptable alternative to normally used reference methods.

Erosion: The wearing away of land surface by wind or water, intensified by land-clearing practices related to farming, residential or industrial development, road building, or logging.

Established Treatment Technologies: Technologies for which cost and performance data are readily available. (See: Innovative treatment technologies.)

Estimated Environmental Concentration: The estimated pesticide concentration in an ecosystem.

Estuary: Region of interaction between rivers and near-shore ocean waters, where tidal action and river flow mix fresh and salt water. Such areas include bays, mouths of rivers, salt marshes, and lagoons. These brackish water ecosystems shelter and feed marine life, birds, and wildlife. (See: wetlands.)

Ethanol: An alternative automotive fuel derived from grain and corn; usually blended with gasoline to form gasohol.

Ethylene Dibromide (EDB): A chemical used as an agricultural fumigant and in certain industrial processes. Extremely toxic and found to be a carcinogen in laboratory animals, EDB has been banned for most agricultural uses in the United States.

Eutrophic Lakes: Shallow, murky bodies of water with concentrations of plant nutrients causing excessive production of algae. (See: dystrophic lakes.)

Eutrophication: The slow aging process during which a lake, estuary, or bay evolves into a bog or marsh and eventually disappears. During the later stages of eutrophication the water body is choked by abundant plant life due to higher levels of nutritive compounds such as nitrogen and phosphorus. Human activities can accelerate the process.

Evaporation Ponds: Areas where sewage sludge is dumped and dried.

Evapotranspiration: The loss of water from the soil both by evaporation and by transpiration from the plants growing in the soil.

Exceedance: Violation of the pollutant levels permitted by environmental protection standards.

Exclusion: In the asbestos program, one of several situations that permit a Local Education Agency (LEA) to delete one or more of the items required by the Asbestos Hazard Emergency Response Act (AHERA); e.g. records of previous asbestos sample collection and analysis may be used by the accredited inspector in lieu of AHERA bulk sampling.

Exclusionary Ordinance: Zoning that excludes classes of persons or businesses from a particular neighborhood or area.

Exempt Solvent: Specific organic compounds not subject to requirements of regulation because they are deemed by EPA to be of negligible photochemical reactivity.

Exempted Aquifer: Underground bodies of water defined in the Underground Injection Control program as aquifers that are potential sources of drinking water though not being used as such, and thus exempted from regulations barring underground injection activities.

Exemption: A state (with primacy) may exempt a public water system from a requirement involving a Maximum Contaminant Level (MCL), treatment technique, or both, if the system cannot comply due to compelling economic or other factors, or because the system was in operation before the requirement or MCL was instituted; and the exemption will not create a public health risk. (See: variance.)

Exotic Species: A species that is not indigenous to a region.

Experimental Use Permit: Obtained by manufacturers for testing new pesticides or uses thereof whenever they conduct experimental field studies to support registration on 10 acres or more of land or one acre or more of water.

Experimental Use Permit: A permit granted by EPA that allows a producer to conduct tests of a new pesticide, product and/or use outside the laboratory. The testing is usually done on ten or more acres of land or water surface.

Explosive Limits: The amounts of vapor in the air that form explosive mixtures; limits are expressed as lower and upper limits and give the range of vapor concentrations in air that will explode if an ignition source is present.

Exports : In solid waste program, municipal solid waste and recyclables transported outside the state or locality where they originated.

Exposure: The amount of radiation or pollutant present in a given environment that represents a potential health threat to living organisms.

Exposure Assessment: Identifying the pathways by which toxicants may reach individuals, estimating how much of a chemical an individual is likely to be exposed to, and estimating the number likely to be exposed.

Exposure Concentration: The concentration of a chemical or other pollutant representing a health threat in a given environment.

Exposure Indicator: A characteristic of the environment measured to provide evidence of the occurrence or magnitude of a response indicator's exposure to a chemical or biological stress.

Exposure Level: The amount (concentration) of a chemical at the absorptive surfaces of an organism.

Exposure Pathway: The path from sources of pollutants via, soil, water, or food to man and other species or settings.

Exposure Route: The way a chemical or pollutant enters an organism after contact; i.e. by ingestion, inhalation, or dermal absorption.

Exposure-Response Relationship: The relationship between exposure level and the incidence of adverse effects.

Extraction Procedure (EP Toxic): Determining toxicity by a procedure which simulates leaching; if a certain concentration of a toxic substance can be leached from a waste, that waste is considered hazardous, i.e."EP Toxic."

Extraction Well: A discharge well used to remove groundwater or air.

Extremely Hazardous Substances: Any of 406 chemicals identified by EPA as toxic, and listed under SARA Title III. The list is subject to periodic revision.

Fabric Filter: A cloth device that catches dust particles from industrial emissions.

Facilities Plans: Plans and studies related to the construction of treatment works necessary to comply with the Clean Water Act or RCRA. A facilities plan investigates needs and provides information on the cost-effectiveness of alternatives, a recommended plan, an environmental assessment of the recommendations, and descriptions of the treatment works, costs, and a completion schedule.

Facility Emergency Coordinator: Representative of a facility covered by environmental law (e.g, a chemical plant) who participates in the emergency reporting process with the Local Emergency Planning Committee (LEPC).

Facultative Bacteria: Bacteria that can live under aerobic or anaerobic conditions.

Feasibility Study: 1. Analysis of the practicability of a proposal; e.g., a description and analysis of potential cleanup alternatives for a site such as one on the National Priorities List. The feasibility study usually recommends selection of a cost-effective alternative. It usually starts as soon as the remedial investigation is underway; together, they are commonly referred to as the "RI/FS." 2. A small-scale investigation of a problem to ascertain whether a proposed research approach is likely to provide useful data.

Fecal Coliform Bacteria: Bacteria found in the intestinal tracts of mammals. Their presence in water or sludge is an indicator of pollution and possible contamination by pathogens.

Federal Implementation Plan: Under current law, a federally implemented plan to achieve attainment of air quality standards, used when a state is unable to develop an adequate plan.

Federal Motor Vehicle Control Program: All federal actions aimed at controlling pollution from motor vehicles by such efforts as establishing and enforcing tailpipe and evaporative emission standards for new vehicles, testing methods development, and guidance to states operating inspection and maintenance programs. Federally designated area that is required to meet and maintain federal ambient air quality standards. May include nearby locations in the same state or nearby states that share common air pollution problems.

Feedlot: A confined area for the controlled feeding of animals. Tends to concentrate large amounts of animal waste that cannot be absorbed by the soil and, hence, may be carried to nearby streams or lakes by rainfall runoff.

Fen: A type of wetland that accumulates peat deposits. Fens are less acidic than bogs, deriving most of their water from groundwater rich in calcium and magnesium. (See: wetlands.)

Ferrous Metals: Magnetic metals derived from iron or steel; products made from ferrous metals include appliances, furniture, containers, and packaging like steel drums and barrels. Recycled products include processing tin/steel cans, strapping, and metals from appliances into new products.

FIFRA Pesticide Ingredient: An ingredient of a pesticide that must be registered with EPA under the Federal Insecticide, Fungicide, and Rodenticide Act. Products making pesticide claims must register under FIFRA and may be subject to labeling and use requirements.

Fill: Man-made deposits of natural soils or rock products and waste materials.

Filling: Depositing dirt, mud or other materials into aquatic areas to create more dry land, usually for agricultural or commercial development purposes, often with ruinous ecological consequences.

Filter Strip: Strip or area of vegetation used for removing sediment, organic matter, and other pollutants from runoff and wastewater.

Filtration: A treatment process, under the control of qualified operators, for removing solid (particulate) matter from water by means of porous media such as sand or a man-made filter; often used to remove particles that contain pathogens.

Financial Assurance for Closure: Documentation or proof that an owner or operator of a facility such as a landfill or other waste repository is capable of paying the projected costs of closing the facility and monitoring it afterwards as provided in RCRA regulations.

Finding of No Significant Impact: A document prepared by a federal agency showing why a proposed action would not have a significant impact on the environment and thus would not require preparation of an Environmental Impact Statement. An FNSI is based on the results of an environmental assessment.

Finished Water: Water is "finished" when it has passed through all the processes in a water treatment plant and is ready to be delivered to consumers.

First Draw: The water that comes out when a tap is first opened, likely to have the highest level of lead contamination from plumbing materials.

Fix a Sample: A sample is "fixed" in the field by adding chemicals that prevent water quality indicators of interest in the sample from changing before laboratory measurements are made.

Fixed-Location Monitoring: Sampling of an environmental or ambient medium for pollutant concentration at one location continuously or repeatedly.

Flammable: Any material that ignites easily and will burn rapidly.

Flare: A control device that burns hazardous materials to prevent their release into the environment; may operate continuously or intermittently, usually on top of a stack.

Flash Point: The lowest temperature at which evaporation of a substance produces sufficient vapor to form an ignitable mixture with air.

Floc: A clump of solids formed in sewage by biological or chemical action.

Flocculation: Process by which clumps of solids in water or sewage aggregate through biological or chemical action so they can be separated from water or sewage.

Floodplain: The flat or nearly flat land along a river or stream or in a tidal area that is covered by water during a flood.

Floor Sweep: Capture of heavier-than-air gases that collect at floor level.

Flow Rate: The rate, expressed in gallons -or liters-per-hour, at which a fluid escapes from a hole or fissure in a tank. Such measurements are also made of liquid waste, effluent, and surface water movement.

Flowable: Pesticide and other formulations in which the active ingredients are finely ground insoluble solids suspended in a liquid. They are mixed with water for application.

Flowmeter: A gauge indicating the velocity of wastewater moving through a treatment plant or of any liquid moving through various industrial processes.

Flue Gas: The air coming out of a chimney after combustion in the burner it is venting. It can include nitrogen oxides, carbon oxides, water vapor, sulfur oxides, particles and many chemical pollutants.

Flue Gas Desulfurization: A technology that employs a sorbent, usually lime or limestone, to remove sulfur dioxide from the gases produced by burning fossil fuels. Flue gas desulfurization is current state-of-the art technology for major SO_2 emitters, like power plants.

Fluidized: A mass of solid particles that is made to flow like a liquid by injection of water or gas is said to have been fluidized. In water treatment, a bed of filter media is fluidized by backwashing water through the filter.

Fluidized Bed Incinerator: An incinerator that uses a bed of hot sand or other granular material to transfer heat directly to waste. Used mainly for destroying municipal sludge.

Flume: A natural or man-made channel that diverts water.

Fluoridation: The addition of a chemical to increase the concentration of fluoride ions in drinking water to reduce the incidence of tooth decay.

Fluorides: Gaseous, solid, or dissolved compounds containing fluorine that result from industrial processes. Excessive amounts in food can lead to fluorosis.

Fluorocarbons (FCs): Any of a number of organic compounds analogous to hydrocarbons in which one or more hydrogen atoms are replaced by fluorine. Once used in the United States as a propellant for domestic aerosols, they are now found mainly in coolants and some industrial processes. FCs containing chlorine are called chlorofluorocarbons (CFCs). They are believed to be modifying the ozone layer in the stratosphere, thereby allowing more harmful solar radiation to reach the Earth's surface.

Flush: 1. To open a cold-water tap to clear out all the water which may have been sitting for a long time in the pipes. In new homes, to flush a system means to send large volumes of water gushing through the unused pipes to remove loose particles of solder and flux. 2. To force large amounts of water through a system to clean out piping or tubing, and storage or process tanks.

Flux: 1. A flowing or flow. 2. A substance used to help metals fuse together.

Fly Ash: Non-combustible residual particles expelled by flue gas.

Fogging: Applying a pesticide by rapidly heating the liquid chemical so that it forms very fine droplets that resemble smoke or fog. Used to destroy mosquitoes, black flies, and similar pests.

Food Chain: A sequence of organisms, each of which uses the next, lower member of the sequence as a food source.

Food Processing Waste: Food residues produced during agricultural and industrial operations.

Food Waste: Uneaten food and food preparation wastes from residences and commercial establishments such as grocery stores, restaurants, and produce stands, institutional cafeterias and kitchens, and industrial sources like employee lunchrooms.

Food Web: The feeding relationships by which energy and nutrients are transferred from one species to another.

Formaldehyde: A colorless, pungent, and irritating gas, CH2O, used chiefly as a disinfectant and preservative and in synthesizing other compounds like resins.

Formulation: The substances comprising all active and inert ingredients in a pesticide.

Fossil Fuel: Fuel derived from ancient organic remains; e.g. peat, coal, crude oil, and natural gas.

Fracture: A break in a rock formation due to structural stresses; e.g. faults, shears, joints, and planes of fracture cleavage.

Free Product: A petroleum hydrocarbon in the liquid free or non aqueous phase. (See: non-aqueous phase liquid.)

Freeboard: 1. Vertical distance from the normal water surface to the top of a confining wall. 2. Vertical distance from the sand surface to the underside of a trough in a sand filter.

Fresh Water: Water that generally contains less than 1,000 milligrams-per-liter of dissolved solids.

Friable: Capable of being crumbled, pulverized, or reduced to powder by hand pressure.

Friable Asbestos: Any material containing more than one-percent asbestos, and that can be crumbled or reduced to powder by hand pressure. (May include previously non-friable material which becomes broken or damaged by mechanical force.)

Fuel Economy Standard: The Corporate Average Fuel Economy Standard (CAFE) effective in 1978. It enhanced the national fuel conservation effort imposing a miles-per-gallon floor for motor vehicles.

Fuel Efficiency: The proportion of energy released by fuel combustion that is converted into useful energy.

Fuel Switching: 1. A precombustion process whereby a low-sulfur coal is used in place of a higher sulfur coal in a power plant to reduce sulfur dioxide emissions. 2. Illegally using leaded gasoline in a motor vehicle designed to use only unleaded.

Fugitive Emissions: Emissions not caught by a capture system.

Fume: Tiny particles trapped in vapor in a gas stream.

Fumigant: A pesticide vaporized to kill pests. Used in buildings and greenhouses.

Functional Equivalent: Term used to describe EPA's decision-making process and its relationship to the environmental review conducted under the National Environmental Policy Act (NEPA). A review is considered functionally equivalent when it addresses the substantive components of a NEPA review.

Fungicide: Pesticides which are used to control, deter, or destroy fungi.

Fungistat: A chemical that keeps fungi from growing.

Fungus (Fungi): Molds, mildews, yeasts, mushrooms, and puffballs, a group of organisms lacking in chlorophyll (i.e. are not photosynthetic) and which are usually non-mobile, filamentous, and multicellular. Some grow in soil, others attach themselves to decaying trees and other plants whence they obtain nutrients. Some are pathogens, others stabilize sewage and digest composted waste.

Furrow Irrigation: Irrigation method in which water travels through the field by means of small channels between each groups of rows.

Future Liability: Refers to potentially responsible parties' obligations to pay for additional response activities beyond those specified in the Record of Decision or Consent Decree.

Game Fish: Species like trout, salmon, or bass, caught for sport. Many of them show more sensitivity to environmental change than "rough" fish.

Garbage: Animal and vegetable waste resulting from the handling, storage, sale, preparation, cooking, and serving of foods.

Gas Chromatograph/Mass Spectrometer: Instrument that identifies the molecular composition and concentrations of various chemicals in water and soil samples.

Gasahol: Mixture of gasoline and ethanol derived from fermented agricultural products containing at least nine percent ethanol. Gasohol emissions contain less carbon monoxide than those from gasoline.

Gasification: Conversion of solid material such as coal into a gas for use as a fuel.

Gasoline Volatility: The property of gasoline whereby it evaporates into a vapor. Gasoline vapor is a mixture of volatile organic compounds.

General Permit: A permit applicable to a class or category of dischargers.

General Reporting Facility: A facility having one or more hazardous chemicals above the 10,000 pound threshold for planning quantities. Such facilities must file MSDS and emergency inventory information with the SERC, LEPC, and local fire departments.

Generally Recognized as Safe (GRAS): Designation by the FDA that a chemical or substance (including certain pesticides) added to food is considered safe by experts, and so is exempted from the usual FFDCA food additive tolerance requirements.

Generator: 1. A facility or mobile source that emits pollutants into the air or releases hazardous waste into water or soil. 2. Any person, by site, whose act or process produces regulated medical waste or whose act first causes such waste to become subject to regulation. Where more than one person (e.g. doctors with separate medical practices) are located in the same building, each business entity is a separate generator.

Genetic Engineering: A process of inserting new genetic information into existing cells in order to modify a specific organism for the purpose of changing one of its characteristics.

Genotoxic: Damaging to DNA; pertaining to agents known to damage DNA.

Geographic Information System (GIS): A computer system designed for storing, manipulating, analyzing, and displaying data in a geographic context.

Geological Log: A detailed description of all underground features (depth, thickness, type of formation) discovered during the drilling of a well.

Geophysical Log: A record of the structure and composition of the earth encountered when drilling a well or similar type of test hold or boring.

Geothermal/Ground Source Heat Pump: These heat pumps are underground coils to transfer heat from the ground to the inside of a building. (See: heat pump; water source heat pump)

Germicide: Any compound that kills disease-causing microorganisms.

Giardia Lamblia: Protozoan in the feces of humans and animals that can cause severe gastrointestinal ailments. It is a common contaminant of surface waters.

Glass Containers: For recycling purposes, containers like bottles and jars for drinks, food, cosmetics and other products. When being recycled, container glass is generally separated into color categories for conversion into new containers, construction materials or fiberglass insulation.

Global Warming: An increase in the near surface temperature of the Earth. Global warming has occurred in the distant past as the result of natural influences, but the term is most often used to refer to the warming predicted to occur as a result of increased emissions of greenhouse gases. Scientists generally agree that the Earth's surface has warmed by about 1 degree Fahrenheit in the past 140 years. The Intergovernmental Panel on Climate Change (IPCC) recently concluded that increased concentrations of greenhouse gases are causing an increase in the Earth's surface temperature and that increased concentrations of sulfate aerosols have led to relative cooling in some regions, generally over and downwind of heavily industrialized areas. (See: climate change)

Global Warming Potential: The ratio of the warming caused by a substance to the warming caused by a similar mass of carbon dioxide. CFC-12, for example, has a GWP of 8,500, while water has a GWP of zero. (See: Class I Substance and Class II Substance.)

Glovebag: A polyethylene or polyvinyl chloride bag-like enclosure affixed around an asbestos-containing source (most often thermal system insulation) permitting the material to be removed while minimizing release of airborne fibers to the surrounding atmosphere.

Gooseneck: A portion of a water service connection between the distribution system water main and a meter. Sometimes called a pigtail.

Grab Sample: A single sample collected at a particular time and place that represents the composition of the water, air, or soil only at that time and place.

Grain Loading: The rate at which particles are emitted from a pollution source. Measurement is made by the number of grains per cubic foot of gas emitted.

Granular Activated Carbon Treatment: A filtering system often used in small water systems and individual homes to remove organics. Also used by municipal water treatment plantsd. GAC can be highly effective in lowering elevated levels of radon in water.

Grasscycling: Source reduction activities in which grass clippings are left on the lawn after mowing.

Grassed Waterway: Natural or constructed watercourse or outlet that is shaped or graded and established in suitable vegetation for the disposal of runoff water without erosion.

Gray Water: Domestic wastewater composed of wash water from kitchen, bathroom, and laundry sinks, tubs, and washers.

Greenhouse Effect: The warming of the Earth's atmosphere attributed to a buildup of carbon dioxide or other gases; some scientists think that this build-up allows the sun's rays to heat the Earth, while making the infra-red radiation atmosphere opaque to infra-red radiation, thereby preventing a counterbalancing loss of heat.

Greenhouse Gas: A gas, such as carbon dioxide or methane, which contributes to potential climate change.

Grinder Pump: A mechanical device that shreds solids and raises sewage to a higher elevation through pressure sewers.

Gross Alpha/Beta Particle Activity: The total radioactivity due to alpha or beta particle emissions as inferred from measurements on a dry sample.

Gross Power-Generation Potential: The installed power generation capacity that landfill gas can support.

Ground Cover: Plants grown to keep soil from eroding.

Ground Water: The supply of fresh water found beneath the Earth's surface, usually in aquifers, which supply wells and springs. Because ground water is a major source of drinking water, there is growing concern over contamination from leaching agricultural or industrial pollutants or leaking underground storage tanks.

Ground Water Under the Direct Influence (UDI) of Surface Water: Any water beneath the surface of the ground with: 1. significant occurence of insects or other microorganisms, algae, or large-diameter pathogens; 2. significant and relatively rapid shifts in water characteristics such as turbidity, temperature, conductivity, or pH which closely correlate to climatological or surface water conditions. Direct influence is determined for individual sources in accordance with criteria established by a state.

Ground-Penetrating Radar: A geophysical method that uses high frequency electromagnetic waves to obtain subsurface information.

Ground-Water Discharge: Ground water entering near coastal waters which has been contaminated by landfill leachate, deep well injection of hazardous wastes, septic tanks, etc.

Ground-Water Disinfection Rule: A 1996 amendment of the Safe Drinking Water Act requiring EPA to promulgate national primary drinking water regulations requiring disinfection as for all public water systems, including surface waters and ground water systems.

Gully Erosion: Severe erosion in which trenches are cut to a depth greater than 30 centimeters (a foot). Generally, ditches deep enough to cross with farm equipment are considered gullies.

Habitat: The place where a population (e.g. human, animal, plant, microorganism) lives and its surroundings, both living and non-living.

Habitat Indicator: A physical attribute of the environment measured to characterize conditions necessary to support an organism, population, or community in the absence of pollutants; e.g. salinity of estuarine waters or substrate type in streams or lakes.

Half-Life: 1. The time required for a pollutant to lose one-half of its original coconcentrationor example, the biochemical half-life of DDT in the environment is 15 years. 2. The time required for half of the atoms of a radioactive element to undergo self-transmutation or decay (half-life of radium is 1620 years). 3. The time required for the elimination of half a total dose from the body.

Halogen: A type of incandescent lamp with higher energy-efficiency that standard ones.

Halon: Bromine-containing compounds with long atmospheric lifetimes whose breakdown in the stratosphere causes depletion of ozone. Halons are used in firefighting.

Hammer Mill: A high-speed machine that uses hammers and cutters to crush, grind, chip, or shred solid waste.

Hard Water: Alkaline water containing dissolved salts that interfere with some industrial processes and prevent soap from sudsing.

Hauler: Garbage collection company that offers complete refuse removal service; many will also collect recyclables.

Hazard: 1. Potential for radiation, a chemical or other pollutant to cause human illness or injury. 2. In the pesticide program, the inherent toxicity of a compound. Hazard identification of a given substances is an informed judgment based on verifiable toxicity data from animal models or human studies.

Hazard Assessment: Evaluating the effects of a stressor or determining a margin of safety for an organism by comparing the concentration which causes toxic effects with an estimate of exposure to the organism.

Hazard Communication Standard: An OSHA regulation that requires chemical manufacturers, suppliers, and importers to assess the hazards of the chemicals that they make, supply, or import, and to inform employers, customers, and workers of these hazards through MSDS information.

Hazard Evaluation: A component of risk evaluation that involves gathering and evaluating data on the types of health injuries or diseases that may be produced by a chemical and on the conditions of exposure under which such health effects are produced.

Hazard Identification: Determining if a chemical or a microbe can cause adverse health effects in humans and what those effects might be.

Hazard Quotient: The ratio of estimated site-specific exposure to a single chemical from a site over a specified period to the estimated daily exposure level, at which no adverse health effects are likely to occur.

Hazard Ratio: A term used to compare an animal's daily dietary intake of a pesticide to its LD 50 value. A ratio greater than 1.0 indicates that the animal is likely to consume an a dose amount which would kill 50 percent of animals of the same species. (See: LD 50 /Lethal Dose.)

Hazardous Air Pollutants: Air pollutants which are not covered by ambient air quality standards but which, as defined in the Clean Air Act, may present a threat of adverse human health effects or adverse environmental effects.Such pollutants include asbestos, beryllium, mercury, benzene, coke oven emissions, radionuclides, and vinyl chloride.

Hazardous Chemical: An EPA designation for any hazardous material requiring an MSDS under OSHA's Hazard Communication Standard. Such substances are capable of producing fires and explosions or adverse health effects like cancer and dermatitis. Hazardous chemicals are distinct from hazardous waste.(See: Hazardous Waste.)

Hazardous Ranking System: The principal screening tool used by EPA to evaluate risks to public health and the environment associated with abandoned or uncontrolled hazardous waste sites. The HRS calculates a score based on the potential of hazardous substances spreading from the site through the air, surface water, or ground water, and on other factors such as density and proximity of human population. This score is the primary factor in deciding if the site should be on the National Priorities List and, if so, what ranking it should have compared to other sites on the list.

Hazardous Substance: 1. Any material that poses a threat to human health and/or the environment. Typical hazardous substances are toxic, corrosive, ignitable, explosive, or chemically reactive. 2. Any substance designated by EPA to be reported if a designated quantity of the substance is spilled in the waters of the United States or is otherwise released into the environment.

Hazardous Waste: By-products of society that can pose a substantial or potential hazard to human health or the environment when improperly managed. Possesses at least one of four characteristics (ignitability, corrosivity, reactivity, or toxicity), or appears on special EPA lists.

Hazardous Waste Landfill: An excavated or engineered site where hazardous waste is deposited and covered.

Hazardous Waste Minimization: Reducing the amount of toxicity or waste produced by a facility via source reduction or environmentally sound recycling.

Hazards Analysis: Procedures used to (1) identify potential sources of release of hazardous materials from fixed facilities or transportation accidents; (2) determine the vulnerability of a geographical area to a release of hazardous materials; and (3) compare hazards to determine which present greater or lesser risks to a community.

Hazards Identification: Providing information on which facilities have extremely hazardous substances, what those chemicals are, how much there is at each facility, how the chemicals are stored, and whether they are used at high temperatures.

Headspace: The vapor mixture trapped above a solid or liquid in a sealed vessel.

Health Advisory Level: A non-regulatory health-based reference level of chemical traces (usually in ppm) in drinking water at which there are no adverse health risks when ingested over various periods of time. Such levels are established for one day, 10 days, long-term and life-time exposure periods. They contain a wide margin of safety.

Health Assessment: An evaluation of available data on existing or potential risks to human health posed by a Superfund site. The Agency for Toxic Substances and Disease Registry (ATSDR) of the Department of Health and Human Services (DHHS) is required to perform such an assessment at every site on the National Priorities List.

Heat Island Effect: A "dome" of elevated temperatures over an urban area caused by structural and pavement heat fluxes, and pollutant emissions.

Heat Pump: An electric device with both heating and cooling capabilities. It extracts heat from one medium at a lower (the heat source) temperature and transfers it to another at a higher temperature (the heat sink), thereby cooling the first and warming the second. (See: geothermal, water source heat pump.)

Heavy Metals: Metallic elements with high atomic weights; (e.g. mercury, chromium, cadmium, arsenic, and lead); can damage living things at low concentrations and tend to accumulate in the food chain.

Heptachlor: An insecticide that was banned on some food products in 1975 and in all of them 1978. It was allowed for use in seed treatment until 1983. More recently it was found in milk and other dairy products in Arkansas and Missouri where dairy cattle were illegally fed treated seed.

Herbicide: A chemical pesticide designed to control or destroy plants, weeds, or grasses.

Herbivore: An animal that feeds on plants.

Heterotrophic Organisms: Species that are dependent on organic matter for food.

High End Exposure (dose) Estimate: An estimate of exposure, or dose level received anyone in a defined population that is greater than the 90th percentile of all individuals in that population, but less than the exposure at the highest percentile in that population. A high end risk descriptor is an estimate of the risk level for such individuals. Note that risk is based on a combination of exposure and susceptibility to the stressor.

High Intensity Discharge: A generic term for mercury vapor, metal halide, and high pressure sodium lamps and fixtures.

High-Density Polyethylene: A material used to make plastic bottles and other products that produces toxic fumes when burned.

High-Level Nuclear Waste Facility: Plant designed to handle disposal of used nuclear fuel, high-level radioactive waste, and plutonium waste.

High-Level Radioactive Waste (HLRW): Waste generated in core fuel of a nuclear reactor, found at nuclear reactors or by nuclear fuel reprocessing; is a serious threat to anyone who comes near the waste without shielding. (See: low-level radioactive waste.)

High-Line Jumpers: Pipes or hoses connected to fire hydrants and laid on top of the ground to provide emergency water service for an isolated portion of a distribution system.

High-Risk Community: A community located within the vicinity of numerous sites of facilities or other potential sources of envienvironmental exposure/health hazards which may result in high levels of exposure to contaminants or pollutants.

High-to-Low-Dose Extrapolation: The process of prediction of low exposure risk to humans and animals from the measured high-exposure-high-risk data involving laboratory animals.

Highest Dose Tested: The highest dose of a chemical or substance tested in a study.

Holding Pond: A pond or reservoir, usually made of earth, built to store polluted runoff.

Holding Time: The maximum amount of time a sample may be stored before analysis.

Hollow Stem Auger Drilling: Conventional drilling method that uses augurs to penetrate the soil. As the augers are rotated, soil cuttings are conveyed to the ground surface via augur spirals. DP tools can be used inside the hollow augers.

Homeowner Water System: Any water system which supplies piped water to a single residence.

Homogeneous Area: In accordance with Asbestos Hazard and Emergency Response Act (AHERA) definitions, an area of surfacing materials, thermal surface insulation, or miscellaneous material that is uniform in color and texture.

Hood Capture Efficiency: Ratio of the emissions captured by a hood and directed into a control or disposal device, expressed as a percent of all emissions.

Host: 1. In genetics, the organism, typically a bacterium, into which a gene from another organism is transplanted. 2. In medicine, an animal infected or parasitized by another organism.

Household Hazardous Waste: Hazardous products used and disposed of by residential as opposed to industrial consumers. Includes paints, stains, varnishes, solvents, pesticides, and other materials or products containing volatile chemicals that can catch fire, react or explode, or that are corrosive or toxic.

Household Waste (Domestic Waste): Solid waste, composed of garbage and rubbish, which normally originates in a private home or apartment house. Domestic waste may contain a significant amount of toxic or hazardous waste.

Human Equivalent Dose: A dose which, when administered to humans, produces an effect equal to that produced by a dose in animals.

Human Exposure Evaluation: Describing the nature and size of the population exposed to a substance and the magnitude and duration of their exposure.

Human Health Risk: The likelihood that a given exposure or series of exposures may have damaged or will damage the health of individuals.

Hydraulic Conductivity: The rate at which water can move through a permeable medium. (i.e. the coefficient of permeability.)

Hydraulic Gradient: In general, the direction of groundwater flow due to changes in the depth of the water table.

Hydrocarbons (HC): Chemical compounds that consist entirely of carbon and hydrogen.

Hydrogen Sulfide (H_2S): Gas emitted during organic decomposition. Also a by-product of oil refining and burning. Smells like rotten eggs and, in heavy concentration, can kill or cause illness.

Hydrogeological Cycle: The natural process recycling water from the atmosphere down to (and through) the earth and back to the atmosphere again.

Hydrogeology: The geology of ground water, with particular emphasis on the chemistry and movement of water.

Hydrologic Cycle: Movement or exchange of water between the atmosphere and earth.

Hydrology: The science dealing with the properties, distribution, and circulation of water.

Hydrolysis: The decomposition of organic compounds by interaction with water.

Hydronic: A ventilation system using heated or cooled water pumped through a building.

Hydrophilic: Having a strong affinity for water.

Hydrophobic: Having a strong aversion for water.

Hydropneumatic: A water system, usually small, in which a water pump is automatically controlled by the pressure in a compressed air tank.

Hypersensitivity Diseases: Diseases characterized by allergic responses to pollutants; diseases most clearly associated with indoor air quality are asthma, rhinitis, and pneumonic hypersensitivity.

Hypolimnion: Bottom waters of a thermally stratified lake. The hypolimnion of a eutrophic lake is usually low or lacking in oxygen.

Hypoxia/Hypoxic Waters: Waters with dissolved oxygen concentrations of less than 2 ppm, the level generally accepted as the minimum required for most marine life to survive and reproduce.

Identification Code or EPA I.D. Number: The unique code assigned to each generator, transporter, and treatment, storage, or disposal facility by regulating agencies to facilitate identification and tracking of chemicals or hazardous waste.

Ignitable: Capable of burning or causing a fire.

IM240: A high-tech, transient dynamometer automobile emissions test that takes up to 240 seconds.

Imhoff Cone: A clear, cone-shaped container used to measure the volume of settleable solids in a specific volume of water.

Immediately Dangerous to Life and Health (IDLH): The maximum level to which a healthy individual can be exposed to a chemical for 30 minutes and escape without suffering irreversible health effects or impairing symptoms. Used as a "level of concern." (See: level of concern.)

Imminent Hazard: One that would likely result in unreasonable adverse effects on humans or the environment or risk unreasonable hazard to an endangered species during the time required for a pesticide registration cancellation proceeding.

Imminent Threat: A high probability that exposure is occurring.

Immiscibility: The inability of two or more substances or liquids to readily dissolve into one another, such as soil and water. Immiscibility The inability of two or more substances or liquids to readily dissolve into one another, such as soil and water.

Impermeable: Not easily penetrated. The property of a material or soil that does not allow, or allows only with great difficulty, the movement or passage of water.

Imports: Municipal solid waste and recyclables that have been transported to a state or locality for processing or final disposition (but that did not originate in that state or locality).

Impoundment: A body of water or sludge confined by a dam, dike, floodgate, or other barrier.

In Situ: In its original place; unmoved unexcavated; remaining at the site or in the subsurface.

In-Line Filtration: Pre-treatment method in which chemicals are mixed by the flowing water; commonly used in pressure filtration installations. Eliminates need for flocculation and sedimentation.

In-Situ Flushing: Introduction of large volumes of water, at times supplemented with cleaning compounds, into soil, waste, or ground water to flush hazardous contaminants from a site.

In-Situ Oxidation: Technology that oxidizes contaminants dissolved in ground water, converting them into insoluble compounds.

In-Situ Stripping: Treatment system that removes or "strips" volatile organic compounds from contaminated ground or surface water by forcing an airstream through the water and causing the compounds to evaporate.

In-Situ Vitrification: Technology that treats contaminated soil in place at extremely high temperatures, at or more than 3000 degrees Fahrenheit.

In Vitro: Testing or action outside an organism (e.g. inside a test tube or culture dish.)

In Vivo: Testing or action inside an organism.

Incident Command Post: A facility located at a safe distance from an emergency site, where the incident commander, key staff, and technical representatives can make decisions and deploy emergency manpower and equipment.

Incident Command System (ICS): The organizational arrangement wherein one person, normally the Fire Chief of the impacted district, is in charge of an integrated, comprehensive emergency response organization and the emergency incident site, backed by an Emergency Operations Center staff with resources, information, and advice.

Incineration: A treatment technology involving destruction of waste by controlled burning at high temperatures; e.g., burning sludge to remove the water and reduce the remaining residues to a safe, non-burnable ash that can be disposed of safely on land, in some waters, or in underground locations.

Incineration at Sea: Disposal of waste by burning at sea on specially-designed incinerator ships.

Incinerator: A furnace for burning waste under controlled conditions.

Incompatible Waste: A waste unsuitable for mixing with another waste or material because it may react to form a hazard.

Indemnification: In the pesticide program, legal requirement that EPA pay certain end-users, dealers, and distributors for the cost of stock on hand at the time a pesticide registration is suspended.

Indicator: In biology, any biological entity or processes, or community whose characteristics show the presence of specific environmental conditions. 2. In chemistry, a substance that shows a visible change, usually of color, at a desired point in a chemical reaction. 3.A device that indicates the result of a measurement; e.g. a pressure gauge or a moveable scale.

Indirect Discharge: Introduction of pollutants from a non-domestic source into a publicly owned waste-treatment system. Indirect dischargers can be commercial or industrial facilities whose wastes enter local sewers.

Indirect Source: Any facility or building, property, road or parking area that attracts motor vehicle traffic and, indirectly, causes pollution.

Indoor Air: The breathable air inside a habitable structure or conveyance.

Indoor Air Pollution: Chemical, physical, or biological contaminants in indoor air.

Indoor Climate: Temperature, humidity, lighting, air flow and noise levels in a habitable structure or conveyance. Indoor climate can affect indoor air pollution.

Industrial Pollution Prevention: Combination of industrial source reduction and toxic chemical use substitution.

Industrial Process Waste: Residues produced during manufacturing operations.

Industrial Sludge: Semi-liquid residue or slurry remaining from treatment of industrial water and wastewater.

Industrial Source Reduction: Practices that reduce the amount of any hazardous substance, pollutant, or contaminant entering any waste stream or otherwise released into the environment. Also reduces the threat to public health and the environment associated with such releases. Term includes equipment or technology modifications, substitution of raw materials, and improvements in housekeeping, maintenance, training or inventory control.

Industrial Waste: Unwanted materials from an industrial operation; may be liquid, sludge, solid, or hazardous waste.

Inert Ingredient: Pesticide components such as solvents, carriers, dispersants, and surfactants that are not active against target pests. Not all inert ingredients are innocuous.

Inertial Separator: A device that uses centrifugal force to separate waste particles.

Infectious Agent: Any organism, such as a pathogenic virus, parasite, or or bacterium, that is capable of invading body tissues, multiplying, and causing disease.

Infectious Waste: Hazardous waste capable of causing infections in humans, including: contaminated animal waste; human blood and blood products; isolation waste, pathological waste; and discarded sharps (needles, scalpels or broken medical instruments).

Infiltration: 1. The penetration of water through the ground surface into sub-surface soil or the penetration of water from the soil into sewer or other pipes through defective joints, connections, or manhole walls. 2. The technique of applying large volumes of waste water to land to penetrate the surface and percolate through the underlying soil. (See: percolation.)

Infiltration Gallery: A sub-surface groundwater collection system, typically shallow in depth, constructed with open-jointed or perforated pipes that discharge collected water into a watertight chamber from which the water is pumped to treatment facilities and into the distribution system. Usually located close to streams or ponds.

Infiltration Rate: The quantity of water that can enter the soil in a specified time interval.

Inflow: Entry of extraneous rain water into a sewer system from sources other than infiltration, such as basement drains, manholes, storm drains, and street washing.

Influent: Water, wastewater, or other liquid flowing into a reservoir, basin, or treatment plant.

Information Collection Request (ICR): A description of information to be gathered in connection with rules, proposed rules, surveys, and guidance documents that contain information-gathering requirements. The ICR describes what information is needed, why it is needed, how it will be collected, and how much collecting it will cost. The ICR is submitted by the EPA to the Office of Management and Budget (OMB) for approval.

Information File: In the Superfund program, a file that contains accurate, up-to-date documents on a Superfund site. The file is usually located in a public building (school, library, or city hall) convenient for local residents.

Inhalable Particles: All dust capable of entering the human respiratory tract.

Initial Compliance Period (Water): The first full three-year compliance period which begins at least 18 months after promulgation.

Injection Well: A well into which fluids are injected for purposes such as waste disposal, improving the recovery of crude oil, or solution mining.

Injection Zone: A geological formation receiving fluids through a well.

Innovative Technologies: New or inventive methods to treat effectively hazardous waste and reduce risks to human health and the environment.

Innovative Treatment Technologies: Technologies whose routine use is inhibited by lack of data on performance and cost. (See: Established treatment technologies.)

Inoculum: 1. Bacteria or fungi injected into compost to start biological action. 2. A medium containing organisms, usually bacteria or a virus, that is introduced into cultures or living organisms.

Inorganic Chemicals: Chemical substances of mineral origin, not of basically carbon structure.

Insecticide: A pesticide compound specifically used to kill or prevent the growth of insects.

Inspection and Maintenance (I/M): 1. Activities to ensure that vehicles' emission controls work properly. 2. Also applies to wastewater treatment plants and other anti-pollution facilities and processes.

Institutional Waste: Waste generated at institutions such as schools, libraries, hospitals, prisons, etc.

Instream Use: Water use taking place within a stream channel; e.g., hydroelectric power generation, navigation, water quality improvement, fish propagation, recreation.

Integrated Exposure Assessment: Cumulative summation (over time) of the magnitude of exposure to a toxic chemical in all media.

Integrated Pest Management (IPM): A mixture of chemical and other, non-pesticide, methods to control pests.

Integrated Waste Management: Using a variety of practices to handle municipal solid waste; can include source reduction, recycling, incineration, and landfilling.

Interceptor Sewers: Large sewer lines that, in a combined system, control the flow of sewage to the treatment plant. In a storm, they allow some of the sewage to flow directly into a receiving stream, thus keeping it from overflowing onto the streets. Also used in separate systems to collect the flows from main and trunk sewers and carry them to treatment points.

Interface: The common boundary between two substances such as a water and a solid, water and a gas, or two liquids such as water and oil.

Interfacial Tension: The strength of the film separating two immiscible fluids (e.g. oil and water) measured in dynes per, or millidynes per centimeter.

Interim (Permit) Status: Period during which treatment, storage and disposal facilities coming under RCRA in 1980 are temporarily permitted to operate while awaiting a permanent permit. Permits issued under these circumstances are usually called "Part A" or "Part B" permits.

Internal Dose: In exposure assessment, the amount of a substance penetrating the absorption barriers (e.g. skin, lung tissue, gastrointestinal tract) of an organism through either physical or biological processes. (See: absorbed dose)

Interstate Carrier Water Supply: A source of water for drinking and sanitary use on planes, buses, trains, and ships operating in more than one state. These sources are federally regulated.

Interstate Commerce Clause: A clause of the U.S. Constitution which reserves to the federal government the right to regulate the conduct of business across state lines. Under this clause, for example, the U.S. Su-

preme Court has ruled that states may not inequitably restrict the disposal of out-of-state wastes in their jurisdictions.

Interstate Waters: Waters that flow across or form part of state or international boundaries; e.g. the Great Lakes, the Mississippi River, or
coastal waters.

Interstitial Monitoring: The continuous surveillance of the space between the walls of an underground storage tank.

Intrastate Product: Pesticide products once registered by states for sale
and use only in the state. All intrastate products have been converted to
full federal registration or canceled.

Inventory (TSCA): Inventory of chemicals produced pursuant to Section
8 (b) of the Toxic Substances Control Act.

Inversion: A layer of warm air that prevents the rise of cooling air and traps
pollutants beneath it; can cause an air pollution episode.

Ion: An electrically charged atom or group of atoms.

Ion Exchange Treatment: A common water-softening method often
found on a large scale at water purification plants that remove some organics and radium by adding calcium oxide or calcium hydroxide to increase the pH to a level where the metals will precipitate out.

Ionization Chamber: A device that measures the intensity of ionizing radiation.

Ionizing Radiation: Radiation that can strip electrons from atoms; e.g.
alpha, beta, and gamma radiation.

IRIS: EPA's Integrated Risk Information System, an electronic data base
containing the Agency's latest descriptive and quantitative regulatory
information on chemical constituents.

Irradiated Food: Food subject to brief radioactivity, usually gamma rays, to
kill insects, bacteria, and mold, and to permit storage without refrigeration.

Irradiation: Exposure to radiation of wavelengths shorter than those of
visible light (gamma, x-ray, or ultra- violet), for medical purposes, to sterilize milk or other foodstuffs, or to induce polymerization of monomers
or vulcanization of rubber.

Irreversible Effect: Effect characterized by the inability of the body to
partially or fully repair injury caused by a toxic agent.

Irrigation: Applying water or wastewater to land areas to supply the water
and nutrient needs of plants.

Irrigation Efficiency: The amount of water stored in the crop root zone
compared to the amount of irrigation water applied.

Irrigation Return Flow: Surface and subsurface water which leaves the field following application of irrigation water.

Irritant: A substance that can cause irritation of the skin, eyes, or respiratory system. Effects may be acute from a single high level exposure, or chronic from repeated low-level exposures to such compounds as chlorine, nitrogen dioxide, and nitric acid.

Isoconcentration: More than one sample point exhibiting the same isolate concentration.

Isopleth: The line or area represented by an isoconcentration.

Isotope: A variation of an element that has the same atomic number of protons but a different weight because of the number of neutrons. Various isotopes of the same element may have different radioactive behaviors, some are highly unstable..

Isotropy: The condition in which the hydraulic or other properties of an aquifer are the same in all directions.

Jar Test: A laboratory procedure that simulates a water treatment plant's coagulation/flocculation units with differing chemical doses, mix speeds, and settling times to estimate the minimum or ideal coagulant dose required to achieve certain water quality goals.

Joint and Several Liability: Under CERCLA, this legal concept relates to the liability for Superfund site cleanup and other costs on the part of more than one potentially responsible party (i.e. if there were several owners or users of a site that became contaminated over the years, they could all be considered potentially liable for cleaning up the site.)

Karst: A geologic formation of irregular limestone deposits with sinks, underground streams, and caverns.

Kinetic Energy: Energy possessed by a moving object or water body.

Kinetic Rate Coefficient: A number that describes the rate at which a water constituent such as a biochemical oxygen demand or dissolved oxygen rises or falls, or at which an air pollutant reacts.

Laboratory Animal Studies: Investigations using animals as surrogates for humans.

Lagoon: 1. A shallow pond where sunlight, bacterial action, and oxygen work to purify wastewater; also used for storage of wastewater or spent nuclear fuel rods. 2. Shallow body of water, often separated from the sea by coral reefs or sandbars.

Land Application: Discharge of wastewater onto the ground for treatment or reuse. (See: irrigation.)

Land Ban: Phasing out of land disposal of most untreated hazardous wastes, as mandated by the 1984 RCRA amendments.

Land Disposal Restrictions: Rules that require hazardous wastes to be treated before disposal on land to destroy or immobilize hazardous constituents that might migrate into soil and ground water.

Land Farming (of Waste): A disposal process in which hazardous waste deposited on or in the soil is degraded naturally by microbes.

Landfills: 1. Sanitary landfills are disposal sites for non-hazardous solid wastes spread in layers, compacted to the smallest practical volume, and covered by material applied at the end of each operating day. 2. Secure chemical landfills are disposal sites for hazardous waste, selected and designed to minimize the chance of release of hazardous substances into the environment.

Landscape: The traits, patterns, and structure of a specific geographic area, including its biological composition, its physical environment, and its anthropogenic or social patterns. An area where interacting ecosystems are grouped and repeated in similar form.

Landscape Characterization: Documentation of the traits and patterns of the essential elements of the landscape.

Landscape Ecology: The study of the distribution patterns of communities and ecosystems, the ecological processes that affect those patterns, and changes in pattern and process over time.

Landscape Indicator: A measurement of the landscape, calculated from mapped or remotely sensed data, used to describe spatial patterns of land use and land cover across a geographic area. Landscape indicators may be useful as measures of certain kinds of environmental degradation such as forest fragmentation.

Langelier Index (LI): An index reflecting the equilibrium pH of a water with respect to calcium and alkalinity; used in stabilizing water to control both corrosion and scale deposition.

Large Quantity Generator: Person or facility generating more than 2200 pounds of hazardous waste per month. Such generators produce about 90 percent of the nation's hazardous waste, and are subject to all RCRA requirements.

Large Water System: A water system that services more than 50,000 customers.

Laser Induced Fluorescence: A method for measuring the relative amount of soil and/or groundwater with an in-situ sensor.

Latency: Time from the first exposure of a chemical until the appearance of a toxic effect.

Lateral Sewers: Pipes that run under city streets and receive the sewage from homes and businesses, as opposed to domestic feeders and main trunk lines.

Laundering Weir: Sedimention basin overflow weir.

LC 50/Lethal Concentration: Median level concentration, a standard measure of toxicity. It tells how much of a substance is needed to kill half of a group of experimental organisms in a given time. (See: LD 50.)

LD 50/ Lethal Dose: The dose of a toxicant or microbe that will kill 50 percent of the test organisms within a designated period. The lower the LD 50, the more toxic the compound.

Ldlo: Lethal dose low; the lowest dose in an animal study at which lethality occurs.

Leachate: Water that collects contaminants as it trickles through wastes, pesticides or fertilizers. Leaching may occur in farming areas, feedlots, and landfills, and may result in hazardous substances entering surface water, ground water, or soil.

Leachate Collection System: A system that gathers leachate and pumps it to the surface for treatment.

Leaching: The process by which soluble constituents are dissolved and filtered through the soil by a percolating fluid. (See: leachate.)

Lead (Pb): A heavy metal that is hazardous to health if breathed or swallowed. Its use in gasoline, paints, and plumbing compounds has been sharply restricted or eliminated by federal laws and regulations. (See: heavy metals.)

Lead Service Line: A service line made of lead which connects the water to the building inlet and any lead fitting connected to it.

Legionella: A genus of bacteria, some species of which have caused a type of pneumonia called Legionaires Disease.

Lethal Concentration 50: Also referred to as LC_{50}, a concentration of a pollutant or effluent at which 50 percent of the test organisms die; a common measure of acute toxicity.

Lethal Dose 50: Also referred to as LD_{50}, the dose of a toxicant that will kill 50 percent of test organisms within a designated period of time; the lower the LD 50, the more toxic the compound.

Level of Concern (LOC): The concentration in air of an extremely hazardous substance above which there may be serious immediate health effects to anyone exposed to it for short periods

Life Cycle of a Product: All stages of a product's development, from extraction of fuel for power to production, marketing, use, and disposal.

Lifetime Average Daily Dose: Figure for estimating excess lifetime cancer risk.

Lifetime Exposure: Total amount of exposure to a substance that a human would receive in a lifetime (usually assumed to be 70 years).

Lift: In a sanitary landfill, a compacted layer of solid waste and the top layer of cover material.

Lifting Station: (See: pumping station.)

Light Non-Aqueous Phase Liquid (LNAPL): A non-aqueous phase liquid with a specific gravity less than 1.0. Because the specific gravity of water is 1.0, most LNAPLs float on top of the water table. Most common petroleum hydrocarbon fuels and lubricating oils are LNAPLs.

Light-Emitting Diode: A long-lasting illumination technology used for exit signs which requires very little power

Limestone Scrubbing: Use of a limestone and water solution to remove gaseous stack-pipe sulfur before it reaches the atmosphere.

Limit of Detection (LOD): The minimum concentration of a substance being analyzed test that has a 99 percent probability of being identified.

Limited Degradation: An environmental policy permitting some degradation of natural systems but terminating at a level well beneath an established health standard.

Limiting Factor: A condition whose absence or excessive concentration, is incompatible with the needs or tolerance of a species or population and which may have a negative influence on their ability to thrive.

Limnology: The study of the physical, chemical, hydrological, and biological aspects of fresh water bodies.

Lindane: A pesticide that causes adverse health effects in domestic water supplies and is toxic to freshwater fish and aquatic life.

Liner: 1. A relatively impermeable barrier designed to keep leachate inside a landfill. Liner materials include plastic and dense clay. 2. An insert or sleeve for sewer pipes to prevent leakage or infiltration.

Lipid Solubility: The maximum concentration of a chemical that will dissolve in fatty substances. Lipid soluble substances are insoluble in water. They will very selectively disperse through the environment via uptake in living tissue.

Liquefaction: Changing a solid into a liquid.

Liquid Injection Incinerator: Commonly used system that relies on high pressure to prepare liquid wastes for incineration by breaking them up into tiny droplets to allow easier combustion.

List: Shorthand term for EPA list of violating facilities or firms debarred from obtaining government contracts because they violated certain sections of the Clean Air or Clean Water Acts. The list is maintained by The Office of Enforcement and Compliance Monitoring.

Listed Waste: Wastes listed as hazardous under RCRA but which have not been subjected to the Toxic Characteristics Listing Process because the dangers they present are considered self-evident.

Lithology: Mineralogy, grain size, texture, and other physical properties of granular soil, sediment, or rock.

Litter: 1. The highly visible portion of solid waste carelessly discarded outside the regular garbage and trash collection and disposal system. 2. leaves and twigs fallen from forest trees.

Littoral Zone: 1. That portion of a body of fresh water extending from the shoreline lakeward to the limit of occupancy of rooted plants. 2. A strip of land along the shoreline between the high and low water levels.

Local Education Agency (LEA): In the asbestos program, an educational agency at the local level that exists primarily to operate schools or to contract for educational services, including primary and secondary public and private schools. A single, unaffiliated school can be considered an LEA for AHERA purposes.

Local Emergency Planning Committee (LEPC): A committee appointed by the state emergency response commission, as required by SARA Title III, to formulate a comprehensive emergency plan for its jurisdiction.

Low Density Polyethylene (LOPE): Plastic material used for both rigid containers and plastic film applications.

Low Emissivity (low-E) Windows: New window technology that lowers the amount of energy loss through windows by inhibiting the transmission of radiant heat while still allowing sufficient light to pass through.

Low NO$_x$ Burners: One of several combustion technologies used to reduce emissions of Nitrogen Oxides (NOx.)

Low-Level Radioactive Waste (LLRW): Wastes less hazardous than most of those associated with a nuclear reactor; generated by hospitals, research laboratories, and certain industries. The Department of Energy, Nuclear Regulatory Commission, and EPA share responsibilities for managing them. (See: high-level radioactive wastes.)

Lower Detection Limit: The smallest signal above background noise an instrument can reliably detect.

Lower Explosive Limit (LEL): The concentration of a compound in air below which the mixture will not catch on fire.

Lowest Acceptable Daily Dose: The largest quantity of a chemical that will not cause a toxic effect, as determined by animal studies.

Lowest Achievable Emission Rate: Under the Clean Air Act, the rate of emissions that reflects (1) the most stringent emission limitation in the implementation plan of any state for such source unless the owner or operator demonstrates such limitations are not achievable; or (2) the most stringent emissions limitation achieved in practice, whichever is more stringent. A proposed new or modified source may not emit pollutants in excess of existing new source standards.

Lowest Observed Adverse Effect Level (LOAEL): The lowest level of a stressor that causes statistically and biologically significant differences in test samples as compared to other samples subjected to no stressor.

Macropores: Secondary soil features such as root holes or desiccation cracks that can create significant conduits for movement of NAPL and dissolved contaminants, or vapor-phase contaminants.

Magnetic Separation: Use of magnets to separate ferrous materials from mixed municipal waste stream.

Major Modification: This term is used to define modifications of major stationary sources of emissions with respect to Prevention of Significant Deterioration and New Source Review under the Clean Air Act.

Major Stationary Sources: Term used to determine the applicability of Prevention of Significant Deterioration and new source regulations. In a nonattainment area, any stationary pollutant source with potential to emit more than 100 tons per year is considered a major stationary source. In PSD areas the cutoff level may be either 100 or 250 tons, depending upon the source.

Majors: Larger publicly owned treatment works (POTWs) with flows equal to at least one million gallons per day (mgd) or servicing a population equivalent to 10,000 persons; certain other POTWs having significant water quality impacts. (See: minors.)

Man-Made (Anthropogenic) Beta Particle and Photon Emitters: All radionuclides emitting beta particles and/or photons listed in Maximum Permissible Body Burdens and Maximum Permissible Concentrations of Radonuclides in Air and Water for Occupational Exposure.

Management Plan: Under the Asbestos Hazard Emergency Response Act (AHERA), a document that each Local Education Agency is required to prepare, describing all activities planned and undertaken by a school to comply with AHERA regulations, including building inspections to identify asbestos-containing materials, response actions, and operations and maintenance programs to minimize the risk of exposure.

Managerial Controls: Methods of nonpoint source pollution control based on decisions about managing agricultural wastes or application times or rates for agrochemicals.

Mandatory Recycling: Programs which by law require consumers to separate trash so that some or all recyclable materials are recovered for recycling rather than going to landfills.

Manifest: A one-page form used by haulers transporting waste that lists EPA identification numbers, type and quantity of waste, the generator it originated from, the transporter that shipped it, and the storage or disposal facility to which it is being shipped. It includes copies for all participants in the shipping process.

Manifest System: Tracking of hazardous waste from "cradle-to-grave" (generation through disposal) with accompanying documents known as manifests.(See: cradle to grave.)

Manual Separation: Hand sorting of recyclable or compostable materials in waste.

Manufacturer's Formulation: A list of substances or component parts as described by the maker of a coating, pesticide, or other product containing chemicals or other substances.

Manufacturing Use Product: Any product intended (labeled) for formulation or repackaging into other pesticide products.

Margin of Safety: Maximum amount of exposure producing no measurable effect in animals (or studied humans) divided by the actual amount of human exposure in a population.

Margin of Exposure (MOE): The ratio of the no-observed adverse-effect level to the estimated exposure dose.

Marine Sanitation Device: Any equipment or process installed on board a vessel to receive, retain, treat, or discharge sewage.

Marsh: A type of wetland that does not accumulate appreciable peat deposits and is dominated by herbaceous vegetation. Marshes may be either fresh or saltwater, tidal or non-tidal. (See: wetlands.)

Material Category: In the asbestos program, broad classification of materials into thermal surfacing insulation, surfacing material, and miscellaneous material.

Material Safety Data Sheet (MSDS): A compilation of information required under the OSHA Communication Standard on the identity of hazardous chemicals, health, and physical hazards, exposure limits, and precautions. Section 311 of SARA requires facilities to submit MSDSs under certain circumstances.

Material Type: Classification of suspect material by its specific use or application; e.g., pipe insulation, fireproofing, and floor tile.

Materials Recovery Facility (MRF): A facility that processes residentially collected mixed recyclables into new products available for market.

Maximally (or Most) Exposed Individual: The person with the highest exposure in a given population.

Maximum Acceptable Toxic Concentration: For a given ecological effects test, the range (or geometric mean) between the No Observable Adverse Effect Level and the Lowest Observable Adverse Effects Level.

Maximum Available Control Technology (MACT): The emission standard for sources of air pollution requiring the maximum reduction of hazardous emissions, taking cost and feasibility into account. Under the Clean Air Act Amendments of 1990, the MACT must not be less than the average emission level achieved by controls on the best performing 12 percent of existing sources, by category of industrial and utility sources.

Maximum Contaminant Level: The maximum permissible level of a contaminant in water delivered to any user of a public system. MCLs are enforceable standards.

Maximum Contaminant Level Goal (MCLG): Under the Safe Drinking Water Act, a non-enforceable concentration of a drinking water contaminant, set at the level at which no known or anticipated adverse effects on human health occur and which allows an adequate safety margin. The MCLG is usually the starting point for determining the regulated Maximum Contaminant Level. (See: maximum contaminant level.)

Maximum Exposure Range: Estimate of exposure or dose level received by an individual in a defined population that is greater than the 98th percentile dose for all individuals in that population, but less than the exposure level received by the person receiving the highest exposure level.

Maximum Residue Level: Comparable to a U.S. tolerance level, the Maximum Residue Level the enforceable limit on food pesticide levels in some countries. Levels are set by the Codex Alimentarius Commission, a United Nations agency managed and funded jointly by the World Health Organization and the Food and Agriculture Organization.

Maximum Tolerated Dose: The maximum dose that an animal species can tolerate for a major portion of its lifetime without significant impairment or toxic effect other than carcinogenicity.

Measure of Effect/ Measurement Endpoint: A measurable characteristic of ecological entity that can be related to an assessment endpoint;

e.g. a laboratory test for eight species meeting certain requirements may serve as a measure of effect for an assessment endpoint, such as survival of fish, aquatic, invertebrate or algal species under acute exposure.

Measure of Exposure: A measurable characteristic of a stressor (such as the specific amount of mercury in a body of water) used to help quantify the exposure of an ecological entity or individual organism.

Mechanical Aeration: Use of mechanical energy to inject air into water to cause a waste stream to absorb oxygen.

Mechanical Separation: Using mechanical means to separate waste into various components.

Mechanical Turbulence: Random irregularities of fluid motion in air caused by buildings or other nonthermal, processes.

Media: Specific environments--air, water, soil--which are the subject of regulatory concern and activities.

Medical Surveillance: A periodic comprehensive review of a worker's health status; acceptable elements of such surveillance program are listed in the Occupational Safety and Health Administration standards for asbestos.

Medical Waste: Any solid waste generated in the diagnosis, treatment, or immunization of human beings or animals, in research pertaining thereto, or in the production or testing of biologicals, excluding hazardous waste identified or listed under 40 CFR Part 261 or any household waste as defined in 40 CFR Sub-section 261.4 (b)(1).

Medium-size Water System: A water system that serves 3,300 to 50,000 customers.

Meniscus: The curved top of a column of liquid in a small tube.

Mercury (Hg): Heavy metal that can accumulate in the environment and is highly toxic if breathed or swallowed. (See:heavy metals.)

Mesotrophic: Reservoirs and lakes which contain moderate quantities of nutrients and are moderately productive in terms of aquatic animal and plant life.

Metabolites: Any substances produced by biological processes, such as those from pesticides.

Metalimnion: The middle layer of a thermally stratified lake or reservoir. In this layer there is a rapid decrease in temperature with depth. Also called thermocline.

Methane: A colorless, nonpoisonous, flammable gas created by anaerobic decomposition of organic compounds. A major component of natural gas used in the home.

Methanol: An alcohol that can be used as an alternative fuel or as a gasoline additive. It is less volatile than gasoline; when blended with gasoline it lowers the carbon monoxide emissions but increases hydrocarbon emissions. Used as pure fuel, its emissions are less ozone-forming than those from gasoline. Poisonous to humans and animals if ingested.

Method 18: An EPA test method which uses gas chromatographic techniques to measure the concentration of volatile organic compounds in a gas stream.

Method 24: An EPA reference method to determine density, water content and total volatile content (water and VOC) of coatings.

Method 25: An EPA reference method to determine the VOC concentration in a gas stream.

Method Detection Limit (MDL): See limit of detection.

Methoxychlor: Pesticide that causes adverse health effects in domestic water supplies and is toxic to freshwater and marine aquatic life.

Methyl Orange Alkalinity: A measure of the total alkalinity in a water sample in which the color of methyl orange reflects the change in level.

Microbial Growth: The amplification or multiplication of microorganisms such as bacteria, algae, diatoms, plankton, and fungi.

Microbial Pesticide: A microorganism that is used to kill a pest, but is of minimum toxicity to humans.

Microclimate: 1. Localized climate conditions within an urban area or neighborhood. 2. The climate around a tree or shrub or a stand of trees.

Microenvironmental Method: A method for sequentially assessing exposure for a series of microenvironments that can be approximated by constant concentrations of a stressor.

Microenvironments: Well-defined surroundings such as the home, office, or kitchen that can be treated as uniform in terms of stressor concentration.

Million-Gallons Per Day (MGD): A measure of water flow.

Minimization: A comprehensive program to minimize or eliminate wastes, usually applied to wastes at their point of origin. (See: waste minimization.)

Mining of an Aquifer: Withdrawal over a period of time of ground water that exceeds the rate of recharge of the aquifer.

Mining Waste: Residues resulting from the extraction of raw materials from the earth.

Minor Source: New emissions sources or modifications to existing emissions sources that do not exceed NAAQS emission levels.

Minors: Publicly owned treatment works with flows less than 1 million gallons per day. (See: majors.)

Miscellaneous ACM: Interior asbestos-containing building material or structural components, members or fixtures, such as floor and ceiling tiles; does not include surfacing materials or thermal system insulation.

Miscellaneous Materials: Interior building materials on structural components, such as floor or ceiling tiles.

Miscible Liquids: Two or more liquids that can be mixed and will remain mixed under normal conditions.

Missed Detection: The situation that occurs when a test indicates that a tank is "tight" when in fact it is leaking.

Mist: Liquid particles measuring 40 to 500 micrometers (pm), are formed by condensation of vapor. By comparison, fog particles are smaller than 40 micrometers (pm).

Mitigation: Measures taken to reduce adverse impacts on the environment.

Mixed Funding: Settlements in which potentially responsible parties and EPA share the cost of a response action.

Mixed Glass: Recovered container glass not sorted into categories (e.g. color, grade).

Mixed Liquor: A mixture of activated sludge and water containing organic matter undergoing activated sludge treatment in an aeration tank.

Mixed Metals: Recovered metals not sorted into categories such as aluminum, tin, or steel cans or ferrous or non-ferrous metals.

Mixed Municipal Waste: Solid waste that has not been sorted into specific categories (such as plastic, glass, yard trimmings, etc.)

Mixed Paper: Recovered paper not sorted into categories such as old magazines, old newspapers, old corrugated boxes, etc.

Mixed Plastic: Recovered plastic unsorted by category.

Mobile Incinerator Systems: Hazardous waste incinerators that can be transported from one site to another.

Mobile Source: Any non-stationary source of air pollution such as cars, trucks, motorcycles, buses, airplanes, and locomotives.

Model Plant: A hypothetical plant design used for developing economic, environmental, and energy impact analyses as support for regulations or regulatory guidelines; first step in exploring the economic impact of a potential NSPS.

Modified Bin Method: Way of calculating the required heating or cooling for a building based on determining how much energy the system would use if outdoor temperatures were within a certain temperature interval and then multiplying the energy use by the time the temperature interval typically occurs.

Modified Source: The enlargement of a major stationary pollutant sources is often referred to as modification, implying that more emissions will occur.

Moisture Content: 1.The amount of water lost from soil upon drying to a constant weight, expressed as the weight per unit of dry soil or as the volume of water per unit bulk volume of the soil. For a fully saturated medium, moisture content indicates the porosity. 2. Water equivalent of snow on the ground; an indicator of snowmelt flood potential.

Molecule: The smallest division of a compound that still retains or exhibits all the properties of the substance.

Molten Salt Reactor: A thermal treatment unit that rapidly heats waste in a heat-conducting fluid bath of carbonate salt.

Monitoring: Periodic or continuous surveillance or testing to determine the level of compliance with statutory requirements and/or pollutant levels in various media or in humans, plants, and animals.

Monitoring Well: 1. A well used to obtain water quality samples or measure groundwater levels. 2. A well drilled at a hazardous waste management facility or Superfund site to collect ground-water samples for the purpose of physical, chemical, or biological analysis to determine the amounts, types, and distribution of contaminants in the groundwater beneath the site.

Monoclonal Antibodies (Also called MABs and MCAs): 1. Man-made (anthropogenic) clones of a molecule, produced in quantity for medical or research purposes. 2. Molecules of living organisms that selectively find and attach to other molecules to which their structure conforms exactly. This could also apply to equivalent activity by chemical molecules.

Monomictic: Lakes and reservoirs which are relatively deep, do not freeze over during winter, and undergo a single stratification and mixing cycle during the year (usually in the fall).

Montreal Protocol: Treaty, signed in 1987, governs stratospheric ozone protection and research, and the production and use of ozone-depleting substances. It provides for the end of production of ozone-depleting substances such as CFCS. Under the Protocol, various research groups continue to assess the ozone layer. The Multilateral Fund provides resources to developing nations to promote the transition to ozone-safe technologies.

Moratorium: During the negotiation process, a period of 60 to 90 days during which EPA and potentially responsible parties may reach settlement but no site response activities can be conducted.

Morbidity: Rate of disease incidence.

Mortality: Death rate.

Most Probable Number: An estimate of microbial density per unit volume of water sample, based on probability theory.

Muck Soils: Earth made from decaying plant materials.

Mudballs: Round material that forms in filters and gradually increases in size when not removed by backwashing.

Mulch: A layer of material (wood chips, straw, leaves, etc.) placed around plants to hold moisture, prevent weed growth, and enrich or sterilize the soil.

Multi-Media Approach: Joint approach to several environmental media, such as air, water, and land.

Multiple Chemical Sensitivity: A diagnostic label for people who suffer multi-system illnesses as a result of contact with, or proximity to, a variety of airborne agents and other substances.

Multiple Use: Use of land for more than one purpose; e.g., grazing of livestock, watershed and wildlife protection, recreation, and timber production. Also applies to use of bodies of water for recreational purposes, fishing, and water supply.

Multistage Remote Sensing: A strategy for landscape characterization that involves gathering and analyzing information at several geographic scales, ranging from generalized levels of detail at the national level through high levels of detail at the local scale.

Municipal Discharge: Discharge of effluent from waste water treatment plants which receive waste water from households, commercial establishments, and industries in the coastal drainage basin. Combined sewer/separate storm overflows are included in this category.

Municipal Sewage: Wastes (mostly liquid) orginating from a community; may be composed of domestic wastewaters and/or industrial discharges.

Municipal Sludge: Semi-liquid residue remaining from the treatment of municipal water and wastewater.

Municipal Solid Waste: Common garbage or trash generated by industries, businesses, institutions, and homes.

Mutagen/Mutagenicity: An agent that causes a permanent genetic change in a cell other than that which occurs during normal growth. Mutagenicity is the capacity of a chemical or physical agent to cause such permanent changes.

National Ambient Air Quality Standards (NAAQS): Standards established by EPA that apply for outdoor air throughout the country. (See: criteria pollutants, state implementation plans, emissions trading.)

National Emissions Standards for Hazardous Air Pollutants (NESHAPS): Emissions standards set by EPA for an air pollutant not covered by NAAQS that may cause an increase in fatalities or in serious, irreversible, or incapacitating illness. Primary standards are designed to protect human health, secondary standards to protect public welfare (e.g. building facades, visibility, crops, and domestic animals).

National Environmental Performance Partnership Agreements: System that allows states to assume greater responsibility for environmental programs based on their relative ability to execute them.

National Estuary Program: A program established under the Clean Water Act Amendments of 1987 to develop and implement conservation and management plans for protecting estuaries and restoring and maintaining their chemical, physical, and biological integrity, as well as controlling point and nonpoint pollution sources.

National Municipal Plan: A policy created in 1984 by EPA and the states in 1984 to bring all publicly owned treatment works (POTWs) into compliance with Clean Water Act requirements.

National Oil and Hazardous Substances Contingency Plan (NOHSCP/NCP): The federal regulation that guides determination of the sites to be corrected under both the Superfund program and the program to prevent or control spills into surface waters or elsewhere.

National Pollutant Discharge Elimination System (NPDES): A provision of the Clean Water Act which prohibits discharge of pollutants into waters of the United States unless a special permit is issued by EPA, a state, or, where delegated, a tribal government on an Indian reservation.

National Priorities List (NPL): EPA's list of the most serious uncontrolled or abandoned hazardous waste sites identified for possible long-term remedial action under Superfund. The list is based primarily on the score a site receives from the Hazard Ranking System. EPA is required to update the NPL at least once a year. A site must be on the NPL to receive money from the Trust Fund for remedial action.

National Response Center: The federal operations center that receives notifications of all releases of oil and hazardous substances into the environment; open 24 hours a day, is operated by the U.S. Coast Guard, which evaluates all reports and notifies the appropriate agency.

National Response Team (NRT): Representatives of 13 federal agencies that, as a team, coordinate federal responses to nationally significant incidents of pollution--an oil spill, a major chemical release, or a—superfund response action--and provide advice and technical assistance to the responding agency(ies) before and during a response action.

National Secondary Drinking Water Regulations: Commonly referred to as NSDWRs.

Navigable Waters: Traditionally, waters sufficiently deep and wide for navigation by all, or specified vessels; such waters in the United States come under federal jurisdiction and are protected by certain provisions of the Clean Water Act.

Necrosis: Death of plant or animal cells or tissues. In plants, necrosis can discolor stems or leaves or kill a plant entirely.

Negotiations (Under Superfund): After potentially responsible parties are identified for a site, EPA coordinates with them to reach a settlement that will result in the PRP paying for or conducting the cleanup under EPA supervision. If negotiations fail, EPA can order the PRP to conduct the cleanup or EPA can pay for the cleanup using Superfund monies and then sue to recover the costs.

Nematocide: A chemical agent which is destructive to nematodes.

Nephelometric: Method of of measuring turbidity in a water sample by passing light through the sample and measuring the amount of the light that is deflected.

Netting: A concept in which all emissions sources in the same area that owned or controlled by a single company are treated as one large source, thereby allowing flexibility in controlling individual sources in order to meet a single emissions standard. (See: bubble.)

Neutralization: Decreasing the acidity or alkalinity of a substance by adding alkaline or acidic materials, respectively.

New Source: Any stationary source built or modified after publication of final or proposed regulations that prescribe a given standard of performance.

New Source Performance Standards (NSPS): Uniform national EPA air emission and water effluent standards which limit the amount of pollution allowed from new sources or from modified existing sources.

New Source Review (NSR): A Clean Air Act requirement that State Implementation Plans must include a permit review that applies to the construction and operation of new and modified stationary sources in nonattainment areas to ensure attainment of national ambient air quality standards.

Nitrate: A compound containing nitrogen that can exist in the atmosphere or as a dissolved gas in water and which can have harmful effects on humans and animals. Nitrates in water can cause severe illness in infants and domestic animals. A plant nutrient and inorganic fertilizer, nitrate is found in septic systems, animal feed lots, agricultural fertilizers, manure, industrial waste waters, sanitary landfills, and garbage dumps.

Nitric Oxide (NO): A gas formed by combustion under high temperature and high pressure in an internal combustion engine; it is converted by sunlight and photochemical processes in ambient air to nitrogen oxide. NO is a precursor of ground-level ozone pollution, or smog..

Nitrification: The process whereby ammonia in wastewater is oxidized to nitrite and then to nitrate by bacterial or chemical reactions.

Nitrilotriacetic Acid (NTA): A compound now replacing phosphates in detergents.

Nitrite: 1. An intermediate in the process of nitrification. 2. Nitrous oxide salts used in food preservation.

Nitrogen Dioxide (NO_2): The result of nitric oxide combining with oxygen in the atmosphere; major component of photochemical smog.

Nitrogen Oxide (NO_x): The result of photochemical reactions of nitric oxide in ambient air; major component of photochemical smog. Product of combustion from transportation and stationary sources and a major contributor to the formation of ozone in the troposphere and to acid deposition.

Nitrogenous Wastes: Animal or vegetable residues that contain significant amounts of nitrogen.

Nitrophenols: Synthetic organopesticides containing carbon, hydrogen, nitrogen, and oxygen.

No Further Remedial Action Planned: Determination made by EPA following a preliminary assessment that a site does not pose a significant risk and so requires no further activity under CERCLA.

No Observable Adverse Effect Level (NOAEL): An exposure level at which there are no statistically or biologically significant increases in the frequency or severity of adverse effects between the exposed population and its appropriate control; some effects may be produced at this level, but they are not considered as adverse, or as precursors to adverse effects. In an experiment with several NOAELs, the regulatory focus is primarily on the highest one, leading to the common usage of the term NOAEL as the highest exposure without adverse effects.

No Till: Planting crops without prior seedbed preparation, into an existing cover crop, sod, or crop residues, and eliminating subsequent tillage operations.

No-Observed-Effect-Level (NOEL): Exposure level at which there are no statistically or biological significant differences in the frequency or severity of any effect in the exposed or control populations.

Noble Metal: Chemically inactive metal such as gold; does not corrode easily.

Noise: Product-level or product-volume changes occurring during a test that are not related to a leak but may be mistaken for one.

Non-Aqueous Phase Liquid (NAPL): Contaminants that remain undiluted as the original bulk liquid in the subsurface, e.g. spilled oil. (See: fee product.)

Non-Attainment Area: Area that does not meet one or more of the National Ambient Air Quality Standards for the criteria pollutants designated in the Clean Air Act.

Non-Binding Allocations of Responsibility (NBAR): A process for EPA to propose a way for potentially responsible parties to allocate costs among themselves.

Non-Community Water System: A public water system that is not a community water system; e.g. the water supply at a camp site or national park.

Non-Compliance Coal: Any coal that emits greater than 3.0 pounds of sulfur dioxide per million BTU when burned. Also known as high-sulfur coal.

Non-Contact Cooling Water: Water used for cooling which does not come into direct contact with any raw material, product, byproduct, or waste.

Non-Conventional Pollutant: Any pollutant not statutorily listed or which is poorly understood by the scientific community.

Non-Degradation: An environmental policy which disallows any lowering of naturally occurring quality regardless of preestablished health standards.

Non-Ferrous Metals: Nonmagnetic metals such as aluminum, lead, and copper. Products made all or in part from such metals include containers, packaging, appliances, furniture, electronic equipment and aluminum foil.

Non-ionizing Electromagnetic Radiation: 1. Radiation that does not change the structure of atoms but does heat tissue and may cause harmful biological effects. 2. Microwaves, radio waves, and low-frequency electromagnetic fields from high-voltage transmission lines.

Non-Methane Hydrocarbon (NMHC): The sum of all hydrocarbon air pollutants except methane; significant precursors to ozone formation.

Non-Methane Organic Gases (NMOG): The sum of all organic air pollutants. Excluding methane; they account for aldehydes, ketones, alcohols, and other pollutants that are not hydrocarbons but are precursors of ozone.

Non-Point Sources: Diffuse pollution sources (i.e. without a single point of origin or not introduced into a receiving stream from a specific outlet). The pollutants are generally carried off the land by storm water. Common non-point sources are agriculture, forestry, urban, mining, construction, dams, channels, land disposal, saltwater intrusion, and city streets.

Non-potable: Water that is unsafe or unpalatable to drink because it contains pollutants, contaminants, minerals, or infective agents.

Non-Road Emissions: Pollutants emitted by combustion engines on farm and construction equipment, gasoline-powered lawn and garden equipment, and power boats and outboard motors.

Non-Transient Non-Community Water System: A public water system that regularly serves at least 25 of the same non-resident persons per day for more than six months per year.

Nondischarging Treatment Plant: A treatment plant that does not discharge treated wastewater into any stream or river. Most are pond systems that dispose of the total flow they receive by means of evaporation or percolation to groundwater, or facilities that dispose of their effluent by recycling or reuse (e.g. spray irrigation or groundwater discharge).

Nonfriable Asbestos-Containing Materials: Any material containing more than one percent asbestos (as determined by Polarized Light Microscopy) that, when dry, cannot be crumbled, pulverized, or reduced to powder by hand pressure.

Nonhazardous Industrial Waste: Industrial process waste in wastewater not considered municipal solid waste or hazardous waste under RARA.

Notice of Deficiency: An EPA request to a facility owner or operator requesting additional information before a preliminary decision on a permit application can be made.

Notice of Intent to Cancel: Notification sent to registrants when EPA decides to cancel registration of a product containing a pesticide.

Notice of Intent to Deny: Notification by EPA of its preliminary intent to deny a permit application.

Notice of Intent to Suspend: Notification sent to a pesticide registrant when EPA decides to suspend product sale and distribution because of failure to submit requested data in a timely and/or acceptable manner, or because of imminent hazard. (See: emergency suspension.)

Nuclear Reactors and Support Facilities: Uranium mills, commercial power reactors, fuel reprocessing plants, and uranium enrichment facilities.

Nuclear Winter: Prediction by some scientists that smoke and debris rising from massive fires of a nuclear war could block sunlight for weeks or months, cooling the earth's surface and producing climate changes that could, for example, negatively affect world agricultural and weather patterns.

Nuclide: An atom characterized by the number of protons, neturons, and energy in the nucleus.

Nutrient: Any substance assimilated by living things that promotes growth. The term is generally applied to nitrogen and phosphorus in wastewater, but is also applied to other essential and trace elements.

Nutrient Pollution: Contamination of water resources by excessive inputs of nutrients. In surface waters, excess algal production is a major concern.

Ocean Discharge Waiver: A variance from Clean Water Act requirements for discharges into marine waters.

Odor Threshold: The minimum odor of a water or air sample that can just be detected after successive dilutions with odorless water. Also called threshold odor.

OECD Guidelines: Testing guidelines prepared by the Organization of Economic and Cooperative Development of the United Nations. They assist in preparation of protocols for studies of toxicology, environmental fate, etc.

Off-Site Facility: A hazardous waste treatment, storage or disposal area that is located away from the generating site.

Office Paper: High grade papers such as copier paper, computer printout, and stationary almost entirely made of uncoated chemical pulp, although some ground wood is used. Such waste is also generated in homes, schools, and elsewhere.

Offsets: A concept whereby emissions from proposed new or modified stationary sources are balanced by reductions from existing sources to stabilize total emissions. (See: bubble, emissions trading, netting)

Offstream Use: Water withdrawn from surface or groundwater sources for use at another place.

Oil and Gas Waste: Gas and oil drilling muds, oil production brines, and other waste associated with exploration for, development and production of crude oil or natural gas.

Oil Desulfurization: Widely used precombustion method for reducing sulfur dioxide emissions from oil-burning power plants. The oil is treated with hydrogen, which removes some of the sulfur by forming hydrogen sulfide gas.

Oil Fingerprinting: A method that identifies sources of oil and allows spills to be traced to their source.

Oil Spill: An accidental or intentional discharge of oil which reaches bodies of water. Can be controlled by chemical dispersion, combustion, mechanical containment, and/or adsorption. Spills from tanks and pipelines can also occur away from water bodies, contaminating the soil, getting into sewer systems and threatening underground water sources.

Oligotrophic Lakes: Deep clear lakes with few nutrients, little organic matter and a high dissolved-oxygen level.

On-Scene Coordinator (OSC): The predesignated EPA, Coast Guard, or Department of Defense official who coordinates and directs Superfund removal actions or Clean Water Act oil- or hazardous-spill response actions.

On-Site Facility: A hazardous waste treatment, storage or disposal area that is located on the generating site.

Onboard Controls: Devices placed on vehicles to capture gasoline vapor during refueling and route it to the engines when the vehicle is starting so that it can be efficiently burned.

Onconogenicity: The capacity to induce cancer.

One-hit Model: A mathematical model based on the biological theory that a single "hit" of some minimum critical amount of a carcinogen at a cellular target such as DNA can start an irreversible series events leading to a tumor.

Opacity: The amount of light obscured by particulate pollution in the air; clear window glass has zero opacity, a brick wall is 100 percent opaque. Opacity is an indicator of changes in performance of particulate control systems.

Open Burning: Uncontrolled fires in an open dump.

Open Dump: An uncovered site used for disposal of waste without environmental controls. (See: dump.)

Operable Unit: Term for each of a number of separate activities undertaken as part of a Superfund site cleanup. A typical operable unit would be removal of drums and tanks from the surface of a site.

Operating Conditions: Conditions specified in a RCRA permit that dictate how an incinerator must operate as it burns different waste types. A trial burn is used to identify operating conditions needed to meet specified performance standards.

Operation and Maintenance: 1. Activities conducted after a Superfund site action is completed to ensure that the action is effective. 2. Actions taken after construction to ensure that facilities constructed to treat waste water will be properly operated and maintained to achieve normative efficiency levels and prescribed effluent limitations in an optimum manner. 3. On-going asbestos management plan in a school or other public building, including regular inspections, various methods of maintaining asbestos in place, and removal when necessary.

Operator Certification: Certification of operators of community and nontransient noncommunity water systems, asbestos specialists, pesticide applicators, hazardous waste transporter, and other such specialists as required by the EPA or a state agency implementing an EPA-approved environmental regulatory program.

Optimal Corrosion Control Treatment: An erosion control treatment that minimizes the lead and copper concentrations at users' taps while also ensuring that the treatment does not cause the water system to violate any national primary drinking water regulations.

Oral Toxicity: Ability of a pesticide to cause injury when ingested.

Organic: 1. Referring to or derived from living organisms. 2. In chemistry, any compound containing carbon.

Organic Chemicals/Compounds: Naturally occuring (animal or plant-produced or synthetic) substances containing mainly carbon, hydrogen, nitrogen, and oxygen.

Organic Matter: Carbonaceous waste contained in plant or animal matter and originating from domestic or industrial sources.

Organism: Any form of animal or plant life.

Organophosphates: Pesticides that contain phosphorus; short-lived, but some can be toxic when first applied.

Organophyllic: A substance that easily combines with organic compounds.

Organotins: Chemical compounds used in anti-foulant paints to protect the hulls of boats and ships, buoys, and pilings from marine organisms such as barnacles.

Original AHERA Inspection/Original Inspection/Inspection: Examination of school buildings arranged by Local Education Agencies to identify asbestos-containing-materials, evaluate their condition, and take samples of materials suspected to contain asbestos; performed by EPA-accredited inspectors.

Original Generation Point: Where regulated medical or other material first becomes waste.

Osmosis: The passage of a liquid from a weak solution to a more concentrated solution across a semipermeable membrane that allows passage of the solvent (water) but not the dissolved solids.

Other Ferrous Metals: Recyclable metals from strapping, furniture, and metal found in tires and consumer electronics but does not include metals found in construction materials or cars, locomotives, and ships. (See: ferrous metals.)

Other Glass: Recyclable glass from furniture, appliances, and consumer electronics. Does not include glass from transportation products (cars trucks or shipping containers) and construction or demolition debris. (See: glass.)

Other Nonferrous Metals: Recyclable nonferrous metals such as lead, copper, and zinc from appliances, consumer electronics, and nonpackaging aluminum products. Does not include nonferrous metals from industrial applications and construction and demolition debris. (See: nonferrous metals.)

Other Paper: For Recyclable paper from books, third-class mail, commercial printing, paper towels, plates and cups; and other nonpackaging paper such as posters, photographic papers, cards and games, milk cartons, folding boxes, bags, wrapping paper, and paperboard. Does not include wrapping paper or shipping cartons.

Other Plastics: Recyclable plastic from appliances, eating utensils, plates, containers, toys, and various kinds of equipment. Does not include heavy-duty plastics such as yielding materials.

Other Solid Waste: Recyclable nonhazardous solid wastes, other than municipal solid waste, covered under Subtitle D of RARA. (See: solid waste.)

Other Wood: Recyclable wood from furniture, consumer electronics cabinets, and other nonpackaging wood products. Does not include lumber and tree stumps recovered from construction and demolition activities, and industrial process waste such as shavings and sawdust.

Outdoor Air Supply: Air brought into a building from outside.

Outfall: The place where effluent is discharged into receiving waters.

Overburden: Rock and soil cleared away before mining.

Overdraft: The pumping of water from a groundwater basin or aquifer in excess of the supply flowing into the basin; results in a depletion or "mining" of the groundwater in the basin. (See: groundwater mining)

Overfire Air: Air forced into the top of an incinerator or boiler to fan the flames.

Overflow Rate: One of the guidelines for design of the settling tanks and clarifers in a treatment plant; used by plant operators to determine if tanks and clarifiers are over or under-used.

Overland Flow: A land application technique that cleanses waste water by allowing it to flow over a sloped surface. As the water flows over the surface, contaminants are absorbed and the water is collected at the bottom of the slope for reuse.

Oversized Regulated Medical Waste: Medical waste that is too large for plastic bags or standard containers.

Overturn: One complete cycle of top to bottom mixing of previously stratified water masses. This phenomenon may occur in spring or fall, or after storms, and results in uniformity of chemical and physical properties of water at all depths.

Oxidant: A collective term for some of the primary constituents of photochemical smog.

Oxidation Pond: A man-made (anthropogenic) body of water in which waste is consumed by bacteria, used most frequently with other waste-treatment processes; a sewage lagoon.

Oxidation: The chemical addition of oxygen to break down pollutants or organizac waste; e.g., destruction of chemicals such as cyanides, phenols, and organic sulfur compounds in sewage by bacterial and chemical means.

Oxidation-Reduction Potential: The electric potential required to transfer electrons from one compound or element (the oxidant) to another compound (the reductant); used as a qualitative measure of the state of oxidation in water treatment systems.

Oxygenated Fuels: Gasoline which has been blended with alcohols or ethers that contain oxygen in order to reduce carbon monoxide and other emissions.

Oxygenated Solvent: An organic solvent containing oxygen as part of the molecular structure. Alcohols and ketones are oxygenated compounds often used as paint solvents.

Ozonation/Ozonator: Application of ozone to water for disinfection or for taste and odor control. The ozonator is the device that does this.

Ozone (O_3): Found in two layers of the atmosphere, the stratosphere and the troposphere. In the stratosphere (the atmospheric layer 7 to 10 miles or more above the earth's surface) ozone is a natural form of oxygen that provides a protective layer shielding the earth from ultraviolet radiation.In the troposphere (the layer extending up 7 to 10 miles from the earth's surface), ozone is a chemical oxidant and major component of photochemical smog. It can seriously impair the respiratory system and is one of the most wide- spread of all the criteria pollutants for which the Clean Air Act required EPA to set standards. Ozone in the troposphere is produced through complex chemical reactions of nitrogen oxides, which are among the primary pollutants emitted by combustion sources; hydrocarbons, released into the atmosphere through the combustion, handling and processing of petroleum products; and sunlight.

Ozone Depletion: Destruction of the stratospheric ozone layer which shields the earth from ultraviolet radiation harmful to life. This destruction of ozone is caused by the breakdown of certain chlorine and/or bromine containing compounds (chlorofluorocarbons or halons), which break down when they reach the stratosphere and then catalytically destroy ozone molecules.

Ozone Hole: A thinning break in the stratospheric ozone layer. Designation of amount of such depletion as an "ozone hole" is made when the detected amount of depletion exceeds fifty percent. Seasonal ozone holes have been observed over both the Antarctic and Arctic regions, part of Canada, and the extreme northeastern United States.

Ozone Layer: The protective layer in the atmosphere, about 15 miles above the ground, that absorbs some of the sun's ultraviolet rays, thereby reducing the amount of potentially harmful radiation that reaches the earth's surface.

Packaging: The assembly of one or more containers and any other components necessary to ensure minimum compliance with a program's storage and shipment packaging requirements. Also, the containers, etc. involved.

Packed Bed Scrubber: An air pollution control device in which emissions pass through alkaline water to neutralize hydrogen chloride gas.

Packed Tower: A pollution control device that forces dirty air through a tower packed with crushed rock or wood chips while liquid is sprayed over the packing material. The pollutants in the air stream either dissolve or chemically react with the liquid.

Packer: An inflatable gland, or balloon, used to create a temporary seal in a borehole, probe hole, well, or drive casing. It is made of rubber or non-reactive materials.

Palatable Water: Water, at a desirable temperature, that is free from objectionable tastes, odors, colors, and turbidity.

Pandemic: A widespread epidemic throughout an area, nation or the world.

Paper: In the recycling business, refers to products and materials, including newspapers, magazines, office papers, corrugated containers, bags and some paperboard packaging that can be recycled into new paper products.

Paper Processor/Plastics Processor: Intermediate facility where recovered paper or plastic products and materials are sorted, decontaminated, and prepared for final recycling.

Parameter: A variable, measurable property whose value is a determinant of the characteristics of a system; e.g. temperature, pressure, and density are parameters of the atmosphere.

Paraquat: A standard herbicide used to kill various types of crops, including marijuana. Causes lung damage if smoke from the crop is inhaled..

Parshall Flume: Device used to measure the flow of water in an open channel.

Part A Permit, Part B Permit: (See: Interim Permit Status.)

Participation Rate: Portion of population participating in a recycling program.

Particle Count: Results of a microscopic examination of treated water with a special "particle counter" that classifies suspended particles by number and size.

Particulate Loading: The mass of particulates per unit volume of air or water.

Particulates: 1. Fine liquid or solid particles such as dust, smoke, mist, fumes, or smog, found in air or emissions. 2. Very small solids suspended in water; they can vary in size, shape, density and electrical charge and can be gathered together by coagulation and flocculation.

Partition Coefficient: Measure of the sorption phenomenon, whereby a pesticide is divided between the soil and water phase; also referred to as adsorption partition coefficient.

Parts Per Billion (ppb)/Parts Per Million (ppm): Units commonly used to express contamination ratios, as in establishing the maximum permissible amount of a contaminant in water, land, or air.

Passive Smoking/Secondhand Smoke: Inhalation of others' tobacco smoke.

Passive Treatment Walls: Technology in which a chemical reaction takes place when contaminated ground water comes in contact with a barrier such as limestone or a wall containing iron filings.

Pathogens: Microorganisms (e.g., bacteria, viruses, or parasites) that can cause disease in humans, animals and plants.

Pathway: The physical course a chemical or pollutant takes from its source to the exposed organism.

Pay-As-You-Throw/Unit-Based Pricing: Systems under which residents pay for municipal waste management and disposal services by weight or volume collected, not a fixed fee.

Peak Electricity Demand: The maximum electricity used to meet the cooling load of a building or buildings in a given area.

Peak Levels: Levels of airborne pollutant contaminants much higher than average or occurring for short periods of time in response to sudden releases.

Percent Saturation: The amount of a substance that is dissolved in a solution compared to the amount that could be dissolved in it.

Perched Water: Zone of unpressurized water held above the water table by impermeable rock or sediment.

Percolating Water: Water that passes through rocks or soil under the force of gravity.

Percolation: 1. The movement of water downward and radially through subsurface soil layers, usually continuing downward to ground water. Can also involve upward movement of water. 2. Slow seepage of water through a filter.

Performance Bond: Cash or securities deposited before a landfill operating permit is issued, which are held to ensure that all requirements for operating ad subsequently closing the landfill are faithful performed. The money is returned to the owner after proper closure of the landfill is completed. If contamination or other problems appear at any time during operation, or upon closure, and are not addressed, the owner must forfeit all or part of the bond which is then used to cover clean-up costs.

Performance Data (For Incinerators): Information collected, during a trial burn, on concentrations of designated organic compounds and pollutants found in incinerator emissions. Data analysis must show that the incinerator meets performance standards under operating conditions specified in the RCRA permit. (See: trial burn; performance standards.)

Performance Standards: 1. Regulatory requirements limiting the concentrations of designated organic compounds, particulate matter, and hydrogen chloride in emissions from incinerators. 2. Operating standards established by EPA for various permitted pollution control systems, asbestos inspections, and various program operations and maintenance requirements.

Periphyton: Microscopic underwater plants and animals that are firmly attached to solid surfaces such as rocks, logs, and pilings.

Permeability: The rate at which liquids pass through soil or other materials in a specified direction.

Permissible Dose: The dose of a chemical that may be received by an individual without the expectation of a significantly harmful result.

Permissible Exposure Limit: Also referred to as PEL, federal limits for workplace exposure to contaminants as established by OSHA.

Permit: An authorization, license, or equivalent control document issued by EPA or an approved state agency to implement the requirements of an environmental regulation; e.g. a permit to operate a wastewater treatment plant or to operate a facility that may generate harmful emissions.

Persistence: Refers to the length of time a compound stays in the environment, once introduced. A compound may persist for less than a second or indefinitely.

Persistent Pesticides: Pesticides that do not break down chemically or break down very slowly and remain in the environment after a growing season.

Personal Air Samples: Air samples taken with a pump that is directly attached to the worker with the collecting filter and cassette placed in the worker's breathing zone (required under OSHA asbestos standards and EPA worker protection rule).

Personal Measurement: A measurement collected from an individual's immediate environment.

Personal Protective Equipment: Clothing and equipment worn by pesticide mixers, loaders and applicators and re-entry workers, hazmat emergency responders, workers cleaning up Superfund sites, et. al., which is worn to reduce their exposure to potentially hazardous chemicals and other pollutants.

Pest: An insect, rodent, nematode, fungus, weed or other form of terrestrial or aquatic plant or animal life that is injurious to health or the environment.

Pest Control Operator: Person or company that applies pesticides as a business (e.g. exterminator); usually describes household services, not agricultural applications.

Pesticide: Substances or mixture there of intended for preventing, destroying, repelling, or mitigating any pest. Also, any substance or mixture intended for use as a plant regulator, defoliant, or desiccant.

Pesticide Regulation Notice: Formal notice to pesticide registrants about important changes in regulatory policy, procedures, regulations.

Pesticide Tolerance: The amount of pesticide residue allowed by law to remain in or on a harvested crop. EPA sets these levels well below the point where the compounds might be harmful to consumers.

PETE (Polyethylene Terepthalate): Thermoplastic material used in plastic soft drink and rigid containers.

Petroleum: Crude oil or any fraction thereof that is liquid under normal conditions of temperature and pressure. The term includes petroleum-based substances comprising a complex blend of hydrocarbons derived from crude oil through the process of separation, conversion, upgrading, and finishing, such as motor fuel, jet oil, lubricants, petroleum solvents, and used oil.

Petroleum Derivatives: Chemicals formed when gasoline breaks down in contact with ground water.

pH: An expression of the intensity of the basic or acid condition of a liquid; may range from 0 to 14, where 0 is the most acid and 7 is neutral. Natural waters usually have a pH between 6.5 and 8.5.

Pharmacokinetics: The study of the way that drugs move through the body after they are swallowed or injected.

Phenolphthalein Alkalinity: The alkalinity in a water sample measured by the amount of standard acid needed to lower the pH to a level of 8.3 as indicated by the change of color of the phenolphthalein from pink to clear.

Phenols: Organic compounds that are byproducts of petroleum refining, tanning, and textile, dye, and resin manufacturing. Low concentrations cause taste and odor problems in water; higher concentrations can kill aquatic life and humans.

Phosphates: Certain chemical compounds containing phosphorus.

Phosphogypsum Piles (Stacks): Principal byproduct generated in production of phosphoric acid from phosphate rock. These piles may generate radioactive radon gas.

Phosphorus: An essential chemical food element that can contribute to the eutrophication of lakes and other water bodies. Increased phosphorus levels result from discharge of phosphorus-containing materials into surface waters.

Phosphorus Plants: Facilities using electric furnaces to produce elemental phosphorous for commercial use, such as high grade phosphoric acid, phosphate-based detergent, and organic chemicals use.

Photochemical Oxidants: Air pollutants formed by the action of sunlight on oxides of nitrogen and hydrocarbons.

Photochemical Smog: Air pollution caused by chemical reactions of various pollutants emitted from different sources. (See: photochemical oxidants.)

Photosynthesis: The manufacture by plants of carbohydrates and oxygen from carbon dioxide mediated by chlorophyll in the presence of sunlight.

Physical and Chemical Treatment: Processes generally used in large-scale wastewater treatment facilities. Physical processes may include air-stripping or filtration. Chemical treatment includes coagulation, chlorination, or ozonation. The term can also refer to treatment of toxic materials in surface and ground waters, oil spills, and some methods of dealing with hazardous materials on or in the ground.

Phytoplankton: That portion of the plankton community comprised of tiny plants; e.g. algae, diatoms.

Phytoremediation: Low-cost remediation option for sites with widely dispersed contamination at low concentrations.

Phytotoxic: Harmful to plants.

Phytotreatment: The cultivation of specialized plants that absorb specific contaminants from the soil through their roots or foliage. This reduces the concentration of contaminants in the soil, but incorporates them into biomasses that may be released back into the environment when the plant dies or is harvested.

Picocuries Per Liter pCi/L): A unit of measure for levels of radon gas; becquerels per cubic meter is metric equivalent.

Piezometer: A nonpumping well, generally of small diameter, for measuring the elevation of a water table.

Pilot Tests: Testing a cleanup technology under actual site conditions to identify potential problems prior to full-scale implementation.

Plankton: Tiny plants and animals that live in water.

Plasma Arc Reactors: devices that use an electric arc to thermally decompose organic and inorganic materials at ultra-high temperatures into gases and a vitrified slag residue. A plasma arc reactor can operate as any of the following:

- integral component of chemical, fuel, or electricity production systems, processing high or medium value organic compounds into a synthetic gas used as a fuel
- materials recovery device, processing scrap to recover metal from the slag
- destruction or incineration system, processing waste materials into slag and gases ignited inside of a secondary combustion chamber that follows the reactor

Plasmid: A circular piece of DNA that exists apart from the chromosome and replicates independently of it. Bacterial plasmids carry information that renders the bacteria resistant to antibiotics. Plasmids are often used in genetic engineering to carry desired genes into organisms.

Plastics: Non-metallic chemoreactive compounds molded into rigid or pliable construction materials, fabrics, etc.

Plate Tower Scrubber: An air pollution control device that neutralizes hydrogen chloride gas by bubbling alkaline water through holes in a series of metal plates.

Plug Flow: Type of flow the occurs in tanks, basins, or reactors when a slug of water moves through without ever dispersing or mixing with the rest of the water flowing through.

Plugging: Act or process of stopping the flow of water, oil, or gas into or out of a formation through a borehole or well penetrating that formation.

Plume: 1. A visible or measurable discharge of a contaminant from a given point of origin. Can be visible or thermal in water, or visible in the air as, for example, a plume of smoke. 2 The area of radiation leaking from a damaged reactor. 3. Area downwind within which a release could be dangerous for those exposed to leaking fumes.

Plutonium: A radioactive metallic element chemically similar to uranium.

PM-10/PM-2.5: PM 10 is measure of particles in the atmosphere with a diameter of less than ten or equal to a nominal 10 micrometers. PM-2.5 is a measure of smaller particles in the air. PM-10 has been the pollutant particulate level standard against which EPA has been measuring Clean Air Act compliance. On the basis of newer scientific findings, the Agency is considering regulations that will make PM-2.5 the new "standard."

Pneumoconiosis: Health conditions characterized by permanent deposition of substantial amounts of particulate matter in the lungs and by the tissue reaction to its presence; can range from relatively harmless forms of sclerosis to the destructive fibrotic effect of silicosis.

Point Source: A stationary location or fixed facility from which pollutants are discharged; any single identifiable source of pollution; e.g. a pipe, ditch, ship, ore pit, factory smokestack.

Point-of-Contact Measurement of Exposure: Estimating exposure by measuring concentrations over time (while the exposure is taking place) at or near the place where it is occurring.

Point-of-Disinfectant Application: The point where disinfectant is applied and water downstream of that point is not subject to recontamination by surface water runoff.

Point-of-Use Treatment Device: Treatment device applied to a single tap to reduce contaminants in the drinking water at the one faucet.

Pollen: The fertilizing element of flowering plants; background air pollutant.

Pollutant: Generally, any substance introduced into the environment that adversely affects the usefulness of a resource or the health of humans, animals, or ecosystems..

Pollutant Pathways: Avenues for distribution of pollutants. In most buildings, for example, HVAC systems are the primary pathways although all building components can interact to affect how air movement distributes pollutants.

Pollutant Standard Index (PSI): Indicator of one or more pollutants that may be used to inform the public about the potential for adverse health effects from air pollution in major cities.

Pollution: Generally, the presence of a substance in the environment that because of its chemical composition or quantity prevents the functioning of natural processes and produces undesirable environmental and health effects. Under the Clean Water Act, for example, the term has been defined as the man-made or man-induced alteration of the physical, biological, chemical, and radiological integrity of water and other media.

Pollution Prevention: 1. Identifying areas, processes, and activities which create excessive waste products or pollutants in order to reduce or prevent them through, alteration, or eliminating a process. Such activities, consistent with the Pollution Prevention Act of 1990, are conducted across all EPA programs and can involve cooperative efforts with such agencies as the Departments of Agriculture and Energy. 2. EPA has initiated a number of voluntary programs in which industrial, or commercial or "partners" join with EPA in promoting activities that conserve energy, conserve and protect water supply, reduce emissions or find ways of utilizing them as energy resources, and reduce the waste stream.

Among these are: Agstar, to reduce methane emissions through manure management. Climate Wise, to lower industrial greenhouse-gas emissions and energy costs. Coalbed Methane Outreach, to boost methane recovery at coal mines. Design for the Environment, to foster including environmental considerations in product design and processes. Energy Star programs, to promote energy efficiency in commercial and residential buildings, office equipment, transformers, computers, office equipment, and home appliances. Environmental Accounting, to help businesses identify environmental costs and factor them into management decision making. Green Chemistry, to promote and recognize cost-effective breakthroughs in chemistry that prevent pollution. Green Lights, to spread the use of energy-efficient lighting technologies. Indoor Environments, to reduce risks from indoor-air pollution. Landfill Methane Outreach, to develop landfill gas-to-energy projects. Natural Gas Star, to reduce methane emissions from the natural gas industry. Ruminant Livestock Methane, to reduce methane emissions from ruminant livestock. Transportation Partners, to reduce carbon dioxide emissions from the transportation sector. Voluntary Aluminum Industrial Partnership, to reduce perfluorocarbon emissions from the primary aluminum industry. WAVE, to promote efficient water use in the lodging industry. Wastewi$e, to reduce business-generated solid waste through prevention, reuse, and recycling. (See: Common Sense Initiative and Project XL.)

Polychlorinated Biphenyls: A group of toxic, persistent chemicals used in electrical transformers and capacitors for insulating purposes, and in gas pipeline systems as lubricant. The sale and new use of these chemicals, also known as PCBs, were banned by law in 1979.

Portal-of-Entry Effect: A local effect produced in the tissue or organ of first contact between a toxicant and the biological system.

Polonium: A radioactive element that occurs in pitchblende and other uranium-containing ores.

Polyelectrolytes: Synthetic chemicals that help solids to clump during sewage treatment.

Polymer: A natural or synthetic chemical structure where two or more like molecules are joined to form a more complex molecular structure (e.g. polyethylene in plastic).

Polyvinyl Chloride (PVC): A tough, environmentally indestructible plastic that releases hydrochloric acid when burned.

Population: A group of interbreeding organisms occupying a particular space; the number of humans or other living creatures in a designated area.

Population at Risk: A population subgroup that is more likely to be exposed to a chemical, or is more sensitive to the chemical, than is the general population.

Porosity: Degree to which soil, gravel, sediment, or rock is permeated with pores or cavities through which water or air can move.

Post-Chlorination: Addition of chlorine to plant effluent for disinfectant purposes after the effluent has been treated.

Post-Closure: The time period following the shutdown of a waste management or manufacturing facility; for monitoring purposes, often considered to be 30 years.

Post-Consumer Materials/Waste: Materials or finished products that have served their intended use and have been diverted or recovered from waste destined for disposal, having completed their lives as consumer items. Postconsumer materials are part of the broader category of recovered materials.

Post-Consumer Recycling: Use of materials generated from residential and consumer waste for new or similar purposes; e.g. converting wastepaper from offices into corrugated boxes or newsprint.

Potable Water: Water that is safe for drinking and cooking.

Potential Dose: The amount of a compound contained in material swallowed, breathed, or applied to the skin.

Potentially Responsible Party (PRP): Any individual or company--including owners, operators, transporters or generators--potentially responsible for, or contributing to a spill or other contamination at a Superfund site. Whenever possible, through administrative and legal actions, EPA requires PRPs to clean up hazardous sites they have contaminated.

Potentiation: The ability of one chemical to increase the effect of another chemical.

Potentiometric Surface: The surface to which water in an aquifer can rise by hydrostatic pressure.

Precautionary Principle: When information about potential risks is incomplete, basing decisions about the best ways to manage or reduce risks on a preference for avoiding unnecessary health risks instead of on unnecessary economic expenditures.

Pre-Consumer Materials/Waste: Materials generated in manufacturing and converting processes such as manufacturing scrap and trimmings and cuttings. Includes print overruns, overissue publications, and obsolete inventories.

Pre-Harvest Interval: The time between the last pesticide application and harvest of the treated crops.

Prechlorination: The addition of chlorine at the headworks of a treatment plant prior to other treatment processes. Done mainly for disinfection and control of tastes, odors, and aquatic growths, and to aid in coagulation and settling,

Precipitate: A substance separated from a solution or suspension by chemical or physical change.

Precipitation: Removal of hazardous solids from liquid waste to permit safe disposal; removal of particles from airborne emissions as in rain (e.g. acid precipitation).

Precipitator: Pollution control device that collects particles from an air stream.

Precursor: In photochemistry, a compound antecedent to a pollutant. For example, volatile organic compounds (VOCs) and nitric oxides of nitrogen react in sunlight to form ozone or other photochemical oxidants. As such, VOCs and oxides of nitrogen are precursors.

Preliminary Assessment: The process of collecting and reviewing available information about a known or suspected waste site or release.

Prescriptive: Water rights which are acquired by diverting water and putting it to use in accordance with specified procedures; e.g. filing a request with a state agency to use unused water in a stream, river, or lake.

Pressed Wood Products: Materials used in building and furniture construction that are made from wood veneers, particles, or fibers bonded together with an adhesive under heat and pressure.

Pressure Sewers: A system of pipes in which water, wastewater, or other liquid is pumped to a higher elevation.

Pressure, Static: In flowing air, the total pressure minus velocity pressure, pushing equally in all directions.

Pressure, Total: In flowing air, the sum of the static and velocity pressures.

Pressure, Velocity: In flowing air, the pressure due to velocity and density of air.

Pretreatment: Processes used to reduce, eliminate, or alter the nature of wastewater pollutants from non-domestic sources before they are discharged into publicly owned treatment works (POTWs).

Prevalent Level Samples: Air samples taken under normal conditions (also known as ambient background samples).

Prevalent Levels: Levels of airborne contaminant occurring under normal conditions.

Prevention of Significant Deterioration (PSD): EPA program in which state and/or federal permits are required in order to restrict emissions from new or modified sources in places where air quality already meets or exceeds primary and secondary ambient air quality standards.

Primacy: Having the primary responsibility for administering and enforcing regulations.

Primary Drinking Water Regulation: Applies to public water systems and specifies a contaminant level, which, in the judgment of the EPA Administrator, will not adversely affect human health.

Primary Effect: An effect where the stressor acts directly on the ecological component of interest, not on other parts of the ecosystem. (See: secondary effect.)

Primary Standards: National ambient air quality standards designed to protect human health with an adequate margin for safety. (See: National Ambient Air Quality Standards, secondary standards.)

Primary Treatment: First stage of wastewater treatment in which solids are removed by screening and settling.

Primary Waste Treatment: First steps in wastewater treatment; screens and sedimentation tanks are used to remove most materials that float or will settle. Primary treatment removes about 30 percent of carbonaceous biochemical oxygen demand from domestic sewage.

Principal Organic Hazardous Constituents (POHCs): Hazardous compounds monitored during an incinerator's trial burn, selected for high concentration in the waste feed and difficulty of combustion.

Prions: Microscopic particles made of protein that can cause disease.

Prior Appropriation: A doctrine of water law that allocates the rights to use water on a first-come, first-served basis.

Probability of Detection : The likelihood, expressed as a percentage, that a test method will correctly identify a leaking tank.

Process Variable: A physical or chemical quantity which is usually measured and controlled in the operation of a water treatment plant or industrial plant.

Process Verification: Verifying that process raw materials, water usage, waste treatment processes, production rate and other facts relative to quantity and quality of pollutants contained in discharges are substantially described in the permit application and the issued permit.

Process Wastewater: Any water that comes into contact with any raw material, product, byproduct, or waste.

Process Weight: Total weight of all materials, including fuel, used in a manufacturing process; used to calculate the allowable particulate emission rate.

Producers: Plants that perform photosynthesis and provide food to consumers.

Product Level: The level of a product in a storage tank.

Product Water: Water that has passed through a water treatment plant and is ready to be delivered to consumers.

Products of Incomplete Combustion (PICs): Organic compounds formed by combustion. Usually generated in small amounts and sometimes toxic, PICs are heat-altered versions of the original material fed into the incinerator (e.g. charcoal is a P.I.C. from burning wood).

Project XL: An EPA initiative to give states and the regulated community the flexibility to develop comprehensive strategies as alternatives to multiple current regulatory requirements in order to exceed compliance and increase overall environmental benefits.

Propellant: Liquid in a self-pressurized pesticide product that expels the active ingredient from its container.

Proportionate Mortality Ratio (PMR): The number of deaths from a specific cause in a specific period of time per 100 deaths from all causes in the same time period.

Proposed Plan: A plan for a site cleanup that is available to the public for comment.

Proteins: Complex nitrogenous organic compounds of high molecular weight made of amino acids; essential for growth and repair of animal tissue. Many, but not all, proteins are enzymes.

Protocol: A series of formal steps for conducting a test.

Protoplast: A membrane-bound cell from which the outer wall has been partially or completely removed. The term often is applied to plant cells.

Protozoa: One-celled animals that are larger and more complex than bacteria. May cause disease.

Public Comment Period: The time allowed for the public to express its views and concerns regarding an action by EPA (e.g. a Federal Register Notice of proposed rule-making, a public notice of a draft permit, or a Notice of Intent to Deny).

Public Health Approach: Regulatory and voluntary focus on effective and feasible risk management actions at the national and community level to reduce human exposures and risks, with priority given to reducing exposures with the biggest impacts in terms of the number affected and severity of effect.

Public Health Context: The incidence, prevalence, and severity of diseases in communities or populations and the factors that account for them, including infections, exposure to pollutants, and other exposures or activities.

Public Hearing: A formal meeting wherein EPA officials hear the public's views and concerns about an EPA action or proposal. EPA is required to consider such comments when evaluating its actions. Public hearings must be held upon request during the public comment period.

Public Notice: 1. Notification by EPA informing the public of Agency actions such as the issuance of a draft permit or scheduling of a hearing. EPA is required to ensure proper public notice, including publication in newspapers and broadcast over radio and television stations. 2. In the safe drinking water program, water suppliers are required to publish and broadcast notices when pollution problems are discovered.

Public Water System: A system that provides piped water for human consumption to at least 15 service connections or regularly serves 25 individuals.

Publicly Owned Treatment Works (POTWs): A waste-treatment works owned by a state, unit of local government, or Indian tribe, usually designed to treat domestic wastewaters.

Pumping Station: Mechanical device installed in sewer or water system or other liquid-carrying pipelines to move the liquids to a higher level.

Pumping Test: A test conducted to determine aquifer or well characteristics.

Purging: Removing stagnant air or water from sampling zone or equipment prior to sample collection.

Putrefaction: Biological decomposition of organic matter; associated with anaerobic conditions.

Putrescible: Able to rot quickly enough to cause odors and attract flies.

Pyrolysis: Decomposition of a chemical by extreme heat.

Qualitative Use Assessment: Report summarizing the major uses of a pesticide including percentage of crop treated, and amount of pesticide used on a site.

Quality Assurance/Quality Control: A system of procedures, checks, audits, and corrective actions to ensure that all EPA research design and performance, environmental monitoring and sampling, and other technical and reporting activities are of the highest achievable quality.

Quench Tank: A water-filled tank used to cool incinerator residues or hot materials during industrial processes.

Real-Time Monitoring: Monitoring and measuring environmental developments with technology and communications systems that provide time-relevant information to the public in an easily understood format people can use in day-to-day decision-making about their health and the environment.

Reasonable Further Progress: Annual incremental reductions in air pollutant emissions as reflected in a State Implementation Plan that EPA deems sufficient to provide for the attainment of the applicable national ambient air quality standards by the statutory deadline.

Reasonable Maximum Exposure: The maximum exposure reasonably expected to occur in a population.

Reasonable Worst Case: An estimate of the individual dose, exposure, or risk level received by an individual in a defined population that is greater than the 90th percentile but less than that received by anyone in the 98th percentile in the same population.

Reasonably Available Control Measures (RACM): A broadly defined term referring to technological and other measures for pollution control.

Reasonably Available Control Technology (RACT): Control technology that is reasonably available, and both technologically and economically feasible. Usually applied to existing sources in nonattainment areas; in most cases is less stringent than new source performance standards.

Recarbonization: Process in which carbon dioxide is bubbled into water being treated to lower the pH.

Receiving Waters: A river, lake, ocean, stream or other watercourse into which wastewater or treated effluent is discharged.

Receptor: Ecological entity exposed to a stressor.

Recharge: The process by which water is added to a zone of saturation, usually by percolation from the soil surface; e.g., the recharge of an aquifer.

Recharge Area: A land area in which water reaches the zone of saturation from surface infiltration, e.g., where rainwater soaks through the earth to reach an aquifer.

Recharge Rate: The quantity of water per unit of time that replenishes or refills an aquifer.

Reclamation: (In recycling) Restoration of materials found in the waste stream to a beneficial use which may be for purposes other than the original use.

Recombinant Bacteria: A microorganism whose genetic makeup has been altered by deliberate introduction of new genetic elements. The offspring of these altered bacteria also contain these new genetic elements; i.e. they "breed true."

Recombinant DNA: The new DNA that is formed by combining pieces of DNA from different organisms or cells.

Recommended Maximum Contaminant Level (RMCL): The maximum level of a contaminant in drinking water at which no known or anticipated adverse effect on human health would occur, and that includes an adequate margin of safety. Recommended levels are nonenforceable health goals. (See: maximum contaminant level.)

Reconstructed Source: Facility in which components are replaced to such an extent that the fixed capital cost of the new components exceeds 50 percent of the capital cost of constructing a comparable brand-new facility. New-source performance standards may be applied to sources reconstructed after the proposal of the standard if it is technologically and economically feasible to meet the standards.

Reconstruction of Dose: Estimating exposure after it has occurred by using evidence within an organism such as chemical levels in tissue or fluids.

Record of Decision (ROD): A public document that explains which cleanup alternative(s) will be used at National Priorities List sites where, under CERCLA, Trust Funds pay for the cleanup.

Recovery Rate: Percentage of usable recycled materials that have been removed from the total amount of municipal solid waste generated in a specific area or by a specific business.

Recycle/Reuse: Minimizing waste generation by recovering and reprocessing usable products that might otherwise become waste (.i.e. recycling of aluminum cans, paper, and bottles, etc.).

Recycling and Reuse Business Assistance Centers: Located in state solid-waste or economic-development agencies, these centers provide recycling businesses with customized and targeted assistance.

Recycling Economic Development Advocates: Individuals hired by state or tribal economic development offices to focus financial, marketing, and permitting resources on creating recycling businesses.

Recycling Mill: Facility where recovered materials are remanufactured into new products.

Recycling Technical Assistance Partnership National Network: A national information-sharing resource designed to help businesses and manufacturers increase their use of recovered materials.

Red Bag Waste: (See: infectious waste.)

Red Border: An EPA document undergoing review before being submitted for final management decision-making.

Red Tide: A proliferation of a marine plankton toxic and often fatal to fish, perhaps stimulated by the addition of nutrients. A tide can be red, green, or brown, depending on the coloration of the plankton.

Redemption Program: Program in which consumers are monetarily compensated for the collection of recyclable materials, generally through prepaid deposits or taxes on beverage containers. In some states or localities legislation has enacted redemption programs to help prevent roadside litter. (See: bottle bill.)

Reduction: The addition of hydrogen, removal of oxygen, or addition of electrons to an element or compound.

Reentry Interval: The period of time immediately following the application of a pesticide during which unprotected workers should not enter a field.

Reference Dose (RfD): The RfD is a numerical estimate of a daily oral exposure to the human population, including sensitive subgroups such as children, that is not likely to cause harmful effects during a lifetime. RfDs are generally used for health effects that are thought to have a threshold or low dose limit for producing effects.

Reformulated Gasoline: Gasoline with a different composition from conventional gasoline (e.g., lower aromatics content) that cuts air pollutants.

Refueling Emissions: Emissions released during vehicle re-fueling.

Refuse: (See: solid waste.)

Refuse Reclamation: Conversion of solid waste into useful products; e.g., composting organic wastes to make soil conditioners or separating aluminum and other metals for recycling.

Regeneration: Manipulation of cells to cause them to develop into whole plants.

Regional Response Team (RRT): Representatives of federal, local, and state agencies who may assist in coordination of activities at the request of the On-Scene Coordinator before and during a significant pollution incident such as an oil spill, major chemical release, or Superfund response.

Registrant: Any manufacturer or formulator who obtains registration for a pesticide active ingredient or product.

Registration: Formal listing with EPA of a new pesticide before it can be sold or distributed. Under the Federal Insecticide, Fungicide, and Rodenticide Act, EPA is responsible for registration (pre-market licensing) of pesticides on the basis of data demonstrating no unreasonable adverse effects on human health or the environment when applied according to approved label directions.

Registration Standards: Published documents which include summary reviews of the data available on a pesticide's active ingredient, data gaps, and the Agency's existing regulatory position on the pesticide.

Regulated Asbestos-Containing Material (RACM): Friable asbestos material or nonfriable ACM that will be or has been subjected to sanding, grinding, cutting, or abrading or has crumbled, or been pulverized or reduced to powder in the course of demolition or renovation operations.

Regulated Medical Waste: Under the Medical Waste Tracking Act of 1988, any solid waste generated in the diagnosis, treatment, or immunization of human beings or animals, in research pertaining thereto, or in the production or testing of biologicals. Included are cultures and stocks of infectious agents; human blood and blood products; human pathological body wastes from surgery and autopsy; contaminated animal carcasses from medical research; waste from patients with communicable diseases; and all used sharp implements, such as needles and scalpels, and certain unused sharps. (See: treated medical waste; untreated medical waste; destroyed medical waste.)

Relative Ecological Sustainability: Ability of an ecosystem to maintain relative ecological integrity indefinitely.

Relative Permeability: The permeability of a rock to gas, NAIL, or water, when any two or more are present.

Relative Risk Assessment: Estimating the risks associated with different stressors or management actions.

Release: Any spilling, leaking, pumping, pouring, emitting, emptying, discharging, injecting, escaping, leaching, dumping, or disposing into the environment of a hazardous or toxic chemical or extremely hazardous substance.

Remedial Action (RA): The actual construction or implementation phase of a Superfund site cleanup that follows remedial design.

Remedial Design: A phase of remedial action that follows the remedial investigation/feasibility study and includes development of engineering drawings and specifications for a site cleanup.

Remedial Investigation: An in-depth study designed to gather data needed to determine the nature and extent of contamination at a Superfund site; establish site cleanup criteria; identify preliminary alternatives for remedial action; and support technical and cost analyses of alternatives. The remedial investigation is usually done with the feasibility study. Together they are usually referred to as the "RI/FS."

Remedial Project Manager (RPM): The EPA or state official responsible for overseeing on-site remedial action.

Remedial Response: Long-term action that stops or substantially reduces a release or threat of a release of hazardous substances that is serious but not an immediate threat to public health.

Remediation: 1. Cleanup or other methods used to remove or contain a toxic spill or hazardous materials from a Superfund site; 2. for the Asbestos Hazard Emergency Response program, abatement methods including evaluation, repair, enclosure, encapsulation, or removal of greater than 3 linear feet or square feet of asbestos-containing materials from a building.

Remote Sensing: The collection and interpretation of information about an object without physical contact with the object; e.g., satellite imaging, aerial photography, and open path measurements.

Removal Action: Short-term immediate actions taken to address releases of hazardous substances that require expedited response. (See: cleanup.)

Renewable Energy Production Incentive (REPI): Incentive established by the Energy Policy Act available to renewable energy power projects owned by a state or local government or nonprofit electric cooperative.

Repeat Compliance Period: Any subsequent compliance period after the initial one.

Reportable Quantity (RQ): Quantity of a hazardous substance that triggers reports under CERCLA. If a substance exceeds its RQ, the release must be reported to the National Response Center, the SERC, and community emergency coordinators for areas likely to be affected.

Repowering: Rebuilding and replacing major components of a power plant instead of building a new one.

Representative Sample: A portion of material or water that is as nearly identical in content and consistency as possible to that in the larger body of material or water being sampled.

Reregistration: The reevaluation and relicensing of existing pesticides originally registered prior to current scientific and regulatory standards. EPA reregisters pesticides through its Registration Standards Program.

Reserve Capacity: Extra treatment capacity built into solid waste and wastewater treatment plants and interceptor sewers to accommodate flow increases due to future population growth.

Reservoir: Any natural or artificial holding area used to store, regulate, or control water.

Residential Use: Pesticide application in and around houses, office buildings, apartment buildings, motels, and other living or working areas.

Residential Waste: Waste generated in single and multi-family homes, including newspapers, clothing, disposable tableware, food packaging, cans, bottles, food scraps, and yard trimmings other than those that are diverted to backyard composting. (See: Household hazardous waste.)

Residual: Amount of a pollutant remaining in the environment after a natural or technological process has taken place; e.g., the sludge remaining after initial wastewater treatment, or particulates remaining in air after it passes through a scrubbing or other process.

Residual Risk: The extent of health risk from air pollutants remaining after application of the Maximum Achievable Control Technology (MACT).

Residual Saturation: Saturation level below which fluid drainage will not occur.

Residue: The dry solids remaining after the evaporation of a sample of water or sludge.

Resistance: For plants and animals, the ability to withstand poor environmental conditions or attacks by chemicals or disease. May be inborn or acquired.

Resource Recovery: The process of obtaining matter or energy from materials formerly discarded.

Response Action: 1. Generic term for actions taken in response to actual or potential health-threatening environmental events such as spills, sudden releases, and asbestos abatement/management problems. 2. A CERCLA-authorized action involving either a short-term removal action or a long-term removal response. This may include but is not limited to: removing hazardous materials from a site to an EPA-approved hazardous waste facility for treatment, containment or treating the waste on-site, identifying and removing the sources of ground-water contamination and halting further migration of contaminants. 3. Any of the following actions taken in school buildings in response to AHERA to reduce the risk of exposure to asbestos: removal, encapsulation, enclosure, repair, and operations and maintenance. (See: cleanup.)

Responsiveness Summary: A summary of oral and/or written public comments received by EPA during a comment period on key EPA documents, and EPA's response to those comments.

Restoration: Measures taken to return a site to pre-violation conditions.

Restricted Entry Interval: The time after a pesticide application during which entry into the treated area is restricted.

Restricted Use: A pesticide may be classified (under FIFRA regulations) for restricted use if it requires special handling because of its toxicity, and, if so, it may be applied only by trained, certified applicators or those under their direct supervision.

Restriction Enzymes: Enzymes that recognize specific regions of a long DNA molecule and cut it at those points.

Retrofit: Addition of a pollution control device on an existing facility without making major changes to the generating plant. Also called backfit.

Reuse: Using a product or component of municipal solid waste in its original form more than once; e.g., refilling a glass bottle that has been returned or using a coffee can to hold nuts and bolts.

Reverse Osmosis: A treatment process used in water systems by adding pressure to force water through a semi-permeable membrane. Reverse osmosis removes most drinking water contaminants. Also used in wastewater treatment. Large-scale reverse osmosis plants are being developed.

Reversible Effect: An effect which is not permanent; especially adverse effects which diminish when exposure to a toxic chemical stops.

Ribonucleic Acid (RNA): A molecule that carries the genetic message from DNA to a cellular protein-producing mechanism.

Rill: A small channel eroded into the soil by surface runoff; can be easily smoothed out or obliterated by normal tillage.

Ringlemann Chart: A series of shaded illustrations used to measure the opacity of air pollution emissions, ranging from light grey through black; used to set and enforce emissions standards.

Riparian Habitat: Areas adjacent to rivers and streams with a differing density, diversity, and productivity of plant and animal species relative to nearby uplands.

Riparian Rights: Entitlement of a land owner to certain uses of water on or bordering the property, including the right to prevent diversion or misuse of upstream waters. Generally a matter of state law.

Risk: A measure of the probability that damage to life, health, property, and/or the environment will occur as a result of a given hazard.

Risk (Adverse) for Endangered Species: Risk to aquatic species if anticipated pesticide residue levels equal one-fifth of LD_{10} or one-tenth of LC_{50}; risk to terrestrial species if anticipated pesticide residue levels equal one-fifth of LC_{10} or one-tenth of LC_{50}.

Risk Assessment: Qualitative and quantitative evaluation of the risk posed to human health and/or the environment by the actual or potential presence and/or use of specific pollutants.

Risk Characterization: The last phase of the risk assessment process that estimates the potential for adverse health or ecological effects to occur from exposure to a stressor and evaluates the uncertainty involved.

Risk Communication: The exchange of information about health or environmental risks among risk assessors and managers, the general public, news media, interest groups, etc.

Risk Estimate: A description of the probability that organisms exposed to a specific dose of a chemical or other pollutant will develop an adverse response, e.g., cancer.

Risk Factor: Characteristics (e.g., race, sex, age, obesity) or variables (e.g., smoking, occupational exposure level) associated with increased probability of a toxic effect.

Risk for Non-Endangered Species: Risk to species if anticipated pesticide residue levels are equal to or greater than LC_{50}.

Risk Management: The process of evaluating and selecting alternative regulatory and non-regulatory responses to risk. The selection process necessarily requires the consideration of legal, economic, and behavioral factors.

Risk-based Targeting: The direction of resources to those areas that have been identified as having the highest potential or actual adverse effect on human health and/or the environment.

Risk-Specific Dose: The dose associated with a specified risk level.

River Basin: The land area drained by a river and its tributaries.

Rodenticide: A chemical or agent used to destroy rats or other rodent pests, or to prevent them from damaging food, crops, etc.

Rotary Kiln Incinerator: An incinerator with a rotating combustion chamber that keeps waste moving, thereby allowing it to vaporize for easier burning.

Rough Fish: Fish not prized for sport or eating, such as gar and suckers. Most are more tolerant of changing environmental conditions than are game or food species.

Route of Exposure: The avenue by which a chemical comes into contact with an organism, e.g., inhalation, ingestion, dermal contact, injection.

Rubbish: Solid waste, excluding food waste and ashes, from homes, institutions, and workplaces.

Run-Off: That part of precipitation, snow melt, or irrigation water that runs off the land into streams or other surface-water. It can carry pollutants from the air and land into receiving waters.

Running Losses: Evaporation of motor vehicle fuel from the fuel tank while the vehicle is in use.

Sacrifical Anode: An easily corroded material deliberately installed in a pipe or intake to give it up (sacrifice it) to corrosion while the rest of the water supply facility remains relatively corrosion-free.

Safe: Condition of exposure under which there is a practical certainty that no harm will result to exposed individuals.

Safe Water: Water that does not contain harmful bacteria, toxic materials, or chemicals, and is considered safe for drinking even if it may have taste, odor, color, and certain mineral problems.

Safe Yield: The annual amount of water that can be taken from a source of supply over a period of years without depleting that source beyond its ability to be replenished naturally in "wet years."

Safener: A chemical added to a pesticide to keep it from injuring plants.

Salinity: The percentage of salt in water.

Salt Water Intrusion: The invasion of fresh surface or ground water by salt water. If it comes from the ocean it may be called sea water intrusion.

Salts: Minerals that water picks up as it passes through the air, over and under the ground, or from households and industry.

Salvage: The utilization of waste materials.

Sampling Frequency: The interval between the collection of successive samples.

Sanctions: Actions taken by the federal government for failure to provide or implement a State Implementation Plan (SIP). Such action may include withholding of highway funds and a ban on construction of new sources of potential pollution.

Sand Filters: Devices that remove some suspended solids from sewage. Air and bacteria decompose additional wastes filtering through the sand so that cleaner water drains from the bed.

Sanitary Landfill: (See: landfills.)

Sanitary Sewers: Underground pipes that carry off only domestic or industrial waste, not storm water.

Sanitary Survey: An on-site review of the water sources, facilities, equipment, operation and maintenance of a public water system to evaluate the adequacy of those elements for producing and distributing safe drinking water.

Sanitary Water (Also known as gray water): Water discharged from sinks, showers, kitchens, or other non-industrial operations, but not from commodes.

Sanitation: Control of physical factors in the human environment that could harm development, health, or survival.

Saprolite: A soft, clay-rich, thoroughly decomposed rock formed in place by chemical weathering of igneous or metamorphic rock. Forms in humid, tropical, or subtropical climates.

Saprophytes: Organisms living on dead or decaying organic matter that help natural decomposition of organic matter in water.

Saturated Zone: The area below the water table where all open spaces are filled with water under pressure equal to or greater than that of the atmosphere.

Saturation: The condition of a liquid when it has taken into solution the maximum possible quantity of a given substance at a given temperature and pressure.

Science Advisory Board (SAB): A group of external scientists who advise EPA on science and policy.

Scrap: Materials discarded from manufacturing operations that may be suitable for reprocessing.

Scrap Metal Processor: Intermediate operating facility where recovered metal is sorted, cleaned of contaminants, and prepared for recycling.

Screening: Use of screens to remove coarse floating and suspended solids from sewage.

Screening Risk Assessment: A risk assessment performed with few data and many assumptions to identify exposures that should be evaluated more carefully for potential risk.

Scrubber: An air pollution device that uses a spray of water or reactant or a dry process to trap pollutants in emissions.

Secondary Drinking Water Regulations: Non-enforceable regulations applying to public water systems and specifying the maximum contamination levels that, in the judgment of EPA, are required to protect the public welfare. These regulations apply to any contaminants that may adversely affect the odor or appearance of such water and consequently may cause people served by the system to discontinue its use.

Secondary Effect: Action of a stressor on supporting components of the ecosystem, which in turn impact the ecological component of concern. (See: primary effect.)

Secondary Materials: Materials that have been manufactured and used at least once and are to be used again.

Secondary Standards: National ambient air quality standards designed to protect welfare, including effects on soils, water, crops, vegetation, man-made (anthropogenic) materials, animals, wildlife, weather, visibility, and climate; damage to property; transportation hazards; economic values, and personal comfort and well-being.

Secondary Treatment: The second step in most publicly owned waste treatment systems in which bacteria consume the organic parts of the waste. It is accomplished by bringing together waste, bacteria, and oxygen in trickling filters or in the activated sludge process. This treatment removes floating and settleable solids and about 90 percent of the oxygen-demanding substances and suspended solids. Disinfection is the final stage of secondary treatment. (See: primary, tertiary treatment.)

Secure Chemical Landfill: (See:landfills.)

Secure Maximum Contaminant Level: Maximum permissible level of a contaminant in water delivered to the free flowing outlet of the ultimate user, or of contamination resulting from corrosion of piping and plumbing caused by water quality.

Sediment: Topsoil, sand, and minerals washed from the land into water, usually after rain or snow melt.

Sediment Yield: The quantity of sediment arriving at a specific location.

Sedimentation: Letting solids settle out of wastewater by gravity during treatment.

Sedimentation Tanks: Wastewater tanks in which floating wastes are skimmed off and settled solids are removed for disposal.

Sediments: Soil, sand, and minerals washed from land into water, usually after rain. They pile up in reservoirs, rivers and harbors, destroying fish and wildlife habitat, and clouding the water so that sunlight cannot reach aquatic plants. Careless farming, mining, and building activities will expose sediment materials, allowing them to wash off the land after rainfall.

Seed Protectant: A chemical applied before planting to protect seeds and seedlings from disease or insects.

Seepage: Percolation of water through the soil from unlined canals, ditches, laterals, watercourses, or water storage facilities.

Selective Pesticide: A chemical designed to affect only certain types of pests, leaving other plants and animals unharmed.

Semi-Confined Aquifer: An aquifer partially confined by soil layers of low permeability through which recharge and discharge can still occur.

Semivolatile Organic Compounds: Organic compounds that volatilize slowly at standard temperature (20 degrees C and 1 atm pressure).

Senescence: The aging process. Sometimes used to describe lakes or other bodies of water in advanced stages of eutrophication. Also used to describe plants and animals.

Septic System: An on-site system designed to treat and dispose of domestic sewage. A typical septic system consists of tank that receives waste from a residence or business and a system of tile lines or a pit for disposal of the liquid effluent (sludge) that remains after decomposition of the solids by bacteria in the tank and must be pumped out periodically.

Septic Tank: An underground storage tank for wastes from homes not connected to a sewer line. Waste goes directly from the home to the tank. (See: septic system.)

Service Connector: The pipe that carries tap water from a public water main to a building.

Service Line Sample: A one-liter sample of water that has been standing for at least 6 hours in a service pipeline and is collected according to federal regulations.

Service Pipe: The pipeline extending from the water main to the building served or to the consumer's system.

Set-Back: Setting a thermometer to a lower temperature when the building is unoccupied to reduce consumption of heating energy. Also refers to setting the thermometer to a higher temperature during unoccupied periods in the cooling season.

Settleable Solids: Material heavy enough to sink to the bottom of a wastewater treatment tank.

Settling Chamber: A series of screens placed in the way of flue gases to slow the stream of air, thus helping gravity to pull particles into a collection device.

Settling Tank: A holding area for wastewater, where heavier particles sink to the bottom for removal and disposal.

7Q10: Seven-day, consecutive low flow with a ten year return frequency; the lowest stream flow for seven consecutive days that would be expected to occur once in ten years.

Sewage: The waste and wastewater produced by residential and commercial sources and discharged into sewers.

Sewage Lagoon: (See: lagoon.)

Sewage Sludge: Sludge produced at a Publicly Owned Treatment Works, the disposal of which is regulated under the Clean Water Act.

Sewer: A channel or conduit that carries wastewater and storm-water runoff from the source to a treatment plant or receiving stream. "Sanitary" sewers carry household, industrial, and commercial waste. "Storm" sewers carry runoff from rain or snow. "Combined" sewers handle both.

Sewerage: The entire system of sewage collection, treatment, and disposal.

Shading Coefficient: The amount of the sun's heat transmitted through a given window compared with that of a standard 1/8- inch-thick single pane of glass under the same conditions.

Sharps: Hypodermic needles, syringes (with or without the attached needle), Pasteur pipettes, scalpel blades, blood vials, needles with attached tubing, and culture dishes used in animal or human patient care or treatment, or in medical, research or industrial laboratories. Also included are other types of broken or unbroken glassware that were in contact with infectious agents, such as used slides and cover slips, and unused hypodermic and suture needles, syringes, and scalpel blades.

Shock Load: The arrival at a water treatment plant of raw water containing unusual amounts of algae, colloidal matter. color, suspended solids, turbidity, or other pollutants.

Short-Circuiting: When some of the water in tanks or basins flows faster than the rest; may result in shorter contact, reaction, or settling times than calculated or presumed.

Sick Building Syndrome: Building whose occupants experience acute health and/or comfort effects that appear to be linked to time spent therein, but where no specific illness or cause can be identified. Complaints may be localized in a particular room or zone, or may spread throughout the building. (See: building-related illness.)

Signal: The volume or product-level change produced by a leak in a tank.

Signal Words: The words used on a pesticide label--Danger, Warning, Caution--to indicate level of toxicity.

Significant Deterioration: Pollution resulting from a new source in previously "clean" areas. (See: prevention of significant deterioration.)

Significant Municipal Facilities: Those publicly owned sewage treatment plants that discharge a million gallons per day or more and are therefore considered by states to have the potential to substantially affect the quality of receiving waters.

Significant Non-Compliance: (See significant violations.)

Significant Potential Source of Contamination: A facility or activity that stores, uses, or produces compounds with potential for significant contaminating impact if released into the source water of a public water supply.

Significant Violations: Violations by point source dischargers of sufficient magnitude or duration to be a regulatory priority.

Silt: Sedimentary materials composed of fine or intermediate-sized mineral particles.

Silviculture: Management of forest land for timber.

Single-Breath Canister: Small one-liter canister designed to capture a single breath. Used in air pollutant ingestion research.

Sink: Place in the environment where a compound or material collects.

Sinking: Controlling oil spills by using an agent to trap the oil and sink it to the bottom of the body of water where the agent and the oil are bio-degraded.

SIP Call: EPA action requiring a state to resubmit all or part of its State Implementation Plan to demonstrate attainment of the require national ambient air quality standards within the statutory deadline. A SIP Revision is a revision of a SIP altered at the request of EPA or on a state's initiative. (See: State Implementation Plan.)

Site: An area or place within the jurisdiction of the EPA and/or a state.

Site Assessment Program: A means of evaluating hazardous waste sites through preliminary assessments and site inspections to develop a Hazard Ranking System score.

Site Inspection: The collection of information from a Superfund site to determine the extent and severity of hazards posed by the site. It follows and is more extensive than a preliminary assessment. The purpose is to gather information necessary to score the site, using the Hazard Ranking System, and to determine if it presents an immediate threat requiring prompt removal.

Site Safety Plan: A crucial element in all removal actions, it includes information on equipment being used, precautions to be taken, and steps to take in the event of an on-site emergency.

Siting: The process of choosing a location for a facility.

Skimming: Using a machine to remove oil or scum from the surface of the water.

Slow Sand Filtration: Passage of raw water through a bed of sand at low velocity, resulting in substantial removal of chemical and biological contaminants.

Sludge: A semi-solid residue from any of a number of air or water treatment processes; can be a hazardous waste.

Sludge Digester: Tank in which complex organic substances like sewage sludges are biologically dredged. During these reactions, energy is released and much of the sewage is converted to methane, carbon dioxide, and water.

Slurry: A watery mixture of insoluble matter resulting from some pollution control techniques.

Small Quantity Generator (SQG-sometimes referred to as "Squeegee"): Persons or enterprises that produce 220-2200 pounds per month of hazardous waste; they are required to keep more records than conditionally exempt generators. The largest category of hazardous waste generators, SQGs, include automotive shops, dry cleaners, photographic developers, and many other small businesses. (See: conditionally exempt generators.)

Smelter: A facility that melts or fuses ore, often with an accompanying chemical change, to separate its metal content. Emissions cause pollution. "Smelting" is the process involved.

Smog: Air pollution typically associated with oxidants. (See: photochemical smog.)

Smoke: Particles suspended in air after incomplete combustion.

Soft Detergents: Cleaning agents that break down in nature.

Soft Water: Any water that does not contain a significant amount of dissolved minerals such as salts of calcium or magnesium.

Soil Adsorption Field: A sub-surface area containing a trench or bed with clean stones and a system of piping through which treated sewage may seep into the surrounding soil for further treatment and disposal.

Soil and Water Conservation Practices: Control measures consisting of managerial, vegetative, and structural practices to reduce the loss of soil and water.

Soil Conditioner: An organic material like humus or compost that helps soil absorb water, build a bacterial community, and take up mineral nutrients.

Soil Erodibility: An indicator of a soil's susceptibility to raindrop impact, runoff, and other erosive processes.

Soil Gas: Gaseous elements and compounds in the small spaces between particles of the earth and soil. Such gases can be moved or driven out under pressure.

Soil Moisture: The water contained in the pore space of the unsaturated zone.

Soil Sterilant: A chemical that temporarily or permanently prevents the growth of all plants and animals,

Solder: Metallic compound used to seal joints between pipes. Until recently, most solder contained 50 percent lead. Use of solder containing more than 0.2 percent lead in pipes carrying drinking water is now prohibited.

Sole-Source Aquifer: An aquifer that supplies 50-percent or more of the drinking water of an area.

Solid Waste: Non-liquid, non-soluble materials ranging from municipal garbage to industrial wastes that contain complex and sometimes hazardous substances. Solid wastes also include sewage sludge, agricultural refuse, demolition wastes, and mining residues. Technically, solid waste also refers to liquids and gases in containers.

Solid Waste Disposal: The final placement of refuse that is not salvaged or recycled.

Solid Waste Management: Supervised handling of waste materials from their source through recovery processes to disposal.

Solidification and Stabilization: Removal of wastewater from a waste or changing it chemically to make it less permeable and susceptible to transport by water.

Solubility: The amount of mass of a compound that will dissolve in a unit volume of solution. Aqueous Solubility is the maximum concentration of a chemical that will dissolve in pure water at a reference temperature.

Soot: Carbon dust formed by incomplete combustion.

Sorption: The action of soaking up or attracting substances; process used in many pollution control systems.

Source Area: The location of liquid hydrocarbons or the zone of highest soil or groundwater concentrations, or both, of the chemical of concern.

Source Characterization Measurements: Measurements made to estimate the rate of release of pollutants into the environment from a source such as an incinerator, landfill, etc.

Source Reduction: Reducing the amount of materials entering the waste stream from a specific source by redesigning products or patterns of production or consumption (e.g., using returnable beverage containers). Synonymous with waste reduction.

Source Separation: Segregating various wastes at the point of generation (e.g., separation of paper, metal and glass from other wastes to make recycling simpler and more efficient).

Source-Water Protection Area: The area delineated by a state for a Public Water Supply or including numerous such suppliers, whether the source is ground water or surface water or both.

Sparge or Sparging: Injection of air below the water table to strip dissolved volatile organic compounds and/or oxygenate ground water to facilitate aerobic biodegradation of organic compounds.

Special Local-Needs Registration: Registration of a pesticide product by a state agency for a specific use that is not federally registered. However, the active ingredient must be federally registered for other uses. The special use is specific to that state and is often minor, thus may not warrant the additional cost of a full federal registration process. SLN registration cannot be issued for new active ingredients, food-use active ingredients without tolerances, or for a canceled registration. The products cannot be shipped across state lines.

Special Review: Formerly known as Rebuttable Presumption Against Registration (RPAR), this is the regulatory process through which existing pesticides suspected of posing unreasonable risks to human health, non-target organisms, or the environment are referred for review by EPA. Such review requires an intensive risk/benefit analysis with opportunity for public comment. If risk is found to outweigh social and economic benefits, regulatory actions can be initiated, ranging from label revisions and use-restriction to cancellation or suspended registration.

Special Waste: Items such as household hazardous waste, bulky wastes (refrigerators, pieces of furniture, etc.) tires, and used oil.

Species: 1. A reproductively isolated aggregate of interbreeding organisms having common attributes and usually designated by a common name. 2. An organism belonging to belonging to such a category.

Specific Conductance: Rapid method of estimating the dissolved solid content of a water supply by testing its capacity to carry an electrical current.

Specific Yield: The amount of water a unit volume of saturated permeable rock will yield when drained by gravity.

Spill Prevention, Containment, and Countermeasures Plan (SPCP): Plan covering the release of hazardous substances as defined in the Clean Water Act.

Spoil: Dirt or rock removed from its original location--destroying the composition of the soil in the process--as in strip-mining, dredging, or construction.

Sprawl: Unplanned development of open land.

Spray Tower Scrubber: A device that sprays alkaline water into a chamber where acid gases are present to aid in neutralizing the gas.

Spring: Ground water seeping out of the earth where the water table intersects the ground surface.

Spring Melt/Thaw: The process whereby warm temperatures melt winter snow and ice. Because various forms of acid deposition may have been stored in the frozen water, the melt can result in abnormally large amounts of acidity entering streams and rivers, sometimes causing fish kills.

Stabilization: Conversion of the active organic matter in sludge into inert, harmless material.

Stabilization Ponds: (See: lagoon.)

Stable Air: A motionless mass of air that holds, instead of dispersing, pollutants.

Stack: A chimney, smokestack, or vertical pipe that discharges used air.

Stack Effect: Air, as in a chimney, that moves upward because it is warmer than the ambient atmosphere.

Stack Effect: Flow of air resulting from warm air rising, creating a positive pressure area at the top of a building and negative pressure area at the bottom. This effect can overpower the mechanical system and disrupt building ventilation and air circulation.

Stack Gas: (See: flue gas.)

Stage II Controls: Systems placed on service station gasoline pumps to control and capture gasoline vapors during refuelling.

Stagnation: Lack of motion in a mass of air or water that holds pollutants in place.

Stakeholder: Any organization, governmental entity, or individual that has a stake in or may be impacted by a given approach to environmental regulation, pollution prevention, energy conservation, etc.

Standard Industrial Classification Code: Also known as SIC Codes, a method of grouping industries with similar products or services and assigning codes to these groups.

Standard Sample: The part of finished drinking water that is examined for the presence of coliform bacteria.

Standards: Norms that impose limits on the amount of pollutants or emissions produced. EPA establishes minimum standards, but states are allowed to be stricter.

Start of a Response Action: The point in time when there is a guarantee or set-aside of funding by EPA, other federal agencies, states or Principal Responsible Parties in order to begin response actions at a Superfund site.

State Emergency Response Commission (SERC): Commission appointed by each state governor according to the requirements of SARA Title III. The SERCs designate emergency planning districts, appoint local emergency planning committees, and supervise and coordinate their activities.

State Environmental Goals and Indication Project: Program to assist state environmental agencies by providing technical and financial assistance in the development of environmental goals and indicators.

State Implementation Plans (SIP): EPA approved state plans for the establishment, regulation, and enforcement of air pollution standards.

State Management Plan: Under FIFRA, a state management plan required by EPA to allow states, tribes, and U.S. territories the flexibility to design and implement ways to protect ground water from the use of certain pesticides.

Static Water Depth: The vertical distance from the centerline of the pump discharge down to the surface level of the free pool while no water is being drawn from the pool or water table.

Static Water Level: 1. Elevation or level of the water table in a well when the pump is not operating. 2. The level or elevation to which water would rise in a tube connected to an artesian aquifer or basin in a conduit under pressure.

Stationary Source: A fixed-site producer of pollution, mainly power plants and other facilities using industrial combustion processes. (See: point source.)

Sterilization: The removal or destruction of all microorganisms, including pathogenic and other bacteria, vegetative forms, and spores.

Sterilizer: One of three groups of anti-microbials registered by EPA for public health uses. EPA considers an antimicrobial to be a sterilizer when it destroys or eliminates all forms of bacteria, viruses, and fungi and their spores. Because spores are considered the most difficult form of microorganism to destroy, EPA considers the term sporicide to be synonymous with sterilizer.

Storage: Temporary holding of waste pending treatment or disposal, as in containers, tanks, waste piles, and surface impoundments.

Storm Sewer: A system of pipes (separate from sanitary sewers) that carries water runoff from buildings and land surfaces.

Stratification: Separating into layers.

Stratigraphy: Study of the formation, composition, and sequence of sediments, whether consolidated or not.

Stratosphere: The portion of the atmosphere 10-to-25 miles above the earth's surface.

Stressors: Physical, chemical, or biological entities that can induce adverse effects on ecosystems or human health.

Strip-Cropping: Growing crops in a systematic arrangement of strips or bands that serve as barriers to wind and water erosion.

Strip-Mining: A process that uses machines to scrape soil or rock away from mineral deposits just under the earth's surface.

Structural Deformation: Distortion in walls of a tank after liquid has been added or removed.

Subchronic: Of intermediate duration, usually used to describe studies or periods of exposure lasting between 5 and 90 days.

Subchronic Exposure: Multiple or continuous exposures lasting for approximately ten percent of an experimental species lifetime, usually over a three-month period.

Submerged Aquatic Vegetation: Vegetation that lives at or below the water surface; an important habitat for young fish and other aquatic organisms.

Subwatershed: Topographic perimeter of the catchment area of a stream tributary.

Sulfur Dioxide (SO2): A pungent, colorless, gasformed primarily by the combustion of fossil fuels; becomes a pollutant when present in large amounts.

Sump: A pit or tank that catches liquid runoff for drainage or disposal.

Superchlorination: Chlorination with doses that are deliberately selected to produce water free of combined residuals so large as to require dechlorination.

Supercritical Water: A type of thermal treatment using moderate temperatures and high pressures to enhance the ability of water to break down large organic molecules into smaller, less toxic ones. Oxygen injected during this process combines with simple organic compounds to form carbon dioxide and water.

Superfund: The program operated under the legislative authority of CERCLA and SARA that funds and carries out EPA solid waste emergency and long-term removal and remedial activities. These activities include establishing the National Priorities List, investigating sites for inclusion on the list, determining their priority, and conducting and/or supervising cleanup and other remedial actions.

Superfund Innovative Technology Evaluation (SITE) Program: EPA program to promote development and use of innovative treatment and site characterization technologies in Superfund site cleanups.

Supplemental Registration: An arrangement whereby a registrant licenses another company to market its pesticide product under the second company's registration.

Supplier of Water: Any person who owns or operates a public water supply.

Surface Impoundment: Treatment, storage, or disposal of liquid hazardous wastes in ponds.

Surface Runoff: Precipitation, snow melt, or irrigation water in excess of what can infiltrate the soil surface and be stored in small surface depressions; a major transporter of non-point source pollutants in rivers, streams, and lakes..

Surface Uranium Mines: Strip mining operations for removal of uranium-bearing ore.

Surface Water: All water naturally open to the atmosphere (rivers, lakes, reservoirs, ponds, streams, impoundments, seas, estuaries, etc.)

Surface-Water Treatment Rule: Rule that specifies maximum contaminant level goals for Giardia lamblia, viruses, and Legionella and promulgates filtration and disinfection requirements for public water systems using surface-water or ground-water sources under the direct influence of surface water. The regulations also specify water quality, treatment, and watershed protection criteria under which filtration may be avoided.

Surfacing ACM: Asbestos-containing material that is sprayed or troweled on or otherwise applied to surfaces, such as acoustical plaster on ceilings and fireproofing materials on structural members.

Surfacing Material: Material sprayed or troweled onto structural members (beams, columns, or decking) for fire protection; or on ceilings or walls for fireproofing, acoustical or decorative purposes. Includes textured plaster, and other textured wall and ceiling surfaces.

Surfactant: A detergent compound that promotes lathering.

Surrogate Data: Data from studies of test organisms or a test substance that are used to estimate the characteristics or effects on another organism or substance.

Surveillance System: A series of monitoring devices designed to check on environmental conditions.

Susceptibility Analysis: An analysis to determine whether a Public Water Supply is subject to significant pollution from known potential sources.

Suspect Material: Building material suspected of containing asbestos; e.g., surfacing material, floor tile, ceiling tile, thermal system insulation.

Suspended Loads: Specific sediment particles maintained in the water column by turbulence and carried with the flow of water.

Suspended Solids: Small particles of solid pollutants that float on the surface of, or are suspended in, sewage or other liquids. They resist removal by conventional means.

Suspension: Suspending the use of a pesticide when EPA deems it necessary to prevent an imminent hazard resulting from its continued use. An emergency suspension takes effect immediately; under an ordinary suspension a registrant can request a hearing before the suspension goes into effect. Such a hearing process might take six months.

Suspension Culture: Cells growing in a liquid nutrient medium.

Swamp: A type of wetland dominated by woody vegetation but without appreciable peat deposits. Swamps may be fresh or salt water and tidal or non-tidal. (See: wetlands.)

Synergism: An interaction of two or more chemicals that results in an effect greater than the sum of their separate effects.

Synthetic Organic Chemicals (SOCs): Man-made (anthropogenic) organic chemicals. Some SOCs are volatile; others tend to stay dissolved in water instead of evaporating.

System With a Single Service Connection: A system that supplies drinking water to consumers via a single service line.

Systemic Pesticide: A chemical absorbed by an organism that interacts with the organism and makes the organism toxic to pests.

Tail Water: The runoff of irrigation water from the lower end of an irrigated field.

Tailings: Residue of raw material or waste separated out during the processing of crops or mineral ores.

Tailpipe Standards: Emissions limitations applicable to mobile source engine exhausts.

Tampering: Adjusting, negating, or removing pollution control equipment on a motor vehicle.

Technical Assistance Grant (TAG): As part of the Superfund program, Technical Assistance Grants of up to $50,000 are provided to citizens' groups to obtain assistance in interpreting information related to cleanups at Superfund sites or those proposed for the National Priorities List. Grants are used by such groups to hire technical advisors to help them understand the site-related technical information for the duration of response activities.

Technical-Grade Active Ingredient (TGA): A pesticide chemical in pure form as it is manufactured prior to being formulated into an end-use product (e.g. wettable powders, granules, emulsifiable concentrates). Registered manufactured products composed of such chemicals are known as Technical Grade Products.

Technology-Based Limitations: Industry-specific effluent limitations based on best available preventive technology applied to a discharge when it will not cause a violation of water quality standards at low stream flows. Usually applied to discharges into large rivers.

Technology-Based Standards: Industry-specific effluent limitations applicable to direct and indirect sources which are developed on a category-by-category basis using statutory factors, not including water-quality effects.

Teratogen: A substance capable of causing birth defects.

Teratogenesis: The introduction of nonhereditary birth defects in a developing fetus by exogenous factors such as physical or chemical agents acting in the womb to interfere with normal embryonic development.

Terracing: Dikes built along the contour of sloping farm land that hold runoff and sediment to reduce erosion.

Tertiary Treatment: Advanced cleaning of wastewater that goes beyond the secondary or biological stage, removing nutrients such as phosphorus, nitrogen, and most BOD and suspended solids.

Theoretical Maximum Residue Contribution: The theoretical maximum amount of a pesticide in the daily diet of an average person. It assumes that the diet is composed of all food items for which there are tolerance-level residues of the pesticide. The TMRC is expressed as milligrams of pesticide/kilograms of body weight/day.

Therapeutic Index: The ratio of the dose required to produce toxic or lethal effects to the dose required to produce nonadverse or therapeutic response.

Thermal Pollution: Discharge of heated water from industrial processes that can kill or injure aquatic organisms.

Thermal Stratification: The formation of layers of different temperatures in a lake or reservoir.

Thermal System Insulation (TSI): Asbestos-containing material applied to pipes, fittings, boilers, breeching, tanks, ducts, or other interior structural components to prevent heat loss or gain or water condensation.

Thermal Treatment: Use of elevated temperatures to treat hazardous wastes. (See: incineration; pyrolysis.)

Thermocline: The middle layer of a thermally stratified lake or reservoir. In this layer, there is a rapid decrease in temperatures in a lake or reservoir.

Threshold: The lowest dose of a chemical at which a specified measurable effect is observed and below which it is not observed.

Threshold: The dose or exposure level below which a significant adverse effect is not expected.

Threshold Level: Time-weighted average pollutant concentration values, exposure beyond which is likely to adversely affect human health. (See: environmental exposure)

Threshold Limit Value (TLV): The concentration of an airborne substance to which an average person can be repeatedly exposed without adverse effects. TLVs may be expressed in three ways: (1) TLV-TWA-- Time weighted average, based on an allowable exposure averaged over a normal 8-hour workday or 40-hour work- week; (2) TLV-STEL--Short-term exposure limit or maximum concentration for a brief specified period of time, depending on a specific chemical (TWA must still be met); and (3) TLV-C--Ceiling Exposure Limit or maximum exposure concentration not to be exceeded under any circumstances. (TWA must still be met.)

Threshold Odor: (See: Odor threshold)

Threshold Planning Quantity: A quantity designated for each chemical on the list of extremely hazardous substances that triggers notification by facilities to the State Emergency Response Commission that such facilities are subject to emergency planning requirements under SARA Title III.

Thropic Levels: A functional classification of species that is based on feeding relationships (e.g. generally aquatic and terrestrial green plants comprise the first thropic level, and herbivores comprise the second.)

Tidal Marsh: Low, flat marshlands traversed by channels and tidal hollows, subject to tidal inundation; normally, the only vegetation present is salt-tolerant bushes and grasses. (See: wetlands.)

Tillage: Plowing, seedbed preparation, and cultivation practices.

Time-weighted Average (TWA): In air sampling, the average air concentration of contaminants during a given period.

Tire Processor: Intermediate operating facility where recovered tires are processed in preparation for recycling.

Tires: As used in recycling, passenger car and truck tires (excludes airplane, bus, motorcycle and special service military, agricultural, off-the-road and-slow speed industrial tires). Car and truck tires are recycled into rubber products such as trash cans, storage containers, rubberized asphalt or used whole for playground and reef construction.

Tolerance Petition: A formal request to establish a new tolerance or modify an existing one.

Tolerances: Permissible residue levels for pesticides in raw agricultural produce and processed foods. Whenever a pesticide is registered for use on a food or a feed crop, a tolerance (or exemption from the tolerance requirement) must be established. EPA establishes the tolerance levels, which are enforced by the Food and Drug Administration and the Department of Agriculture.

Tonnage: The amount of waste that a landfill accepts, usually expressed in tons per month. The rate at which a landfill accepts waste is limited by the landfill's permit.

Topography: The physical features of a surface area including relative elevations and the position of natural and man-made (anthropogenic) features.

Total Dissolved Phosphorous: The total phosphorous content of all material that will pass through a filter, which is determined as orthophosphate without prior digestion or hydrolysis. Also called soluble P. or ortho P.

Total Dissolved Solids (TDS): All material that passes the standard glass river filter; now called total filtrable residue. Term is used to reflect salinity.

Total Maximum Daily Load (TMDL): A calculation of the highest amount of a pollutant that a water body can receive and safely meet water quality standards set by the state, territory, or authorized tribe.

Total Petroleum Hydrocarbons (TPH): Measure of the concentration or mass of petroleum hydrocarbon constituents present in a given amount of soil or water. The word "total" is a misnomer--few, if any, of the procedures for quantifying hydrocarbons can measure all of them in a given sample. Volatile ones are usually lost in the process and not quantified and non-petroleum hydrocarbons sometimes appear in the analysis.

Total Recovered Petroleum Hydrocarbon: A method for measuring petroleum hydrocarbons in samples of soil or water.

Total Suspended Particles (TSP): A method of monitoring airborne particulate matter by total weight.

Total Suspended Solids (TSS): A measure of the suspended solids in wastewater, effluent, or water bodies, determined by tests for "total suspended non-filterable solids." (See: suspended solids.)

Toxaphene: Chemical that causes adverse health effects in domestic water supplies and is toxic to fresh water and marine aquatic life.

Toxic Chemical: Any chemical listed in EPA rules as "Toxic Chemicals Subject to Section 313 of the Emergency Planning and Community Right-to-Know Act of 1986."

Toxic Chemical Release Form: Information form required of facilities that manufacture, process, or use (in quantities above a specific amount) chemicals listed under SARA Title III.

Toxic Chemical Use Substitution: Replacing toxic chemicals with less harmful chemicals in industrial processes.

Toxic Cloud: Airborne plume of gases, vapors, fumes, or aerosols containing toxic materials.

Toxic Concentration: The concentration at which a substance produces a toxic effect.

Toxic Dose: The dose level at which a substance produces a toxic effect.

Toxic Pollutants: Materials that cause death, disease, or birth defects in organisms that ingest or absorb them. The quantities and exposures necessary to cause these effects can vary widely.

Toxic Release Inventory: Database of toxic releases in the United States compiled from SARA Title III Section 313 reports.

Toxic Substance: A chemical or mixture that may present an unreasonable risk of injury to health or the environment.

Toxic Waste: A waste that can produce injury if inhaled, swallowed, or absorbed through the skin.

Toxicant: A harmful substance or agent that may injure an exposed organism.

Toxicity: The degree to which a substance or mixture of substances can harm humans or animals. *Acute toxicity* involves harmful effects in an organism through a single or short-term exposure. *Chronic toxicity* is the ability of a substance or mixture of substances to cause harmful effects over an extended period, usually upon repeated or continuous exposure sometimes lasting for the entire life of the exposed organism. *Subchronic toxicity* is the ability of the substance to cause effects for more than one year but less than the lifetime of the exposed organism.

Toxicity Assessment: Characterization of the toxicological properties and effects of a chemical, with special emphasis on establishment of dose-response characteristics.

Toxicity Testing: Biological testing (usually with an invertebrate, fish, or small mammal) to determine the adverse effects of a compound or effluent.

Toxicological Profile: An examination, summary, and interpretation of a hazardous substance to determine levels of exposure and associated health effects.

Transboundary Pollutants: Air pollution that travels from one jurisdiction to another, often crossing state or international boundaries. Also applies to water pollution.

Transfer Station: Facility where solid waste is transferred from collection vehicles to larger trucks or rail cars for longer distance transport.

Transient Water System: A non-community water system that does not serve 25 of the same nonresidents per day for more than six months per year.

Transmission Lines: Pipelines that transport raw water from its source to a water treatment plant, then to the distribution grid system.

Transmissivity: The ability of an aquifer to transmit water.

Transpiration: The process by which water vapor is lost to the atmosphere from living plants. The term can also be applied to the quantity of water thus dissipated.

Transportation Control Measures (TCMs): Steps taken by a locality to reduce vehicular emission and improve air quality by reducing or changing the flow of traffic; e.g. bus and HOV lanes, carpooling and other forms of ride-shairing, public transit, bicycle lanes.

Transporter: Hauling firm that picks up properly packaged and labeled hazardous waste from generators and transports it to designated facilities for treatment, storage, or disposal. Transporters are subject to EPA and DOT hazardous waste regulations.

Trash: Material considered worthless or offensive that is thrown away. Generally defined as dry waste material, but in common usage it is a synonym for garbage, rubbish, or refuse.

Trash-to-Energy Plan: Burning trash to produce energy.

Treatability Studies: Tests of potential cleanup technologies conducted in a laboratory (See: bench-scale tests.)

Treated Regulated Medical Waste: Medical waste treated to substantially reduce or eliminate its pathogenicity, but that has not yet been destroyed.

Treated Wastewater: Wastewater that has been subjected to one or more physical, chemical, and biological processes to reduce its potential of being health hazard.

Treatment: (1) Any method, technique, or process designed to remove solids and/or pollutants from solid waste, waste-streams, effluents, and air emissions. (2) Methods used to change the biological character or composition of any regulated medical waste so as to substantially reduce or eliminate its potential for causing disease.

Treatment Plant: A structure built to treat wastewater before discharging it into the environment.

Treatment, Storage, and Disposal Facility: Site where a hazardous substance is treated, stored, or disposed of. TSD facilities are regulated by EPA and states under RCRA.

Tremie: Device used to place concrete or grout under water.

Trial Burn: An incinerator test in which emissions are monitored for the presence of specific organic compounds, particulates, and hydrogen chloride.

Trichloroethylene (TCE): A stable, low boiling-point colorless liquid, toxic if inhaled. Used as a solvent or metal degreasing agent, and in other industrial applications.

Trickle Irrigation: Method in which water drips to the soil from perforated tubes or emitters.

Trickling Filter: A coarse treatment system in which wastewater is trickled over a bed of stones or other material covered with bacteria that break down the organic waste and produce clean water.

Trihalomethane (THM): One of a family of organic compounds named as derivative of methane. THMs are generally by-products of chlorination of drinking water that contains organic material.

Troposhpere: The layer of the atmosphere closest to the earth's surface.

Trust Fund (CERCLA): A fund set up under the Comprehensive Environmental Response, Compensation and Liability Act (CERCLA) to help pay for cleanup of hazardous waste sites and for legal action to force those responsible for the sites to clean them up.

Tube Settler: Device using bundles of tubes to let solids in water settle to the bottom for removal by conventional sludge collection means; sometimes used in sedimentation basins and clarifiers to improve particle removal.

Tuberculation: Development or formation of small mounds of corrosion products on the inside of iron pipe. These tubercules roughen the inside of the pipe, increasing its resistance to water flow.

Tundra: A type of treeless ecosystem dominated by lichens, mosses, grasses, and woody plants. Tundra is found at high latitudes (arctic tundra) and high altitudes (alpine tundra). Arctic tundra is underlain by permafrost and is usually water saturated. (See: wetlands.)

Turbidimeter: A device that measures the cloudiness of suspended solids in a liquid; a measure of the quantity of suspended solids.

Turbidity: 1. Haziness in air caused by the presence of particles and pollutants. 2. A cloudy condition in water due to suspended silt or organic matter.

Ultra Clean Coal (UCC): Coal that is washed, ground into fine particles, then chemically treated to remove sulfur, ash, silicone, and other substances; usually briquetted and coated with a sealant made from coal.

Ultraviolet Rays: Radiation from the sun that can be useful or potentially harmful. UV rays from one part of the spectrum (UV-A) enhance plant life. UV rays from other parts of the spectrum (UV-B) can cause skin cancer or other tissue damage. The ozone layer in the atmosphere partly shields us from ultraviolet rays reaching the earth's surface.

Uncertainty Factor: One of several factors used in calculating the reference dose from experimental data. UFs are intended to account for (1) the variation in sensitivity among humans; (2) the uncertainty in extrapolating animal data to humans; (3) the uncertainty in extrapolating data obtained in a study that covers less than the full life of the exposed animal or human; and (4) the uncertainty in using LOAEL data rather than NOAEL data.

Unconfined Aquifer: An aquifer containing water that is not under pressure; the water level in a well is the same as the water table outside the well.

Underground Injection Control (UIC): The program under the Safe Drinking Water Act that regulates the use of wells to pump fluids into the ground.

Underground Injection Wells: Steel- and concrete-encased shafts into which hazardous waste is deposited by force and under pressure.

Underground Sources of Drinking Water: Aquifers currently being used as a source of drinking water or those capable of supplying a public water system. They have a total dissolved solids content of 10,000 milligrams per liter or less, and are not "exempted aquifers." (See: exempted aquifer.)

Underground Storage Tank (UST): A tank located at least partially underground and designed to hold gasoline or other petroleum products or chemicals.

Unreasonable Risk: Under the Federal Insecticide, Fungicide, and Rodenticide Act (FIFRA), "unreasonable adverse effects" means any unreasonable risk to man or the environment, taking into account the medical, economic, social, and environmental costs and benefits of any pesticide.

Unsaturated Zone: The area above the water table where soil pores are not fully saturated, although some water may be present.

Upper Detection Limit: The largest concentration that an instrument can reliably detect.

Uranium Mill Tailings Piles: Former uranium ore processing sites that contain leftover radioactive materials (wastes), including radium and unrecovered uranium.

Uranium Mill-Tailings Waste Piles: Licensed active mills with tailings piles and evaporation ponds created by acid or alkaline leaching processes.

Urban Runoff: Storm water from city streets and adjacent domestic or commercial properties that carries pollutants of various kinds into the sewer systems and receiving waters.

Urea-Formaldehyde Foam Insulation: A material once used to conserve energy by sealing crawl spaces, attics, etc.; no longer used because emissions were found to be a health hazard.

Use Cluster: A set of competing chemicals, processes, and/or technologies that can substitute for one another in performing a particular function.

Used Oil: Spent motor oil from passenger cars and trucks collected at specified locations for recycling (not included in the category of municipal solid waste).

User Fee: Fee collected from only those persons who use a particular service, as compared to one collected from the public in general.

Utility Load: The total electricity demand for a utility district.

Vadose Zone: The zone between land surface and the water table within which the moisture content is less than saturation (except in the capillary fringe) and pressure is less than atmospheric. Soil pore space also typically contains air or other gases. The capillary fringe is included in the vadose zone. (See: Unsaturated Zone.)

Valued Environmental Attributes/Components: Those aspects(components/processes/functions) of ecosystems, human health, and environmental welfare considered to be important and potentially at risk from human activity or natural hazards. Similar to the term "valued environmental components" used in environmental impact assessment.

Vapor: The gas given off by substances that are solids or liquids at ordinary atmospheric pressure and temperatures.

Vapor Capture System: Any combination of hoods and ventilation system that captures or contains organic vapors so they may be directed to an abatement or recovery device.

Vapor Dispersion: The movement of vapor clouds in air due to wind, thermal action, gravity spreading, and mixing.

Vapor Plumes: Flue gases visible because they contain water droplets.

Vapor Pressure: A measure of a substance's propensity to evaporate, vapor pressure is the force per unit area exerted by vapor in an equilibrium state with surroundings at a given pressure. It increases exponentially with an increase in temperature. A relative measure of chemical volatility, vapor pressure is used to calculate water partition coefficients and volatilization rate constants.

Vapor Recovery System: A system by which the volatile gases from gasoline are captured instead of being released into the atmosphere.

Variance: Government permission for a delay or exception in the application of a given law, ordinance, or regulation.

Vector: 1. An organism, often an insect or rodent, that carries disease. 2. Plasmids, viruses, or bacteria used to transport genes into a host cell. A gene is placed in the vector; the vector then "infects" the bacterium.

Vegetative Controls: Non-point source pollution control practices that involve vegetative cover to reduce erosion and minimize loss of pollutants.

Vehicle Miles Travelled (VMT): A measure of the extent of motor vehicle operation; the total number of vehicle miles travelled within a specific geographic area over a given period of time.

Ventilation Rate: The rate at which indoor air enters and leaves a building. Expressed as the number of changes of outdoor air per unit of time (air changes per hour (ACH), or the rate at which a volume of outdoor air enters in cubic feet per minute (CFM).

Ventilation/Suction: The act of admitting fresh air into a space in order to replace stale or contaminated air; achieved by blowing air into the space. Similarly, suction represents the admission of fresh air into an interior space by lowering the pressure outside of the space, thereby drawing the contaminated air outward.

Venturi Scrubbers: Air pollution control devices that use water to remove particulate matter from emissions.

Vinyl Chloride: A chemical compound, used in producing some plastics, that is believed to be oncogenic.

Virgin Materials: Resources extracted from nature in their raw form, such as timber or metal ore.

Viscosity: The molecular friction within a fluid that produces flow resistance.

Volatile: Any substance that evaporates readily.

Volatile Liquids: Liquids which easily vaporize or evaporate at room temperature.

Volatile Organic Compound (VOC): Any organic compound that participates in atmospheric photochemical reactions except those designated by EPA as having negligible photochemical reactivity.

Volatile Solids: Those solids in water or other liquids that are lost on ignition of the dry solids at 550° centigrade.

Volatile Synthetic Organic Chemicals: Chemicals that tend to volatilize or evaporate.

Volume Reduction: Processing waste materials to decrease the amount of space they occupy, usually by compacting, shredding, incineration, or composting.

Volumetric Tank Test: One of several tests to determine the physical integrity of a storage tank; the volume of fluid in the tank is measured directly or calculated from product-level changes. A marked drop in volume indicates a leak.

Vulnerability Analysis: Assessment of elements in the community that are susceptible to damage if hazardous materials are released.

Vulnerable Zone: An area over which the airborne concentration of a chemical accidentally released could reach the level of concern.

Xenobiota: Any biotum displaced from its normal habitat; a chemical foreign to a biological system.

Yard Waste: The part of solid waste composed of grass clippings, leaves, twigs, branches, and other garden refuse.

Yellow-Boy: Iron oxide flocculant (clumps of solids in waste or water); usually observed as orange-yellow deposits in surface streams with excess iron content. (See: floc, flocculation.)

Yield: The quantity of water (expressed as a rate of flow or total quantity per year) that can be collected for a given use from surface or groundwater sources.

Zero Air: Atmospheric air purified to contain less than 0.1 ppm total hydrocarbons.

Zooplankton: Small (often microscopic) free-floating aquatic plants or animals.

Zone of Saturation: The layer beneath the surface of the land containing openings that may fill with water.

ACRONYMS

A&I: Alternative and Innovative (Wastewater Treatment System)

AA: Accountable Area; Adverse Action; Advices of Allowance; Assistant Administrator; Associate Administrator; Atomic Absorption

AAEE: American Academy of Environmental Engineers

AANWR: Alaskan Arctic National Wildlife Refuge

AAP: Asbestos Action Program

AAPCO: American Association of Pesticide Control Officials

AARC: Alliance for Acid Rain Control

ABEL: EPA's computer model for analyzing a violator's ability to pay a civil penalty.

ABES: Alliance for Balanced Environmental Solutions

AC: Actual Commitment. Advisory Circular

A&C: Abatement and Control

ACA: American Conservation Association

ACBM: Asbestos-Containing Building Material

ACE: Alliance for Clean Energy

ACE: Any Credible Evidence

ACEEE: American Council for an Energy Efficient Economy

ACFM: Actual Cubic Feet Per Minute

ACL: Alternate Concentration Limit. Analytical Chemistry Laboratory

ACM: Asbestos-Containing Material

ACP: Agriculture Control Program (Water Quality Management); ACP: Air Carcinogen Policy

ACQUIRE: Aquatic Information Retrieval

ACQR: Air Quality Control Region

ACS: American Chemical Society; Annual Commitment System

ACT: Action

ACTS: Asbestos Contractor Tracking System

ACWA: American Clean Water Association

ACWM: Asbestos-Containing Waste Material

ADABA: Acceptable Data Base

ADB: Applications Data Base

ADI: Acceptable Daily Intake

ADP: AHERA Designated Person; Automated Data Processing

ADQ: Audits of Data Quality

ADR: Alternate Dispute Resolution

ADSS: Air Data Screening System

ADT: Average Daily Traffic

AEA: Atomic Energy Act

AEC: Associate Enforcement Counsels

AEE: Alliance for Environmental Education

AEERL: Air and Energy Engineering Research Laboratory
AEM: Acoustic Emission Monitoring
AERE: Association of Environmental and Resource Economists
AES: Auger Electron Spectrometry
AFA: American Forestry Association
AFCA: Area Fuel Consumption Allocation
AFCEE: Air Force Center for Environmental Excellence
AFS: AIRS Facility Subsystem; Air Facility System
AFSICR: Air Facilities System—Information Collection Request
AFUG: AIRS Facility Users Group
AH: Allowance Holders
AHERA: Asbestos Hazard Emergency Response Act
AHU: Air Handling Unit
AI: Active Ingredient
AIC: Active to Inert Conversion
AICUZ: Air Installation Compatible Use Zones
AID: Agency for International Development
AIHC: American Industrial Health Council
AIP: Auto Ignition Point
AIRMON: Atmospheric Integrated Research Monitoring Network
AIRS: Aerometric Information Retrieval System
AL: Acceptable Level
ALA: Delta-Aminolevulinic Acid
ALA-O: Delta-Aminolevulinic Acid Dehydrates
ALAPO: Association of Local Air Pollution Control Officers
ALARA: As Low As Reasonably Achievable
ALC: Application Limiting Constituent
ALJ: Administrative Law Judge
ALMS: Atomic Line Molecular Spectroscopy
ALR: Action Leakage Rate
AMBIENS: Atmospheric Mass Balance of Industrially Emitted and Natural Sulfur
AMOS: Air Management Oversight System
AMPS: Automatic Mapping and Planning System
AMSA: Association of Metropolitan Sewer Agencies
ANC: Acid Neutralizing Capacity
ANPR: Advance Notice of Proposed Rulemaking
ANRHRD: Air, Noise, & Radiation Health Research Division/ORD
ANSS: American Nature Study Society
AO: Administrative Orders

AOAC: Association of Official Analytical Chemists
AOC: Abnormal Operating Conditions
AOD: Argon-Oxygen Decarbonization
AOML: Atlantic Oceanographic and Meteorological Laboratory
AP: Accounting Point
APA: Administrative Procedures Act
APCA: Air Pollution Control Association
APCD: Air Pollution Control District
APDS: Automated Procurement Documentation System
APHA: American Public Health Association
APRAC: Urban Diffusion Model for Carbon Monoxide from Motor Vehicle Traffic
APTI: Air Pollution Training Institute
APWA: American Public Works Association
AQ-7: Non-reactive Pollutant Modelling
AQCCT: Air-Quality Criteria and Control Techniques
AQCP: Air Quality Control Program
AQCR: Air-Quality Control Region
AQD: Air-Quality Digest
AQDHS: Air-Quality Data Handling System
AQDM: Air-Quality Display Model
AQMA: Air-Quality Maintenance Area
AQMD: Air Quality Management District
AQMP: Air-Quality Maintenance Plan; Air-Quality Management Plan
AQSM: Air-Quality Simulation Model
AQTAD: Air-Quality Technical Assistance Demonstration
AR: Administrative Record
A&R: Air and Radiation
ARA: Assistant Regional Administrator; Associate Regional Administrator
ARAC: Acid Rain Advisory Committee
ARAR: Applicable or Relevant and Appropriate Standards, Limitations, Criteria, and Requirements
ARB: Air Resources Board
ARC: Agency Ranking Committee
ARCC: American Rivers Conservation Council
ARCS: Alternative Remedial Contract Strategy
ARG: American Resources Group
ARIP: Accidental Release Information Program
ARL: Air Resources Laboratory
ARM: Air Resources Management

ARNEWS: Acid Rain National Early Warning Systems
ARO: Alternate Regulatory Option
ARRP: Acid Rain Research Program
ARRPA: Air Resources Regional Pollution Assessment Model
ARS: Agricultural Research Service
ARZ: Auto Restricted Zone
AS: Area Source
ASC: Area Source Category
ASDWA: Association of State Drinking Water Administrators
ASHAA: Asbestos in Schools Hazard Abatement Act
ASHRAE: American Society of Heating, Refrigerating, and Air-Conditioning Engineers
ASIWCPA: Association of State and Interstate Water Pollution Control Administrators
ASMDHS: Airshed Model Data Handling System
ASRL: Atmospheric Sciences Research Laboratory
AST: Advanced Secondary (Wastewater) Treatment; Above Ground Storage Tank
ASTHO: Association of State and Territorial Health Officers
ASTM: American Society for Testing and Materials
ASTSWMO: Association of State and Territorial Solid Waste Management Officials
AT: Advanced Treatment. Alpha Track Detection
ATERIS: Air Toxics Exposure and Risk Information System
ATS: Action Tracking System; Allowance Tracking System
ATSDR: Agency for Toxic Substances and Disease Registry
ATTF: Air Toxics Task Force
AUSM: Advanced Utility Simulation Model
A/WPR: Air/Water Pollution Report
AWRA: American Water Resources Association
AWT: Advanced Wastewater Treatment
AWWA: American Water Works Association
AWWARF: American Water Works Association Research Foundation.
BAA: Board of Assistance Appeals
BAC: Bioremediation Action Committee; Biotechnology Advisory Committee
BACM: Best Available Control Measures
BACT: Best Available Control Technology
BADT: Best Available Demonstrated Technology
BAF: Bioaccumulation Factor

BaP: Benzo(a)Pyrene
BAP: Benefits Analysis Program
BART: Best Available Retrofit Technology
BASIS: Battelle's Automated Search Information System
BAT: Best Available Technology
BATEA: Best Available Treatment Economically Achievable
BCT: Best Control Technology
BCPCT: Best Conventional Pollutant Control Technology
BDAT: Best Demonstrated Achievable Technology
BDCT: Best Demonstrated Control Technology
BDT: Best Demonstrated Technology
BEJ: Best Engineering Judgement. Best Expert Judgment
BF: Bonafide Notice of Intent to Manufacture or Import (IMD/OTS)
BIA: Bureau of Indian Affairs
BID: Background Information Document. Buoyancy Induced Dispersion
BIOPLUME: Model to Predict the Maximum Extent of Existing Plumes
BMP: Best Management Practice(s)
BMR: Baseline Monitoring Report
BO: Budget Obligations
BOA: Basic Ordering Agreement (Contracts)
BOD: Biochemical Oxygen Demand. Biological Oxygen Demand
BOF: Basic Oxygen Furnace
BOP: Basic Oxygen Process; Bureau of Prisons
BOPF: Basic Oxygen Process Furnace
BOYSNC: Beginning of Year Significant Non-Compliers
BP: Boiling Point
BPJ: Best Professional Judgment
BPT: Best Practicable Technology. Pest Practicable Treatment
BPWTT: Best Practical Wastewater Treatment Technology
BRI: Building-Related Illness
BRS: Bibliographic Retrieval Service
BSI: British Standards Institute
BSO: Benzene Soluble Organics
BTZ: Below the Treatment Zone
BUN: Blood Urea Nitrogen
CA: Citizen Act. Competition Advocate. Cooperative Agreements. Corrective Action, Compliance Assistance
CAA: Clean Air Act; Compliance Assurance Agreement
CAAA: Clean Air Act Amendments
CAC: Compliance Assistance Coordinator

CACDS: Compliance Assistance Conclusion Data Sheet

CAER: Community Awareness and Emergency Response

CAFE: Corporate Average Fuel Economy

CAFO: Concentrated Animal Feedlot; Consent Agreement/Final Order

CAG: Carcinogenic Assessment Group

CAIR: Clean Air Interstate Rule: Comprehensive Assessment of Information Rule

CALINE: California Line Source Model

CAM: Compliance Assurance Monitoring rule; Compliance Assurance Monitoring

CAMP: Continuous Air Monitoring Program

CAN: Common Account Number

CAO: Corrective Action Order

CAP: Corrective Action Plan. Cost Allocation Procedure. Criteria Air Pollutant

CAPMoN: Canadian Air and Precipitation Monitoring Network

CAR: Corrective Action Report

CAS: Center for Automotive Safety; Chemical Abstract Service

CASAC: Clean Air Scientific Advisory Committee

CASLP: Conference on Alternative State and Local Practices

CASTNet: Clean Air Status and Trends Network

CATS: Corrective Action Tracking System

CAU: Carbon Adsorption Unit; Command Arithmetic Unit

CB: Continuous Bubbler

CBA: Chesapeake Bay Agreement. Cost Benefit Analysis

CBD: Central Business District

CBEP: Community Based Environmental Project

CBI: Compliance Biomonitoring Inspection; Confidential Business Information

CBOD: Carbonaceous Biochemical Oxygen Demand

CBP: Chesapeake Bay Program; County Business Patterns; Bureau of Customs and Border Protection

CCA: Competition in Contracting Act

CCAA: Canadian Clean Air Act

CCAP: Center for Clean Air Policy; Climate Change Action Plan

CCDS: Case Conclusion Data Sheet

CCEA: Conventional Combustion Environmental Assessment

CCHW: Citizens Clearinghouse for Hazardous Wastes

CCID: Confidential Chemicals Identification System

CCMS/NATO: Committee on Challenges of a Modern Society/North Atlantic Treaty Organization

CCP: Composite Correction Plan

CC/RTS: Chemical Collection/ Request Tracking System

CCTP: Clean Coal Technology Program

CD: Climatological Data

CDB: Consolidated Data Base

CDBA: Central Data Base Administrator

CDBG: Community Development Block Grant

CDD: Chlorinated dibenzo-p-dioxin

CDF: Chlorinated dibenzofuran

CDHS: Comprehensive Data Handling System

CDI: Case Development Inspection

CDM: Climatological Dispersion Model; Comprehensive Data Management

CDMQC: Climatological Dispersion Model with Calibration and Source Contribution

CDNS: Climatological Data National Summary

CDP: Census Designated Places

CDS: Compliance Data System

CE: Categorical Exclusion. Conditionally Exempt Generator

CEA: Cooperative Enforcement Agreement; Cost and Economic Assessment

CEAT: Contractor Evidence Audit Team

CEARC: Canadian Environmental Assessment Research Council

CEB: Chemical Element Balance

CEC: Commission for Environmental Cooperation

CECATS: CSB Existing Chemicals Assessment Tracking System

CEE: Center for Environmental Education

CEEM: Center for Energy and Environmental Management

CEI: Compliance Evaluation Inspection

CELRF: Canadian Environmental Law Research Foundation

CEM: Continuous Emission Monitoring

CEMS: Continuous Emission Monitoring System

CEPA: Canadian Environmental Protection Act

CEPP: Chemical Emergency Preparedness Plan

CEQ: Council on Environmental Quality

CERCLA: Comprehensive Environmental Response, Compensation, and Liability Act (1980)

CERCLIS: Comprehensive Environmental Response, Compensation, and Liability Information System
CERT: Certificate of Eligibility
CESQG: Conditionally Exempt Small Quantity Generator
CEST: Community Environmental Service Teams
CF: Conservation Foundation
CFC: Chlorofluorocarbons
CFM: Chlorofluoromethanes
CFR: Code of Federal Regulations
CHABA: Committee on Hearing and Bio-Acoustics
CHAMP: Community Health Air Monitoring Program
CHEMNET: Chemical Industry Emergency Mutual Aid Network
CHESS: Community Health and Environmental Surveillance System
CHIP: Chemical Hazard Information Profiles
CI: Compression Ignition. Confidence Interval
CIAQ: Council on Indoor Air Quality
CIBL: Convective Internal Boundary Layer
CICA: Competition in Contracting Act
CICIS: Chemicals in Commerce Information System
CID: Criminal Investigations Division
CIDRS: Cascade Impactor Data Reduction System
CIMI: Committee on Integrity and Management Improvement
CIP: Compliance Incentive Programs
CIS: Chemical Information System. Contracts Information System
CKD: Cement Kiln Dust
CKRC: Cement Kiln Recycling Coalition
CLC: Capacity Limiting Constituents
CLEANS: Clinical Laboratory for Evaluation and Assessment of Toxic Substances
CLEVER: Clinical Laboratory for Evaluation and Validation of Epidemiologic Research
CLF: Conservation Law Foundation
CLI: Consumer Labelling Initiative
CLIPS: Chemical List Index and Processing System
CLP: Contract Laboratory Program
CM: Corrective Measure
CMA: Chemical Manufacturers Association
CMB: Chemical Mass Balance
CME: Comprehensive Monitoring Evaluation
CMEL: Comprehensive Monitoring Evaluation Log

CMEP: Critical Mass Energy Project
CMS: Compliance Monitoring Strategy
CNG: Compressedd Natural Gas
COCO: Contractor-Owned/ Contractor-Operated
COD: Chemical Oxygen Demand
COH: Coefficient Of Haze
CPDA: Chemical Producers and Distributor Association
CPF: Carcinogenic Potency Factor
CPO: Certified Project Officer
CQA: Construction Quality Assurance
CR: Continuous Radon Monitoring
CROP: Consolidated Rules of Practice
CRP: Child-Resistant Packaging; Conservation Reserve Program
CRR: Center for Renewable Resources
CRSTER: Single Source Dispersion Model
CSCT: Committee for Site Characterization
CSGWPP: Comprehensive State Ground Water Protection Program
CSI: Common Sense Initiative; Compliance Sampling Inspection
CSIN: Chemical Substances Information Network
CSMA: Chemical Specialties Manufacturers Association
CSO: Combined Sewer Overflow
CSPA: Council of State Planning Agencies
CSRL: Center for the Study of Responsive Law
CSS: Combined Sewer Systems
CTARC: Chemical Testing and Assessment Research Commission
CTG: Control Techniques Guidelines
CTSA: Cleaner TechnologiesSubstitutess Assessment
CUPA: Certified Unified Program Agencies
CV: Chemical Vocabulary
CVS: Constant Volume Sampler
CW: Continuous working-level monitoring
CWA: Clean Water Act (aka FWPCA)
CWAP: Clean Water Action Project
CWTC: Chemical Waste Transportation Council
CZMA: Coastal Zone Management Act
CZARA: Coastal Zone Management Act Reauthorization Amendments
DAPSS: Document and Personnel Security System (IMD)
DBP: Disinfection By-Product
DCI: Data Call-In
DCO: Delayed Compliance Order

DCO: Document Control Officer
DDT: DichloroDiphenylTrichloroethane
DERs: Data Evaluation Records
DES: Diethylstilbesterol
DfE: Design for the Environment
DI: Diagnostic Inspection
DMR: Discharge Monitoring Report
DNA: Deoxyribonucleic acid
DNAPL: Dense Non-Aqueous Phase Liquid
DO: Dissolved Oxygen
DOW: Defenders Of Wildlife
DPA: Deepwater Ports Act
DPD: Method of Measuring Chlorine Residual in Water
DQO: Data Quality Objective
DRE: Destruction and Removal Efficiency
DRES: Dietary Risk Evaluation System
DRMS: Defense Reutilization and Marketing Service
DRR: Data Review Record
DS: Dichotomous Sampler
DSAP: Data Self Auditing Program
DSCF: Dry Standard Cubic Feet
DSCM: Dry Standard Cubic Meter
DSS: Decision Support System; Domestic Sewage Study
DT: Detectors (radon) damaged or lost; Detention Time
DU: Decision Unit. Ducks Unlimited; Dobson Unit
DUC: Decision Unit Coordinator
DWEL: Drinking Water Equivalent Level
DWS: Drinking Water Standard
DWSRF: Drinking Water State Revolving Fund
EA: Endangerment Assessment; Enforcement Agreement; Environmental
    Action; Environmental Assessment;. Environmental Audit
EAF: Electric Arc Furnaces
EAG: Exposure Assessment Group
EAO: Emergency Administrative Order
EAP: Environmental Action Plan
EAR: Environmental Auditing Roundtable
EASI: Environmental Alliance for Senior Involvement
EB: Emissions Balancing
EC: Emulsifiable Concentrate; Environment Canada; Effective Concentra-
    tion

ECA: Economic Community for Africa
ECAP: Employee Counselling and Assistance Program
ECD: Electron Capture Detector
ECHH: Electro-Catalytic Hyper-Heaters
ECHO: Enforcement and Compliance History Online
ECL: Environmental Chemical Laboratory
ECOS: Environmental Council of the States
ECR: Enforcement Case Review
ECRA: Economic Cleanup Responsibility Act
ED: Effective Dose
EDA: Emergency Declaration Area
EDB: Ethylene Dibromide
EDC: Ethylene Dichloride
EDD: Enforcement Decision Document
EDF: Environmental Defense Fund
EDRS: Enforcement Document Retrieval System
EDS: Electronic Data System; Energy Data System
EDTA: Ethylene Diamine Triacetic Acid
EDX: Electronic Data Exchange
EDZ: Emission Density Zoning
EEA: Energy and Environmental Analysis
EECs: Estimated Environmental Concentrations
EER: Excess Emission Report
EERL: Eastern Environmental Radiation Laboratory
EERU: Environmental Emergency Response Unit
EESI: Environment and Energy Study Institute
EESL: Environmental Ecological and Support Laboratory
EETFC: Environmental Effects, Transport, and Fate Committee
EF: Emission Factor
EFO: Equivalent Field Office
EFTC: European Fluorocarbon Technical Committee
EGR: Exhaust Gas Recirculation
EH: Redox Potential
EHC: Environmental Health Committee
EHS: Extremely Hazardous Substance
EI: Emissions Inventory
EIA: Environmental Impact Assessment. Economic Impact Assessment
EIL: Environmental Impairment Liability
EIR: Endangerment Information Report; Environmental Impact Report
EIS: Environmental Impact Statement; Environmental Inventory System

EIS/AS: Emissions Inventory System/Area Source

EIS/PS: Emissions Inventory System/Point Source

EJ: Environmental Justice

EJAC: Environmental Justice Areas of Concern

EJSEAT: Environmental Justice Strategic Enforcement Assessment Tool

EKMA: Empirical Kinetic Modeling Approach

EL: Exposure Level

ELI: Environmental Law Institute

ELR: Environmental Law Reporter

EM: Electromagnetic Conductivity

EMAP: Environmental Mapping and Assessment Program

EMAS: Enforcement Management and Accountability System

EMP: Environmental Management Practices

EMR: Environmental Management Report; Environmental Management Reviews

EMS: Enforcement Management System; Environmental Management System

EMSL: Environmental Monitoring Support Systems Laboratory

EMTS: Environmental Monitoring Testing Site; Exposure Monitoring Test Site

EnPA: Environmental Performance Agreement

EO: Ethylene Oxide

EOC: Emergency Operating Center

EOF: Emergency Operations Facility (RTP)

EOP: End Of Pipe

EOT: Emergency Operations Team

EP: Earth Protectors; Environmental Profile; End-use Product; Experimental Product; Extraction Procedure

EPAA: Environmental Programs Assistance Act

EPA: Environmental Protection Agency

EPAAR: EPA Acquisition Regulations

EPCA: Energy Policy and Conservation Act

EPACT: Environmental Policy Act

EPACASR: EPA Chemical Activities Status Report

EPCRA: Emergency Planning and Community Right to Know Act

EPD: Emergency Planning District

EPI: Environmental Policy Institute

EPIC: Environmental Photographic Interpretation Center

EPNL: Effective Perceived Noise Level

EPRI: Electric Power Research Institute

EPTC: Extraction Procedure Toxicity Characteristic

EQIP: Environmental Quality Incentives Program

ER: Ecosystem Restoration; Electrical Resistivity

ERA: Economic Regulatory Agency

ERAMS: Environmental Radiation Ambient Monitoring System

ERC: Emergency Response Commission. Emissions Reduction Credit, Environmental Research Center

ERCS: Emergency Response Cleanup Services

ERDA: Energy Research and Development Administration

ERD&DAA: Environmental Research, Development and Demonstration Authorization Act

ERL: Environmental Research Laboratory

ERNS: Emergency Response Notification System

ERP: Enforcement Response Policy; Environmental Results Program

ERT: Emergency Response Team

ERTAQ: ERT Air Quality Model

ES: Enforcement Strategy

ESA: Endangered Species Act. Environmentally Sensitive Area

ESC: Endangered Species Committee

ESCA: Electron Spectroscopy for Chemical Analysis

ESCAP: Economic and Social Commission for Asia and the Pacific

ESD: Explanations of Significant Differences

ESECA: Energy Supply and Environmental Coordination Act

ESH: Environmental Safety and Health

ESP: Electrostatic Precipitators

ET: Emissions Trading

ETI: Environmental Technology Initiative

ETP: Emissions Trading Policy

ETS: Emissions Tracking System; Environmental Tobacco Smoke

ETV: Environmental Technology Verification Program

EUP: End-Use Product; Experimental Use Permit

EWCC: Environmental Workforce Coordinating Committee

EXAMS: Exposure Analysis Modeling System

ExEx: Expected Exceedance

FACA: Federal Advisory Committee Act

FAN: Fixed Account Number

FATES: FIFRA and TSCA Enforcement System

FBC: Fluidized Bed Combustion

FCC: Fluid Catalytic Converter

FCCC: Framework Convention on Climate Change

FCCU: Fluid Catalytic Cracking Unit

FCE: Full Compliance Evaluation

FCO: Federal Coordinating Officer (in disaster areas); Forms Control Officer

FDF: Fundamentally Different Factors

FDL: Final Determination Letter

FDO: Fee Determination Official

FE: Fugitive Emissions

FEDS: Federal Energy Data System

FEFx: Forced Expiratory Flow

FEIS: Fugitive Emissions Information System

FEL: Frank Effect Level

FEMA: Federal Emergency Management Agency

FEPCA: Federal Environmental Pesticide Control Act; enacted as amendments to FIFRA.

FERC: Federal Energy Regulatory Commission

FES: Factor Evaluation System

FEV: Forced Expiratory Volume

FEVı: Forced Expiratory Volume--one second; Front End Volatility Index

FF: Federal Facilities

FFAR: Fuel and Fuel Additive Registration

FFDCA: Federal Food, Drug, and Cosmetic Act

FFEO: Federal Facilities Enforcement Office

FFF: Firm Financial Facility

FFFSG: Fossil-Fuel-Fired Steam Generator

FFIS: Federal Facilities Information System

FFP: Firm Fixed Price

FGD: Flue-Gas Desulfurization

FID: Flame Ionization Detector

FIFRA: Federal Insecticide, Fungicide, and Rodenticide Act

FIM: Friable Insulation Material

FINDS: Facility Index System

FIP: Final Implementation Plan

FIPS: Federal Information Procedures System

FIT: Field Investigation Team

FLETC: Federal Law Enforcement Training Center

FLM: Federal Land Manager

FLP: Flash Point

FLPMA: Federal Land Policy and Management Act

FMAP: Financial Management Assistance Project

F/M: Food to Microorganism Ratio
FML: Flexible Membrane Liner
FMP: Facility Management Plan
FMP: Financial Management Plan
FMS: Financial Management System
FMVCP: Federal Motor Vehicle Control Program
FOE: Friends Of the Earth
FOIA: Freedom Of Information Act
FOISD: Fiber Optic Isolated Spherical Dipole Antenna
FONSI: Finding Of No Significant Impact
FORAST: Forest Response to Anthropogenic Stress
FP: Fine Particulate
FPA: Federal Pesticide Act
FPAS: Foreign Purchase Acknowledgement Statements
FPD: Flame Photometric Detector
FPEIS: Fine Particulate Emissions Information System
FPM: Federal Personnel Manual
FPPA: Federal Pollution Prevention Act
FPR: Federal Procurement Regulation
FPRS: Federal Program Resources Statement; Formal Planning and Supporting System
FQPA: Food Quality Protection Act
FR: Federal Register. Final Rulemaking
FRA: Federal Register Act
FREDS: Flexible Regional Emissions Data System
FRES: Forest Range Environmental Study
FRM: Federal Reference Methods
FRN: Federal Register Notice. Final Rulemaking Notice
FRP: Facility Response Plan
FRS: Formal Reporting System
FS: Feasibility Study
FSA: Food Security Act
FSS: Facility Status Sheet; Federal Supply Schedule
FTE: Full-Time Equivalent
FTP: Federal Test Procedure (for motor vehicles)
FTS: File Transfer Service
FTTS: FIFRA/TSCA Tracking System
FUA: Fuel Use Act
FURS: Federal Underground Injection Control Reporting System
FVMP: Federal Visibility Monitoring Program

FWCA: Fish and Wildlife Coordination Act
FWPCA: Federal Water Pollution and Control Act (aka CWA). Federal Water Pollution and Control Administration
FY: Fiscal Year
GAAP: Generally Accepted Accounting Principles
GAC: Granular Activated Carbon
GACT: Granular Activated Carbon Treatment
GAO: Government Accountability Office
GAW: Global Atmospheric Watch
GCC: Global Climate Convention
GC/MS: Gas Chromatograph/ Mass Spectograph
GCVTC: Grand Canyon Visibility Transport Commission
GCWR: Gross Combination Weight Rating
GDE: Generic Data Exemption
GEI: Geographic Enforcement Initiative
GEMI: Global Environmental Management Initiative
GEMS: Global Environmental Monitoring System; Graphical Exposure Modeling System
GEP: Good Engineering Practice
GFF: Glass Fiber Filter
GFO: Grant Funding Order
GFP: Government-Furnished Property
GICS: Grant Information and Control System
GIS: Geographic Information Systems; Global Indexing System
GLC: Gas Liquid Chromatography
GLERL: Great Lakes Environmental Research Laboratory
GLNPO: Great Lakes National Program Office
GLP: Good Laboratory Practices
GLWQA: Great Lakes Water Quality Agreement
GMCC: Global Monitoring for Climatic Change
GME: Groundwater Monitoring Evaluation
G/MI: Grams per mile
GOCO: Government-Owned/ Contractor-Operated
GOGO: Government-Owned/ Government-Operated
GOP: General Operating Procedures
GOPO: Government-Owned/ Privately-Operated
GPAD: Gallons-per-acre per-day
GPG: Grams-per-Gallon
GPR: Ground-Penetrating Radar
GPRA: Government Performance and Results Act

GPS: Groundwater Protection Strategy
GR: Grab Radon Sampling
GRAS: Generally Recognized as Safe
GRCDA: Government Refuse Collection and Disposal Association
GRGL: Groundwater Residue Guidance Level
GT: Gas Turbine
GTN: Global Trend Network
GTR: Government Transportation Request
GVP: Gasoline Vapor Pressure
GVW: Gross Vehicle Weight
GVWR: Gross Vehicle Weight Rating
GW: Grab Working-Level Sampling. Groundwater
GWDR: Ground Water Disinfection Rule
GWM: Groundwater Monitoring
GWP: Global Warming Potential
GWPC: Ground Water Protection Council
GWPS: Groundwater Protection Standard; Groundwater Protection Strategy
HA: Health Advisory
HAD: Health Assessment Document
HAP: Hazardous Air Pollutant
HAPEMS: Hazardous Air Pollutant Enforcement Management System
HAPPS: Hazardous Air Pollutant Prioritization System
HATREMS: Hazardous and Trace Emissions System
HAZMAT: Hazardous Materials
HAZOP: Hazard and Operability Study
HBFC: Hydrobromofluorocarbon
HC: Hazardous Constituents; Hydrocarbon
HCCPD: Hexachlorocyclo-pentadiene
HCFC: Hydrochlorofluorocarbon
HCP: Hypothermal Coal Process
HDD: Heavy-Duty Diesel
HDDT: Heavy-duty Diesel Truck
HDDV: Heavy-Duty Diesel Vehicle
HDE: Heavy-Duty Engine
HDG: Heavy-Duty Gasoline-Powered Vehicle
HDGT: Heavy-Duty Gasoline Truck
HDGV: Heavy-Duty Gasoline Vehicle
HDPE: High Density Polyethylene
HDT: Highest Dose Tested in a study. Heavy-Duty Truck

HDV: Heavy-Duty Vehicle
HEAL: Human Exposure Assessment Location
HECC: House Energy and Commerce Committee
HEI: Health Effects Institute
HEM: Human Exposure Modeling
HEPA: High-Efficiency Particulate Air
HEPA: Highly Efficient Particulate Air Filter
HERS: Hyperion Energy Recovery System
HFC: Hydrofluorocarbon
HHDDV: Heavy Heavy-Duty Diesel Vehicle
HHE: Human Health and the Environment
HHV: Higher Heating Value
HI: Hazard Index
HI-VOL: High-Volume Sampler
HIWAY: A Line Source Model for Gaseous Pollutants
HLRW: High Level Radioactive Waste
HMIS: Hazardous Materials Information System
HMS: Highway Mobile Source
HMTA: Hazardous Materials Transportation Act
HMTR: Hazardous Materials Transportation Regulations
HOC: Halogenated Organic Carbons
HON: Hazardous Organic NESHAP
HOV: High-Occupancy Vehicle
HP: Horse Power
HPLC: High-Performance Liquid Chromatography
HPMS: Highway Performance Monitoring System
HPV: High Priority Violator
HQ: Headquarters
HQCDO: Headquarters Case Development Officer
HRS: Hazardous Ranking System
HRUP: High-Risk Urban Problem
HSDB: Hazardous Substance Data Base
HSL: Hazardous Substance List
HSWA: Hazardous and Solid Waste Amendments
HT: Hypothermally Treated
HTP: High Temperature and Pressure
HUD: Housing and Urban Development
HVAC: Heating, Ventilation, and Air-Conditioning system
HVIO: High Volume Industrial Organics
HW: Hazardous Waste

HWDMS: Hazardous Waste Data Management System
HWGTF: Hazardous Waste Groundwater Task Force; Hazardous Waste Groundwater Test Facility
HWIR: Hazardous Waste Identification Rule
HWLT: Hazardous Waste Land Treatment
HWM: Hazardous Waste Management
HWRTF: Hazardous Waste Restrictions Task Force
HWTC: Hazardous Waste Treatment Council
I/A: Innovative/Alternative
IA: Interagency Agreement
IAAC: Interagency Assessment Advisory Committee
IAC: Innovative Action Council
IADN: Integrated Atmospheric Deposition Network
IAG: Interagency Agreement
IAP: Incentive Awards Program. Indoor Air Pollution
IAQ: Indoor Air Quality
IARC: International Agency for Research on Cancer
IATDB: Interim Air Toxics Data Base
IBSIN: Innovations in Building Sustainable Industries
IBT: Industrial Biotest Laboratory
IC: Internal Combustion
ICAIR: Interdisciplinary Planning and Information Research
ICAP: Inductively Coupled Argon Plasma
ICB: Information Collection Budget
ICBN: International Commission on the Biological Effects of Noise
ICCP: International Climate Change Partnership
ICDS: Inspection Conclusion Data Sheet
ICE: Industrial Combustion Emissions Model. Internal Combustion Engine
ICIS: Integrated Compliance Information System
ICIS—NPDES: Integrated Compliance Information System—National Pollutant Discharge Elimination System
ICP: Inductively Coupled Plasma
ICR: Information Collection Request
ICRE: Ignitability, Corrosivity, Reactivity, Extraction
ICRP: International Commission on Radiological Protection
ICRU: International Commission of Radiological Units and Measurements
ICS: Incident Command System. Institute for Chemical Studies; Intermittent Control Strategies.; Intermittent Control System
ICWM: Institute for Chemical Waste Management
IDEA: Integrated Data for Enforcement Analysis

IDLH: Immediately Dangerous to Life and Health
IEB: International Environment Bureau
IEMP: Integrated Environmental Management Project
IES: Institute for Environmental Studies
IFB: Invitation for Bid
IFCAM: Industrial Fuel Choice Analysis Model
IFCS: International Forum on Chemical Safety
IFIS: Industry File Information System
IFMS: Integrated Financial Management System
IFPP: Industrial Fugitive Process Particulate
IG: Inspector General
IGCC: Integrated Gasification Combined Cycle
IGCI: Industrial Gas Cleaning Institute
IIS: Inflationary Impact Statement
IINERT: In-Place Inactivation and Natural Restoration Technologies
IJC: International Joint Commission (on Great Lakes)
I/M: Inspection/Maintenance
IMM: Intersection Midblock Model
IMPACT: Integrated Model of Plumes and Atmosphere in Complex Terrain
IMPROVE: Interagency Monitoring of Protected Visual Environment
INECE: International Network for Environmental Compliance and Enforcement
INPUFF: Gaussian Puff Dispersion Model
INT: Intermittent
IOB: Iron Ore Beneficiation
IOU: Input/Output Unit
IPCS: International Program on Chemical Safety
IP: Inhalable Particles
IPM: Inhalable Particulate Matter. Integrated Pest Management
IPOD: ICIS Policy on Demand
IPP: Implementation Planning Program. Integrated Plotting Package; Inter-media Priority Pollutant (document); Independent Power Producer
IPCC: Intergovernmental Panel on Climate Change
IPM: Integrated Pest Management
IRG: Interagency Review Group
IRLG: Interagency Regulatory Liaison Group (Composed of EPA, CPSC, FDA, and OSHA)

IRIS: Instructional Resources Information System. Integrated Risk Information System

IRM: Intermediate Remedial Measures

IRMC: Inter-Regulatory Risk Management Council

IRP: Installation Restoration Program

IRPTC: International Register of Potentially Toxic Chemicals

IRR: Institute of Resource Recovery

IRS: International Referral Systems

IS: Interim Status

ISAM: Indexed Sequential File Access Method

ISC: Industrial Source Complex

ISCL: Interim Status Compliance Letter

ISCLT: Industrial Source Complex Long Term Model

ISCST: Industrial Source Complex Short Term Model

ISD: Interim Status Document

ISE: Ion-specific electrode

ISMAP: Indirect Source Model for Air Pollution

ISO: International Organization for Standardization

ISPF: (IBM) Interactive System Productivity Facility

ISS: Interim Status Standards

ITC:Innovative Technology Council

ITC: Interagency Testing Committee

ITRC: Interstate Technology Regulatory Coordination

ITRD: Innovative Treatment Remediation Demonstration

IU: Industrial Users (non-domestic)

IUP: Intended Use Plan

IUR: Inventory Update Rule

IWC: In-Stream Waste Concentration

IWS: Ionizing Wet Scrubber

JAPCA: Journal of Air Pollution Control Association

JCL: Job Control Language

JEC: Joint Economic Committee

JECFA: Joint Expert Committee of Food Additives

JEIOG: Joint Emissions Inventory Oversight Group

JLC: Justification for Limited Competition

JMPR: Joint Meeting on Pesticide Residues

JNCP: Justification for Non-Competitive Procurement

JOFOC: Justification for Other Than Full and Open Competition

JPA: Joint Permitting Agreement

JSD: Jackson Structured Design

JSP: Jackson Structured Programming
JTU: Jackson Turbidity Unit
LAA: Lead Agency Attorney
LADD: Lifetime Average Daily Dose; Lowest Acceptable Daily Dose
LAER: Lowest Achievable Emission Rate
LAI: Laboratory Audit Inspection
LAMP: Lake Acidification Mitigation Project
LBP: Lead-Based Paint
LC: Lethal Concentration. Liquid Chromatography
LCA: Life Cycle Assessment
LCD: Local Climatological Data
LCL: Lower Control Limit
LCM: Life Cycle Management
LCRS: Leachate Collection and Removal System
LD: Land Disposal. Light Duty
LD Lo: The lowest dosage of a toxic substance that kills test organisms.
LDAR: Leak Detection and Repair
LDC: London Dumping Convention
LDCRS: Leachate Detection, Collection, and Removal System
LDD: Light-Duty Diesel
LDDT: Light-Duty Diesel Truck
LDDV: Light-Duty Diesel Vehicle
LDGT: Light-Duty Gasoline Truck
LDIP: Laboratory Data Integrity Program
LDR: Land Disposal Restrictions
LDRTF: Land Disposal Restrictions Task Force
LDS: Leak Detection System
LDT: Lowest Dose Tested. Light-Duty Truck
LDV: Light-Duty Vehicle
LEA: Local Education Authority
LEL: Lowest Effect Level. Lower Explosive Limit
LEP: Laboratory Evaluation Program
LEPC: Local Emergency Planning Committee
LERC: Local Emergency Response Committee
LEV: Low Emissions Vehicle
LFG: Landfill Gas
LFL: Lower Flammability Limit
LGEAN: Local Government Environmental Assistance Network
LGR: Local Governments Reimbursement Program
LHDDV: Light Heavy-Duty Diesel Vehicle

LI: Langelier Index
LIDAR: Light Detection and Ranging
LIMB: Limestone-Injection Multi-Stage Burner
LLRW: Low Level Radioactive Waste
LMFBR: Liquid Metal Fast Breeder Reactor
LMOP: Landfill Methane Outreach Program
LNAPL: Light Non-Aqueous Phase Liquid
LOAEL: Lowest-Observed-Adverse-Effect-Level
LOD: Limit of Detection
LQER: Lesser Quantity Emission Rates
LQG: Large Quantity Generator
LRTAP: Long Range Transboundary Air Pollution
LUIS: Label Use Information System
MAC: Mobile Air Conditioner
MACT: Maximum Achievable Control Technology
MAPSIM: Mesoscale Air Pollution Simulation Model
MATC: Maximum Acceptable Toxic Concentration
MBAS: Methylene-Blue-Active Substances
MCL: Maximum Contaminant Level
MCLG: Maximum Contaminant Level Goal
MCS: Multiple Chemical Sensitivity
MDL: Method Detection Limit
MDR: Minimum Data Requirements
MEC: Model Energy Code
MEI: Maximally (or most) Exposed Individual
MEP: Multiple Extraction Procedure
MHDDV: Medium Heavy-Duty Diesel Vehicle
MOA: Memorandum of Agreement
MOBILE5A: Mobile Source Emission Factor Model
MOE: Margin Of Exposure
MOS: Margin of Safety
MP: Manufacturing-use Product; Melting Point
MPCA: Microbial Pest Control Agent
MPI: Maximum Permitted Intake
MPN: Maximum Possible Number
MPWC: Multiprocess Wet Cleaning
MRBMA: Mercury-Containing and Rechargeable Battery Management Act
MRF: Materials Recovery Facility
MRID: Master Record Identification number
MRL: Maximum-Residue Limit (Pesticide Tolerance)

MS4: Municipal Separate Storm Sewer System
MSW: Municipal Solid Waste
MTBE: Methyl tertiary butyl ether
MTD: Maximum Tolerated Dose
MUP: Manufacturing-Use Product
MUTA: Mutagenicity
MWC: Machine Wet Cleaning
NAA: Nonattainment Area
NAAEC: North American Agreement on Environmental Cooperation
NAAQS: National Ambient Air Quality Standards
NACA: National Agricultural Chemicals Association
NACEPT: National Advisory Council for Environmental Policy and Technology
NADP/NTN: National Atmospheric Deposition Program/National Trends Network
NAMS: National Air Monitoring Stations
NAPAP: National Acid Precipitation Assessment Program
NAPL: Non-Aqueous Phase Liquid
NAPS: National Air Pollution Surveillance
NARA: National Agrichemical Retailers Association
NARSTO: North American Research Strategy for Tropospheric Ozone
NAS: National Academy of Sciences
NASA: National Aeronautics and Space Administration
NASDA: National Association of State Departments of Agriculture
NCAMP: National Coalition Against the Misuse of Pesticides
NCEPI: National Center for Environmental Publications and Information
NCWS: Non-Community Water System
NEDS: National Emissions Data System
NEIC: National Enforcement Investigations Center
NEJAC: National Environmental Justice Advisory Council
NEPA: National Environmental Policy Act
NEPI: National Environmental Policy Institute
NEPPS: National Environmental Performance Partnership System
NESHAP: National Emission Standard for Hazardous Air Pollutants
NIEHS: National Institute for Environmental Health Sciences
NETA: National Environmental Training Association
NETI: National Enforcement Training Institute
NFRAP: No Further Remedial Action Planned
NICT: National Incident Coordination Team
NIOSH: National Institute of Occupational Safety and Health

NIPDWR: National Interim Primary Drinking Water Regulations
NISAC: National Industrial Security Advisory Committee
NMHC: Nonmethane Hydrocarbons
NMOC: Non-Methane Organic Component
NMVOC: Non-methane Volatile Organic Chemicals
NO: Nitric Oxide
NO²: Nitrogen Dioxide
NOA: Notice of Arrival
NOAA: National Oceanographic and Atmospheric Agency
NOAC: Nature of Action Code
NOAEL: No Observable Adverse Effect Level
NOEL: No Observable Effect Level
NOIC: Notice of Intent to Cancel
NOIS: Notice of Intent to Suspend
N2O: Nitrous Oxide
NOV: Notice of Violation
NOx: Nitrogen Oxides
NORM: Naturally Occurring Radioactive Material
NPCA: National Pest Control Association>
NPDES: National Pollutant Discharge Elimination System
NPHAP: National Pesticide Hazard Assessment Program
NPIRS: National Pesticide Information Retrieval System
NPL: National Priorities List
NPM: National Program Manager
NPMS: National Performance Measures Strategy
NPTN: National Pesticide Telecommunications Network
NRC: National Response Center
NRD: Natural Resource Damage
NRDC: Natural Resources Defense Council
NSDWR: National Secondary Drinking Water Regulations
NSEC: National System for Emergency Coordination
NSEP: National System for Emergency Preparedness
NSPS: New Source Performance Standards
NSR: New Source Review
NSR/PSD: National Source Review/Prevention of Significant Deterioration
NTI: National Toxics Inventory
NTIS: National Technical Information Service
NTNCWS: Non-Transient Non-Community Water System
NTP: National Toxicology Program; National Training Plan

NTU: Nephlometric Turbidity Unit
O3: Ozone
OAM: Operation and Maintenance
OAP: Office of Administration and Policy
OAQPS: Office of Air Quality Planning and Standards
OC: Office of Compliance
OCD: Offshore and Coastal Dispersion
OCE: Office of Civil Enforcement
OCEFT: Office of Criminal Enforcement, Forensics and Training
OCFO: Office of Chief Financial Officer
OCIR: Office of Congressional and Intergovernmental Relations
ODP: Ozone-Depleting Potential
ODS: Ozone-Depleting Substances
OECA: Office of Enforcement and Compliance Assurance
OECD: Organization for Economic Cooperation and Development
OEJ: Office of Environmental Justice
OF: Optional Form
OGD: Office of Grants and Disbarment
OI: Order for Information
OIG: Office of the Inspector General
OLC: Office of Legal Counsel
OLTS: On Line Tracking System
O&M: Operations and Maintenance
OMB: Office of Management and Budget
OPP: Office of Pesticide Programs
OPPTS: Office of Prevention, Pesticides, and Toxic Substances
ORE: Office of Regulatory Enforcement
ORM: Other Regulated Material
ORP: Oxidation-Reduction Potential
OTAG: Ozone Transport Assessment Group
OTC: Ozone Transport Commission
OTIS: Online Tracking Information System
OTR: Ozone Transport Region
P2: Pollution Prevention
PAG: Pesticide Assignment Guidelines
PAH: Polynuclear Aromatic Hydrocarbons
PAI: Performance Audit Inspection (CWA); Pure Active Ingredient compound
PAM: Pesticide Analytical Manual
PAMS: Photochemical Assessment Monitoring Stations

PAT: Permit Assistance Team (RCRA)
PATS: Pesticide Action Tracking System; Pesticides Analytical Transport Solution
Pb: Lead
PBA: Preliminary Benefit Analysis (BEAD)
PBT: Persistent Bio-Accumulative Toxics
PCA: Principle Component Analysis
PCB: Polychlorinated Biphenyl
PCE: Perchloroethylene; Partial Compliance Evaluation
PCM: Phase Contrast Microscopy
PCN: Policy Criteria Notice
PCO: Pest Control Operator
PCS: Permit Compliance System
PCSD: President's Council on Sustainable Development
PDCI: Product Data Call-In
PEI: Production Establishment Inspections
PFA: Preliminary Financial Assessments
PFC: Perfluorated Carbon
PFCRA: Program Fraud Civil Remedies Act
PHC: Principal Hazardous Constituent
PHI: Pre-Harvest Interval
PHSA: Public Health Service Act
PI: Preliminary Injunction. Program Information
PIC: Products of Incomplete Combustion
PIGS: Pesticides in Groundwater Strategy
PIMS: Pesticide Incident Monitoring System
PIN: Pesticide Information Network
PIN: Procurement Information Notice
PIP: Public Involvement Program
PIPQUIC: Program Integration Project Queries Used in Interactive Command
PIRG: Public Interest Research Group
PIRT: Pretreatment Implementation Review Task Force
PIT: Permit Improvement Team
PITS: Project Information Tracking System
PLIRRA: Pollution Liability Insurance and Risk Retention Act
PLM: Polarized Light Microscopy
PLUVUE: Plume Visibility Model
PM: Particulate Matter
PMAS: Photochemical Assessment Monitoring Stations

PM2.5: Particulate Matter Smaller than 2.5 Micrometers in Diameter
PM10: Particulate Matter (nominally 10m and less)
PM15: Particulate Matter (nominally 15m and less)
PMEL: Pacific Marine Environmental Laboratory
PMN: Premanufacture Notification
PMNF: Premanufacture Notification Form
PMR: Pollutant Mass Rate
PMR: Proportionate Mortality Ratio
PMRS: Performance Management and Recognition System
PMS: Program Management System
PNA: Polynuclear Aromatic Hydrocarbons
PO: Project Officer
POC: Point Of Compliance
POE: Point Of Exposure
POGO: Privately-Owned/ Government-Operated
POHC: Principal Organic Hazardous Constituent
POI: Point Of Interception
POLREP:Pollution Report
POM: Particulate Organic Matter. Polycyclic Organic Matter
POP: Persistent Organic Pollutant
POR: Program of Requirements
POTW: Publicly Owned Treatment Works
POV: Privately Owned Vehicle
PP: Program Planning
PPA: Planned Program Accomplishment; Performance Partnership Agreement
PPB: Parts Per Billion
PPE: Personal Protective Equipment
PPG: Performance Partnership Grant
PPIC: Pesticide Programs Information Center
PPIS: Pesticide Product Information System; Pollution Prevention Incentives for States
PPMAP: Power Planning Modeling Application Procedure
PPM/PPB: Parts per million/ parts per billion
PPSP: Power Plant Siting Program
PPT: Parts Per Trillion
PPTH: Parts Per Thousand
PQUA: Preliminary Quantitative Usage Analysis
PR: Pesticide Regulation Notice; Preliminary Review
PRA: Paperwork Reduction Act; Planned Regulatory Action

PRATS: Pesticides Regulatory Action Tracking System
PRC: Planning Research Corporation
PRI: Periodic Reinvestigation
PRM: Prevention Reference Manuals
PRN: Pesticide Registration Notice
PRP: Potentially Responsible Party
PRZM: Pesticide Root Zone Model
PS: Point Source
PSAM: Point Source Ambient Monitoring
PSC: Program Site Coordinator
PSD: Prevention of Significant Deterioration
PSES: Pretreatment Standards for Existing Sources
PSI: Pollutant Standards Index; Pounds Per Square Inch; Pressure Per Square Inch
PSIG: Pressure Per Square Inch Gauge
PSM: Point Source Monitoring
PSNS: Pretreatment Standards for New Sources
PSU: Primary Sampling Unit
PTDIS: Single Stack Meteorological Model in EPA UNAMAP Series
PTE: Potential to Emit
PTFE: Polytetrafluoroethylene (Teflon)
PTMAX: Single Stack Meteorological Model in EPA UNAMAP series
PTPLU: Point Source Gaussian Diffusion Model
PUC: Public Utility Commission
PV: Project Verification
PVC: Polyvinyl Chloride
PWB: Printed Wiring Board
PWS: Public Water Supply/ System
PWSS: Public Water Supply System; Public Water System Supervision
QAC: Quality Assurance Coordinator
QA/QC: Quality Assistance/ Quality Control
QAMIS: Quality Assurance Management and Information System
QAO: Quality Assurance Officer
QAPP: Quality Assurance Program (or Project) Plan
QAT: Quality Action Team
QBTU: Quadrillion British Thermal Units
QC: Quality Control
QCA: Quiet Communities Act
QCI: Quality Control Index
QCP: Quiet Community Program

QL: Quantification Limit
QNCR: Quarterly Noncompliance Report
QUA: Qualitative Use Assessment
QUIPE: Quarterly Update for Inspector in Pesticide Enforcement

RA: Reasonable Alternative; Regulatory Alternatives; Regulatory Analysis; Remedial Action; Resource Allocation; Risk Analysis; Risk Assessment
RAATS: RCRA Administrate Action Tracking System
RAC: Radiation Advisory Committee. Raw Agricultural Commodity; Regional Asbestos Coordinator. Response Action Coordinator
RACM: Reasonably Available Control Measures
RACT: Reasonably Available Control Technology
RAD: Radiation Adsorbed Dose (unit of measurement of radiation absorbed by humans)
RADM: Random Walk Advection and Dispersion Model; Regional Acid Deposition Model
RAM: Urban Air Quality Model for Point and Area Source in EPA UNA-MAP Series
RAMP: Rural Abandoned Mine Program
RAMS: Regional Air Monitoring System
RAP: Radon Action Program; Registration Assessment Panel; Remedial Accomplishment Plan; Response Action Plan
RAPS: Regional Air Pollution Study
RARG: Regulatory Analysis Review Group
RAS: Routine Analytical Service
RAT: Relative Accuracy Test
RB: Request for Bid
RBAC: Re-use Business Assistance Center
RBC: Red Blood Cell
RC: Responsibility Center
RCC: Radiation Coordinating Council
RCDO: Regional Case Development Officer
RCO: Regional Compliance Officer
RCP: Research Centers Program
RCRA: Resource Conservation and Recovery Act
RCRAInfo: Resource Conservation and Recovery Act Information
RCRIS: Resource Conservation and Recovery Information System
RD/RA: Remedial Design/ Remedial Action
R&D: Research and Development
RD&D: Research, Development and Demonstration

RDF: Refuse-Derived Fuel
RDNA: Recombinant DNA
RDU: Regional Decision Units
RDV: Reference Dose Values
RE: Reasonable Efforts; Reportable Event
REAP: Regional Enforcement Activities Plan
RECAP: Regional Enforcement and Compliance Assurance Program
REE: Rare Earth Elements
REEP: Review of Environmental Effects of Pollutants
RECLAIM: Regional Clean Air Initiatives Marker
RED: Reregistration Eligibility Decision Document
REDA: Recycling Economic Development Advocate
ReFIT: Reinvention for Innovative Technologies
REI: Restricted Entry Interval
REM: (Roentgen Equivalent Man)
REM/FIT: Remedial/Field Investigation Team
REMS: RCRA Enforcement Management System
REP: Reasonable Efforts Program
REPS: Regional Emissions Projection System
RESOLVE: Center for Environmental Conflict Resolution
RF: Response Factor
RFA: Regulatory Flexibility Act
RFB: Request for Bid
RfC: Reference Concentration
RFD: Reference Dose Values
RFI: Remedial Field Investigation
RFP: Reasonable Further Programs. Request for Proposal
RHRS: Revised Hazard Ranking System
RI: Reconnaissance Inspection
RI: Remedial Investigation
RIA: Regulatory Impact Analysis; Regulatory Impact Assessment
RIC: Radon Information Center
RICC: Retirement Information and Counseling Center
RICO: Racketeer Influenced and Corrupt Organizations Act
RI/FS: Remedial Investigation/ Feasibility Study
RIM: Regulatory Interpretation Memorandum
RIN: Regulatory Identifier Number
RIP: RCRA Implementation Plan
RISC: Regulatory Information Service Center
RJE: Remote Job Entry

RLL: Rapid and Large Leakage (Rate)

RMCL: Recommended Maximum Contaminant Level (this phrase being discontinued in favor of MCLG)

RMDHS: Regional Model Data Handling System

RMIS: Resources Management Information System

RMP: Risk Management Plan

RNA: Ribonucleic Acid

ROADCHEM: Roadway Version that Includes Chemical Reactions of BI, NO_2, and O_3

ROADWAY: A Model to Predict Pollutant Concentrations Near a Roadway

ROC: Record Of Communication

RODS: Records Of Decision System

ROG: Reactive Organic Gases

ROLLBACK: A Proportional Reduction Model

ROM: Regional Oxidant Model

ROMCOE: Rocky Mountain Center on Environment

ROP: Rate of Progress; Regional Oversight Policy

ROPA: Record Of Procurement Action

ROSA: Regional Ozone Study Area

RP: Radon Progeny Integrated Sampling. Respirable Particulates. Responsible Party

RPAR: Rebuttable Presumption Against Registration

RPM: Reactive Plume Model. Remedial Project Manager

RQ: Reportable Quantities

RRC: Regional Response Center

RR+P: Renovation, Repair and Painting

RRT: Regional Response Team; Requisite Remedial Technology

RS: Registration Standard

RSCC: Regional Sample Control Center

RSD: Risk-Specific Dose

RSE: Removal Site Evaluation

RTCM: Reasonable Transportation Control Measure

RTDF: Remediation Technologies Development Forum

RTDM: Rough Terrain Diffusion Model

RTECS: Registry of Toxic Effects of Chemical Substances

RTM: Regional Transport Model

RTP: Research Triangle Park

RUP: Restricted Use Pesticide

RVP: Reid Vapor Pressure

RWC: Residential Wood Combustion
S&A: Sampling and Analysis. Surveillance and Analysis
SAAP: Special Appropriations Act Projects
SAB: Science Advisory Board
SAC: Suspended and Cancelled Pesticides; Special Agent-in-Charge
SAEWG: Standing Air Emissions Work Group
SAIC: Special-Agents-In-Charge
SAIP: Systems Acquisition and Implementation Program
SAMI: Southern Appalachian Mountains Initiative
SAMWG: Standing Air Monitoring Work Group
SANE: Sulfur and Nitrogen Emissions
SANSS: Structure and Nomenclature Search System
SAP: Scientific Advisory Panel
SAR: Start Action Request. Structural Activity Relationship (of a qualitative
    assessment)
SARA: Superfund Amendments and Reauthorization Act of 1986
SAROAD: Storage and Retrieval Of Aerometric Data
SAS: Special Analytical Service. Statistical Analysis System
SASS: Source Assessment Sampling System
SAV: Submerged Aquatic Vegetation
SBC: Single Breath Cannister
SC: Sierra Club
SCAP: Superfund Consolidated Accomplishments Plan
SCBA: Self-Contained Breathing Apparatus
SCC: Source Classification Code
SCD/SWDC: Soil or Soil and Water Conservation District
SCFM: Standard Cubic Feet Per Minute
SCLDF: Sierra Club Legal Defense Fund
SCR: Selective Catalytic Reduction
SCRAM: State Consolidated RCRA Authorization Manual
SCRC: Superfund Community Relations Coordinator
SCS: Supplementary Control Strategy/System
SCSA: Soil Conservation Society of America
SCSP: Storm and Combined Sewer Program
SCW: Supercritical Water Oxidation
SDC: Systems Decision Plan
SDWA: Safe Drinking Water Act
SDWIS: Safe Drinking Water Information System
SDWIS/ODS: Safe Drinking Water Information System/Operational Data
    System

SBS: Sick Building Syndrome
SEA: State Enforcement Agreement
SEA: State/EPA Agreement
SEAM: Surface, Environment, and Mining
SEAS: Strategic Environmental Assessment System
SEC: Securities and Exchange Commission
SEDS: State Energy Data System
SEE: Senior Environmental Employment
SEGIP: State Environmental Goals and Improvement Project
SEIA: Socioeconomic Impact Analysis
SEM: Standard Error of the Means
SEP: Standard Evaluation Procedures; Supplementary Environmental Project
SEPWC: Senate Environment and Public Works Committee
SERC: State Emergency Planning Commission
SES: Secondary Emissions Standard
SETAC: Society for Environmental Toxicology and Chemistry
SETS: Site Enforcement Tracking System
SF: Standard Form. Superfund
SFA: Spectral Flame Analyzers
SFDS: Sanitary Facility Data System
SFFAS: Superfund Financial Assessment System
SFIP: Sector Facility Indexing Project
SFIREG: State FIFRA Issues Research and Evaluation Group
SFS: State Funding Study
SGTM: State Grant Template Measures
SHORTZ: Short Term Terrain Model
SHWL: Seasonal High Water Level
SI: International System of Units. Site Inspection. Surveillance Index. Spark Ignition
SIC: Standard Industrial Classification
SICEA: Steel Industry Compliance Extension Act
SIMS: Secondary Ion-Mass Spectrometry
SIP: State Implementation Plan
SITE: Superfund Innovative Technology Evaluation
SITS: Strategy Implementation Teams
SJVAPCD: San Joaquin Valley Air Pollution Control District
SLAMS: State/Local Air Monitoring Station
SLN: Special Local Need
SLPD: Special Litigation and Projects Division

SLSM: Simple Line Source Model
SM: Synthetic Minor
SMART: Simple Maintenance of ARTS
SMCL: Secondary Maximum Contaminant Level
SMCRA: Surface Mining Control and Reclamation Act
SME: Subject Matter Expert
SMO: Sample Management Office
SMOA: Superfund Memorandum of Agreement
SMP: State Management Plan
SMR: Standardized Mortality Ratio
SMSA: Standard Metropolitan Statistical Area
SNA: System Network Architecture
SNAAQS: Secondary National Ambient Air Quality Standards
SNAP: Significant New Alternatives Project; Significant Noncompliance Action Program
SNARL: Suggested No Adverse Response Level
SNC: Significant Noncompliers; Significant Noncompliance
SNUR: Significant New Use Rule
SNY: SNC Yes
SO^2: Sulfur Dioxide
SOC: Synthetic Organic Chemicals; Significant Operational Compliance
SOCMI: Synthetic Organic Chemicals Manufacturing Industry
SOFC: Solid Oxide Fuel Cell
SOTDAT: Source Test Data
SOW: Scope Of Work
SPAR: Status of Permit Application Report
SPCC: Spill Prevention, Containment, and Countermeasure
SPE: Secondary Particulate Emissions
SPF: Structured Programming Facility
SPI: Strategic Planning Initiative
SPLMD: Soil-pore Liquid Monitoring Device
SPMS: Strategic Planning and Management System; Special Purpose Monitoring Stations
SPOC: Single Point Of Contact
SPS: State Permit System
SPSS: Statistical Package for the Social Sciences
SPUR: Software Package for Unique Reports
SQBE: Small Quantity Burner Exemption
SQG: Small Quantity Generator
SR: Special Review

SRAP: Superfund Remedial Accomplishment Plan

SRC: Solvent-Refined Coal

SRF: State Revolving Fund; State Review Framework

SRM: Standard Reference Method

SRP: Special Review Procedure

SRR: Second Round Review. Submission Review Record

SRTS: Service Request Tracking System

SS: Settleable Solids. Superfund Surcharge. Suspended Solids

SSA: Sole Source Aquifer

SSAC: Soil Site Assimilated Capacity

SSC: State Superfund Contracts

SSD: Standards Support Document

SSEIS: Standard Support and Environmental Impact Statement;. Stationary Source Emissions and Inventory System.

SSI: Size Selective Inlet

SSMS: Spark Source Mass Spectrometry

SSO: Sanitary Sewer Overflow; Source Selection Official

SSRP: Source Reduction Review Project

SSTS: Section Seven Tracking System

SSURO: Stop Sale, Use and Removal Order

STAG: State and Tribal Assistance Grant

STALAPCO: State and Local Air-Pollution Control Officials

STAPPA: State and Territorial Air Pollution

STAR: Stability Wind Rose. State Acid Rain Projects

STARS: Strategic Targeted Activities for Results System

STEL: Short Term Exposure Limit

STEM: Scanning Transmission-Electron Microscope

STN: Scientific and Technical Information Network

STORET: Storage and Retrieval of Water-Related Data

STP: Sewage Treatment Plant. Standard Temperature and Pressure

STTF: Small Town Task Force (EPA)

SUP: Standard Unit of Processing

SURE: Sulfate Regional Experiment Program

SV: Sampling Visit; Significant Violater

SW: Slow Wave

SWAP: Source Water Assessment Program

SWARF: Waste from Metal Grinding Process

SWC: Settlement With Conditions

SWDA: Solid Waste Disposal Act

SWIE: Southern Waste Information Exchange

SWMU: Solid Waste Management Unit

SWPA: Source Water Protection Area

SWQPPP: Source Water Quality Protection Partnership Petitions

SWPPP: Stormwater Pollution Prevention Plan

SWTR: Surface Water Treatment Rule

SYSOP: Systems Operator

TAD: Technical Assistance Document

TAG: Technical Assistance Grant

TALMS: Tunable Atomic Line Molecular Spectroscopy

TAMS: Toxic Air Monitoring System

TAMTAC: Toxic Air Monitoring System Advisory Committee

TAP: Technical Assistance Program

TAPDS: Toxic Air Pollutant Data System

TAS: Tolerance Assessment System

TBT: Tributyltin

TC: Target Concentration. Technical Center. Toxicity Characteristics. Toxic Concentration:

TCDD: Dioxin (Tetrachlorodibenzo-p-dioxin)

TCDF: Tetrachlorodi-benzofurans

TCE: Trichloroethylene

TCF: Total Chlorine Free

TCLP: Total Concentrate Leachate Procedure. Toxicity Characteristic Leachate Procedure

TCM: Transportation Control Measure

TCP: Transportation Control Plan; Trichloropropane;

TCRI: Toxic Chemical Release Inventory

TD: Toxic Dose

TDS: Total Dissolved Solids

TEAM: Total Exposure Assessment Model

TEC: Technical Evaluation Committee

TED: Turtle Excluder Devices

TEG: Tetraethylene Glycol

TEGD: Technical Enforcement Guidance Document

TEL: Tetraethyl Lead

TEM: Texas Episodic Model

TEP: Typical End-use Product. Technical Evaluation Panel

TERA: TSCA Environmental Release Application

TES: Technical Enforcement Support

TEXIN: Texas Intersection Air Quality Model

TGO: Total Gross Output

TGAI: Technical Grade of the Active Ingredient
TGP: Technical Grade Product
THC: Total Hydrocarbons
THM: Trihalomethane
TI: Temporary Intermittent
TI: Therapeutic Index
TIBL: Thermal Internal Boundary Layer
TIC: Technical Information Coordinator. Tentatively Identified Compounds
TIM: Technical Information Manager
TIP: Technical Information Package
TIP: Transportation Improvement Program
TIS: Tolerance Index System
TISE: Take It Somewhere Else
TITC: Toxic Substance Control Act Interagency Testing Committee
TLV: Threshold Limit Value
TLV-C: TLV-Ceiling
TLV-STEL: TLV-Short Term Exposure Limit
TLV-TWA: TLV-Time Weighted Average
TMDL: Total Maximum Daily Limit; Total Maximum Daily Load
TMRC: Theoretical Maximum Residue Contribution
TNCWS: Transient Non-Community Water System
TNT: Trinitrotoluene
TO: Task Order
TOA: Trace Organic Analysis
TOC: Total Organic Carbon/ Compound
TOX: Tetradichloroxylene
TP: Technical Product; Total Particulates
TPC: Testing Priorities Committee
TPI: Technical Proposal Instructions
TPQ: Threshold Planning Quantity
TPSIS: Transportation Planning Support Information System
TPTH: Triphenyltinhydroxide
TPY: Tons Per Year
TQM: Total Quality Management
T-R: Transformer-Rectifier
TRC: Technical Review Committee
TRD: Technical Review Document
TRI: Toxic Release Inventory
TRIP: Toxic Release Inventory Program

TRIS: Toxic Chemical Release Inventory System
TRLN: Triangle Research Library Network
TRO: Temporary Restraining Order
TSA: Technical Systems Audit
TSCA: Toxic Substances Control Act
TSCATS: TSCA Test Submissions Database
TSCC: Toxic Substances Coordinating Committee
TSD: Technical Support Document; Treatment, Storage and Disposal
TSDF: Treatment, Storage, and Disposal Facility
TSDG: Toxic Substances Dialogue Group
TSI: Thermal System Insulation
TSM: Transportation System Management
TSO: Time Sharing Option
TSP: Total Suspended Particulates
TSS: Total Suspended (non-filterable) Solids
TTFA: Target Transformation Factor Analysis
TTHM: Total Trihalomethane
TTN: Technology Transfer Network
TTO: Total Toxic Organics
TTY: Teletypewriter
TVA: Tennessee Valley Authority
TVOC: Total Volatile Organic Compounds
TWA: Time Weighted Average
TWS: Transient Water System
UAC: User Advisory Committee
UAM: Urban Airshed Model
UAO: Unilateral Administrative Order
UAPSP: Utility Acid Precipitation Study Program
UAQI: Uniform Air Quality Index
UARG: Utility Air Regulatory Group
UCC: Ultra Clean Coal
UCCI: Urea-Formaldehyde Foam Insulation
UCL: Upper Control Limit
UDMH: Unsymmetrical Dimethyl Hydrazine
UEL: Upper Explosive Limit
UF: Uncertainty Factor
UFL: Upper Flammability Limit
ug/m3: Micrograms Per Cubic Meter
UIC: Underground Injection Control
ULEV: Ultra Low Emission Vehicles

UMTRCA: Uranium Mill Tailings Radiation Control Act
UNAMAP: Users' Network for Applied Modeling of Air Pollution
UNECE: United Nations Economic Commission for Europe
UNEP: United Nations Environment Program
UNICOR: trade name of Federal Prison Industries
UPDS: Unified Program Database System
USC: Unified Soil Classification
USDA: United States Department of Agriculture
USDW: Underground Sources of Drinking Water
USFS: United States Forest Service
UST: Underground Storage Tank
UTM: Universal Transverse Mercator
UTP: Urban Transportation Planning
UV: Ultraviolet
UVA, UVB, UVC: Ultraviolet Radiation Bands
UZM: Unsaturated Zone Monitoring
VALLEY: Meteorological Model to Calculate Concentrations on Elevated Terrain
VCM: Vinyl Chloride Monomer
VCP: Voluntary Cleanup Program
VE: Visual Emissions
VEO: Visible Emission Observation
VHS: Vertical and Horizontal Spread Model
VHT: Vehicle-Hours of Travel
VISTTA: Visibility Impairment from Sulfur Transformation and Transport in the Atmosphere
VKT: Vehicle Kilometers Traveled
VMT: Vehicle Miles Traveled
VOC: Volatile Organic Compounds
VOS: Vehicle Operating Survey
VOST: Volatile Organic Sampling Train
VP: Vapor Pressure
VSD: Virtually Safe Dose
VSI: Visual Site Inspection
VSS: Volatile Suspended Solids
WA: Work Assignment
WADTF: Western Atmospheric Deposition Task Force
WAP: Waste Analysis Plan
WAVE: Water Alliances for Environmental Efficiency
WB: Wet Bulb

WCED: World Commission on Environment and Development
WDROP: Distribution Register of Organic Pollutants in Water
WENDB: Water Enforcement National Data Base
WERL: Water Engineering Research Laboratory
WET: Whole Effluent Toxicity test
WHO: World Health Organization
WHP: Wellhead Protection Program
WHPA: Wellhead Protection Area
WHWT: Water and Hazardous Waste Team
WICEM: World Industry Conference on Environmental Management
WL: Warning Letter; Working Level (radon measurement)
WLA/TMDL: Wasteload Allocation/Total Maximum Daily Load
WLM: Working Level Months
WMO: World Meteorological Organization
WP: Wettable Powder
WPCF: Water Pollution Control Federation
WQS: Water Quality Standard
WRC: Water Resources Council
WRDA: Water Resources Development Act
WRI: World Resources Institute
WS: Work Status
WSF: Water Soluble Fraction
WSRA: Wild and Scenic Rivers Act
WSTB: Water Sciences and Technology Board
WSTP: Wastewater Sewage Treatment Plant
WW: Wet Weather
WWEMA: Waste and Wastewater Equipment Manufacturers Association
WWF: World Wildlife Fund
WWTP: Wastewater Treatment Plant
WWTU: Wastewater Treatment Unit
ZEV: Zero Emissions Vehicle
ZHE: Zero Headspace Extractor
ZOI: Zone Of Incorporation
ZRL: Zero Risk Level

Appendix C: Resources

American Water Works Association
Public Affairs Department
6666 West Quincy Avenue
Denver, CO 80235
Phone (303) 794-7711
www.awwa.org

Association of Metropolitan Water Agencies
1620 I Street NW Suite 500
Washington, DC 20006
Phone (202) 331-2820
Fax (202) 785-1845
www.amwa.net

Association of State Drinking Water Administrators
1401 Wilson Blvd. Suite 1225
Arlington, VA 22209
Phone (703) 812-9505
www.asdwa.org

Clean Water Action
4455 Connecticut Avenue NW Suite A300
Washington, DC 20008
Phone (202) 895-0420

www.cleanwater.org

Consumer Federation of America
1620 I Street NW Suite 200
Washington, DC 20006
Phone (202) 387-6121
www.consumerfed.org

The Groundwater Foundation
P.O. Box 22558
Lincoln, NE 68542 Phone
(800) 858-4844
www.groundwater.org

The Ground Water Protection Council
13308 N. Mac Arthur Oklahoma City,
OK 73142
Phone (405) 516-4972
www.gwpc.org

International Bottled Water Association
1700 Diagonal Road Suite 650
Alexandria, VA 22314
Phone (703) 683-5213
Information Hotline 1-800-WATER-11
ibwainfo@bottledwater.org

National Association of Regulatory Utility Commissioners
1101 Vermont Ave NW Suite 200
Washington, DC 20005
Phone (202) 898-2200
www.naruc.org

National Association of Water Companies
2001 L Street NW Suite 850
Washington, DC 20036
Phone (202) 833-8383
www.nawc.org

National Drinking Water Clearinghouse

West Virginia University
P.O. Box 6064
Morgantown, WV 26506
Phone (800) 624-8301
www.ndwc.wvu.edu

National Ground Water Association
601 Dempsey Rd
Westerville, OH 43081-8978
Phone: (800) 551-7379
www.ngwa.org

National Rural Water Association
2915 South 13th Street
Duncan, OK 73533
Phone (580) 252-0629
www.nrwa.org

Natural Resources Defense Council
40 West 20th Street
New York, NY 10011
Phone (212) 727-2700
www.nrdc.org

NSF International
P.O. Box 130140
789 North Dixboro Road
Ann Arbor, MI 48113
Phone (800) NSF-MARK

www.nsf.org Rural Community Assistance Program
1522 K Street NW Suite
400 Washington, DC 20005
Phone (800) 321-7227
www.rcap.org

Underwriters Laboratories Corporate Headquarters
2600 N.W. Lake Road
Camas, WA 98607
Phone (877) 854-3577

www.ul.com

Water Quality Association
4151 Naperville Road
Lisle, IL 60532
Phone (630) 505-0160
www.wqa.org

U.S. Environmental Protection Agency Water Resource Center
1200 Pennsylvania Avenue NW RC-4100T
Washington, DC 20460
SDWA Hotline (800) 426-4791
www.epa.gov/safewater

Water Systems Council National Programs Office
101 30th Street NW Suite 500
Washington, D.C. 20007
Phone: (202) 625-4387
Wellcare Hotline 888-395-1033
www.watersystems council.org

EPA Region 1
(CT, ME, MA, NH, RI, VT)
Phone (888) 372-7341
Phone (617) 918-1614

EPA Region 2
(NJ, NY, PR, VI)
Phone (212) 637-3000

EPA Region 3
(DE, DC, MD, PA, VA, WV)
Phone (215) 814-5000

EPA Region 4
(AL, FL, GA, KY, MS, NC, SC, TN)
Phone (404) 562-9900

EPA Region 5

(IL, IN, MI, MN, OH, WI)
Phone (312) 353-2000 EPA

EPA Region 6
(AR, LA, NM, OK, TX)
Phone (214) 665-2200

EPA Region 7
(IA, KS, MO, NE)
Phone (913) 551-7003

EPA Region 8
(CO, MT, ND, SD, UT, WY)
Phone (303) 312-6312

EPA Region 9
(AZ, CA, HI, NW, AS GU)
Phone (415) 947-8000

EPA Region 10
(AK, ID, OR, WA)
Phone (206) 553-1200